# COMMUNITY DEVELOPMENT:
# BREAKING THE CYCLE OF POVERTY

## FIFTH EDITION

# COMMUNITY DEVELOPMENT: BREAKING THE CYCLE OF POVERTY

## FIFTH EDITION

**Hennie Swanepoel and Frik de Beer**

JUTA

*Community Development: Breaking the cycle of poverty*
First published 1989
Second Edition 1992
Third Edition 1997
Fourth Edition 2006
Fifth Edition 2011
Reprinted 2012

Juta and Co Ltd, © 2011

PO Box 24309, Lansdowne, South Africa 7779

ISBN: 978 0 70218 875 6

Project managed by Corina Pelser
Editing by Cindy Taylor
Proofreading by Juta
Indexing by Melanie Blignaut, Jennifer Stern and authors
Typeset by Unwembi
Cover design by WaterBerry Designs cc
Print management by Print Communications

# CONTENTS

## PREFACE (FOURTH EDITION)

In 1989 *Community Development, Putting plans into action* was published under the name of one of us. Since then it was revised in a second edition in 1992 and extensively revised in a third edition in 1997. It has now become necessary to revise it again. We have worked together on many projects and have published a number of works. It has become difficult for us to distinguish intellectual property of either one of us. Further, it was time to really extend the work to a proper handbook for practitioners and students alike; a rather big task. So, 'putting plans into action' has been reworked. Not by one of us, but by both, and just to show that this is really a new work, we have altered the title slightly.

We would like to dedicate this work to one another in recognition of the specific role each has played in a partnership stretching back over twenty five years. We would also like to dedicate this work to our spouses, Kittie and Linda, who have given us space for and support in all our endeavours. Finally, we would like to dedicate it to the many community development workers who have crossed our paths and, in the process, have shaped our ideas and broaden our horizons.

## PREFACE (FIFTH EDITION)

It was over a Wimpy breakfast in Braamfontein, Johannesburg that the idea of this book emerged. We were on our way to facilitate training of a group of local level community development workers and speculated on how the community development workers can be supported after completing the training. The book seemed a good idea. The revised fifth edition was conceived further north and later in the day, over lunch at Huckleberry's in Magnolia Dell, Pretoria. We identified some gaps that needed to be filled; we also considered the usefulness of the book for community development students and practitioners and identified themes for inclusion. The response and ideas for further improvement from those who use the book is eagerly awaited.

Our partnership as authors now stretches over 30 years. The partnership and our academic endeavours have been supported in all these years by Kittie and Linda. To both we yet again express our thanks and gratitude. Finally, as always, we dedicate this book to the many community development workers and members of communities who have crossed our paths and, in the process, have shaped our ideas and broaden our horizons.

# INTRODUCTION (FOURTH EDITION)

Community development must be the most abused form of development over the last five decades. It was used to placate unsatisfied people; get development done in a cheap way, soften up the people before the government's bulldozers moved in; indoctrinate the people to get their blessing for programmes that had very little benefits for them; and westernise especially women to demonstrate that they too subscribe to the western notion of the wholesome wife.

The basic points of departure of community development nearly fifty years ago were crude, but not bad; even less so were they evil. Yet, in the hands of powerful people community development became a tool of marginalisation and disempowerment. The basic tenets of community development should have been developed in an evolutionary way and should have been followed by adapted techniques and methodologies. Unfortunately, however, community development was nearly wiped off the map before it found a rebirth through the basic needs approach and such other approaches. It must be noted that these new approaches were the result of opposition against the modernisation paradigm that became more than a paradigm by being elevated to an ideology by policy makers all over the world and also in South Africa. This sounds a definite warning to today's policy makers: if community development is still seen within this outdated and discredited paradigm, there is not chance of success, even if the technique and methodology are perfect. The masses, especially in South Africa, have awakened and if proponents of community development do not take cognisance of it, it will be spurned by those who are supposed to be the beneficiaries.

Community development must find a home within two other paradigms and they are that of participation and of sustainable development. Very few institutions concerned with development will oppose the idea of participation, but the interpretation of participation may be questionable. A liberal viewpoint on participation will just not have the required results. The liberal viewpoint sees participation as something given to the poor by the authority or NGO working for the alleviation of poverty. It is a paternalistic view in that the local people are guided to accept more and more responsibility as and when they are judged by their "guides" to be ready for it. It does recognise the learning process, but the learning is done by the poor and the teaching is done by the development institution. People are supposed to be introduced to the techniques of planning, implementation and maintenance. Their position is seen as one of assisting the planners, as one of contributing indigenous knowledge to the planning package. The reasons given for the necessity of this participation have to do with the value it may have for the development effort and that it will ensure a continuous involvement of the people. The human being is clearly in service of development. His/her 'participation' will hopefully benefit the project. This viewpoint of participation is in line with the modernisation paradigm and is therefore just as outdated and discredited.

Following the ideas of Freire, Gran and Korten our viewpoint is that empowerment must be a bottom-up process. In other words, the people must take empowerment. But this taking of empowerment is still a process and can be carried by community development. Community development therefore becomes the vehicle, not for physical outputs as has been the view in the past, but for the very human process of empowerment. The role of the authorities or NGOs in community development is then an enabling and supportive one. The main objective of this role must be to create space for communities and to provide the necessary information to the communities so that their empowerment will be meaningful.

With this supportive role people's capacity will be built, not to assist planners and developers from outside, but to take full responsibility for their own development. The end result will be that people will enjoy ownership of development which they will execute in a responsible and enlightened way.

The paradigm of sustainable development also requires the empowerment of the people to be responsible for their own development. According to sustainable development the local development effort must be in harmony with the local ecology. The local people are the experts on that local ecology. They will know and understand the subtleties of their area best. Guidelines can be drawn on a national or regional level, but they must leave scope for the uniqueness of local development to fit in with the local ecology for the sake of sustainability.

From this it is clear that we emphasise the human factor in community development. And by human factor we not only mean the basic concrete needs of people. Community development must involve a process in which the capacity of people is built so that they can take responsibility for their own development through which their human dignity is enhanced. The physical outputs of this process are secondary, even incidental. Primary and foremost is the freeing of people through development so that they can take responsibility for all other development concerning them.

It is also clear that this process of community development is political. The taking of power and the resulting decision-making on the utilisation of scarce resources are political acts. The efforts in the past to separate development from politics as if politics will adulterate development, is a vestige from the liberal modernisation view and is simply impossible to realise in practice. In our country the intense role of civics some years ago in local development confirms this view and it must be admitted, perhaps reluctantly, that there is nothing that anyone can do about it. Development is part of local politics, whether anyone wants it like that or not. Therefore, this political process of development should be supported rather than disclaimed, ignored or opposed.

A further consequence of our viewpoint is that the learning process through community development requires adaptive administration of development, not only on the local level, but also on all other levels. It is important that the local process will create structures for itself within which to operate. Take note that these structures must be the result of the process — it must evolve from the process. It cannot be created beforehand according to an accepted model. That will be restrictive for the process. The structures that will evolve from the process will be unique because they will evolve from a unique process to further carry that unique process.

In their supportive role of this process the authorities or NGOs must themselves follow an adaptive mode of administration. This may represent the single most serious obstacle in the way of community development. Bureaucracies, whether public or private, find it extremely difficult to change their own structures. But it needs a change to become supportive instead of being the primary role-player, to enable decision-making instead of making the decisions, to enhance ownership instead of being the owner of development. It therefore needs a re-assessment of philosophies, missions, policies, strategies and structures and it needs for this re-assessment to become a continuous process of adaptation.

This book has been written with this viewpoint in mind. We would like to see new professionals backed by adaptive organisations giving their all to eradicate poverty. We hope that this book will play a role in achieving this.

Hennie and Frik
2006

## INTRODUCTION (FIFTH EDITION)

Our point of departure and 'articles of faith' as expressed in the introduction to the fourth edition remain unchanged. What we did in the revision was to strengthen some theoretical aspects, include a brief history and better explain some practical aspects. While some may argue (correctly) that the Millennium Development Goals are past their sell-by date, they still perform an important function as an umbrella for investigating and explaining development objectives in the international or global arena. These we now address. Sustainability and compassion are identified as principles for community development and are explained in Chapter 6. The progression in the debate and origins of community development is illustrated with reference to Max Neef's Human Scale Development and Sen's Capability Approach. These approaches have gained prominence internationally and community development workers should know about them.

The UK Department for International Development and other development actors from the North are increasingly supporting research into and the use of the social enterprise sector in promoting development. Though we have some reservations about the theoretical sharpness of this concept we briefly introduce it in this edition. If the North gets its way, as we think they may, more will be heard about the social enterprise sector in terms of development support. Finally we revised the chapter on co-ordination in development, added a discussion on specific PRAP techniques and fine-tuned the chapter on planning and implementation.

In South Africa community development has gained more prominence and support from government, private and NGO sectors over the past decade. We trust that this may enhance community development as a profession. We would like, as stated in the previous edition, to see new professionals in community development backed by adaptive organisations giving their all to eradicate poverty. We hope that this revised edition will play a role in achieving this.

Hennie and Frik
2011

# SECTION A
## THE DEVELOPMENT CONTEXT

# CHAPTER 1

# POVERTY, ILL-BEING AND WELLBEING

Poverty is like heat; you cannot see it; you can only feel it; so, to know poverty you have to go through it (words by a poor person living in Ethiopia, quoted by Narayan, Chambers, Shah & Petesch 2000:33).

## 1.1 INTRODUCTION

Even though most people recognise poverty when they see it, it is difficult to define in universal terms and often impossible to attach figures, numbers or amounts to it. Because poverty is a relative concept, you cannot give it a precise description. Poverty is a relative term because it can either describe the situation of an individual or a family, or it can describe a whole community or society. In cases where poverty in a community or society is the exception, we talk about individual poverty. Therefore, when an individual and his/her family experience deprivation and hardship, we say they are an example of individual poverty, especially if they are the only family or one of only a few families that are poor. People as poor as those discussed in the first three case studies (*The story of Sipho*, *Francisco's story* and *A desperate woman*) are found in all communities. In some communities only a few such people are found., but if there are hundreds or even thousands of other families in a similar situation, we can no longer describe it as individual poverty; then it becomes societal or community poverty. So, if many or even the majority of people are poor, we talk about societal or community poverty. Some people also talk of mass poverty where a whole country or large parts of society and communities suffer poverty. Our concern is with this type of poverty. The few poor people in a relatively prosperous community can be looked after by the community through actions by welfare- and faith-based organisations. Community or mass poverty, however, needs more than that. That is why community development workers (CDWs) concern themselves with societal or community poverty and not individual poverty. In South Africa, where some areas experience unemployment of up to 50 per cent and even more, societal poverty or mass poverty is the order of the day.

But not all people are equally poor. Put differently, the level of ill-being differs between individuals, communities and countries. What we are talking about here is the classification of poverty as *absolute* or *relative* poverty.

Absolute poverty is best illustrated in a situation where the next meal (or its absence) means the difference between life and death; or, as Sen (1981:12) puts it: 'Starvation, clearly, is the most telling aspect of poverty'. People with incomes so low that food, shelter and personal necessities cannot be maintained find themselves in a position of absolute poverty (earning less than US$1.25 per day). By 2005 about 25 per cent (1.4 billion people) in the world lived in absolute poverty, of which 85 per cent lived in rural areas, predominantly of the Third World (Chen & Ravallion, 2008:33).

Amongst the absolute poor one finds the chronic poor—in 2005 it was reported that between 300 and 420 million people of the world are trapped in chronic poverty. They are poor for all or most of their lives and pass on the poverty to their children (Chronic Poverty Research Centre, 2005:v).

Relative poverty is 'poverty defined in relation to social norms and standard of living in a particular context' (DFID, 2001:184). Relative poverty can include the ability of a person to participate in social activities, even if they are not necessary for survival; it can, however, also refer to the overall distribution of resources within, or between, different countries. Relative poverty is therefore an expression of the poverty of one entity in relation to another entity. For example: in relation to South Africa, Lesotho is poor. In relation to the United States of America, South Africa is the poorer country. In relation to the average American family, the African-American family suffers poverty or deprivation; while in relation to an African-American family, an average Malawian family is poor.

Relative poverty is not a kind of poverty that is different from absolute poverty, but should rather be seen as supplementary to the definition of absolute poverty. The concept 'relative poverty' refers to people whose basic needs are met, but who, in terms of their social environment, still experience some disadvantages. In other words, while managing to survive, some people are materially disadvantaged compared with others living in the same community or society.

Whether people are absolutely or relatively poor, some action needs to be taken to improve their position. Yet, in practice, poverty alleviation measures often lead to only a short-term relief, after which the beneficiaries return to their previous balance or equilibrium of poverty. The CDW needs to be aware of this 'danger' in order to plan projects to overcome the tendency of returning to the equilibrium of poverty. A return to the equilibrium of poverty means that the chronic poor will remain chronically poor and pass the poverty on to their children.

## 1.2 UNDERSTANDING THE SOCIO-ECONOMIC CONTEXT OF DEVELOPMENT

> Dirty water is responsible for four-fifths of all sickness and one out of every three deaths in the world today (Goutier 1994:49).

The world population is estimated to be 7 billion people by 2012 (About.com.Geography, Accessed on 8 March 2011). Of this number, at least 1.4 billion live on less than US$1.25 a day (Chen & Ravallion, 2008:33). The socio-economic situation of the world population is illustrated in Table 1.1 on the next page.

Table 1.1    Serious deprivations in many aspects of life in developing countries

### Health

968 million people without access to improved water sources (1998)

2.4 billion people without access to basic sanitation (1998)

34 million people living with HIV/AIDS (end of 2000)

2.2 million people dying annually from indoor air pollution (1996)

### Education

854 million illiterate adults, 543 million of them women (2000)

325 million children out of school at the primary and secondary levels, 183 million of them girls (2000)

### Income poverty

1.2 billion people living on less than US$1 a day (1993 PPP US$), 2.8 billion on less than US$2 a day (1998)

### Children

163 million underweight children under age five (1998)

11 million children under five dying annually from preventable causes (1998)

Adapted from UNDP 2001

### If the world were a village of 100 people...

At least 18 villagers would be unable to read or write but 33 would have cellular phones and 16 would be online on the Internet.

27 villagers would be under 15 years of age and 7 would be over 64 years old.

There would be an equal number of males and females.

There would be 18 cars in the village.

63 villagers would have inadequate sanitation.

30 villagers would be unemployed or underemployed while of those 70 who would work:

- 28 would work in agriculture
- 14 would work in industry (secondary sector), and
- the remaining 28 would work in the service sector (tertiary sector).

53 villagers would live on less than two U.S. dollars a day.

One villager would have AIDS, 26 villagers would smoke, and 14 villagers would be obese.

By the end of a year, one villager would die and two new villagers would be born so thus the population would climb to 101.

Adapted from About.com.Geography (Accessed on 8 March 2011)

Information in the box illustrates the general socio-economic condition of the 'global village'. In specific areas of the Third World the picture is bleaker, with high rates of unemployment, poor service delivery, high infant mortality and food insecurity amongst others (see 1.3 below).

## 1.3   THE DEPRIVATION TRAP

Behind the cold statistics in Table 1.1 are real people fighting a daily battle to survive the deprivation trap in which they find themselves (see Chambers, 1983: 111 et seq). The majority of people in this trap live in rural areas and squatter settlements on the outskirts of cities and towns. Case Study 3: *A desperate woman*, illustrates some of the challenges faced by the poor to survive the deprivation trap.

Figure 1.1 on page 6, taken from Chambers (1983:112), shows how the clusters or groups of deprivation interact to form a trap. Each arrow points in two directions indicating that each cluster influences the other. For example: the arrow between physical weakness and powerlessness shows that it is not just a matter of physical weakness leading to powerlessness, but that powerlessness can, in turn, lead to physical weakness.

> Poverty is a strong determinant of the others. It contributes to physical weakness through lack of food, small bodies, malnutrition leading to low immune response to infections, and inability to reach or pay for health services; to isolation because of the inability to pay the cost of schooling, to buy a radio or a bicycle, to afford to travel to look for work, or to live near the village centre or a main road; to vulnerability through lack of assets to pay large expenses or to meet contingencies; and to powerlessness because lack of wealth goes with low status: the poor have no voice (Chambers 1983:111).

Isolation, powerlessness and physical weakness render people vulnerable: vulnerability in the physical sense to disease, and psychologically to abuse and the destruction of self-esteem. People are vulnerable to unscrupulous landlords and uncaring officials, and to the forces of nature that may bring droughts or floods.

The poor have limited access to information, services, labour organisations, opportunities and to opinion leaders and policymakers. Poverty renders them voiceless and powerless. Their powerlessness is exacerbated by physical weakness. Poor hygiene, malnutrition and under-nourishment, lack of education and life skills cause physical weakness: the consequences are among others poor school performance and an inability to perform manual work. In 1996/97, 27 per cent of the Botswana population and 43 per cent of the population of Angola suffered from under-nourishment (UNDP, 2001:164).

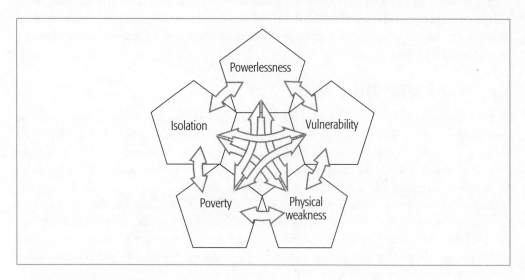

Figure 1.1    **The Deprivation Trap**

To break the hold of the deprivation trap (or cycle of poverty) over poor people, the links in the chain of the trap need to be broken. The CDW should consider at which point intervention can be considered (in co-operation with the community!) by analysing the community in terms of the deprivation trap.

▶ Poverty is caused by lack of assets, be it land, money or job-related skills.
▶ Vulnerability is seen in the lack of reserves and choices, and the ease with which poor people can be coerced.
▶ Isolation is often in a geographical sense, but also shown by the lack of education and exclusion from systems and structures.
▶ The powerlessness of the poor is illustrated by lack of social and economic influence and the ease by which they can be exploited by others.
▶ Physical weakness is seen in the lack of physical strength of individuals and chronic illness.

A community development project cannot address, nor should it, all these issues at once. Yet, understanding of the issues and its manifestations in a specific community can help in identifying a focus for a project. At this point a word of caution is appropriate. While we work with and address problems, issues and shortcomings in the community, this should be done by working with the assets and building on them, in finding solutions. The importance of assets and an asset-based approach to community development is discussed in Chapter 19.

The plight of the poor is illustrated in Case Study 1: *The story of Sipho*, where the situation of a child-headed household is explained. Case Study 2: *Francisco's story*, shows how the clusters of the deprivation trap keep a family from rising from their poverty.

The impact of the deprivation trap and how it keeps people from improving their lives can be illustrated with examples about shelter, employment or lack of employment opportunities, water, drainage and sewage, health facilities, nutrition, education and the stagnant local economy. However, the CDW should not only identify characteristics of the deprivation trap but also look beyond and identify positive aspects — the assets in poor communities — on which development can be based. In the discussion of the deprivation trap below, some examples of community-assets are briefly introduced.

## 1.3.1    Shelter

In urban areas many people build shacks in squatter or informal settlements. Some shacks are quite neat and safe to live in, but many leak rain and dust, have bad or inadequate foundations, and almost all are too small for the number of people living in them. In rural areas the shelters built with traditional building materials need a lot of maintenance. Because of a shortage of these materials (eg of thatch during droughts) it is difficult for people to maintain their dwellings properly. Also, they invariably do not have the time or physical strength to spend on repairing their homes.

Because people are poor, it is difficult for them to build proper houses in a short time. Living in poor conditions affects their health; and it is difficult for an unhealthy person to find—and keep—a job. The rural poor have an added problem: because they are 'out of sight', officials do not know of their problems. The rural poor are consequently isolated. They are isolated from urban areas where social and economic infrastructure and services are available. The isolation is caused by distance, poor roads and telecommunications, and by their poverty which renders communication impossible or unaffordable. Their isolation is compounded by the tendency of government to invest in urban areas and neglect integrated urban-rural development.

Yet the housing created by the people, in spite of shortcomings, represents an asset on which further community development can be based. Small investments over many years, sometimes decades, lead to improvements of housing and represents large capital investments—assets controlled by the poor. De Soto (1989:18—19) illustrates this point in discussing housing in Lima, Peru. To obtain shelter people occupied land, built houses, installed infrastructure and only then obtained legal ownership—quite the reverse of the traditional process. The people, mostly migrants moving to the city, invested between 1960—1984 US$8 319.8 million in their own housing compared to the US$173.6 million invested by government.

## 1.3.2    Unemployment

The isolation of people in the deprivation trap contributes to their experience of poverty and powerlessness. Unemployment is both a cause and a result of the poverty situation in which people find themselves. It is a cause, since without a job people have no income and cannot pay for proper housing, food, medical care and education for them and their children. It is a result because poor health caused by an unbalanced diet, poor housing and lack of appropriate education (all on account of poverty) prevents people from finding and keeping gainful employment.

Unemployment is in many instances also the result of isolation, physical weakness and vulnerability. Because of distance and poor communication, the poor are isolated from the job market. They find it difficult to gain access to employment opportunities. An unbalanced diet and prolonged illness lead to physical weakness. Physical weakness increases vulnerability to other diseases, for example, tuberculosis (TB), HIV/AIDS and malaria break down a person's natural immune system. At another level, the poor are also vulnerable to exploitation by employers and people in positions of power. As they have nothing to bargain with, the poor are powerless. See also 1.3.7 below on the stagnant local economy and local economic development.

### 1.3.3    Water, drainage and sewage

The absence or inadequate provision of water, and poor drainage and sewage services pose serious health problems. Lack of safe drinking water is one of the clearest signs of poverty. People, and especially children, suffer poor health as a result of drinking unsafe water. With no proper sewage system (for instance pit latrines) rainwater washes sewage on the surface into streams and stagnant pools. Diseases flourish and spread under such conditions. In urban squatter areas the problem is worse because of the population density. In rural areas, however, the same problem occurs, but is perhaps also less visible to people from outside the settlements. Prolonged and repeated illness leaves the victims physically weak.

Yet, even infrastructure development projects to address sanitation needs are not beyond community development. In Karachi, Pakistan, the Orangi Pilot Projects through research, organisation and commitment, made it possible for the communities to lay self-financed and self-managed underground sewage lines involving almost 70 000 houses (Ekins, 1992:190).

### 1.3.4    Health facilities

Because of the mushrooming of urban settlements and the long distances between scattered villages in rural areas, the provision of healthcare facilities lags far behind. Preventive primary healthcare facilities need to be expanded. Curative facilities provided by large clinics and hospitals are situated long distances from where the poor find themselves. Transport facilities, such as ambulance services to health centres, are not adequate.

On the other hand, poverty contributes to the squalor in which many people live and this leaves them vulnerable to disease. It limits their access to proper medical care, contributing to their physical weakness caused by prolonged illness and/or inadequate medical care. They are vulnerable to disease (eg tuberculosis) and they are also vulnerable as far as the employment market is concerned, because to find, and keep a job, is difficult for a sickly, uneducated person with little access to proper transport.

Combined with poverty, these factors keep households like trapped mice in the deprivation trap. One factor reinforces the other.

### 1.3.5    Food security

Access to food depends on the purchasing power of the money that people earn, their access to land to grow food crops, foraging, such as occur in rural areas and the support in kind received from other members of communities. The coping strategies of households may include migration to places perceived to offer jobs (mainly urban areas) and obtaining various grants for the indigent and vulnerable (children, disabled and the elderly) provided by governments.

In the absence of food security, too little food and food of low nutritional value forms the diet of poor people. Balanced nutritious meals are important for the cognitive development (perception, thinking and learning) of children and adults. Even before birth, nutrition affects the development of a child. Undernutrition of the mother negatively affects brain development and may cause permanent and irreversible damage to the baby. Breast feeding of babies leads to higher IQ development, and fewer cases of rashes and bacterial infections. Iron deficiency during the early years of a child can cause permanent damage to the brain. Iodine deficiency in the early years is associated with reduced cognition and achievement in school-age children. Poorly nourished children are more prone to infections, may be sick more often and are likely to be frequently absent from school.

The lack of food security and under- and malnourishment experienced by the poor (and especially their children) contributes to *physical weakness*. Physical weakness makes people *vulnerable*, it may keep them from finding well-paid jobs and generally makes them *powerless*.

## 1.3.6 Education

The relationship between the ability of a child to learn and the need for nutritious food is illustrated above. Weak, under- and malnourished children have a clear disadvantage at school. They may have lacked brain development at an early stage and may regularly be absent from school, making their disadvantage worse.

The lack of or inability to obtain education keeps people in a position of vulnerability and powerlessness. Education is viewed as one of the most effective preventive weapons against HIV/AIDS. Knowledge of this disease lowers the vulnerability and powerlessness of people. Education helps to prepare people in finding or creating their own jobs. In this way it helps to combat poverty. A lack of education makes it difficult for people to escape the deprivation trap.

Education has many advantages for the individual and for society. For the individual, education can improve health and nutrition. Better education means better chances of obtaining jobs with better earnings. Inequality is reduced through education, especially where girls have equal access to opportunities.

For society, education means a skilled workforce and improved productivity. It consequently should support the eradication of poverty by increasing incomes.

In many poor areas, informal and private schools and early childhood development centres are established by people. This is a community-based asset that can, with proper support, develop into real resources in the fight against poverty.

## 1.3.7 Stagnant local economy

Lack of economic development at the local level contributes to high levels of unemployment and consequently, poverty. In urban squatter and informal settlements unemployment rates of 70—80 per cent are common. These areas are home to many migrants from rural and peri-urban areas, and migrants from cities that experience economic slumps. In Africa, migration between countries in search of jobs and social services contributes to the growth of squatter and informal settlements. These settlements are mostly 'labour reservoirs' for the closest city and because of their relative *isolation* and lack of proper education, the inhabitants have little access to proper jobs and remain poor, vulnerable and powerless.

In poor areas much entrepreneurship is shown by people who run small enterprises and hairdressers, motor mechanics, spaza shops and shebeens abound. These are assets that, with proper local economic development (LED) support and infrastructure, can make a meaningful contribution to combat and eradicate poverty.

## 1.4 FROM ILL-BEING TO WELLBEING

### 1.4.1 Ill-being

'We are above the dead and below the living' says one of the 20 000 poor respondents who participated in the Voices of the Poor Project (Narayan et al, 2000:33). To be poor is to suffer from ill-being. The condition of ill-being is not the same as not having money. Conversely, to be developed (wellbeing) is not the same as having money. Poverty and development have many more than simple material definitions. In our first three case studies people are caught in the deprivation trap and suffer from ill-being. The condition of ill-being can be measured in at least the following five dimensions, each explained according to some characteristics as indicated (Narayan et al, 2000:31–37).

> *Material lack and want*: of food, livelihood assets and money, housing and shelter;
>
> *Physical ill-being*: characterised by hunger, pain and discomfort, exhaustion and poverty of time;
>
> *Bad social relations*: manifested by exclusion, rejection, isolation and loneliness;
>
> *Insecurity, vulnerability, worry and fear*: characterised by stress, risks and defencelessness; and
>
> *Powerlessness, helplessness, frustration and anger*: manifested in political impotence.

### 1.4.2 Wellbeing

The condition of wellbeing can be measured in at least the following five dimensions, each explained according to some characteristics as indicated below (Narayan et al, 2000:25–28).

> *Material wellbeing*: having enough food, assets, work;
>
> *Bodily wellbeing*: possessing good health and appearance, being in good physical condition;
>
> *Social wellbeing*: being able to care for children, maintaining selfrespect and dignity, living in peace and harmony with family and community;
>
> *Security*: characterised by civil peace, physical safety and a secure environment, personal physical security, lawfulness and access to justice, security in old age and confidence in the future ; and
>
> *Freedom of choice and action* in all aspects of life.

Case Study 4: *The story of Thembalihle*, illustrates how a situation of ill-being is turned around into wellbeing for the family.

Earlier we said that community poverty is associated with factors such as poor housing, a lack of safe water, a lack of sanitation services, poor educational facilities and little opportunity for employment.

Ill-being gives a portrait of the person or community in the deprivation trap. Wellbeing shows how that person or community looks when they escape from the deprivation trap.

A development model has to build on and execute government policies and strategies. Examples of such models are the South African Integrated Development Plan, aimed at sustainable municipal development in a sound environment, and the Integrated Sustainable Rural Development Programme, aimed at rural development.

## 1.5    THE EQUILIBRIUM OF POVERTY

Attempts at alleviating poverty may bring some relief, but soon the balance or equilibrium returns and the poor remain as poor as before. In Chapter 6 we argue that development must bring release, not relief from poverty.

Galbraith (1979) argues that in a poor society or community any progress (in economic terms) is soon cancelled out due, for example, to an increased birth rate or a natural disaster. Accordingly, the fruits of successful development such as job creation are nullified by an uncontrolled increase in population numbers. These forces operate in such a way that they return the people to a situation more or less the same as before the development project. Improvements in the socio-economic position of a community or society are thus obliterated by some force or another operating in society. The poor community or society comes to accept their poverty as normal—they accommodate their poverty.

Savings that might accrue from development aid are often spent on means of survival and not invested in productive enterprises. A country may, for example, invest development aid in the building of social infrastructure such as schools or hospitals, or the paying of public service salaries, in which case no long-term interest will be earned or job opportunities created. A small-scale farmer may be granted a loan to buy farming equipment, but decides to rather spend it on school fees: no income is generated and the loan must be paid back. Once the surplus money of the household is depleted, it automatically returns to its previous level of subsistence; thus the balance (equilibrium) of poverty is restored. Accepting this position is what is called accommodation to a culture of poverty. It is a survival attitude inside the deprivation trap. It is clear that CDWs must instil in poor people an anti-equilibrium attitude; a will to fight the situation in which poverty thrives, even against all the odds.

The equilibrium of poverty points to the presence of chronic poverty. 'Some poverty passes from one generation to another as if the offspring sucks it from the mother's breast' (a group of disabled Ugandan women quoted in Chronic Poverty Research Centre 2005: vi). For the chronic poor to escape, much more is needed than equal opportunities. For them, specific and targeted programmes are required. According to the Chronic Poverty Research Centre (2005:50), such support should include policies and strategies that: prioritise livelihood security; ensure chronically poor people can take up opportunities; take empowerment seriously and recognise obligations to provide resources.

It is the task of the CWDs to be well-informed about government policies and strategies that will benefit the poor and the chronically poor. It is also their task to find resources made available and assist poor and chronically poor communities in gaining access to them.

## 1.6   CONCLUSION

In the African context, poverty and the resulting ill-being affect the masses, not just the individual. Masses of poor people are trapped in deprivation and it is extremely difficult for them to break free of this trap. In fact, the tendency exists for poverty to constantly reintroduce itself in new guises, thus ensuring that equilibrium of ill-being continues. It is developers' greatest task—no—it is their only task to break the deprivation trap and to bring about disequilibrium in the poverty situation. In the final instance it is human beings that must be released from the trap. They must be given the chance to look after their own wellbeing in a self-reliant way. It is the task of CWDs to guide and enable them to do so.

# CHAPTER 2

# THE DEVELOPMENT ENVIRONMENT

## 2.1 INTRODUCTION

Societal and individual poverty (see Chapter 1) is caused, perpetuated or even intensified by natural, social, economic, political, psychological and cultural factors that are present in all societies and communities. All these factors must be studied and their interdependence understood to know the environment in which poverty eradication and development must be addressed. Each environment has stumbling blocks to development; yet each environment also has resources (or assets) that must be identified and then applied in the struggle against poverty.

The struggle against mass poverty does not consist, however, of isolated attempts by individual countries in the world. The fight against poverty has become a major factor on the world agenda and is to some extent driven by protocols and agreements reached at the United Nations and supported by member countries. The most important item currently on the world 'development agenda' is the Millennium Development Goals (MDGs).

## 2.2 THE GLOBAL CONTEXT OF POLICY FORMULATION FOR DEVELOPMENT

The MDGs provide a good framework from which to consider the development environment. These goals were identified and supported by most members of the United Nations (UN:2011). In 2000 when the goals were approved, the aim was to half most of the identified indicators of poverty by 2015. In reality very few, if any, of the goals will be achieved by this date. Eight goals have been identified and these break down into **21 quantifiable targets** that are measured by **60 indicators**.

The goals and targets are (UN:2011):

**Goal 1:** Eradicate extreme hunger and poverty. The targets of this goal are to increase income, increase employment and reduce the number of people who suffer from hunger.

**Goal 2:** Achieve universal primary education. The target of this goal is to ensure that all children (boys and girls) complete a full course of primary schooling.

**Goal 3:** Promote gender equality and empower women. The target of this goal is to eliminate gender disparity at school level.

**Goal 4:** Reduce child mortality. The target of this goal is to reduce by two thirds the child mortality rate among children under five.

**Goal 5:** Improve maternal health. The targets of this goal are to reduce by two thirds the maternal mortality rate and to achieve by 2015 universal reproductive health.

**Goal 6:** Combat HIV/AIDS, malaria and other diseases. The targets are to halt and reverse the spread of HIV/AIDS, achieve by 2010 universal access to treatment for HIV/AIDS for those who need it and finally, to halt and begin reverse the incidence of malaria and other major diseases.

**Goal 7:** Ensure environmental sustainability. The targets are to integrate the principles of sustainable development into country policies and programmes; reverse the loss of environmental resources; reduce biodiversity loss; reduce by half the number of people without sustainable access to safe drinking water and basic sanitation; and to achieve significant improvements in lives of at least 100 million slum dwellers by 2010.

**Goal 8:** Develop a Global Partnership for Development. The targets are to develop an open rule-based predictable and non-discriminatory trading and financial system; address the special needs of the least developed countries; address the special needs of landlocked developing countries and small island developing states; and deal comprehensively with the debt problem of developing countries.

**According to the UNDP (2001):** 'The MDGs ... provide a framework for the entire international community to work together towards a common end—making sure that human development reaches everyone, everywhere. If these goals are achieved, world poverty will be cut by half, tens of millions of lives will be saved, and billions more people will have the opportunity to benefit from the global economy'.

The MDGs address all aspects of human development. If they are achieved it would be possible to say that the deprivation trap (see Chapter 1) has been broken and that people experience wellbeing.

All the United Nations agencies work towards the achievement of these goals, but implementation is nationally planned and driven. A prerequisite for the successful implementation of the MDGs is for governments to regulate the environments and to create circumstances that will enhance or facilitate development to take place and poverty to be eradicated. The context in which development takes place is directly dependent on the degree to which development initiatives are supported by aspects such as policy and regulatory frameworks.

Countries and governments do not operate in isolation, unaffected by the world outside. Attempts by a government to regulate the various environments through policy are influenced by the world; by the global context within which we all live.

Laws are made in the parliament of a country to give guidance and to help establish the rules according to which society conducts its affairs. These laws attempt to promote development according to the prescriptions of the Constitution. In a democratic country people are elected to represent the population (the electorate) and their will in parliament. The elected representatives must ensure that the needs and aspirations of the people in society are expressed in the laws that govern the country.

Policy formulation occurs in a country according to a process in which people are elected, political parties function (eg congresses) and debate in the media takes place. Eventually these actions lead to the enactment of laws (De Coning & Fick, 1995).

But it is not only activities and debate within a country that influence policy formulation. With the increased use of information technology (IT) and improved transport systems, the world has become a smaller place—so small that some people call it the global village. In our global village, because information and people travel at such speed, an incident in one corner of the world tends to affect the rest of the world. A military and political crisis in the Arab world, for example, usually results in an increase in the price of crude oil. The popular uprising and overthrow of governments in Tunisia and Egypt early in 2011 are examples of the international impact of instability in one part of the world on the rest. In both instances change occurred as 'revolutions by social media' (Crovitz, 2011). These revolutions spread through the Arab world, also to Libya and caused major upsets in the world oil trade, influencing the economies of most countries of the world. When the price of oil increases, the rest of the world suffers. Such a rise influences the value of a country's currency and has an effect on the inflation rate. As a consequence of the unrest in the Arab world, a situation over which most other countries have no control, policies need to be formulated to make provision for its effects on the economy of a specific country.

Many other examples of activities in the global village can be cited as having influenced policy formulation in a country. The earthquake and Tsunami that hit Japan in 2011 had immediate effects on the stock exchange and, consequently, the economies of most countries. It is said, for example, that if the American stock exchange sneezes the rest of the world catches a cold. While policy needs to be formulated to address the specific needs and aspirations of a specific society, it cannot be done without taking into account what is happening in the world outside—in the global village (Olivier, 2004).

## 2.3 THE LOCAL DEVELOPMENT ENVIRONMENT

How does the global context affect the local environment where community development workers (CDWs) are active? A rise in oil price caused by unrest in the Arab world affects the price of petrol and therefore the whole economy of individual countries. It influences the price of food, transport and income. On the positive side, an internationally agreed framework such as the MDGs focuses attention on urgent development issues and supports political will and policy-making in individual countries that are geared towards human development.

Awareness of the global context should assist the CDW in understanding the wider context of development. It is, however, important to understand and know how to interpret conditions in the local development environment to design strategies that will be successful in the local environment. The existing situation is therefore of vital importance for development projects. Some of the aspects within this existing situation that need attention are the organisational and institutional, the socio-economic and physical environment, the prevailing educational system, culture and religion.

These aspects either support and strengthen development, or they hinder it. If they support it, an enabling environment exists. Policy, regulations and structures must be committed and geared towards accommodating community initiatives. If they are not, they are disabling for the process. See Case Study 10: *The project that had its fences brought down*. It serves little purpose to try and motivate the stakeholders to participate on a long-term basis if realities such as policies and laws and structures make it very difficult for them to participate meaningfully. These difficulties are compounded by a socio-economic and cultural environment that is often already disabling in its own right. It is hoped that the enabling environment set by formal aspects such as laws, policy and structures will gradually erode the disabling informal social and cultural environment and make it more enabling for community participation and initiative. If the formal aspects are disabling, however, there is very little hope that the socio-economic and cultural environment would become supportive.

The local development environment is the context in which communities organise and projects take place. This context influences development and is—at the same time—influenced by development taking place within its borders. Actually, the development environment consists of, or presents itself in a number of types of environment. These types of environment have a profound influence on communication and thus on development. Environments that should be taken note of are discussed below.

### 2.3.1    Political environment

To be effective the CDW must know and understand the local political environment. The political environment consists of political leaders and political groupings with political activities such as meetings and marches. Political communication consists of messages about political orientation and policy preferences. There can also be, and usually is, conflict and strife in the political environment.

Political forces are at work in all communities. In rural areas traditional leaders still play an important role in organising and deciding on events and actions within the community. In other areas, especially in urban and peri-urban areas, democratic structures and warlords play their political roles. In South Africa, for example, opposing political groups are found in many communities; they may be aligned to existing power structures (be they traditional or democratic) or they may form a party-based organisation within the community. Sometimes opposing groups reach mutual agreement for the sake of development in the community. In many areas, however, animosity and even violence are often present.

Political differences in a community can render it incapable of agreeing on development projects. On the other hand, political agreement can be beneficial to the elite—those with external contacts—but to the exclusion of the chronic poor who still find themselves isolated and vulnerable. Case Study 12: *The divided community*, gives an example of how destructive politics can be. The political situation is not an excuse to withdraw from the community, but it is important that the CDWs will not be naive and think that they can facilitate development without the impact of politics.

### 2.3.2    Social environment

The social environment consists of institutions such as the primary institution of the family and the secondary institutions such as the school and church, and clubs and interest groups (see Chapter 3). There are also informal institutions such as friendships. Families are represented in many of the secondary institutions and families also tend to communicate with one another, but there is a social layering that means that some families will interact with one another and not with others.

All communities are organised: they have, for instance, power structures, schools, interest groups and civic organisations. How the organisations are structured and how they relate to one another (interact), form the social environment within which community development takes place. In fact, the existence of such organisations and forms of interaction is proof that the community itself is already busy with community development. As part of the social environment, one also finds negative factors such as delinquency, power struggles, group forming and antisocial behaviour such as prostitution, drug abuse and child abuse.

In many poor communities the presence of people suffering from HIV/AIDS is an important factor in the social environment. Not only is it a health issue but it affects social relationships; it contributes to the growth of child-headed households and it tests to the extreme the household livelihood strategies and survival of families.

Crime is another factor in the social environment which negatively affects the whole community.

### 2.3.3  Cultural environment

The cultural environment consists of the values and mores of a society. These values and mores are often spoken of as the traditions of the people. According to these traditions people have a place in society and certain obligations towards society, while they can expect that the society will guide them and provide a living environment for them—as long as they are true to the traditions. If an information message looks as if it wants to change tradition or is critical of traditional values, it has an uphill battle to be accepted (see Chapter 13).

Culture creates or contains taboos and provides a framework according to which people act and react to daily life. It is not necessarily true that culture creates stumbling blocks for development. In fact, in some situations cultural practices may be beneficial to the success of development efforts.

The Grameen Bank in Bangladesh operates on the principle of group organisation, specifically targeting the rural poor of which women are in the majority. In some villages the groups consist only of women and these groups do not accept male members, a decision: '… rooted in the extremely oppressive power structure as far as poor women are concerned' (Ekins 1992:123—124). In this instance a cultural practice negatively impacting on women was—through organisation and solidarity of the women—overcome in favour of development. Another example is given by Diale (2009) where the project committee has its meetings outdoors, where the male members sit in the shade of a large tree while the female members sit some metres away in the shade of a small bush.

### 2.3.4  Economic environment

Every community has its own economy that is manifested to a large extent in the informal system, but also in employment in the formal system. The society is also economically layered so that you will find very poor people (the chronic poor), poor people and those who are better off. The economic environment is very important in community development and the management of scarce resources.

The economic context refers to rate of employment, presence and activity of commerce and industry, and the presence and scope of informal economic activity. The level of activity of the economy can be measured by aspects such as the ability to pay for (municipal) services and daily needs (food, clothing, education). In the poorest areas the unemployment rate is high and the level of informal sector activity is consequently also high. Though activity in the informal economic sector mostly escapes scrutiny (and tax collection!) by the tax collector and population census officials, it contributes significantly to the economy and the local economic environment in poor communities. There are usually very few shops, workshops and factories present. These are usually found some distance away, closer to the urban centre. Public transport is rarely adequate and people often have to use taxis, which they cannot afford.

The presence of infrastructure also gives an indication of the level of economic activity. In rural and in urban areas where the poor live, the infrastructure is most often either not developed, or badly maintained. The economic environment poses some of the most difficult and tangible challenges for community leaders and CDWs.

### 2.3.5 Psychological environment

People experience life in their own peculiar way. This abstract manifestation of their experience of reality is known as the psychological make-up of people. This make-up can be negative where people live under stress or where they find themselves in a strange environment, for example migrants experiencing city life. In most African cities and towns, and especially in South Africa, migrants from neighbouring countries are increasing and their mere presence make a claim on the social and economic resources available. Their presence also impacts on the psychology of local people and contributes to xenophobic attitudes and conduct. Negative reaction from the local population leaves psychological scars of fear, feelings of rejection and apathy on these migrants. The psychological make-up of people will, to a large extent, influence their participation and the extent to which they will be prepared to assume responsibility.

The psychological environment is something abstract that we tend to ignore. It consists of the attitude people display towards life around them. Poor people who spend their time in a battle for survival often feel apathy towards people or institutions trying to persuade them to 'do something'.

Lack of self-esteem is another psychological characteristic of people caught in a poverty situation. They often believe that they lack the ability to 'do something'. Hence they become more and more dependent on aid from government or NGO welfare assistance. They are not prepared to take risks because if they fail (for instance in an agricultural project), they stand to lose a lot. Having experienced negative situations in the past, they are often distrustful of strangers and even people they know who might come up with new ideas. The psychological environment of the poor is strongly influenced by experiences of the past.

## 2.4   CONCLUSION

Development does not take place in a vacuum and the same applies to the work of CDWs. In the first place the facilitation of development efforts is influenced by politics, culture, economics, and the psychological make-up of the people. In the second place the development efforts can have some effect on the environment. If this effect is for the worse, one must put a question mark to that development, because an unsustainable environment is hardly going to assist the poor to break out of the deprivation trap.

When we talk about the environment within which development takes place, we must also be careful not to remain at the micro or local level because the world has shrunk to the extent that it has become the stage on which our efforts take place.

The political environment poses one of the most difficult challenges facing leaders and CDWs. Development is about gaining access to resources to satisfy needs; essentially this is part of the political process and cannot be ignored by those involved in development.

There is a cultural environment in all communities and among all people. Culture determines the norms and values of people and is also adapted or changed by people as the need arises.

It is essential, therefore, to keep in mind that population growth is not the only important factor in the over-utilisation of the environment. Equally important is people's access to resources, and sound economic and political management and leadership provided by the governments of developing countries.

# CHAPTER 3
# STAKEHOLDERS IN COMMUNITY DEVELOPMENT

## 3.1 INTRODUCTION

It is the interest a person or a group has in achieving some goals that guides participation in action and projects. In their lives people interact in different ways with those around them and may belong to different organisations. Once they have an interest or stake in an activity or project, the individual or organisation becomes a stakeholder in it. In community development, stakeholders can be identified at the levels of government, private sector, non-governmental organisations and community sector stakeholders. Of course, strictly speaking, the community sector stakeholders are also in the non-governmental sector. Yet, because the community sector is so important, we classify and discuss them separately. Stakeholders can also be classified according to functional areas (or areas of analysis) such as political, economic, legal or social (Jütting, 2003:13). One can, for example, classify the National Department of Social Development as a governmental institution working in the social functional area.

According to Jütting (2003:11) a stakeholder, or institution:

 include(s) any form of constraint that human beings devise to shape human interaction. These constraints include both what individuals are prohibited from doing and, sometimes, under what conditions some individuals are permitted to undertake certain activities.

What this means is that the conduct of individuals, groups and organisations in society is regulated by socially agreed upon rules and understandings which may be recorded or not. Typically then; the stakeholder organisation operates according to some laws, rules and guidelines, usually contained in constitutions, laws and operational procedures. In less formal organisations such rules may not be in a written format but the members would agree between them about it.

One stakeholder who deserves special attention in this book is the community development worker (CDW). The CDW is a 'cross-cutting' sector, meaning that its representatives are found in the public, private, non-governmental organisation (NGO), community and social enterprise sectors. CDWs play an important part in networking and co-ordinating development activities in communities.

In addition to being able to identify and describe the various stakeholders, we also need to know about their interaction with one another, and the difficulties around such interaction —or as we call it here—co-ordination and collaboration. This chapter is consequently devoted to an introduction of the various types of stakeholders and an overview of ways of co-ordinating the development activities and projects of stakeholders.

## 3.2 IDENTIFYING STAKEHOLDERS

A stakeholder, or role-player in poverty eradication, is a person, a group or an institution that performs a certain task. A stakeholder may be actively doing something or may have an untapped potential to perform a function. An active stakeholder is, for instance, a school, a town clerk, a utility supplier (eg electricity), a church group or a civic organisation. To outsiders some stakeholders may not seem to be doing anything, but they have the potential for action, for example informal organisations like stokvels.[1]

In Kenya the Chama 'a group of people with a common interest in coming together' plays a role similar to stokvels (Kilongi, 2011). In reality these stakeholders are, or may become, active in their own way, in poverty alleviation and eradication.

Stakeholders may be classified into four main groups or sectors: public sector, private sector, NGO sector, and popular or community-based sector. The fifth sector, represented in all four above is the CDW sector.

### 3.2.1  Public sector stakeholders

The public sector consists of national, provincial and local government. The national government is organised according to broad functional areas with departments dealing with issues such as social development, land affairs, environmental affairs, water affairs, forestry and agriculture.

Provincial government has certain specified competencies at provincial level. In South Africa provincial government has competencies over functional areas such as education, health and roadworks. To perform these functions specific departments are established.

In South Africa local government has wide-ranging powers and responsibilities for— amongst others—social and people development, local economic development and—in the metropoles—also local policing.

Parastatals (eg Eskom) are providing utility services. While they form part of the public sector their services are usually commercialised; which means they aim to at least recover cost of services provided.

### 3.2.2  Private sector stakeholders

The private sector consists of stakeholders or groups active in commerce, industry and mining. Here we find industries, or factories, manufacturing consumer goods. Commerce, consisting of shops, banks and services such as dry cleaning and motor repairs also fall within the private sector. And finally, commerce and industry associations such as the National African Federated Chamber of Commerce (NAFCOC) are important stakeholders in the private sector.

Apart from big corporations, the private sector contains small, medium and micro-enterprises (SMMEs). In South Africa it is estimated that SMMEs represent 97.5 per cent of all business enterprises and employ 55 per cent of the country's labour force (Mutezo, 2005:32). SMMEs may be part of the formal economy meeting legal registration requirements, or they may be part of the informal economic sector.

Some authors argue that the informal sector (eg hawkers, shebeens, prostitutes) also fall within the private sector. While privately owned enterprises in this sector are usually small, they are not regulated by laws and are poorly developed. In the Tshwane area, for instance, only 15 per cent of the entrepreneurs in this sector make a profit equal to, or slightly higher, than the minimum level of living (MLL) of R2000 in 2005 (Beeld, 2005:21).

### 3.2.3  Non-government (civil society) stakeholders

This sector consists of organisations that are not in any way dependent on, or responsible to either the public or private sectors. Usually NGOs come into existence to address specific problems, for example health, education or housing. More often, though, they address a number of problems in the field of development. Examples of NGO or civil society stakeholders are local government associations, development institutions, international, national and local development organisations and advocacy organisations such as the Treatment Action Campaign (TAC) in South Africa.

NGOs have social or economic development aims and are non-profit organisations. They depend on grants from large corporations, government aid agencies and donations from the public.

### 3.2.4  Popular or community-based sector stakeholders

The popular sector, also called the community-based sector, consists of organisations founded and run by individuals or groups within communities. Examples of community-based organisations (CBOs) are women's clubs, youth clubs, ratepayers' associations, farmers' cooperatives, burial societies and sports clubs; faith-based groupings such as choirs, prayer groups and care groups; more formal organisations such as clinic committees and school committees; political associations, groupings and parties and traditional leaders and structures.

CBOs are at the grassroots level, and grapple daily with issues of development. In the way we approach community development in this book, they are the small groups and the building blocks around which 'community' can be identified.

### 3.2.5  Social enterprise sector

A more recent development is the emergence of what is called the social enterprise sector. One way of looking at social enterprise is to say that it attempts to unify business principles with social ventures. According to Martin and Osberg (2007) an understanding of the concept of 'social entrepreneur' depends on understanding what an entrepreneur is. They view an entrepreneur as a person with 'an exceptional ability to see and seize upon new opportunities, the commitment and drive required to pursue them, and an unflinching willingness to bear the inherent risks' (Martin and Osberg, 2007:31). To get to a definition of social enterprise they distinguish social activism (eg the Ghandian movement) from social service provision (a school or clinic). Whereas social activism works on a grand scale, attempting to change the equilibrium of social service delivery to have it replaced by something better (but at a large scale), social service delivery works within the equilibrium and attempts to alleviate and assist with social development issues. Social entrepreneurship combines the grand scale of social activism, within the social field, with the drive and risk taking of an entrepreneur. The social entrepreneur works in the social field but attempts on a grand scale—and taking the accompanying risk—to make changes that will disturb the equilibrium and create a new equilibrium at a higher level of services. According to their definition of the social entrepreneur, Martin and Osberg (2007:39) say that the social entrepreneur should be understood

> … as someone who targets an unfortunate but stable equilibrium that causes the neglect, marginalization, or suffering of a segment of humanity; who brings to bear on this situation his or her inspiration, direct action, creativity, courage, and fortitude; and who aims for and ultimately affects the establishment of a new stable equilibrium that secures permanent benefit for the targeted group and society at large.

The Grameen Bank in Bangladesh is cited as an example of a social enterprise because it has social development aims, works with and for poor people but uses business principles to achieve its objectives. The social enterprise sector is thus a hybrid, lying somewhere between the private sector and the NGO sector.

### 3.2.6    CDWs

CDWs do not work in a vacuum. They and their organisations are part of a group of stakeholders and, as such, they need to take a certain position and represent it. We have heard many times that we must be prepared before we start doing anything. A CDW's operational strategy is his/her preparation for the work as CDW (see Chapter 17 for more on the operational strategy of the CDW). This operational strategy reflects the CDW's relationship with the organisation he/she works for. We can safely say that the relationship between the CDW and his/her organisation determines what the CDW will do and how he/she will do it. It is this relationship between CDWs and their organisations, that we will contemplate further.

The operational strategy is guided by the relationship between the CDW and his/her organisation. It is also influenced by the expectations held of each other. The relationship between the CDW and his/her organisation is determined by, among others:

▶ the law;
▶ training; and
▶ human resource practices.

The national Constitution and the laws laid down in terms of it, provide the framework or guidelines according to which a government institution functions. The law usually spells out what policy goals need to be achieved by certain institutions. Of course, NGOs and CBOs determine their goals somewhat differently since they are not established in terms of a statute. Yet, they too have to abide by the Constitution and work within the parameters set by laws.

In South Africa the following are examples of laws that influence and set guidelines for the work done by CDWs:

The Constitution of the Republic of South Africa, 1996 (Act 108 of 1996). In section 152 references are made to the encouragement of community involvement as an aim of local government. In fact, the constitution is very specific on the aims when it states that local government must aim to: 'promote social and economic development' (sec 152 (1c) and: ' a municipality must ... promote the social and economic development of the community' (sec 153 a).

▶ The Development Facilitation Act, 1995 (Act 67 of 1995) requires of local government to be development oriented.
▶ The Act on Municipal Demarcation, 1998 (Act 27 of 1998), Municipal Structures Act, 1998 (Act 117 of 1998) and the Municipal Systems Act, 2000 (Act 32 of 2000) all contribute to development aims of the government.

With training, certain values, skills and attitudes can be engendered within employees. Training that is interactive will probably achieve the best results. Yet, it is not only the CDWs who need training.

Middle and top management also need training on topics similar to those the CDWs are exposed to. The managers especially need to be trained to understand their role as facilitators and enablers of CDWs. If they do not grasp how this role should work, CDWs will have an uphill battle in achieving the goals set for community development. Training as a tool to establish and strengthen a healthy relationship between the employee CDW and his/her organisation, applies equally to employees in government, private and NGO institutions. Development training is dealt with in detail in Chapters 22 and 23.

Following standard human resource practices encourages an atmosphere of transparency and fairness. Employees know the rules that apply to their remuneration and benefits. They also know the expectations and have the tools to perform optimally. Yet, sometimes the most important tool—a job description—is weak or non-existent and then the CDW is expected to perform in a void. In all types of organisation, the setting of a clear, well-organised and negotiated job description is crucial for the achievement of optimum results. Middle and senior managers must understand the contents of the job description and also know what is required of them as managers or 'enablers' in terms of support needed, to make CDWs effective in doing their job. In addition, the necessary hardware, logistical support and maintenance must be available for CDWs to do their work.

## 3.3 THE ORGANISATION AS AN ENABLER OF COMMUNITY DEVELOPMENT

Stakeholders (institutions) responsible for working towards an enabling environment, including policy making, work in an uncertain and ever-changing environment. These institutions should therefore be of a special orientation to be successful in their quest for an enabling environment. Their orientation should be one of readiness to adapt to ever-changing situations. Adaptiveness is a concept which you will meet throughout the book.

It is in direct contradiction to blueprint planning. See Chapter 20 for a detailed discussion of the different approaches to planning.

An adaptive approach requires complete organisational and procedural changes. Management should be fluid, open to change and adaptable. Structures should give space for manoeuvring and should be flexible, allowing new actions where and when necessary.

An adaptive orientation will identify the following necessities in order to ensure an enabling environment for CDWs (Rondinelli, 1993:158):

▶ Adjusting planning procedures and methods of administration to the political dynamics of local policy-making. Circumstances differ from one area to another; stakeholders also differ. While national policies such as the Integrated Development Plan (IDP) give guidelines and steps to follow, these must be applied flexibly to suit local circumstances.

▶ Increasing the responsiveness of bureaucracies engaged in development activities. This means networking and personal contact with relevant stakeholders from all spheres: government, private sector, NGOs and CBOs. Since the CDW does not have power to force responsiveness, other methods, such as good interpersonal skills, must be used.

▶ Adopting a learning approach to planning and administration. This will allow communities to participate and learn by doing. The CDW must be actively aware of his/her role and responsibility in facilitating learning by community members.

▶ Developing widespread and appropriate forms of administrative capacity within the community and its committees.

▶ Decentralising authority for development planning and administration. The CDW is not the leader and decision-maker in the community. He/she must foster capacity and provide information for the community leadership to become masters of their own development planning and administration.

▶ Relying on adjunctive and strategic rather than comprehensive and control-oriented planning. CDWs invariably work in communities trapped in deprivation (see Chapter 1). They therefore work with people exposed to uncertainty and fear, with few resources available for 'development'. In this situation comprehensive planning will fail as there is no guarantee that a project will be completed successfully. The CDW knows where he/she is going (thus has a blueprint in mind) and will know how to communicate and achieve the end-result through adjunctive and strategic planning. He/she will also be prepared to adapt his/her 'blueprint' as required by circumstances.

▶ Encouraging error detection and correction rather than suppression and punishment. In working with people this is a most important guideline to adhere to. The operational strategy must be clear on corrective measures to be taken when error is discovered. As important as detection and correction are, sometimes punishment may be called for if mistakes are made on purpose. The strategy also needs to deal with the nuts and bolts of punishment within a community group.

Sustainable and equitable community development requires strengthening administrative capacity of relevant institutions. It implies expanding participation, strengthening a wide variety of public and private organisations, and increasing the access of individuals to resources and opportunities. Case Study 11: *The project that was taken over*, illustrates the enabling organisation doing too much and going in the wrong direction.

## 3.4   CAPACITY BUILDING AS ENABLING MECHANISM

Understanding and working with group dynamics requires knowledge and experience. This should be obtained through capacity building, an important goal of the CDW. Capacity building means the strengthening of personal and institutional ability to undertake tasks. In the context of community development (which is ideally a responsibility of local government), this includes the necessary functions of governance, other local government related activities, increasing access to resources, improving power relationships between all parties involved, increasing the general awareness of local communities regarding resources management, development in general and the ability to secure an enabling environment for promoting stakeholder participation.

The capacity building needs of the stakeholders are directly related not only to the existing skills levels of the stakeholders and the desired level of appropriate skills, but also to the relevance of their skills to the organisational requirements. Different levels of capacity building would be needed for different stakeholders and categories of stakeholders. The level and focus of the capacity building process would depend on the skills level of the participating stakeholders, their expected roles and the needs of the forum.

Capacity building must be contextually appropriate. The capacity building process should also take cognisance of and accommodate the variety of societal, economic and cultural differences found in the typical developing society. Capacity building also needs to be grounded in the contextual realities of local government within a specific municipal area.

Developing the level and focus of a capacity building process would be dependent upon an analysis of the existing skills of the participants, compared to the functional, personal and organisational skills required. It should also recognise and accommodate the personality traits of the participants.

It is very important that any capacity building process be developed in consultation with the participants involved in the process. This will ensure high levels of relevance and acceptance by stakeholders.

All stakeholders from communities and from relevant government institutions (local, provincial and national) should undergo some form of capacity building. It must be recognised that the level and focus of the capacity building process will differ from group to group and even on an individual basis. The specific role, functions and responsibilities of individuals or groups combined with existing levels of skill, knowledge and awareness, will serve as a basis to determine the type of capacity building that will be required.

Capacity building must be understood as an integral part of an ongoing process that seeks to acquire, transfer and match skills and competence of people to equip and enable them to enter into a range of situations with stable abilities, independence and self-confidence, allowing them to actively engage in seeking agreements and solutions that work for them.

Within the context of local development and participation in organisational activities, this would mean that they would acquire sufficient knowledge, competencies and skills to allow an understanding of the core principles involved; the needs, interests and concerns of other stakeholders and to actively engage in working towards shared goals.

There is only one way to ensure that capacity building takes place and that is to ensure that there exists a structure for it and that able people staff the structure. One of the great dangers regarding capacity building is that it will take place haphazardly by uncommitted and ill trained trainers, who have no one to report to and have no support system to assist them. Such training is mostly a waste of time and leads to immense frustration.

## 3.5 FINDING WAYS TO CO-ORDINATE COMMUNITY DEVELOPMENT

In any community all or most of the above stakeholders will be found. They all have an interest—a stake—in proposed or intended poverty alleviation and poverty eradication projects. The CDW, the government official, or the altruistic NGO approaching a community to facilitate development must be sure to clearly identify and promote participation of all stakeholders in identifying, planning, implementing and evaluating any development project in the area. In addition, stakeholders identified must be brought together and systems designed and implemented that harness them, focus energies and make possible collaboration between them and co-ordination of all their efforts.

Acceptable and applicable mechanisms for the co-ordination of community development should be based on knowledge gained from the literature that reflects mostly on the practical situation, practical examples from research and experience, and the needs and experiences of the relevant stakeholders. To be successful, it should be appropriate to the empirical reality and be backed and supported by a policy and by political support. In general, very few of these inputs exist. The literature on the co-ordination of community development is almost non-existent and—where available—mostly superficial.

### 3.5.1 Understanding the environment in which co-ordination must take place

It is clear that the environment is tremendously complicated. In fact, it is very hard to talk of an environment. Actually there are various environments with different political, social, cultural, economic and psychological realities (see Chapter 2). This complexity makes it very important to know the environment in detail, to know the role-players, the situations and the potential conflicts. Through co-ordination a seemingly unworkable situation must be made to work, a potentially explosive situation must be defused and the diversity of stakeholders must be utilised in a positive manner to the great advantage of local people.

We can say that the following principles should form a basis for identifying a co-ordination environment:

▶ Co-ordination is an essential management function and tool in a varied and complex environment.
▶ There is a firm commitment to a transparent and effective relationship with all stakeholders and impacted audiences.
▶ Accountability to the people in a local government area is a key element of a co-ordination strategy.
▶ There is a commitment to empowering target audiences.
▶ The co-ordination strategy must be seen at all times as part of a wider strategy.
▶ An analysis of the co-ordination environment and the challenges that the co-ordination strategy must concentrate on, have certain priorities. These priorities will be determined by the stakeholders and the way in which those in power (politicians and officials) relate to local communities and civil society.

In more detail these themes are as follows:

▶ All three spheres of government are forging partnerships with communities to act decisively in order to improve their lives.
▶ Community participation is a key to equity, efficiency and sustainability of local government.
▶ Community development is the key to socio-economic development in the municipal area.

These principles and themes will be concretised through forging linkages. Linkages are more than mere co-ordination activities. While they are forged through co-ordination and quite often kept alive through co-ordination, they are more than just that. They are structures that must be created and formalised. A linkage can consist of a loose organisation with, say, one meeting per month, or it can be a partnership to share information on the internet. Linkages can consist of focus groups, or beehives, for local government relevant institutions that are not necessarily part of the institutions, but interact with them in various ways. The important aspect in this case is that some linkage structure must exist and be used. This linkage structure must also fit the situation, in other words, it must conform to the criterion of appropriateness.

With the diverse nature of the target audiences in mind any co-ordination structure will have to be innovative and include all stakeholders.

### 3.5.2 Preparing the way for co-ordination: establishing discussion forums

The establishment and management of forums must be a participatory process through the medium of workshops followed by small task teams to each attend to a specific aspect of the brief. Guidelines must be formulated and agreed upon by all stakeholders involved.

Once forums have been established they begin a survival struggle that can last for a long time. It is important to realise that groups such as forums are naturally frail and that they need, among others, support to continue to exist, never mind making a success of their task. It needs knowledge and understanding of the psychology and dynamics of such groups in order to facilitate them (see Chapter 11 for more on group dynamics).

### 3.5.3 Constraints and barriers to co-ordination

Practical examples of (successful) co-ordination are not well documented. Empirical reality in South Africa was, and still is, in flux and a policy and political support for co-ordinating community development is only now in a process of taking shape.

When designing mechanisms for co-ordinating community development, three simple, but very important questions must be asked and clearly answered:

▶ Who are the stakeholders that need to be co-ordinated?
▶ Who are the owners of the envisaged development?
▶ What is community development?

The answer to the first question will vary from one situation to another, but—generally speaking—the stakeholders will include a community group, local, regional and central government, NGOs and the private sector. However, only if agreement on the answers to the second and third questions is reached, can we make headway in determining appropriate mechanisms for co-ordinating community development. Regardless of the rhetoric to the contrary, politicians, officials, aid agencies and private sector stakeholders often regard development projects as 'theirs' and not belonging to the affected community. As long as this spirit prevails and as long as communities are not allowed to take ownership of community development projects, efforts at developing acceptable and applicable mechanisms of co-ordination will fail. Furthermore, in many circles, community development is still perceived as a line function, that is creating clubs and promoting sewing and knitting classes for 'idle women'. Community development as a process of empowerment (as we argue in Chapter 6) to be applied by all professionals in line functions, needs to be recognised before any attempt at co-ordinating community development will succeed. When ownership belongs to the people, the matter of co-ordination will become less of an issue. Development will not belong to a ministry or other line functionary and therefore the duty of establishing co-ordination will not lie with any of them, but with the community.

### 3.5.4    Practices of co-ordination in community development

Due to a perception that attempts at co-ordination have mostly failed, the concept is used less often in recent literature. Authors use the concept co-operation and more frequently, collaboration. In this chapter no attempt will be made to debate the philosophical and analytical differences between them; we rather use them as synonyms, with the meaning of a framework for collective development action (Selsky, 1991).

The literature on co-ordination deals with principles, preconditions and stumbling blocks on a macro level. Co-ordination of development projects is dealt with in some detail but inter-agency co-ordination receives scant attention (see Cusworth & Franks, 1993; Blunt, 1990; Franks, 1989; Honadle & Cooper, 1989). As Selsky (1991) says 'Development in inter-organisational settings is poorly conceptualised in the literature'. Case studies and analysis of co-ordination are rarely found in the literature.

The available literature shows that co-ordination cannot be enforced. At the same time it cannot be successful without certain structures (see Khosa, 1991 and Kingma, 1994). But the mere existence of structures is not a guarantee for co-ordination. The one and perhaps only, certain thing about co-ordination is that it is extremely difficult to accomplish (Swanepoel, 1993). The work of Lippitt and Van Til (1981) gives a useful framework for developing mechanisms for co-ordination. They identify a number of constraints or barriers to co-ordination or 'collaboration' as they put it. These are the following:

- Organisations and institutions are kept apart to maintain fair play.
- An ethos exists in which competition and independence is the rule.
- It takes so much time and effort to establish co-ordination that it is regarded by many as not worth the trouble.
- Institutions survive because they maintain their turf.
- In society emphasis is put on the individual's rights and a strong ego is built.
- The idea of negotiation and compromise is seen as negative.
- The bad name of the 'committee' is a way to express distrust in co-ordination.

A further constraint is that of communication. The one factor that makes co-ordination succeed or fail is the ability, or lack of it, of people to communicate.

These constraints are all present in any given situation. Add to that the fact of the sectorally or functionally structured government institutions, and it becomes obvious why co-ordination is such a difficult goal to achieve (Swanepoel, 1986:49). Holdcroft (1982:222) talks of this separateness of institutions as the 'battle of departments' which renders co-ordination, let alone integration, impossible.

Yet, co-ordination is an absolute necessity if one thinks of community development as a total transformation. If this holistic character of development is recognised and acknowledged, if it is accepted that it should touch the total milieu and the hearts and minds of people, then one can talk of the necessity of a total systems approach (Armor et al, 1979:276). In such an approach, according to Swanepoel (1985(a):101):

> [...] all the participating organisations, be they governmental or private, have the same goals and objectives which they strive to obtain through an interrelated and integrated programme.

Lippitt and Van Til (1981) suggest a six-step process to establish co-ordination. The six steps are as follows:

### Step one: Establishing the preconditions for co-ordination
Co-ordination begins with a vision or idea how something will be better if two or more organisations work together. Without this vision co-ordination will not materialise. The initiation of co-ordinative activity is both a highly personal and idiosyncratic event with structural determinants.

### Step two: Testing the co-ordinative waters
The articulation of co-ordinative potential must be followed by a fuller exploration of the idea's viability. Four tests are suggested in this regard: assuring that the proposed co-ordination does not threaten organisational domain; assuring that the proposed co-ordination does not threaten organisational autonomy; sketching an image of potential domain consensus; and checking limits of pre-existing co-ordinative networks.

### Step three: Initiating the idea of co-ordination
From the very first conversation that broached the idea of co-ordination, attention is required to the mood and setting of the exploratory discussion. If parties to the proposed co-ordination do not see it as a necessary way of problem solving they will not easily become part of the process.

### Step four: Defining the co-ordinative venture
Clear definitions of member and team roles need to be developed. Co-ordination will work best if a clearly identifiable co-ordinative team can be developed. As this team comes into existence, it must be able to show that it can act independently of the several organisational loyalties its members carry. As they learn to trust and work with each other, the group begins to draw a social contract of their co-ordinative venture.

### Step five: Invigorating the co-ordinative process
Co-ordination has its low points and pitfalls. Surmounting them requires insight, patience, sensitivity and perspective. There are two things that are playing a role in the invigoration of co-ordination. They are the following:

> ▶ The greater the complementarity of functions between the co-ordinative venture and the individual members, the greater the likelihood of co-ordinated action.
> ▶ The larger the co-ordinating group, the more likely it is that an uncooperative coalition will develop within it.

**Step six: Evaluating the co-ordinative experience**

Co-ordinative ventures should be evaluated even more frequently than more established organisational ventures. The validity of the initial idea that brought the co-ordination into existence requires renewal and review.

This whole process is fascinating and thought provoking when one thinks of the South African situation. The reason why co-ordination was so often a failure in this country lies perhaps in the fact that the care with establishing co-ordination as suggested above, was to a large extent absent. One could summarise from this that the ground for co-ordination must be carefully prepared; that the co-ordination venture must be nurtured all the time; that the venture should not be a threat to any participating organisation; and that co-ordination must be absolutely necessary before it is attempted.

**To the above we can add a seventh step:** that of establishing a legal body such as a trust for facilitating co-ordination. To establish a legal body the following should be considered:

> ▶ investigate the desirability of one legal body community, district or municipality;
> ▶ investigate the legal ramification/requirement for establishing such a body;
> ▶ investigate and list the functions to be performed by the legal body; and
> ▶ establish the legal body in terms of the guidelines gleaned from the previous steps.

If the ownership of community development is turned around so that it rests with the community, it seems very important that supportive and enabling organisations work together as a team (Swanepoel 1993). It is also important to note that if the ownership of projects is in the hands of the community, the community will be the initiator of co-ordination. This means that the community will have to follow the suggestions made by Lippitt and Van Til. This may be a daunting task which will require careful thought and study.

## 3.6 CONCLUSION

CDWs never work in isolation. There are always a number of stakeholders present in any development environment. Hopefully, most of them will be friendly, but there may be a few who are not. Much of the co-ordination problems of the past and also the present are the result of a misplaced view by many of the stakeholders from the government, private and non-governmental cadres that development projects belong to them. It then becomes a turf war in the development environment with the concomitant lack of any collaboration, the duplication of activities and expenses, and quite often the bewilderment of those who are supposed to be the owners of projects—the community. But even if all agree that the projects belong to the people, it will still be difficult to establish collaboration and to develop it. One needs wisdom and tenacity to be successful.

Case Study 20: *The story of KwaMpofu*, gives an idea of the various stakeholders present in a specific area and the presence and lack of co-ordination at the same time.

The community at large is the most important stakeholder in poverty alleviation. The community knows its own needs, resources and capabilities. It is the community that will win— or lose—the most in any attempt at development or poverty eradication.

## Endnote

1. A stokvel is a women's club where members pay an equal amount of money each month to a central fund and one member then receives the large amount when it is her turn. Some stokvels also lend small amounts of money to members or help them with funeral expenses.

**SECTION B**
THE PROCESS OF
COMMUNITY DEVELOPMENT

# CHAPTER 4

# THE ORIGINS OF COMMUNITY DEVELOPMENT

## 4.1   INTRODUCTION

Historically, a number of key themes stand out which can be tied to the history of community development. These are, inter alia, participation, project management, training, community, co-ordination and funding. These themes formed the debating points around which the 'idea' of community development evolved and developed. Community development is referred to as an idea because it has no firm, precise and generally agreed upon meaning (Cornwell 1986:219).

This then is what the history of community development points out: in spite of attempts over the past 50 years by practitioners and academics to give meaning to the concept, no generally accepted definition of community development has evolved. What did happen, though, was that ideas about development crystallised into what was regarded as radical viewpoints some years ago, but are now the accepted approach towards poverty eradication.

## 4.2   EARLY HISTORY

The practice of what we may loosely call community development dates back to the history of the early civilisations when mankind initiated actions from which groups or parts of groups benefited in some or other way.  But we are interested in the more recent origin of community development which is attributed by some American authors to the practice of agricultural extension, instituted in 1870 in some Mid-Western states of the USA  (De Beer & Swanepoel, 1998:2).

Some (Phifer et al, 1980) give a different explanation of the origin of community development. According to them, it originated in the USA in 1908 with the *Country Life Commission* report and the 1914 Smith-Lever-Act in terms of which the *Co-operative Extension Service* came into being. With this exercise the aim was to establish community organisation in order to promote better living, better farming, more education, more happiness and better citizenship (Phifer et al, 1980:19—20).  According to Cornwell (1986:12) the aims of the *Co-operative Extension Service* concur with the aims attributed in recent literature to community development, although the development of leadership did not feature.

While these community organisation efforts remind us of community development, a more realistic starting point for explaining the origin of community development is perhaps the attempts by the *Institute for Rural Reconstruction* created in 1921 in India. The aim of this institute was:

> ... to bring back life in all its completeness, making the villagers self-reliant and self-respectful, acquainted with the cultural tradition of their own country and competent to make an efficient use of modern resources for the fullest development of their physical, social, economic and intellectual conditions (Brokensha & Hodge, 1969:40–41).

This programme emphasised the use of local resources and the need for an integrated approach towards development.

The Gandhian rural reconstruction experiment which started in 1931 was similar in approach to the Institute for Rural Reconstruction, with an emphasis on self-sufficiency and attitude change as pre-requisites for community development (Brokensha & Hodge, 1969: 41).

The British Colonial Office incorporated the gist of the rural reconstruction programmes into subsequent colonial development approaches. It was, however, not until 1944 that this policy took shape. Community development formed an important part of British colonial policy, not only in India but also in the African colonies. By the end of the 1940s, the term community development was in use world wide. By then it was used to denote government programmes aimed at the stimulation of local initiative for community self-development efforts (Cornwell, 1986: 16).

According to Monaheng (2000:126) influences on the character of community development came from the launching of India's community development programme after its independence in 1947 and this occurrence also stimulated community development efforts in neighbouring Asian countries and further afield in the Third World. To Korten (1980:481) it was a Ford Foundation funded project in the Ettawah district of Uttar Pradesh, India in 1948 that brought community development into prominence in the late and post-colonial era. This pilot project involved 64 villages and established the village level worker as a key role player. The Ettawah project concentrated on increasing productivity in agricultural and local industry. It did, however, also address needs of the local population like education, health and sanitation. The spectacular success of the project (an increase of 165 per cent in production in the first four years) was attributed to the problem oriented framework within which needs were identified, the strong personality of the project leader and the fact that carefully selected and well trained officials were responsible for implementation.

The success of the Ettawah project contributed to the establishment of India's national development programme. With American aid the programme was launched in 1952.

The programme's eventual failure was measured in terms of its inability to encourage community initiative and a failure to develop local leadership. In the end the elite benefitted more than the poor villagers at whom the programmes were initially aimed (De Beer & Swanepoel, 1998:3).

The popularity of community development reached a peak during the 1950s and 1960s. This period coincided with the time of the Cold War; a period during which the United States regarded community development as a tool or method through which democracy could be established and communism kept at bay. In Greece, Korea and Burma community development programmes were used in the reconstruction of community facilities, the creation of jobs for demobilised soldiers and to combat poverty (Cornwell, 1986:17). By the early 1960s community development programmes were in place in more than sixty countries and in more than half of those countries the community development programmes represented the national development efforts. This was perhaps reason for its problems later on. Community development did not work as well on the macro-level as it did on the micro-level.

## 4.3  THEMATIC DEVELOPMENT

Community development programmes were not nearly as successful as was envisaged and this lack of success forced academics, officials and policy makers to think again. Disappointment with the lack of success with community development led to the emergence of 'new' or 'alternative' approaches. On closer scrutiny it becomes apparent, however, that the new approaches basically represented a change in emphasis on the themes underlying community development (De Beer & Swanepoel, 1998:13).

The early practice of community development emphasised the means or method to bring about change. *Method* is consequently one of the themes constantly present in the earlier writings on community development. The method usually entailed the use of a change agent such as a community development worker (CDW) who had as aim the stimulation of the participation of 'the community' in development projects. Most often such projects were decided on and planned by 'outsiders'—be it government agents or non-governmental organisations (NGOs)—who decided on the needs of the people. So, to these people community development was a method and a tool to bring about 'desired change' according to their view.

In reaction to this emphasis others saw community development as a process in which local (or community) groups take the initiative to formulate objectives involving changes in their living conditions (Roberts, 1979:39). We can see that the process idea gives more initiative and freedom to the ordinary people to begin a process, while the method idea wants the change agent to apply a certain method in order to generate the necessary result (De Beer & Swanepoel, 1998:4). Roberts' idea of community development as a process stemming from community initiative is supported by others such as Brokensha & Hodge (1969:48) who argue that community development is:

> ... the educational process by which people change themselves and their behavior and acquire new skills and confidence through working in cooperation ...

Yet, even if this process approach seems liberal, the emphasis is still wrong if judged in terms of our views today. The onus is on the poor to change, and not primarily their situation, but their behaviour. Nothing or very little is made of the approach and objective of the CDW and whoever he/she represents.

The method/process debate has, however, become stale and lost its vigour. In the subsequent debate on community development the focus moved more towards the question of whether the community is the master or client in development.

In the mid 1970s a variation on the theme of community development occurred when the Basic Needs Approach (BNA) was developed by the World Bank and the International Labour Organisation (ILO). With this shift in emphasis came a broader concern to eradicate poverty and a shift from a preoccupation with means to a renewed awareness of ends. According to Cornwell (1986:23) this shift represents a radical change from emphasising the *method* to emphasising the attainment of concrete objectives identified by the poor. In other words, we are again dealing with method and process.

The BNA attaches fundamental importance to poverty eradication within a short period as one of the main objectives of development. It defines poverty not in terms of income, but as the inability to meet certain basic human needs on the part of identifiable groups of human beings. Poverty is characterised by hunger and malnutrition, by ill health, by lack of education, safe water, sanitation and decent shelter. A vital aspect of the elimination of poverty, then, consists in securing access to these goods and services for the poor.

While focusing on the *what* (basic needs), the BNA never really developed a methodology of *how* to achieve the satisfaction of basic needs. Consequently, in the early 1980s it lost its appeal as a separate approach towards the development of Third World/poor communities. It fulfilled the role of a guiding principle and objective. It surfaced, however, again as part of the more elaborate people-centred approach which we will discuss later on.

The BNA did, however, contribute towards the debate on the process character of community development. Wisner (1988:27) for example, distinguishes between a strong (radical) and a weak (liberal) version of BNA: '... the weak BNA either imposes a set of needs on the poor from the outside and/or limits the radical potential of participation'. By contrast, when the poor collectively reflect on their needs, a radical BNA manifests itself. 'In this process, the poor themselves define and control their own struggle. The development project becomes, in other words, radically participatory' (Wisner, 1988:26). This theme was carried further in the third variant of community development, ie participatory development. One of the biggest proponents of participatory development, Gran (1983:327) defines the concept as:

> ... the self-sustaining process to engage free men and women in activities that meet their basic needs and, beyond that, realise individually defined human potential within socially defined limits ...

## 4.4 RADICALISED APPROACH

The radical viewpoint of the BNA marked an early era of questioning of the commonly held truth about community development. Within the participatory development debate we can differentiate two distinct schools of thought: on the one hand the advocates of the liberal or humanistic views and on the other the advocates of a radical participatory development. The latter group argues that participation can only be effective if it is direct and allows ultimate control to communities to decide their own affairs. Scope must be allowed for the production of new knowledge, the mapping out of new directions and the design of new organisational methods; all of which are to engender an upward progression from the bottom to management level (Oakley & Marsden, 1984:13). Since the middle 1980s the radical approach has gained ground and has come to dominate the debate on community development.

The radical viewpoint takes the debate away from the mobilisation of community resources, community organisation and involvement in pre-planned projects, to issues of powerlessness, decision-making and empowerment. The debate on the more radical version of participation coincided with or stimulated the development of even more variants of community development: the learning process approach, people-centred approach, human scale development and empowerment. The debate on these approaches, it must be stressed, blends to such an extent that it becomes difficult to disentangle concepts, let alone understand the meaning attached to them in different settings. For analytical purposes, and as far as it is distinguishable, the broad outlines of these variants will nevertheless be discussed here.

The (social) learning process approach (LPA) aims to meet the need for '... a flexible, sustained, experimental, action based capacity building style of assistance ...' (Korten, 1980:484). It is a bottom-up approach, avoiding the restrictions of a blueprint (top-down) approach. Consequently, it envisages development programmes arising from a learning process in which the local people and programme staff have an equal share and in which their knowledge and resources are shared to establish a programme.

The logical result of using the LPA should be greater emphasis on the autonomy of the poor, their right to decision-making and their empowerment. According to Gran (1983: 345) the success story of the LPA has proved that '... people can lead their own change processes. They can be the actors, not merely the subjects of change'.

The people-centred or empowerment strategy builds on the participatory approach and LPA; it also represents a further development of the BNA. The components integral to a people-centred approach are:

> population participation in development;
> the need for sustainable development; and
> the support and advocacy of the people's role in development by the bureaucracy, NGOs and voluntary organisations.

The people's role becomes clear in the empowerment strategy's definition of development, formulated by Korten (1990:67) as:

> ... a process by which the members of a society increase their potential and institutional capacities to mobilize and manage resources to produce sustainable and justly distributed improvements in their quality of life consistent with their own aspirations.

This definition places the decision as to what development is in the hands of the community—outsiders do not prescribe to a community or a society. The emphasis is on a long-term process whereby those who are involved in it develop the ability to manage and utilise local resources to their own benefit. Moser (1983: 3) sees people-centred or empowerment strategies as aiming at capacity building; in this instance participation is not a means, but becomes an end in itself:

> ... the objective is not a fixed, quantifiable development goal but a process whose outcome is an increasingly 'meaningful' participation in the development process.

In the people-centred or empowerment strategy, institutions, as in the past, play a very important, but vastly different role. What is required from the bureaucracy, for instance, is a change in its role from 'giver of good things' to that of enabler; a role that relates to the premises of adaptive administration. The bureaucracy, to succeed, needs to open itself and become in the words of Denis Goulet 'institutionally vulnerable' (Goulet, 1974:37—38). Korten (1991:17) identifies four generic principles which would enable bureaucracies to promote participatory, people-centred or empowerment development:

- Assistance to each individual community group should be designed and managed as a discrete activity with its own specifications and time table responsive to the particular situation of that group, based on a careful study of existing practices, technical capacities, resource availabilities and power structures.
- The emphasis should be on community control and management of the resource, with every aspect of the intervention geared to this outcome. This should include provision for legal confirmation of the resources management group as an autonomous body with legal rights.
- Actual design of the facilities does not take place until the beneficiaries are fully prepared to make their needs and preferences known and, once completed, is not implemented until formally accepted by an association of the beneficiaries.
- Organising takes account of and works within existing social and organisational structures to the extent possible, while building member strength from the bottom up to ensure broadly based participation by the actual producers and avoid domination by traditional leaders.

The Human Scale Development (HSD) approach (Max-Neef, 1991) shows many similarities with the people-centred approach. HSD evolved mainly in Latin America under the strong inspiration of Max-Neef. In this approach a distinction is made between needs and satisfiers. Needs are viewed to be universal and basic: not only material needs are addressed, but individual and community needs dominate this model. Satisfiers are those aspects that are contextually defined and may differ from one place to another. Both needs and satisfiers are addressed in HSD, since the human being is viewed as a whole, responsible for his/her own development within the norms of society.

A related approach also acknowledging the central place of the human being is the Capabilities Approach emphasised by the Indian development philosopher Amartya Sen. This approach was influenced by the work of Adam Smith, Karl Marx and the Greek philosopher Aristotle (Clark, 2005:2). The Capabilities Approach provides a framework to tackle human development and addresses poverty and inequality and consists of two core concepts: functionings and capabilities. Functionings refer to a person's state of being and doing. Capabilities refer to real or effective opportunities to achieve functionings. The Capabilities Approach sees development as a process of expanding people's human capabilities. This, then, is an approach that places human development—and not, for instance, economic development—at the centre. Human beings and their development become an end in itself and not a means to other ends. In the field of development 'capabilities', according to Sen, do not refer to income, resources, goods, emotions or the satisfaction of preferences. It refers to 'what people are effectively able to do and be' or the freedom 'to enjoy valuable beings and doings' (Robeyns, 2005:91).

Sen does not provide a list of specific capabilities; what he does is to stress the role of activity and freedom in people's ability to make their own choices.

Over the years, practitioners and theorists of the international 'community development movement' have departed from a strong emphasis on centralised government decision-making and a reliance on international financial power as a driving force behind people's involvement. As part of the historical development described above, what is known as 'Another Development', evolved in the late 1980s and early 1990s. Ekins (1992:100) says the following about this:

'Another Development' has emerged as a clear and coherent system of developmental analysis to contrast with the top-down, finance oriented economism of conventional development strategies.

The five main characteristics of 'Another Development' are that it is:

▶ need-oriented and addresses material and non-material human needs;
▶ endogenous in that every society's values and vision of the future should determine development;
▶ self-reliant in that the power and energy in every society's natural and cultural environment are used for development;
▶ ecologically pure because planning and action occur within the confines of the ecology; and
▶ based on structural transformation of social relationships, economic activities and power relationships (Nerfin, 1977:10)

## 4.5   CONCLUSION

In the coming years all these approaches, from BNA to 'Another Development', will probably dominate the debate on development. A confluence of these debates into yet another debate is possible. Much more debate will go into the questions of needs and poverty, relief and release from the deprivation trap, centralisation versus decentralisation, a redefinition of the role of bureaucracy, a closer scrutiny of the role of NGOs, more emphasis on the role of the social enterprise sector and the question of empowerment and ownership in terms of control over community resources and sustainable development.

# CHAPTER 5

# THE FEATURES AND OUTCOMES OF COMMUNITY DEVELOPMENT

## 5.1 INTRODUCTION

One can be busy with various kinds of development or betterment or change. Some of the principles discussed in the next chapter will also be true for or relevant to these different forms of change, but the combination of those principles as a unit is true only for what is known all over the world as community development. These principles inform, even sculpt, the features and outcomes of community development. In this chapter we will look at these features and the end results of community development and will show how the principles play a role in their formulation.

## 5.2 THE FEATURES OF COMMUNITY DEVELOPMENT

### 5.2.1 An integrated approach

The most fundamental characteristic of community development is that it follows an integrated approach to the problems of poverty and development, these being the eradication of poverty (Monaheng, 2000:127). Integration in community development has two major implications (Monaheng, 2000:127). The first is that the problems of development are multifaceted and that they should be tackled together in a co-ordinated fashion. It emphasises the fact that social, political and cultural aspects should be treated together with the economic aspects, because they are all interrelated. The second element of integration is that different role-players should co-ordinate their efforts. Government agencies, non-governmental organisations and community based organisations should work hand in hand in order to optimise the impact of their efforts and to avoid duplication and conflict. See Chapter 3 for a further discussion of this. In fact, community development cannot be sectoralised. A person who has a need for health services invariably also has a need for other basics such as clean water and a balanced diet (Swanepoel, 2000:72).

### 5.2.2 Collective action

Community development is not the action of an individual or of a few individuals. The individual is important, and it is therefore a collective activity in that a group of people sharing a mutual problem, need, sentiment or concern, act together and in concert and share a certain responsibility for the action. Such a collective action is a human activity, dealing with human problems and needs. It is also a voluntary action. Not all people who stand to gain from community development will act together. There is a personal freedom for individuals to join the collective activity or not. Community development workers (CDWs) are sometimes disheartened by the small number of people who seem willing to participate in collective action to solve problems and address needs. However, the positive outcome of this is that the freedom of the individual is respected, no one is forced to participate in community development, further, those participating are truly committed and, finally, a small group is, in fact, very strong when it comes to addressing abstract human needs, participating in the true sense of the word and learning from the activity. Collective action means that a group of people that can be defined as exclusive will be involved. The exclusivity of the group enhances the learning process because the same people are involved throughout and learn to work as a team. This does not mean that individualism is banned from projects. There are examples of projects also favouring the individual. The individual inputs are also very important in group action because that is how the group grows as an entity, the individual inputs being the building blocks for whatever venture. See Case Study 18: *Food garden in Mapayeni*.

### 5.2.3 Needs orientation

Projects are sometimes built around interests or hobbies. The large majority of these never come to fruition. People don't have the strength, energy or the commitment for those types of actions. The better vehicle to proceed with that type of activity is the club, which has a different set-up and different procedures from a project. Without a need or the perception of a need, community development cannot take place. This need or perception of a need must be heartfelt among the people who must participate in the project. People are not going to rally together around needs that have been identified by some expert and one which they find intangible. Therefore, needs identification is a prerequisite for action—it is the first step to be taken before a project commences (Adejunmobi, 1990:226; Jeppe, 1985:28).

A project without a clearly defined need is a dead project. This needs identification exercise is a participatory process because it is the people who must identify the need before they will organise themselves to do something about the need (Monaheng, 2000:127). A project with a need that is not perceived or understood by the people is a dead project. A community development project is not aimed at vague, ill-defined or broad, abstract needs. People will not rally together for the eradication of vaguely felt needs and such a project will have limited hope for success.

A perception of need, crisis and urgency must underline community action for it to be purposeful. The principle of release is important here (see Chapter 6). Relief cannot engender the same commitment and enthusiasm as release. A 'total transformation' is much more of a war cry than 'some improvement'.

There are dangers attached to participatory needs identification. There is a right and a wrong way in which to go about it and, unfortunately, the wrong way may often sound the easier and more official way. The needs identification aspect will be discussed in later chapters; suffice to say here that the principle of ownership is very important in this process.

If needs identification becomes the drawing up of a shopping list for some development agency to attend to, the process is heading for disaster. People must be the owners of their situation. They must realise that they have a certain need and they must decide that they are going to do something about it. In other words, they must take ownership of the action as well as the need. Of vital importance is the fact that if they have taken ownership of the need, it is so much easier to also take ownership of the action.

Another aspect of needs identification is that it is basically a negative activity. Poor people are negative about their situation and their chances to improve it. It is very interesting with how much ease a group of people from a deprived area can enumerate their needs. If they are then asked to identify their assets they usually find it very difficult. One of the psychological manifestations of poverty is a negative self-perception. Needs identification lies easily within this psychological characteristic.

If something is not done about this negative self-perception, needs identification will remain a finite, isolated process that will make participants more aware of their dire situation and will bring about a heightened sense of negative self-perception. CDWs must regard it as one of their prime tasks to change the negative self-perception to a positive one. CDWs must also realise that this change is a process and an arduous one at that.

Finally, it is important to realise that needs identification can lead to expectations. It is fine if people's expectations are raised because they have decided to do something about their situation. It is, however, sad if people's ingrained dependency on do-gooders raise their expectations that something will be done for them every time that they are facilitated to identify their needs. Recurrent disappointments every time that their expectations are not met hardens their negative self-perception and makes them suspicious of all potential development initiators and reluctant to react positively to inputs from these people such as CDWs. See Case Study 16: *The felt and the real need.*

### 5.2.4   Objective orientation

Each identified concrete need must be addressed by trying to realise a concrete objective. Because community development is born of a need, it is obvious that it must be directed at an objective addressing that specific need. Projects are by definition activities or sets of organisational measures aimed at or associated with clear objectives (Morgan 1983:330). Just as needs are not vaguely felt and broadly described, objectives are precise and concrete. Preciseness is the first requirement. A community development project cannot have a vague objective. Take the example of establishing a crèche. Where is the crèche to be situated? Whose children may attend it? How many children will it accommodate? Answering these questions will lead a group to describe their objective precisely.

The second requirement is that an objective must be concrete. A project's objective cannot be a better life. Every participant's concept of a better life will be unique and therefore different from others' concept. Besides, how is a plan to be devised and implemented for a better life? People's norms and values influence their perceptions. If an objective is stated broadly or vaguely or in the abstract, the chances are that diverse perceptions and interpretations will make collective action very difficult.

### 5.2.5    Action at grassroots level

Community development is not a method whereby the elite, government officials or experts keep the people busy by involving them in worthwhile actions. Neither does it consist of huge infrastructural projects where the community is confronted with ready-made blueprints from engineers or professional planners. It is primarily a process in which ordinary people play the leading part, with government, experts and the elite playing a facilitating role. Community development is really grassroots oriented in the sense that the main role-players are just ordinary and, usually, poor people. One must be careful not to put barriers in a project that successfully keep the poor out. If projects are meant for the 'enterprising members of a community' we are not really at the very grassroots and we are not touching the poor. If a local government is involved in a project as role-player, the ordinary people are not necessarily present. The local government may look as if it is grassroots, but it is rather somewhere slightly higher, such as the grass blades.

Because they are grassroots oriented, community development efforts are small, simple and address the basic needs of those at this level. This last aspect is of great importance. The needs at grassroots level must be tackled. Community development is not meant to fulfil the needs of a community over the whole spectrum. With the principle of simplicity in mind, we can safely say that community development seeks simplicity, avoids complexity and lies at the micro-level.

### 5.2.6    Asset based

Community development is not an action whereby local people draw up shopping lists for government agencies to fulfil. Community development makes use of the assets to its disposal. That is why no community development project can go without the identification of local assets. Those assets come from a very broad spectrum. It covers natural assets such as, for example, soil and water. But it also includes infrastructural assets such as roads, electricity, buildings and a sanitary system. The most important of all assets, though, are human beings and their ability to organise. This is what makes community development different and is what makes development management different from any other management. It is not a kind of development by demand or command. It is a development making use of the available resources, especially human resources in order to reach the objective. The beauty of this is that as the assets are used, they improve. This is especially true of the humans and their organisational skills. The whole activity is therefore geared to build the assets for better use in future.

### 5.2.7    Democratic

The concept of community development gives a special meaning to community. It first tells us that community is regarded as various kinds of vehicle to carry development forward (see Sihlongonyane, 2001). It also emphasises that the third sphere of government which is tied to the community in a special way, is involved. This sphere of government, known as local government, has a special function in developmental government. Community development forms part of this democratic activity. Community development also forms part of the local government's Integrated Development Planning and, as such, it is a democratic activity.

However, community development has a special democratic function in that it extends democracy beyond the ordinary three sphere government structure. It gives a lower than grassroots opportunity to the poorest of the poor, the most deprived, the isolated and vulnerable and the politically weak to participate in a democratic action that will give true meaning to their democratic rights as citizens.

## 5.3    THE OUTCOMES OF COMMUNITY DEVELOPMENT

Not all community development projects are a success. In fact, quite a large percentage never reach their objectives. Many reasons can be given for the failure of projects. These reasons must be sought at the running of projects, not at characteristics of community development. It was alleged in the past that community development does not work, but it will not work if the approach is wrong and the activities flowing from that approach are therefore also wrong. To blame community development for that is to throw the baby out with the bath water. Community development has all the attributes needed for positive results. The following are a few of those positive results.

### 5.3.1    Awareness creation

Communities gain a lot by the awareness that is being generated through community development. This does not mean that communities are ordinarily lacking awareness. Community development, however, encourages a certain kind of awareness. People become aware of themselves in terms of their environment; their needs and their resources. They also become aware of positive objectives that will change their situation. Community development, therefore, changes people's apathy into a positive disposition from the victims of poverty to active participants to eradicate the need.

A community is normally aware of its situation of need, but if people go through a community development process they start to see themselves as an active organism that is able to, and does, change its environment. This positive awareness ties in with the first principle that abstract human needs, such as that of self-reliance, are fulfilled at the same time as concrete needs. It also underlies the idea of asset-based development.

### 5.3.2    Further development

Community development projects quite often spark off further activity that can lead to the setting and reaching of further goals which bring about further development. Success in attaining goals that they have set for themselves does something very positive to people. They become aware of further needs and they set new objectives to address those needs. We see clearly that this leads to the fulfilment of abstract human needs. Apart from the confidence they gain, they have an enthusiasm born out of optimism to tackle further problems or needs. In this way one successful project can easily lead to another project.

But quite often projects that have been successfully completed are in fact not at an end. What was established through a project must be managed and maintained. It must be used or sold or adapted for changing circumstances. A project may have a continuous marketing and/or bookkeeping function. In short, a project's establishing function may end once the objective has been reached, but then its management function may still continue. We see clearly that this leads to the fulfilment of abstract human needs. Apart from the confidence they gain, they have an enthusiasm born out of optimism, to tackle further problems and needs.

### 5.3.3   Demonstration effect

Projects have an influence that spans much wider than only the project and those participating in it. It broadcasts its effect over a wide area so that people become aware of its success. Poor people are, justifiably, concerned about the risk that goes with any project. A successful project tends to allay fears, not only among the participants, but also among observers from outside. A successful project demonstrates to all that people who stand together and work together can bring about changes that will make a difference. A successful project usually leads to similar projects being launched in the area. In a few cases to note, this has become an avalanche with projects springing up everywhere. Apart from the physical results of such a dramatic growth in projects, it also has a psychological effect on people, so that the threat and risk of poverty become less of an issue and new ideas to cope with old problems become uppermost in their minds. When this happens a community can very quickly look after its own development efforts and will only need some expert advice from time to time. In these cases there is genuine ownership by the people of the local development efforts. See Case Study 17: *Mothers of the mountain community.*

### 5.3.4   Learning

The learning process in community development projects has a wider reach than only the project. The participants learn to be successful in many other spheres. The organisational sphere is a good example. A community's organisation becomes more efficient, more effective and develops the ability to expand — the outcome of the learning process in Korten's mind (1980).

The Participatory Rapid Appraisal and Planning (PRAP—see Chapter 18) process opens many opportunities to observe through research and to learn through observation. The participants, including the CDWs, learn not only what is—the context, but also what should—the activity of poverty eradication. The participants in community development also learn skills. A project can be in service of skills training such as sewing, but usually the learning is not an end in itself, but is in service of the project. Then people learn to organise, to plan, to implement and to evaluate. They can also learn more specialised skills tied in with the project such as agriculture, nursing, horticulture, masonry, bookkeeping and welding. In summary we can say that community development will continuously improve the ability of the people to deal with the challenges confronting them (Monaheng 2000:128).

One of the most important things participants learn is communication. It is the life blood of any project and if people do not learn quickly to communicate, the project is doomed. See Case Study 18: *Food garden in Mapayeni.*

### 5.3.5   Community building

Community development greatly strengthens a community. This strengthening takes place at both the abstract and concrete levels. People become more self-sufficient and self-reliant, which does a lot to their dignity. But they also learn how to organise more effectively. In other words, they learn how to run projects and their leadership structures develop accordingly.

Through the improvement of organisational skill, institution building also takes place. Institutions become adaptable and development oriented. Through these institutions, leadership is fostered and developed. According to Korten (1991:15) enhancing institutional capabilities is one of the most important human objectives of community development.

The importance of linkages in society is often negated or simply forgotten. Community development forges new linkages between institutions, between individuals and between institutions and individuals. Existing linkages are consequently strengthened. The isolation of poor communities is addressed by the creation of external linkages between communities or between communities and various authorities and agencies.

True leadership can gain much from community development. Existing leaders are enabled to lead more effectively and new leaders (especially on the project level) are thrust to the fore through institutions and project activities. Leadership is enhanced specifically through skills attainment. The skills we are talking about lie at two levels. First, there are organisational skills such as organising, negotiating, planning and evaluating. Second, there are also many other hard skills such as agriculture, horticulture, building, arts and crafts, health care, child care and needlework. All these skills are necessary ingredients of a self-sufficient community. Added to this is the fact that the results of projects lead to improvement in health, education, child care, sanitation and housing, to name but a few. Quite a few types of projects create jobs and/or generate incomes and this has a direct bearing on overcoming crime and antisocial behaviour.

## 5.4   CONCLUSION

Community development is a collective grassroots action to tackle felt concrete needs. Because it is so directed to everyday needs, it is not utopian. Its ideals are never grand and idyllic. Yet, community development achieves much more than what it sets out to do. It may involve only a handful of people, but its effects will touch many more. It may entail a simple action not requiring much skill and insight, but people participating will find that they have gained much more than what the simple activity would initially promise.

Finally, it is important to remember that it is a human activity with the goal to transform the lives of the poor, not on a grand scale or in action leading to glory, but bit by bit through small and simple activities of human beings.

A community development project is not aimed at vague, ill-defined or broad, abstract needs. People must be helped to move to the point where they will see themselves as capable of doing something about their position. People's norms and values influence their perceptions. An awareness of itself in terms of objectives is one of the greatest strengths a community can enjoy.

# CHAPTER 6

# THE PRINCIPLES OF COMMUNITY DEVELOPMENT

## 6.1 INTRODUCTION

Thousands of people calling themselves community development workers (CDWs), community facilitators, development officers or social ecologists are busy with 'development work' in deprived areas. Their job entails organising local people around projects that address real or perceived problems among the people. These workers come from different backgrounds and different training regimes and may represent as wide a spectrum as engineering, education, health, agriculture, religion, child care and culture. These people do not come into this job with the same point of departure, following the same set of rules or moving within the same parameters. It therefore becomes extremely important to bring some order to the chaos, to provide a universal set of principles, both at the ethical and practical level, to serve as guiding lights to the varied multitude.

This chapter will endeavour to do just that by first looking at certain ethical principles which hold universal importance. All practitioners, whether they are social workers or engineers, should abide by these principles. The practical repercussions of abiding by these principles are covered under the practical principles.

## 6.2 ETHICAL PRINCIPLES

### 6.2.1 Human orientation

People in the 'deprivation trap' have basic physical needs that are not being met. (See Chapter 1 and Chambers (1983) for a discussion of the deprivation trap.) People caught in this trap, who have unfulfilled, basic physical or concrete needs such as food, clean water, clothing and shelter, also have needs that are not, strictly speaking, physical, such as happiness, self-reliance and human dignity. In fact, people's physical and abstract needs go hand in hand and are present at the same time.

The principle that must be followed here is that—while people's concrete needs are addressed and, hopefully, fulfilled—their abstract human needs must also be fulfilled. One cannot separate the physical aspects of a project from the abstract human aspects. They must go hand in hand otherwise we do not have development. Does this mean that every project must have a double objective; one lying within the concrete sphere and one found in the abstract humanities? Not necessarily, but projects should be planned and formulated in such a way that the process of abstract objective attainment flows naturally from the process to address physical and concrete needs.

Poor people are not going to participate in projects with vague abstract objectives. Their concern is with a concrete need or problem and that is what they will concentrate on. But this action of the participants must take place in such a way that the abstract needs are also addressed. This responsibility falls squarely within the ambit of the CDW, who must ensure that every project succeeds in both these objectives; without confronting the participants with the objectives. You cannot tell participants that they must launch a project to improve their human dignity. These abstract objectives lie on a subtler plain, but may not be neglected for that reason. For the CDW this means that, as people strive to meet their basic physical needs, they realise many of their abstract, human needs. CDWs must ensure that the assessment of projects also provides answers to the attainment of these abstract goals.

It also means that, under no circumstances, may we address the basic physical needs to the detriment of the people's human dignity and other abstract human needs; such as happiness and contentment. The human fabric of people may never suffer as a result of so-called physical development. Those who are tasked to mobilise people must make it their objective not only to mobilise people for physical development, but also to help people gain in self-reliance, happiness, fulfilment and eventually human dignity. People may not be ignored, bypassed or be forced into, or made dependent on, development projects addressing their physical needs.

The most important abstract human need is dignity. Essama-Nssah (2004) sees it as a necessity of public policy to enable the citizens to choose to lead fulfilled lives This entails functioning properly as a human being or exercising fully the capabilities that are characteristically human (see Chapter 4 on the Capabilities Approach). The characterisation of a fulfilled life boils down to identifying human capabilities that make such a life possible. The core idea is that of human beings as dignified free beings who shape their own life in co-operation and reciprocity with others, rather than being passively shaped or pushed around in the manner of a 'flock' or 'herd' of animals. A life that is really human is one that is shaped throughout by these human powers of practical reason and sociability.

Nussbaum (2000:78—80), lists the following central human capabilities as an indicator of human dignity:

- *Life*: The ability to avoid premature death;
- *Bodily health*: The ability to have good health with adequate nourishment and shelter;
- *Bodily integrity*;
- *Senses, imagination and thought*: The ability to use these to imagine, think and reason in a truly human way;
- *Emotions*: The ability to have attachments to things and people outside oneself;
- *Practical reason*: The ability to conceive of the good and engage in critical reflection about the formulation and implementation of one's life plan;
- *Affiliation*: The ability to live with and towards others, and to engage in various social interactions with dignity and respect;
- *Other species*: The ability to live with concern about the world of nature;

▶ *Play*: The ability to enjoy recreational activities; and
▶ *Control over one's environment*: both political and material.

You can compare this list with the characteristics of wellbeing as discussed in Chapter 1. Physical improvements to an area can have negative effects on people and can harm their human dignity. Dignity is promoted by giving people recognition; by recognising them as capable of making their own decisions and accepting responsibility for their decisions. Dignity is enhanced when people become self-reliant and self-sufficient; when they become capable of organising themselves and engendering and maintaining benevolent and farsighted leadership. In other words, it grows as people fulfil their potential (Gran, 1983:327). People must progress in realising their inner potential while working to fulfil their physical needs.

A further important aspect of this principle is that human beings do not live in a vacuum. Human beings live in an environment that is physical, but there is also an abstract environment such as a social, political, economic and cultural milieu of immense importance to human beings. Furthermore, people carry with them a oneness that influences their whole existence. Their needs are part of this oneness and can therefore not be separated. Their health needs cannot be separated from their educational and their social needs. Development agencies must be careful not to create tension within people by dividing their needs into sectors that can create a dichotomy leading, for example, to problems of existentialism.

In our efforts to address poverty and fulfil basic needs, it is apt to remember that the human being is more important than his/her needs (see Chapter 4 on the basic needs approach). CDWs should not trample on human beings or bedevil their environment in their rush to do something about their needs. A well-meaning, but misguided, stampede by government agencies, NGOs and other well-wishers will trample the views of the people. In spite of the great need among poor people, it is always wise to approach development with caution. Case Study 5 is about a dam that can bring hardship and illustrates this principle of community development. Case Study 23: *The old chief's story*, shows how a well-meaning, but misguided approach can engender negative reactions.

### 6.2.2  Participation

We are mobilising people to participate in development efforts or projects, but we must have a clear view of what participation really means; what it really is. We cannot mobilise people and then limit or prescribe their participation. That is tokenism. Participation does not mean involvement. When we involve people in projects, we allow them in, under certain conditions, to take part in certain actions in a prescribed way. This whole process is then pre-planned and prescribed by the CDWs and their organisations. When people are mobilised to participate, they do so fully; in all aspects of the project. Then they become part of the decision-making and planning of the project. They are part of the implementation and evaluation of the project. And, if need be, they decide on project course adaptations to keep a project on track; in short, they then participate fully in the management of the project.

The 'buzz value' of participation is so great that debate on whether it is good or bad has ceased. The liberal view of participation sees it as good, especially if it is organised and orderly. The liberal view emphasises two points. The first point is that, through participation, a solid, local knowledge base is used for development. Local people, who have lived in deprivation for years, surviving the hardships of their poverty, have a certain ingrained knowledge that outsiders do not have. Their 'common sense' knowledge of environmental dynamics can be of immense value to development efforts. Developers who do not use this knowledge base to the full are placing limitations on projects. The second point is that it has now been established that people who do not participate in their own development have no affinity for development efforts and their results. The huge problem of sustaining development and maintaining facilities can be solved by having the local people fully present.

Although legitimate, these are not and cannot be the only reasons for participation. We must also take note of the radical view on participation (see Chapter 4 on the radical approach to participation). According to this view participation becomes a way of ensuring equity. Often, the poorest of the poor do not get their fair share of the fruits of development. Therefore, participation must include them (Gran, 1983:2). Further, we must realise that it is the democratic right of people to participate in matters affecting their future. Every adult, whether relatively poor, poor, or the poorest of the poor, has a right to be part of the decision-making mechanism affecting his/her development (De Beer & Swanepoel, 1998:20–24). When people are mobilised to participate in a project, they are not just there to make them feel part of the project; they are not present so that we can make use of their local practical knowledge; they are not there to do the physical work. They are there because it is their democratic right to be there and to make decisions regarding the project that involves their future. The guiding principle is quite clear: Don't mobilise people to play a minor role in a project and to fill a subordinate position in relation to professionals, bureaucrats and donors. If the people are not the main role-players there is something wrong with their participation.

What do people of a community do when they participate? In what do they participate? Is the people's participation limited to an advisory role? If the local people act only as advisors to the planners and decision-makers, we cannot talk of participation. Power must accompany participation (El Sherbini, 1986:9). As far back as the 1960s, Arnstein (1969) declared that participation without power 'is an empty and frustrating process for the powerless'. People do not like advisory roles. But worse can happen; under the banner of participation, people can be used as cheap labour.
Blanchet (2001) quotes Colin when he says:

> 'Participation' may simply mean taking part in an initiative without really being its instigator or leader. In this case those participating have no power, but simply a role to play, a task to complete.

The excuse is often made that ordinary people are not capable of anything other than physical labour, that decision-making and planning are outside the ambit of ordinary people because participation is seen as interfering with the effective provision of basic needs (Spalding, 1990:105). It is necessary for CDWs to facilitate the ordinary people's full participation through enabling strategies. They must also guard against the subtle undermining of the participation of the poor so that it becomes co-option (Sowman & Gawith, 1994). Participation can only be meaningful if it goes with empowerment. Development decision-making will be governed by perceptions of power and how these perceptions can be changed

(Gran, 1983:23; Guaraldo Choguill, 1996). See Case Study 6: *The parson who became a painter*. This case study illustrates what can happen if people do not really participate in a project.

### 6.2.3   Empowerment

People use the term empowerment very loosely. If they teach people a skill they say that they have empowered them. If they give them representation on a council or committee they call it empowerment. Basically, though, empowerment refers to political power. We must be very careful that our mobilisation does not lead to tokenism. Tokenism—or window-dressing—means that people are apparently mobilised, involved or placed on committees just so that it looks good. Sometimes people are mobilised just to do some physical work and then they are taught various skills in order to do that labour and this is then called empowerment. But empowerment does not mean having certain skills or having a certain token representation. That is an extremely thin and shallow view. Empowerment is to have decision-making power (Taconni & Tisdell, 1993:413). And, yes, they do need certain skills to make those decisions, so skills do come into it, but not as the primary ingredient of empowerment. It is only a tool of enablement.

Associated with the skills needed for decision-making is the fact that people can only make enlightened decisions if they have the correct information. Therefore, empowerment also includes information or knowledge, but then in service of the people's responsibility to make wise and informed decisions.

The guiding principle is that mobilisation must aim at giving people the power or the right to make decisions and not to stop there, but continue a supportive function by providing the necessary information to make good decision-making possible. This can be regarded as one of the primary roles of CDWs. They and their organisations should be reservoirs of information to provide communities and committees with relevant, unadulterated and fresh information.

Softer options for empowerment, such as skills training and co-option, abound for the simple reason that empowerment can cause vulnerability among the development agencies and loosen their grip on the process of development. To what extent should agencies 'let go'? Are there limits to the power of project steering committees? By whom and to what extent should the steering committee's work be supervised, overseen and assessed? These are not simple issues. But the issue of empowerment cannot be put on the back burner because of these questions. Development agencies must approach the issue with open minds and in the spirit of the new professionalism of Chambers (1983). Case Study 7: The community hall with no purpose, is a case in point where the people's inputs were not heeded because they were not empowered. You will find a similar situation in Case Study 20: *The story of KwaMpofu*.

### 6.2.4   Ownership

Too often mobilisation is done in a spirit of inviting the people to come and join someone else's activity, to treat people as guests on someone else's property. This, of course, is altogether wrong.

People must have the power to make decisions. It is their destiny, it is their future, and it is their development. This is clear and straightforward logic. Because the people are the owners no one else can be the main role-player. All other role-players must be there to support and to assist the people in carrying out their owner's responsibility.

Development agencies who regard development projects as their property will find that they are forever going to be burdened with the responsibility of the project's smooth progress and if they are successful in doing this, they may find one day that the people have 'stolen' their project.

The principle tells us that mobilisation is not about inviting people to join some outsider's project or effort on the terms and conditions of that other someone. This is token participation, token empowerment and token ownership maintained by established interests that are threatened by the mass ownership of development (Wisner, 1988:294). Mobilisation is to activate people to take up the responsibilities of ownership and manage their future through their project. This principle also warns us that development agencies should never assume ownership at first with the idea to transfer it later on 'when the people are ready'. Apart from the fact that it is paternalistic for development agencies to decide when people are ready, this approach is fraught with danger because ownership transfer does not take place easily. A CDW who emphasises from the start that it is the people's effort to address their problems will find that people are at first reluctant to accept this ownership or are unsure of what the ownership entails, but as they go along they become more and more aware of their special position and what it means in practical terms. Then their acceptance of ownership is a natural process facilitated by the CDW. Because every owner wants to regard the ownership as long-term, a project's life can be so much longer because its life is being sustained by the owners. At the same time we should not be blind to the fact that ownership claims can cause strife and animosities. Whitehead, Kriel and Richter (2005) found that the issue of ownership of the project arose as a point of contention throughout. Case Study 19: *Stealing or taking ownership*, illustrates the wrong and the correct perception.

### 6.2.5   Sustainability

Human beings and their communities are an integral part of the natural environment. If the natural environment is under threat or is damaged for one or other reason, humans will also be under threat or will be harmed. This fact is the basis on which this principle of sustainability is built. The golden rule is that no community development project should harm the environment.

Sustainable development does not comprise a single universal goal. It is rather a broad direction which is context specific. It means different things to different people according to the context (Elliott, 1994:1—6).

What is important about this seeking of answers to issues regarding sustainability is that it is the result of a revolutionary paradigm shift in science and development practice. We call this shift the view on holism. This simply means that the human being and the rest of nature form a oneness, a whole and from this we can argue that if this whole is not managed properly, all living things will suffer. Popularised in the 1920s, it was claimed that the whole was more than the sum of the parts. This claim moves the emphasis away from the parts in the direction of the whole as a collective and self-regulating unit. A core component of holism is structure determinism that implies basically that the structure and patterns of the whole determine the course thereof. We should take a look at our planet as a whole and examine our existing patterns with regard to affecting the environment (Treurnicht, 2000:67).

The accepted definition of sustainable development is that it is development that meets the needs of the present without compromising the ability of future generations to meet their own needs. If we meet the needs of the present through projects, but we compromise the ability of future generations to meet their own needs, then we have broken this principle. The big question, however, is 'How can we address the needs existing now without jeopardising future generations?' This is a real problem that requires deep thought and wise actions. It is unrealistic to expect poor people to conserve resources for the future when they are struggling to survive (Elliott, 1994:39). The trend today is based on the realisation that knowledge, culture and the environment seldom operate in isolation. There should be ample opportunity for knowledge systems to share information in a reciprocal way. Because no knowledge system is complete, there should always be space to learn and adapt. The problem with this approach is that there is seldom real space for reciprocal relationships (Treurnicht, 2000:86). Unfortunately one knowledge system is usually dominating the other with a resulting limiting of reciprocal learning.

Approaches to sustainability occur with varying degrees of a preferable mix. Any development process in a social and environmental system needs particular inputs and outputs to maintain equilibrium and to grow and sustain itself over time. Growth and progress is seldom an unlimited process that can be sustained indefinitely. Any environmental system can only handle so much pressure before imbalances start to occur. This is precisely the reason why sustainable development at grassroots level is so vitally important. Those knowledge systems that have helped to sustain environmental systems over long periods of time should be revitalised for promoting sustainable development where possible. Many civilisations before ours have come and gone or perhaps have changed into something completely different. We will have to live within the limits of our natural system. People-centred development will have to take note of the limits of our natural system otherwise it may destroy the resource base crucial for our survival.

The point of departure is that the local context with its own unique needs and dynamics is a determining variable in development. The people are the professionals because they have indigenous coping strategies that help them to make the most of their local environment (enabling setting). Participation is a key in the whole issue of context. New approaches to grassroots level development deal with local dynamics finding operationalisation in participation.

Any system, whether a social or natural one, needs a certain measure of stability in order to cope with a specific challenge. Usually coping with a challenge means to bring about changes. We therefore have the apparent anomaly that you need stability in order to change. If stability is not present it is unlikely that change will be accepted. A manifestation of that stability is that the people themselves should control the process of development. They should determine the tempo and direction of the change. They will give meaning to the whole process so that it becomes much more than an externally induced change. This does not mean that all local development will automatically be sustainable and in harmony with the natural system. The chances are, however, that some local role players will want to protect that which is to their own good and in their own interest. The central focus in this regard is therefore who should manage environmental problems; who should decide how to address these problems. See Case Study 24: *Water to waste*.

A further requirement for sustainability is that all development efforts should be experimental. Through learning from reality, through obtaining wisdom through experience, CDWs and the local people can build on appropriate structures that will be sympathetic to future needs. Learning for sustainable development should be open ended and people should realise that collectively and individually they seldom have the knowledge to approach development with confidence. They have to realise their own limitations. This goes for indigenous people and western experts.

### 6.2.6    Release

The real goal of development is to eradicate poverty, not to address poverty or deal with some of the manifestations of poverty. Put in another way, development wants to free people from the deprivation trap. Development efforts are efforts to break the deprivation trap so that people can become free. We are therefore talking about a vicious attack on the current situation in order to bring radical change. Development is not an effort to bring some relief to poor people or to improve their situation somewhat. Such efforts would rather fit in with welfare and betterment programmes.

The negative spin-off of such efforts is that they make the people increasingly dependent on their benefactors because their need for relief does not stop. Relief and improvement will not free people. The objective of these efforts is not to free people, but to help them to survive in their situation. Relieving efforts therefore tend to perpetuate the poverty situation. Therefore, one should be rather critical and alert in one's judgement of so-called development efforts. Development agencies and their CDWs should gain clarity on whether their efforts try to address the symptoms of the situation without doing anything about the status quo. The direct opposite of this approach focuses on the whole person (the first principle) in his/her environment and on a total transformation so that his/her situation as a whole can be drastically changed or transformed.

If the whole person is to be the target of development, and if development aims to meet his/her abstract needs of self-reliance and dignity, (the first principle) then it must be more than a relief operation. Development becomes an effort at releasing the whole person from the jaws of poverty. Projects often tend to maintain the status quo and this forces them to restrict themselves to bringing short-term or repetitive relief to a situation without addressing its causes. These efforts try to bring relief to trapped people without the slightest effort to free them from the trap. Transforming efforts, on the other hand, do not try to bring relief. They attempt to release people from the trap so that, free and self-reliant, they can gradually improve the situation themselves. It is obvious, therefore, that transforming efforts are long-term activities that bring radical change to people's lives over a period of time. Case Study 17: *Mothers of the mountain community*, illustrates this process of transformation and release.

## 6.3    PRACTICAL PRINCIPLES

A transforming, releasing approach and policy must also be carried out by transforming releasing actions. Appropriate actions are just as important as appropriate policies and approaches. In other words, you need to follow and respect certain practical principles in order to carry out the ethical principles.

### 6.3.1    Learning

The first of these practical principles goes without saying, but in our western culture we have become so conditioned to ideas of excellence, perfection and professionalism that we need to be reminded of this axiom, namely that by continuously striving to fulfil their needs, people learn to realise their objectives more easily. This simple truism underpins the principle of learning. Participation in a project therefore brings about learning. This is another important reason why people should participate in projects. And it is not only the poor people who learn. All role-players, whether government, NGOs or CBOs, learn as they go along.

No one role-player is the teacher. All are students and the teacher's position is taken up by the prevailing circumstances. This principle tells us something of the spirit in which community development projects should be approached. (See the principle of compassion.) It is clear that there is no place for elitism; that so-called professional aloofness is quite out of place. It is also clear that CDWs should approach their task with humility, aware of the fact that there is a lot to learn for them and that much of that will come from ordinary simple people.

The learning process approach has as aim to meet the need for '... a flexible, sustained, experimental, action based capacity building style of assistance ...' (Korten, 1980:484). It is a bottom-up approach, avoiding the restrictions of a blueprint (top-down) approach. You can read more about this approach in Chapter 4. Consequently, it envisages community development projects arising from a learning process in which the local people and project staff have an equal share and in which their knowledge and resources are shared to establish a project, a process of 'bottom-up-learning' in Korten's words. Such a project can only result when unity can be attained between:

- the needs of the 'target group' and the results of a project, (ie the project must address their 'felt' needs);
- the formulation of needs and the power (of participants) to make decisions, (ie the participants must be in a position to decide on their needs and on what to do about it); and
- the objectives of the project and the capacity of the institution (responsible for the project), (ie the institution must have the capacity to reach the objective).

An organisation must meet certain requirements in order to be able to do all these things. According to Korten (1980: 498) this approach requires:

> ... organisations with a well developed capacity for responsive anticipatory adaptation—organisations that (a) embrace error; (b) plan with the people; and (c) link knowledge building with action.

The logical result of using this approach should be greater emphasis on the autonomy of the poor, their right to decision-making and their empowerment. According to Gran (1983: 345) the success story of the learning approach has proved that '... people can lead their own change processes. They can be the actors, not merely the subjects of change'.

This principle has certain strong consequences for development. An important one is that non-negotiable or pre-selected frameworks cannot curtail learning. The moment that a development agency approaches this task with certain set procedures and a decision-making mechanism that is removed from the people, the process of learning is impeded, in fact, is just about wiped out.

Development agencies must send their CDWs to communities with an empty agenda. They should come into a community with a clean slate (Korten, 1980); with nothing to offer than themselves, their compassion and their willingness to become involved through a learning process in the people's efforts to break free of the deprivation trap. In later chapters we will look at practical ways to accomplish this.

The principle here is quite clear, namely that CDWs should create as many learning opportunities as possible. See Case Study 16: *The felt and the real need.* There may be shorter and quicker routes to objective attainment, but if we want the results of projects to be permanent and the transformation of the situation lasting, then the longer and perhaps more arduous route of learning is the only way to bring self-reliance and eventually self-sufficiency.

### 6.3.2 Compassion

By now it must be quite clear that CDWs must be unique people with a broad range of skills that are carried by something that is akin to sympathy or empathy. The facilitating and enabling task of the CDWs is simply not just another job. The most skilful CDW will still find it quite impossible to fulfil all these other principles if he or she misses the principle of compassion. An easy explanation of compassion is that the person with compassion stands in the shoes of the object of his or her compassion. While people find themselves in the deprivation trap the CDWs should also experience that entrapment. It is clear that this principle demands that aloofness on the side of the CDWs should be totally absent. It also demands that human dignity and happiness should be uppermost in their minds. The objective of CDWs and their organisations should not be just to help poor people gain some objective they had identified themselves. Yes, they should help, but the objective must be so much broader because the CDW and enabling institution must be driven by compassion. For this reason one finds emphasis on aspects such as human orientation, sustainability and release. For this reason CDWs are prompted to use research methodologies where the people 'receive the stick', where they obtain the responsibility to learn through their own efforts.

Compassion also has got a very practical benefit. That is that compassion wins friends, compassion draws out a response that makes co-operation within a project possible.

### 6.3.3 Adaptiveness

If the principle of learning is followed, one cannot be anything but adaptive. Adaptiveness is in direct contradiction to blueprint planning. Blueprint planning is technical, clean, precise, comprehensive, but inflexible. The learning takes place before planning begins. Learning consists of community profiles and feasibility studies. The situation in which development must take place is stable. Planning and implementation are the prerogatives of the professional planner and engineer. Their success is measured through cost-benefit analysis and impact studies. In this scenario there is no place for adaptiveness and for learning as you progress. There is also no place for ordinary community members — most definitely not to make decisions (Swanepoel, 2000:91). Professional planners are removed from reality, not only in mind, but also in body (Korten, 1980:499). Most important however, is that the blueprint approach simply cannot work in a situation where the poor are present and where it is the distinct objective to help them to break from the deprivation trap (Rondinelli, 1993:90 et seq).

This does not mean that there is no place for feasibility studies, cost-benefit analysis and impact studies. But it does mean that those tools must firstly, be adapted to the poverty, learning situation. Secondly, they must become the property of the participating poor who must be able to use them, and, thirdly, they are not the only tools, therefore they have a specific function that will not jeopardise the participation of the poor. There are other planning and evaluation tools just as well suited or even better suited to the situation.

Adaptive administration encapsulates bottom-up decision-making participation by communities and an improved responsiveness, creativity and innovative ability of institutions. Adaptive administration is characterised by partnership action with the aims of reducing the dependence of communities, to set democratic processes in action and to enhance human potential. The partnership can be described as follows: Decisions on development strategies and the availability and allocation of resources are taken at central level, while decisions on implementation are taken locally in consultation with the communities concerned. CDWs treat the population as partners in the definition and solution of problems. Evaluation is based on process and results; development personnel are considered responsible for any improvement in the local communities' capacity for participation.

The principle of adaptiveness requires a change of mindset. It demands a willingness to learn as you go along. It stands for experimentation and therefore disjointed, sometimes dirty, short-term, trial and error planning and implementation. When the mindset conducive to this is achieved, the principle also requires complete organisational and procedural changes. Management should be fluid, changeable and adaptable. Structures should give space for manoeuvring and should be flexible, allowing new actions where and when necessary (De Beer & Swanepoel, 1998:103). Adaptive institutions by definition will be highly adaptable to a wide variety of problems with no universally prescribed design and will be built on culturally accepted arrangements, practices and behaviour, but at the same time will try to transfer traditional practices and behaviour into more suitable arrangements.

### 6.3.4  Simplicity

The principle of simplicity contrasts sharply with the notion that 'bigger is better'. We tend to go for the big, the complex and the sophisticated. Gellert and Lynch (2003:22) explain this as follows:

> The faith in technology and belief in domination of nature central to modernisation ideology easily lead to a specific bias toward large scale on the part of international lending institutions, construction firms, and monumentalist states.

The situation of mass poverty is such that it seems that only large projects will make a dent. Also, it is politically expedient to tackle the problems of poverty in a big and grandiose way.

Chambers (1978:211) talks of the big project trap and says that the learning, releasing approach is not suited to complex techniques. When the opportunity for learning and participation is curtailed, the very humanistic nature of development is in jeopardy. The enhancement of self-reliance and dignity becomes more remote. At the same time the release from poverty becomes less of an issue. Adaptiveness is much more difficult to attain with complex projects. We can say that all the principles that we have thus far discussed are jeopardised by large, complex and sophisticated projects. Does that mean that these principles are only of relevance to small and simple projects? Not necessarily, but it means that large projects should be broken down in smaller parts where the learning process can be enhanced. It also means that technical content should be explained to lay people so that they can make sense of it and still make informed decisions. Gunton (2003:518) says that the impact of large projects should be assessed beforehand. These projects can generate significant growth, but the growth is not necessarily beneficial to the region. Gellert and Lynch (2003:15) add to this line of thinking when they argue that displacement is intrinsic to megaproject development. The principle is quite clear, namely that the smaller and simpler a project the easier it is to get long-lasting results. Therefore, if we want to adhere to all the principles that we have discussed so far, it is necessary to keep projects simple, at least as simple as can be, but when a project is of necessity large and sophisticated, CDWs should be aware of the warning signs and be focused to make the best of a difficult situation. Case Study 8: Small is better, illustrates the principle of simplicity.

This principle also tells us something about our approach to development efforts. It is again a matter of mindset. Chambers (1993:27) phrases the necessity for a different approach as follows:

> [T]he right starting point is not the means but the end, not the library but the village, not the methodology of appraisal but the poorer rural people. Starting from them rather than from the cost-benefit paradigm, and trying to see what approaches will help them rather than consummate the training project appraisal which many economists have received, leads away from complex procedures and towards the conclusion that for these purposes true sophistication lies in simplicity: in short, that simple is optimal.

## 6.4    CONCLUSION

The principles that we have discussed in this chapter are not objectives. They are not aims to be attained somewhere in the future. They are absolutely necessary to make community development work as it should work with the result of freeing people from the deprivation trap.

Projects provide a concrete structure that makes it possible to have funds allocated or donated to the project. Because projects are well structured they provide scope for various roles to be played and they arrange these roles into a viable entity so that the roles will be mutually supportive and will serve the same purpose. But projects can be used for all the wrong reasons and do more damage than good. So, in order to be this good foundation for development and in order to accomplish what it sets out to do, it is necessary that projects follow the guiding principles discussed in this chapter. The ethical principles must inform the approach towards development even before projects are established, but also during the life of projects. The practical principles must guide the implementation of development so that the poor will reap the benefits.

People must progress in realising their inner potential while working to fulfil their physical needs. The huge problem of sustaining development and maintaining facilities can be solved by making the local people owners. Empowerment is therefore a mixture between the right to make decisions and the ability to make decisions.

People must have ownership of their own development. They must be the owners of their own destiny. Relief and improvement will not free people. The objective of these efforts is not to free people, but to help them to survive in their situation.

To create as many learning opportunities as possible can be regarded as another of the prime tasks of the CDW.

# CHAPTER 7

# THE COMMUNITY AS MAIN ACTOR IN COMMUNITY DEVELOPMENT

## 7.1 INTRODUCTION

Community is usually defined in terms of geographic locality, of shared interests or needs, or in terms of deprivation and disadvantage. In our (African) situation, implicit in the use of the concept is either the (sometimes romantic) image of the traditional African village or, because of its prominence and visibility, the urban squatter or informal settlement (De Beer & Swanepoel, 1998:17). These groupings of people, be it rural village or urban informal settlement, are always seen as poor or deprived or disadvantaged and are described as receivers or non-receivers of services as targets for development and as beneficiaries. Unfortunately they are not often seen as very important role-players in their own development.

This chapter will describe and discuss these groupings specifically as role-players, in other words, mobilised to do rather than prompted to receive. We have already seen in a previous chapter that to do means much more than only physical labour, and this chapter will reiterate that.

## 7.2 THE MEANING OF COMMUNITY

A community is a unique, living entity and, like its people, it undergoes continuous physical and psychological change. It also interacts with its own individuals, its environment and other communities (Brokensha & Hodge, 1969). Societies consist of individuals and institutions. Institutions are groupings of people sharing common characteristics, circumstances or goals. They are in varying degrees organised and include families, schools, churches and various interest groups, such as burial societies and sport clubs. Most have a certain hierarchical structure. These various institutions are bound together by people and by interests. They also interact with one another in ways that suit their interests. A community, therefore, is not an easily defined, isolated or permanent entity that can be approached and organised for community development purposes. We can safely say that community development workers (CDWs) do not necessarily enter a community. More often than not they enter an inhabited area.

Edwards and Jones (1976:12) define community in terms of geography:

> ... a grouping of people who reside in a specific locality and who exercise some degree of local autonomy in organizing their social life in such a way that they can, from that locality base, satisfy the full range of their daily needs.

This definition is open to criticism. What degree or measure of local autonomy are they talking about? Many entities practising community development have very little autonomy and would be disqualified in terms of this definition (De Beer, 1984:43). It would be a mistake to see community as homogenous with shared norms and values (Sihlongonyane, 2001:38). Similarly, it would be exceptional to find a community that is able to 'satisfy the full range of their daily needs' from local resources. The important thing is that this definition describes a community as 'all the people' residing in a certain locality. When we regard the community as a role-player or stakeholders in development we cannot view it as the entire populace. First, any community will be represented by a political structure such as a ward with a councillor. Second, it will never happen that the whole community will share the same concern, the same level of deprivation, the same sense of urgency because of a certain need or problem.

We prefer not to see the community as the entire populace in a certain locality for other reasons of incorrect use. The first is that there is a notion that the community is intrinsically good. This has been challenged by those who argue that it is morally and culturally narrow-minded, oppressive to women, outsiders and minorities and not harmonious as sometimes painted (Sihlongonyane, 2001:38). The second is that the community is often given a false sense of identity when political parties or senior government officers claim that they have consulted the community. In other words, 'it can be used as an agent of stereotyping, in order to legitimise state or sectional interests' (Sihlongonyane, 2001:38).

CDWs sometimes fall into the trap of trying to organise the whole community for which they are responsible. This is impossible, and therefore a waste of time. The best attempts to organise a whole community will only yield small groups of willing participants. CDWs might well spare themselves a lot of unnecessary work and frustration by starting with small groups. The rule should be to work from the inside outwards, to start with one group and one project. The learning process that takes place and its demonstration effect will allow other action groups to be established for further projects.

Therefore, only those who share a maximum of concern will come together and work together to address that need. Roberts (1979:27), who views the concept as part of community development, emphasises shared interests and concern:

The community exists when a group of people perceives common needs and problems, acquires a sense of identity, and has a common set of objectives.

Now we are dealing with a group within the larger group and they are an entity because they share a common need or problem that they want addressed. White's (1982:19) assumption that community projects involve the participation of the organised community as such, does not hold water for the simple reason that all individuals of a given community will never be in close association with a project for various reasons, such as that they do not share the concern, that they do not believe that anything can be done about the concern, that they do not have the time to participate, or that they are simply one of a majority of individuals with no sense of society or community.

While we have indicated in a previous chapter that ordinary people play a primary role in community development, we can now say that those ordinary people do not represent the whole community. Our use of the term 'community' refers to that group of ordinary concerned people. We are in concert with the UN who suggests 'small communities of individuals 'at the lowest level of aggregation at which people organise for common effort' (De Beer & Swanepoel 1998:18).

It is important to emphasise that a lot of assumptions regarding community are wrong, misleading and outright dangerous to the success of community development. Communities are not homogeneous entities where all work together in a spirit of sharing. Very few individuals will share the notion of the common good for society. Communities for our purposes can consist of spatially separated people who share common needs and values. Regarding this larger society, it is important to realise that the society is not asleep, waiting to be woken by the CDW. Neither is society at its last breath waiting to be redeemed by the CDW. Society is busy with a rational existence that makes sense to its citizens.

## 7.3    COMMUNITY AS ROLE-PLAYER

It is dangerous to see the community as a role-player or just one of a number of stakeholders. The danger lies in the fact that the community is either the main role-player or our principles discussed in an earlier chapter fly out of the window. As we have shown in Chapter 6, participation is an elusive concept. However, it is quite often made elusive in order to weaken the meaning. The word is used by those opting for a systems-maintaining, a conforming kind of participation. It is also recognised as a liberal, even conservative approach with an absence of 'participatory experiences from self-reliant grassroots organizations' (Burbidge, 1988:188). On the other hand, the word is also used by those who equate it with power. They are regarded as the radicals or those in favour of systems-transformation. Wisner (1988:14) distinguishes between a 'strong' and a 'weak' interpretation of participation. The strong interpretation:

> ... advocated a new style of development which was radically participatory and in which land reform, asset redistribution and other necessary preconditions set the stage for the poor to take control of their own development, usually through grassroots organizations ... On the other side was the 'weak' interpretation of participatory development ... [that] saw participation as a limited, formalized process, stripped of the political volatility of direct popular involvement.

> This division between systems-maintaining, weak or conservative interpretations and systems-transforming, strong or radical interpretations is of pivotal importance in the debate on participatory development. The debate distinguishes between two analytical groupings, the 'participation as involvement' and the 'empowerment' schools (De Beer & Swanepoel, 1998:20).

To us, involvement refers to co-option, or at best the mobilisation of communities to be involved in the execution of top-down determined development plans and projects (De Beer & Swanepoel, 1998:22). This is simply not good enough. In this instance the community is not the main role-player. When the community becomes the main role-player, the other role-players and their roles become clearer. Government and other NGOs will still give support and material assistance to communities. Aid agencies have a role to play, as does the private sector. Finding the appropriate role for each and accommodating the various roles is part of the question addressed by empowerment. It is not a matter of the community versus the rest, but of the community and the rest.

What is needed is true decentralisation of decision-making processes:

> ... decision-making must truly be returned to the people, who have both the capacity and the right to inject into the process the richness – including subjectivity – of their values and needs (Korten, 1984:301).

There are three types of grouping suited to becoming action groups for community development projects.

### 7.3.1    The interest group

An interest group can act as an action group. The sewing club can launch a project to provide every child with a jersey for the winter. A youth club can launch a city-cleaning project; and a farmers' association can launch a woodlot project. If an interest group decides to start a community development project, it cannot do so as part of its normal functions. A community development project is too intense and requires too much attention to be treated as just one of many activities to be undertaken by that interest group. The interest group will be well advised to give a smaller group of people, perhaps those with a special interest in that type of project, responsibility for the project. Such a group can then function as a subcommittee of the interest group's executive and can report to it at regular intervals.

The advantage of an existing interest group is that it is already established. It is already organised and has a structure and a way of doing things. It has an infrastructure that can be used for a project. The sewing club that wants to provide every child with a jersey will use its knitting machines for the job and will buy the wool or yarn from its regular supplier. The members of an interest group also know one another and are used to working together. It will not be necessary to go through an initial period of finding and accepting one another as will be the case with newly formed groups.

The disadvantage of existing interest groups is that they may be busy with so many things that the community development project is given little attention, or it may be so dedicated to its primary objective that the community development project's objective may be regarded as secondary. A church deciding to launch a project is a good example. The church's normal interest and occupation, that is religion, may take up so much of its time and attention that the community development project is neglected. There is another disadvantage attached to established structures and functions. While they may have tremendous advantages, they may be so entrenched in their ways that the learning process cannot proceed properly. If this happens, the principle of adaptiveness is not adhered to.

### 7.3.2    The ad hoc group

The second type of group that can fulfil the role of an action group in a community development project is the ad hoc group of concerned individuals united by a common need. When individuals start finding common ground with others around a certain issue, they are becoming a group of concerned citizens. The next step will be to talk among themselves about possible solutions to their common problem and the final step will be taken, when, together, they decide to do something about it collectively. They will then have reached the stage where they can start to act as an action group for a community development project. The fact that they share a common characteristic (eg mothers of babies) will not make them a potential action group. The necessary ingredient is not the common characteristic, but the fact that they are all concerned about the same thing. Their concern is the important criterion.

The main weakness of this type of group is the newness of association. Members may not know one another very well and a system of working together may be absent. It may take quite some time for them to gel as a group and only then can a concerted effort begin. The CDW should make it his/her special task to form such a group of individuals into a group that can work together in a community development project.

### 7.3.3    The elected committee

It may happen that a relatively large group of people present at perhaps a public meeting for a ward or constituency will decide on a project and will then elect a development committee immediately or later to address the identified problem or a project steering committee to launch and run a project. The advantage of such a group is that it usually has a relatively clear brief. It can therefore start with its work immediately. The disadvantages are that it may have such narrow parameters that it has little freedom of learning and adaptation. Such a committee may consist of representatives of various groupings within a community and this may make it very difficult to operate simply because rivalries and animosities may exist among the members. There may be experts in this group, which can be a good or a bad thing.

The other type of elected committee usually acts in a more permanent way. That is the clinic committee or water or schools committee. These committees are not created specifically to launch projects. They are elected to look after the interests of institutions such as clinics and schools or to improve a service such as water reticulation or sewage. In this role these committees can decide to launch some project or projects or even a programme consisting of a few projects.

## 7.4    CONCLUSION

It is clear that the action group in a community development project cannot be an amorphous mass of individuals. It must be possible to define it in terms of certain criteria. The most important criteria will be a common, genuine concern and a committed membership. It is also clear that in most poverty environments the size of a group and the proximity of its members are important aspects determining the ease with which it will operate. The larger the group, the more difficult it will be to identify a common need and objective. The further they live from one another the more difficult it will be for them to come together for collective action. Chapter 11 deals with groups in more detail.

Community development is meant for communities. The action, including planning and decision-making takes place at grassroots level with ordinary people. Just as the need is something experienced, felt and identified by the ordinary people, so is the action to address that need taken by the people. The community is therefore the main role-player and all other agencies or stakeholders, be they governmental, non-governmental or private sector, play a supporting, aiding and facilitating role as it is illustrated in the next chapter when the CDW is discussed.

# CHAPTER 8

# THE PLACE AND ROLE OF COMMUNITY DEVELOPMENT WORKERS

## 8.1 INTRODUCTION

Community development workers (CDWs) need not be professionals, but quite often they are. A CDW can be a specialist professional, such as an agricultural extension officer, an engineer, a social worker, teacher, nurse or occupational therapist. These professionals will not be called CDWs, but will operate under their occupational titles. A second category of professionals will be generalist CDWs, who usually have a co-ordinating task and who concern themselves mostly with the mobilisation of people for development and the running of development projects. These so-called generalists comprise many people not trained for a specific task, who have been appointed to the bottom of the departmental hierarchy by government departments and provincial and local governments. These people need immediate and appropriate training so that they can get to grips with their jobs. In the NGO cadre there are also professional specialists with a keen interest in community development and then there are volunteers who may have some specialist training or who may have no specific training for what they are doing.

From these facts we can conclude that CDWs are either employed by government, or they are volunteers or employees of NGOs. They are either employed or tasked to play a broad, general facilitating role in community development, or they are specialists in various fields who can play the role of CDW if a project is about their speciality. They are, in other words, executing their line functions, but through projects. When we deal with the place, attitude and role of the CDW in this chapter we try to include all these different types of workers.

The extremely vulnerable position of the poor and the great difficulties they encounter in breaking out of the deprivation trap make it essential that CDWs act as resources to these people. The role of resource can be either over-played or under-played. In most instances it is over-played in that the CDW is more, or becomes more, than only a resource. The tendency is always to overplay the role: to be too forceful, to take leadership, to do things by oneself. In most cases overplaying the role is the result of a poor perception of the CDW's task and role or an inconsiderate attitude. Even if the attitude is right, the situation is such that it invites overplay. To compound the situation, few people will see anything wrong in playing a more forceful and primary role, especially if the action group lacks vitality.

Yet, it is of critical importance that the role should never be overplayed because then the opportunity is taken away from the people to take charge and responsibility for their own fate. It also leads to a situation where it will be very difficult for the CDW to 'get rid' of a project, so to speak. People will either be fairly satisfied with the CDW's execution of the role of owner or manager, or they will feel themselves obliged to leave things as they are because it is the 'right thing' to do. But, in the meantime, our ethical principles are ignored; with very bad consequences.

The fact is that the position and role of the CDW is precarious and difficult and for that reason attention must be paid to this role. It is clear that they can be resources only if they are very careful regarding their position, their goals and attitudes and the roles they play.

## 8.2 ETHICAL GUIDELINES

CDWs do not yet work under a formal code of ethics. If, however, they are specialist professionals such as nurses, teachers and social workers, they will have their own code of ethics for their professions.

Any set of ethical guidelines is based, roughly, on the following beliefs:

▶ Every human being has unique value and potential, irrespective of origin, ethnicity, sex, age, beliefs, socio-economic and legal status.
▶ Each individual has the right to the fulfilment of his/her innate and acquired skills.
▶ The professional has got a responsibility to devote his/her knowledge and skills to the benefit of each individual, group, community and mankind.
▶ The professional has got a primary obligation to render service professionally.

The following acts or omissions are, usually regarded as improper:

▶ Negligent performance of duties.
▶ Execution of duties in a manner which does not comply with generally accepted standards.
▶ Behaviour which is detrimental to the occupation as such.
▶ Being guilty of dishonesty in the execution of his/her duties.
▶ Receiving or agreeing to receive direct or indirect compensation or any other form of incentive other than a normal salary.
▶ Refusing without sufficient cause, to render services which he/she took on or for which he/she was employed.
▶ Failure to keep a record of acts performed, money managed, and fees charged in all matters dealt with by him/her in his/her professional capacity.
▶ The receipt of any bribe, or agreement to receive any bribe in connection with any matter which is directly or indirectly related to his/her duties.
▶ Direct or indirect criticism of the work of a colleague, or a professional person he/she has dealt with in the execution of his/her duty.
▶ Casting of reflections directly or indirectly upon the probity professional reputation, skill, competence, knowledge or qualifications of a colleague or such other professional person.

- ▶ Breaching his/her contract of service or behaviour that would justify his/her summary dismissal at common law.
- ▶ Practising or carrying on from his/her offices any business, trade, work or occupation apart from his/her ordinary job.

## 8.3   POSITION

CDWs occupy very delicate and at the same time, difficult positions. If we remind ourselves that CDWs usually have more expertise than the people, are usually better educated than they are, are better able to organise and plan, are in a better position to anticipate the outcome of actions, and are equipped with more external links, it seems quite natural that they take up leadership positions. Yet, this is the last thing they should do. CDWs must never accept positions that lead to situations of dependency between them and the people. They may, therefore, not accept leadership positions.

Their position may never put the people's primacy in jeopardy (Swanepoel & De Beer, 1996:32). The community fills the primary position and CDWs hold secondary positions. Because many of them are specialists there are those among them who expect the people from a poor and less sophisticated community to respond to them in a sheep-like way. They do not see that they should respond to the community's needs and that they should honour the community's views on the matter (Gow & Vansant, 1983:429). It is again, as we have seen in a previous chapter, a matter of ownership. As long as the CDW regards a project as his/her property, people will be invited on the CDW's terms and conditions. In fact, the roles should be reversed and the CDW should respond to the invitation from the people to become involved in their effort.

It will be to the advantage of the CDW to play his/her role with the utmost care from the moment of entry. The people should realise from the outset that no activity and no organised effort will ever belong to the CDW. It is not a matter of gradually transferring ownership — that is, if not impossible, then at least a very difficult task. CDWs should never talk of 'my' or 'our' project. Just as the needs and problems are those of the people, to the same extent efforts to address them should be the property and responsibility of the people.

## 8.4   GOALS

It may sound strange, but the CDW's goals are not to fulfil people's concrete needs. Although people address their concrete needs in projects and therefore have concrete objectives, it is dangerous for CDWs to make the concrete objectives their own because they can then begin to pull the community along towards the concrete objective at the pace of the CDW. It is natural that the CDW wants the community to reach their concrete objectives, but that is not paramount for him/her, even in the case of a specialist line functionary such as an agricultural extension officer. The CDW's goals lie on another, perhaps less concrete level. His/her goals are as follows:

- ▶ To enable the people to fulfil their abstract human needs. In other words, the CDW is interested in an enhanced human dignity among the poor, a lasting self-reliance that softens their dependency, a positive self-perception that bodes well for efforts to break out of the deprivation trap, and a general air of happiness and content that tells us that people are becoming free of the deprivation trap. The CDW's goals lie on an altogether different (perhaps higher) plain. It will be a happy day for community development if more CDWs and the organisations employing them will realise and understand this aspect.

▶ To enhance the learning process. The growth in self-reliance, dignity and contentment is the result of a vigorous learning process where each and everyone learns as much as there is to be learnt so that the next step, the next effort, the next project will be better. If the CDW shares the concrete goals of the people, he/she may be tempted to take short cuts in order to reach the goal sooner; in fact, is that not what efficiency is all about? But if the CDW's goals lie on a different plain, he/she will not mind going the longer route through learning opportunities.

▶ To help the people achieve meaningful empowerment. In the final analysis, development should be more than mere service delivery. It should follow a path and produce results that are ensured by careful decision-making by those nearest to the situation. In order to make this possible, the CDW's whole effort should be aimed at providing the people with the information they need to make informed decisions.

▶ To fulfil the first principle is, in a way, to fulfil them all because the abstract human needs such as self-reliance, happiness and dignity lie at the heart of empowerment and release. To enhance the learning process is the practical way to enable people to fulfil those needs while they learn to cope with the situation. Eventually, the end result is true empowerment that transcends the scope of the liberal and often overused meaning of the word.

## 8.5    ATTITUDE

The attitude of the CDW is of prime importance. The correct attitude opens doors while the wrong attitude closes them. The wrong attitude can also cause misunderstanding among the people regarding the CDW's role and obligations. Good planning, reliable funding and prompt action are all ingredients necessary for success, but the attitude of the CDW is more important. The following are a number of important guidelines addressed to the CDW regarding his/her attitude:

▶ Don't regard yourself as a superhuman who will save the people. You are not superhuman and it is not your job to save the people.

▶ Never regard your job as mundane. What you do can decide whether people live on in abject poverty or are released from the deprivation trap.

▶ Have respect for the knowledge and wisdom of the people. The fact that some of them are illiterate and most of them are not well educated does not mean that any of them are stupid.

▶ Respect the people's views and feelings. These things are dear to them and disrespect will solicit the wrong reaction. If you respect their knowledge and wisdom, you will also respect the people's views and feelings. Their views and feelings are usually informed by their culture and world view which are valuable resources in the fight against poverty. (See Case Study 9: *The daughter of hope.*)

▶ Respect the people as human beings. They already suffer a lack of human dignity and quite often they have a negative self-perception that should not be made worse by your attitude.

▶ Have and show compassion for people who are suffering in poverty. Compassion is not only to have sympathy for people. It is a willingness to share their situation and their experience of that situation. It is the willingness to stand in the shoes of other people. Aloofness never goes down well, but compassion generates a willingness to accept the CDWs and work with them. It is very difficult to react negatively to compassion. On the other hand, absence of compassion will frustrate the CDW and will make of him/her the type of person that poor people will not trust and accept as someone to help them fight against poverty (See Chapter 6).

▶ Guard against paternalism (and often 'maternalism'). The people are not children awaiting your kind, benevolent, but strict leadership. See Case Study 21: *The loving teacher*.

▶ Don't underestimate people and don't belittle them. The CDW comes to them with an empty slate and only him/herself to offer.

▶ Regard yourself as the people's servant and supporter. This will take care of your position vis-à-vis theirs.

▶ Be humble. Poor people are usually very humble and you should not stand out while you are among them. See Case Study 22: *Brutal force among the cabbage plants*, as an illustration of the opposite attitude. Your humility will also give credence to their leadership because your position will not be a threat to them.

▶ Align yourself with the people's success. They are so seldom successful in a spectacular kind of way and they therefore get so little credit for anything, that you can acknowledge their accomplishments, even if they are small. In this way you can build their dignity.

We can conclude that it takes a certain type of person to be a successful CDW. In a later chapter we will see that people at peace with themselves and those who do not mistrust all other people are usually good communicators. We can say the same of being a successful CDW. Hopefully, the right people will fill most of the CDW positions. The case study in Chapter 17 about Miss Najafi reveals the place and attitude of the CDW and the kind of person needed for the job. Case Study 22: *Brutal force among the cabbage plants*, illustrates the wrong attitude.

Morris, (1970:173) describes this required attitude practically, yet pertinently:

> When the agent's confidence as an expert is tempered by an effective respect for the perceptions, wants and desires of persons in the developing area, then he has begun the transformation from expert into development agent.

To Morris (1970:174) the CDW is 'concerned with inducing change ... but at the same time tempering that change by the wishes and pacing of the society and individuals involved'.

## 8.6 ROLE

The CDW's role is quite difficult to describe because any word that describes a role or function can be misinterpreted or can have a broader or narrower meaning for different people. When we deal with the following five categories of role, we must be aware of the fact that all these roles can be played in different ways. We will try to show a more acceptable way of playing these roles in terms of the principles and the attitude of the CDW, and also point to the wrong way of seeing them.

### 8.6.1 Guide

CDWs' views and perspectives are much broader and longer term than those of the people they work with. They usually have a better idea what the consequences of any action might be. They are also more aware of pitfalls and obstacles than are the people. It is therefore their task to guide the people through those pitfalls towards objectives that may be somewhat murky to the people. But they do this cognisant of their own limitations. CDWs do not know everything. They are also a part of the learning process. They do not have answers to all problems. All this is enough reason to play their role as guide in a specific way. Don't try to be smart all the time. Furthermore, the people should never become dependent on them. This is another very good reason for a specific approach towards this role. It simply means that CDWs' role as guide is more contextual, that is providing understanding within a certain situation and it therefore does not entitle them to lead from the front. They are not guiding blind or crippled people and they are themselves far from perfect. At best CDWs make discoveries with the people as they go along.

### 8.6.2 Adviser

Because of their greater knowledge and broader view, CDWs must give advice. But the role of adviser is also limited. Its sole purpose is to motivate and enable therefore this advice should be in the form of information on the possible choices people can make and the probable consequences of each choice. If we keep in mind what the goals of the CDW are and when we realise that those tie in with the principles discussed in Chapter 6, it is clear that advice should never take the form of telling people what to do and what not to do. See Case Study 14: *The case of the community worker who met his match*. It should never take the responsibility for making decisions away from the people; it should only motivate and enable them to make those decisions.

Empowerment becomes hollow rhetoric if people are starved of information so that they cannot make informed decisions. CDWs should act as conduits, passing information on to the people. But a conduit should be connected to a reliable source. The question is whether CDWs are linked to reliable sources of information. In this age of computerised information systems it should be possible to serve even remote communities with the necessary information. But are they linked to these sources? If they are starved of information, it is impossible for CDWs to empower the people through information. CDWs and their organisations should make sure that they are linked to reliable sources of up to date information so that they can extend that access to the groups of people they work with (see Chapter 13 for more detail).

### 8.6.3 Advocate

CDWs have contacts with the outside world that communities usually lack. They also know which channels to follow while the situation may look like a maze to the ordinary people. The

CDWs know how to deal with the authorities, where to go and who to see to get approvals and obtain concessions. They may therefore be valuable to the community if they use their links and point out the correct channels. This does not mean that community facilitators should always represent the people to the outside world. They should play this role only if the situation demands it and all concerned are convinced that that is the best option. In any case a CDW should never go it alone. One or more people should be delegated to accompany the CDW so that the learning opportunity can be utilised. They remain conduits through which information flows.

They can also play an advocacy role in helping their group to complete a business plan or project proposal. The contents of these documents are so important that the CDW can play a vital role. The professional appearance of such a document is also very important and could make good use of the CDW's contribution. This does not mean that the CDW should complete these documents on his/her own. The completion of these documents can be a very good learning opportunity.

Sometimes it is also necessary for CDWs to defend the people's wishes, interests, and actions and their right to autonomy against outside misunderstanding, jealousy, bureaucracy and apathy.

In Case Study 7: *A community hall with no purpose*, the CDWs did not play this role well enough.

Again this role can be misunderstood. CDWs do not act independently from their groups. They remain conduits through which messages can travel to and from communities. They are not the people's 'Foreign Affairs Ministers'. They do not have that legal standing and therefore they may not compromise the people in any way.

### 8.6.4    Enabler

CDWs aim to enable the people to fulfil their abstract human needs, to enhance their learning processes and to help them gain meaningful empowerment. For this reason, they are present primarily to enable the people to do what should be done.

Through all of these activities CDWs must foster a climate for the people to act. They must create space for the people to move forward. This provision of climate and space is not a hectic role. In their enabling role CDWs are catalysts—they are there to make things happen without being active themselves. CDWs will be well advised to calm their role-playing down. People do not want to be pressurised into action. To them every step forward is an accomplishment. So, the CDW's actions can never be accomplishing, but must remain enabling, establishing opportunities without enforcing them. Case Study 18: *Food garden in Mapayeni*, gives a good example of a CDW who enables.

### 8.6.5    Facilitator

The primary concern of CDWs is to help the people make rational decisions, to enable them to participate fully, to assist them in taking the initiative, to help them to discover their resources, and to help them to plan and to implement. The three operative verbs used here, 'help', 'enable', and 'assist', make it clear that this role is the fulfilment of the attitude a CDW should harbour. This role differs vastly from the situation that is the rule rather than the exception where the CDW overplays his/her hand by making the decisions, taking the initiative and doing the planning and allowing the people to assist him/her. Unfortunately, this is not a facilitator's role. Instead, it describes the role of leader or boss or manager where participation, empowerment and ownership are liberal 'concessions', the measure of which is decided upon by the initiating organisation. A facilitator cannot be but in the background, cannot play any other than a secondary role and cannot do anything else than assisting and enabling.

## 8.7 CONCLUSION

The place and role of the CDW can be described as very delicate. It can be nearly impossible to fulfil if the correct attitude is not present. The CDW will be well advised to approach these roles and his/her position with the attitude Korten (1980) suggests: 'All I have is myself to offer'. Case Study 15: *The inspector whose help was dumped*, shows what we can learn from the mistakes of a CDW as summarised here:

▶ Those working in NGOs often come from the affluent part of society and often they do not share the language and culture of the poor.
▶ CDWs hold behind-the-scenes positions.
▶ CDWs might find themselves forced to champion the causes of the people, sometimes in the face of opposition from all and sundry, including their superiors.
▶ In their enabling role CDWs must remove obstacles, steer clear of trouble, and provide know-how to make it possible for people to act.
▶ The CDW has a very difficult role to play and it is easy to play it wrongly.

# CHAPTER 9

# PARTICIPATORY DECISION-MAKING AND MANAGEMENT

## 9.1 INTRODUCTION

No one can deny that participation in activities that affect your future and that of your children is a democratic right. This clearly means that no politician and no official has the right to decide when people should participate and to what extent they should do so. The local, provincial and national governments are there to serve the people, not the other way around; therefore the primary role-players, also in decision-making, are the people, not the government. It is, however, easier to say than to facilitate these things. People, especially if they are poor, not well educated and unsophisticated, find it very difficult to make decisions that they can defend as logical and reasonable. On the other hand, there are people and parties who prefer that the poor and the ordinary remain in the background and play the docile role of beneficiaries.

## 9.2 PARTICIPATORY MANAGEMENT

### 9.2.1 Goals of participation

The process of participation has got the following broad goals:

▶ The active participation of individuals and groups in the promotion of their own well-being through actions that will lead to effective problem-solving.
▶ Individual and group participation in decisions about the type of projects that are required in a community. Three specific and essential aims are served by ensuring participation on this level. They are:
  – the enhancement of the capacity of communities to make informed decisions and prioritise needs;
  – the promotion of the legitimacy of any institutional structure that is formed within a community; and
  – the promotion of ongoing participation of the community in the planning and monitoring of existing services, facilities and projects and the extension or alteration of such services or facilities.
▶ The final level of participation seeks the active mobilisation of community resources and assets (human and natural) for the promotion of project objectives.

With the above in mind we can say that centralised decision-making does not work. Centralised decision-making carries very little accountability and therefore decision-makers are removed from the very real human situation influenced by their decisions. When development processes do not take the local structures into consideration, an institutional vacuum is created. There is no institutional support for development processes with the result that efforts collapse as soon as benefactors start to withdraw structural support. Finally, we can say that there is no holistic approach by centralised, non-participatory decision-making. Development efforts are fragmentary, quite often contradictory and nearly always in competition with each other to the detriment of those who need the help.

Having said this, we can go back to the principles of community development that we have covered in a previous chapter. We should concentrate on flexibility, go for simplicity and move step-by-step. We must be focused on the local situation and therefore be socially sensitive and responsive to the local human needs and wishes. Eventually we can emphasise that development cannot take place in a vacuum. We need local structures created by the people to carry the development. Participation and learning and ownership cannot take place within a chaotic situation. For this reason all these activities must be structured. We must remember that the structures are there to serve the purposes already mentioned. They must therefore be appropriate for the task and they must be the means to an end, not the end in itself.

Participatory decision-making is crucial. Local knowledge and skills should be used through participation. Local people are the experts on their own situation and this expertise should be used.

The public service, including the local government, will not be the only development role-player. The responsibility will be shared with the private sector, community organisations, trade unions, other stakeholders and the community at large. Service delivery will therefore become developmental, will address the poverty situation of the people and will therefore, be founded on the creation of government-community partnership.

### 9.2.2 Participation in projects

Participatory management of projects means that the people who are going to be affected by the change the project aims to bring, should be full partners in the initiation of the project and should play a leading role in the management of the project. When we look at the world around us it becomes clear that local people have a much better understanding of their own circumstances, needs and aspirations than anybody on the outside. People can make better decisions within the framework of their own understanding of their situation. But this is only one reason why local people should participate. The other, more important reason is that it is their democratic right to participate in decisions affecting their lives. Excluding people from participating in issues that affect their lives is a violation of their human right and therefore of their human dignity.

Community participation means that local people must take part in the management of their own lives and their own environments, in this instance within projects. Community participation in project management includes:

▶ identifying and making decisions on issues, needs and problems they consider important or believe need to change;

- implementing projects aimed at changing unacceptable situations in a positive way;
- evaluating and adjusting the project and its processes in order to see if they are successful in addressing their needs and in changing their circumstances for the better; and
- Taking full responsibility for and control over projects and processes they have embarked upon.

The community development worker (CDW) is the enabler of this participation and, in being the enabler, he/she must make sure that the following aspects receive attention:

- The people must have a need to address through a project. They will not participate just because a project serves a good cause and they will not participate just because the project looks interesting. People must have a real need before they will pledge themselves to do something. (See Chapter 5)
- The people must be motivated. One of the most important tasks of facilitation is to motivate. There must be a vision that the people share and they must be eager to fulfil their aspirations. (See Chapter 13)
- There must be as few hindrances as possible in the way of participation. Animosities, jealousy, favouritism and opportunism must be absent if a climate for participation is to be created. But also, from the official side, the people must be given the freedom to participate. Departmental rules and regulations and bureaucratic red tape can easily act as demotivators and can make it difficult or unpleasant to participate. (See Chapter 13)
- There must be regular feedback to the people. Unfortunately all people cannot directly participate in project management. For that reason it is mostly an elected committee, a representative body, that does the day to day management on behalf of the people. But that does not mean that the bulk of the people must be disempowered by ignoring them. They must still have the power to call a halt to actions by their representatives and to contribute their ideas, meanings, concerns and suggestions to the process.
- The project must eventually ensure concrete visible benefits to the community or to a group of people who have a common need. One project that does not deliver anticipated benefits makes the acceptance of future projects by the people very difficult. On the other hand, a project with visible and obvious benefits acts as a motivator for future projects. (See Chapter 5)

Management of a project consists of four discrete responsibilities or actions. They are planning, implementation, evaluation and control. Development management, though, does much more than that. Development management is the management of development that includes the management of the project, but reaches much further. We can say that development management differs from ordinary management in that it has got to:

- adapt to a very dynamic, and therefore constantly changing environment;
- deal with a situation where new needs appear all the time;
- ensure the effective participation of the people who are touched by the project; and
- include and support existing institutional structures in the development process.

This is a tall order and that is why development management is never easy.

A further very important aspect of development management is that it must integrate community inputs and technical inputs. The fact that it must be integrated, immediately tells us that the two are not in opposition or that the one automatically nullifies the other. These two types of inputs are equally important and it is the task of development management to optimise both.

Community inputs consist of the following:

▶ *Participation*: In terms of input, participation in all aspects related to planning, implementation and evaluation is essential as it points to the *process* of community input and not as a once-off activity.

▶ *Local knowledge*: Local people are guardians to a wealth of information that, once unleashed, can work wonders. This local, indigenous information by far exceeds any academic or book-gained knowledge outsiders may have access to. This information is a crucial aspect of community-based development management.

▶ *Local skills*: Whilst local people have access to indigenous knowledge they also have indigenous skills that are not necessarily inferior to any technical skills and are quite often better suited to the situation than technical skills. Many actions in any development project need the type of skills that can readily be found among local people. In these instances technical skills are unnecessary and can even be inappropriate.
Participatory management does not mean that the community should be managed. The whole idea of participatory projects is that the community should not be managed from outside. Participatory management can therefore only mean to organise and to enable the community to take charge of its own affairs. This reflects specifically on sustainability, cost recovery and the implementation of government policy.

### 9.2.3 Important aspects regarding participatory management

▶ *Short and long term sustainability*: Sustainability means the opposite of what frequently happens in development situations in Third World countries. This is that a lot of money is spent on projects, a number of arrangements are made and usually a lot of effort is put into the matter, just to find that the whole effort grinds to a halt before real benefits have been reaped. Participatory management is meant to prevent this situation. This can only happen if development efforts are maintained through a system of management. Through this management process the community must be put in a position where it can continuously take responsibility for what has been started.
Sustainability is also dependent on a notion of long-term commitment. Quite often, in Third World situations, there is a strong realisation of the short-term needs of people. Projects are then aimed to bring relief in the short term and very little arrangements are made to sustain the benefits over the long term.
As for long-term sustainability, people must be helped to see beyond their immediate needs. They must also realise that they cannot redress all their problems in the short term. Although development should bear fruit in the short term, it is equally important

to realise that the totality of the problem can only be addressed over the long term. Sustainability therefore becomes extremely important to ensure that the totality of the problem receives attention in the long term. Further, it is also of extreme importance that what has been started should be successfully completed. An effort should therefore be sustained until it bears the fruit expected of it and must then be further maintained in order to continue to bear fruit.

▶ *Cost recovery*: The initial financial outlay for and the continuous maintenance of any community project must at least be partially recovered by the users of the new service. A cost-recovery mechanism must therefore form part of the planning of any project. It is obvious that this part of a project is part of the long-term aspects and is therefore dependent on the sustainability of the project. It is therefore clear that one of the most important reasons for participatory management is to ensure a healthy cost recovery in the long term.

▶ *Government policy*: Government policy is dependent on long-term commitments and can only come to fruition in the long-term. Government policy is also dependent on a well-organised system through which it can be implemented, and it sets the targets, determines the scope of and identifies the strategy through which development efforts are to be launched in deprived areas. Unfortunately government policy must be implemented before it means much and for, that reason, an organised community is necessary to put policies into practice (Mmakola, 1996:20). Participatory management therefore helps to ensure that government policy is implemented.

▶ *Participatory management—the concept*: To be understood, participatory management must be seen in its entirety, as discussed earlier in this chapter. It is not meant as something whereby the government, on any of the three spheres runs and controls the community. Participatory management is done by the community itself. It refers to the self-reliance of a community to organise itself in such a fashion that policies can be implemented, projects can be initiated and sustained and the necessary cost recovery can take place. It therefore means that a community can organise itself to take responsibility for itself. If a community can begin to do this it is en route to being free of the shackles of deprivation and poverty that bound it before. See Case study 17: *Mothers of the mountain community*.

▶ *Monitoring and evaluation*: Sustainability must be maintained through a participatory management system that works. It is not enough to have a policy and strategy in place, to have the determination to do something about the situation and to announce the imminent launch of projects and then not to do anything about it. For that reason monitoring and evaluation must play such an important part. It is only through monitoring and evaluation that we can really determine whether the initial plans have been put in practice and whether they are being carried out according to the plans. It is also the task of monitoring and evaluation to ensure that the direction is correct. In other words, monitoring and evaluation also ensure that the initial plans were on target and suggest course changes when necessary. The most important condition for monitoring and evaluation is that it must be orderly. It is a process, using selected and previously accepted criteria and indicators to tell us whether an effort is still on track and tell us all other aspects of that effort such as whether it maintains the time frame and whether it really addresses the problems as identified initially.

Planning and implementation without participation is a sure method to extend costs, stir up political unrest, ensure lack of progress, and cause rifts in the community. Real participation adds quality and co-operation and eventually brings together (perhaps with a measure of strife) a number of diverse players in an issue-based process towards achieving acceptable solutions.

Not only does the constitution indicate that the participation of communities and community groups in the matters of local government should be encouraged, experience elsewhere and in South Africa has shown the vital importance of community participation in projects. In summary, communities should participate in management of their projects for the following reasons:

▶ Through participation both concrete and abstract needs of participants are fulfilled.
▶ It encourages a learning process in which people participate and take the initiative from the start by participating in needs identification and decision-making.
▶ Collective action that includes collective decision-making is stimulated.
▶ If communities do participate, development is needs oriented.
▶ Because communities work towards addressing needs, they focus on achieving objectives.
▶ It involves people at grassroots level and through this process provides an opportunity for ordinary people to participate.
▶ It brings about awareness among people about their own situation and their ability to address their situation themselves.
▶ It leads to community building by encouraging leadership skills, institutional development and organisational ability.
▶ People gain awareness and power for further developmental activities.
▶ After all, it is the people's democratic right to participate in decision-making.

## 9.3    GROUP DECISION-MAKING

It is clear that development-relevant institutions need group decision-making, but it is necessary to manage such a process. The manager of such a process should know that it has advantages and disadvantages. We will first look at the advantages (Massie & Douglas, 1981:178):

▶ Individual specialists can approach a problem from different viewpoints in the group.
▶ Co-ordination of activities and decisions of separate departments can be achieved through interaction and joint decision-making in groups.
▶ Motivation of individual members to carry out decisions may be increased by the feeling of being part of the decision-making process.
▶ Groups provide a means by which personnel members can be trained in decision-making.
▶ Groups permit representation of different interest groups in the decision-making process.

▶ Groups provide the opportunity for experts from outside an organisation to be made part of the decision-making process.

▶ Groups may also be a way to democratise decision-making by drawing members of the public into these groups so that their preferences, fears and knowledge are part of the process.

▶ Group decisions are a good method to use for creative thinking because fragmentary ideas from individuals usually start a chain reaction in the minds of others so that a decision is built like a jigsaw puzzle.

The disadvantages are the following:

▶ Considering the value of the time of each individual member, groups are expensive.

▶ The length of time it takes a group to come to a decision makes prompt decision-making difficult.

▶ Group action may lead to compromise and indecision.

▶ Group decision-making can be a sham where very senior people or outside experts are present.

▶ Group decisions may lead to a situation where no one takes responsibility for a decision.

Some guidelines for successful group decision-making are as follows (Massie & Douglas, 1981:179—180):

▶ The physical layout, size of the group and general atmosphere are important factors determining the effectiveness of decision-making.

▶ Threat reduction is an important objective in the planning of group action so that the group will shift from interpersonal problems to group goals. The golden rule should be: No personal attacks allowed!

▶ The best group leadership is performed by the entire group. It is not the job of the chairperson, the CDW or any formal leader. A group that functions well tends to function informally with no single person providing all the leadership.

▶ The group should explicitly formulate goals. They should not be fenced in by predetermined rules, but should rather be guided by their own predetermination of goals.

▶ The group should formulate an agenda, but it should never be regarded as a blueprint.

▶ The decision-making process should continue until the group formulates a consensus upon which it can formulate a solution. If the group action results in a minority opinion, the group has failed to maximise its effectiveness. So, voting is not a solution when we cannot quickly find consensus.

▶ Any group should be made aware of the interaction process by which it arrives at solutions. The individual members must be made aware of their individual and collective role and responsibility. In this manner the skill of being a member of a group becomes a distinguishable skill that can be developed.

▶ Group members should be made aware of problem-solving and decision-making models and then they can choose a model that suits their situation or they can devise their own process.

▶ It is important that a group obtains the necessary information that will enable it to make enlightened decisions.

▶ It goes without saying that a manager, executive or official may never ignore or override the decision made by a group.

## 9.4 THE NEED FOR INFORMATION IN DECISION-MAKING

You cannot make informed decisions if you do not receive the necessary relevant information. For this reason information dissemination is part of the mobilisation and empowerment drive. No community lives in isolation. There is a constant flow of information to a community. This information covers many aspects of life and can also be of an interpretative nature. In other words, the information explains something. Information can also be of a motivational nature. and political information is usually of this nature, but; for example, development management could also carry motivational information. See Chapter 13 for more about information dissemination.

In a development-relevant situation a process of regular ongoing communication is required once stakeholders have been identified to ensure that effective linkages can be established for their participation. Both the mechanisms for communicating and the content of communication will need to be based on the needs of each stakeholder group, as well as on the particular stage of the process. Most of the information will be project-related, but then still with different objectives in mind.

### 9.4.1 Motivational information

Information should not speak only to the minds of people, but also to their hearts. Their commitment to the project and their organisational obligations must be established and for that purpose motivational information is needed.

### 9.4.2 Organisational information

People like stakeholders find themselves within organisations and that one organisation exists within another. It is therefore necessary to know how organisations work and what organisational obligations exist for stakeholders, for example, the obligation to attend meetings.

### 9.4.3 Management information

People such as the stakeholders will fulfil certain managerial functions within development-relevant institutions. They will also have linkages with managers and management systems, and they need to know and understand how these work.

### 9.4.4 Professional/technical information

This is the information that stakeholders need in order to make informed decisions because most of their decisions will be of a technical nature. This does not mean that the other types of information will not also contribute to their forming opinions and making decisions.

All this information must be channelled to the target audience and for that you need communication channels. These channels must satisfy certain requirements. They must be without obstruction because obstructions hinder or stop the flow of information. They must not be too long because long channels take longer to disseminate information and can slow down the flow to a trickle. They must be clean and no pollution of the information must be possible. Information gets polluted because the senders or handlers of information are not careful. Sometimes information gets polluted because someone has an ulterior motive, such as political or financial expediency. One of the most important requirements is that the channels must be connected to a source of information.

There are many information channels to a community—from mass media, such as television, radio and newspapers, to small interest groups with much focused interests. In our case, one would make use of mass media and other large distributors of information, such as schools, only at the beginning of entry to announce and introduce something to the larger public. But as the development-relevant institutions become established and the stakeholders become involved, it seems that more specific channels, such as the stakeholder groupings and the various structures regarding development projects, would be the ideal information channels.

## 9.5  CONCLUSION

There may be easier ways of decision-making than participatory. And because of that, one is tempted to take a short cut. But participatory decision-making is so part of the new-look development, so integral to adaptiveness and learning, that there is not really any short cut. Instead of looking for short cuts, CDWs should rather look for ways and means to manage this process so successfully that participatory decision-making becomes the only way of decision-making.

The CDW must champion the cause of the poor and as such must do everything to ensure that the poor will make enlightened and reasonable decisions.

Just as a water pipe can only provide water to the tap if it is connected to a reservoir, so communication channels can only provide information if they are connected to a source.

Problem-solving can be tackled incorrectly from the start or many smaller things can go wrong during problem-solving.

**SKILLS FOR COMMUNITY DEVELOPMENT**

# CHAPTER 10

# COMMUNICATION SKILLS

## 10.1 INTRODUCTION

Talking to other people, reading a book or newspaper, watching television, bargaining about the price of something, making an appointment, enjoying a joke with friends—these are all part of our daily communication that links us to our environment and makes our existence meaningful. Communication can be regarded as the activity humans do most and it can be seen as the activity that affects humans most.

It is quite obvious that communication is very important to all of us. If we are good communicators it will affect our lives and those of other people positively. In effect, it will shape our lives and when we have a hand in influencing other people positively it will in turn help us to become more effective communicators. Communication is improved by discovering better and more effective ways of relating to others and having them relate to us. It is clear that human communication is the vehicle through which interpersonal relationships are developed and destroyed.

If communication is so important in our daily lives, we can imagine how important it is in development projects where a number of people, usually as an organised group, are actively and emotionally involved in decision-making and executing those decisions. We can safely say that community development projects succeed or fail according the communication that takes place within them. That is why it is so important to spend some time on this aspect.

## 10.2 A COMMUNICATION MODEL

Let us look at the ingredients of communication in order to understand it better.

First, there is a **sender**, or source, or origin, of communication. Communication must start from somewhere. I start talking to you. The television announces a new programme. The newspaper has a heading that catches my eye. So, the communication originates with the sender.

Second, there is a **receiver** or target. Communication is directed at someone or at a group of people or at a certain type of person. If I say: 'How are you today, Margaret?' the receiver or target of my communication is Margaret. If a notice in the newspaper says: 'To all those who want to start a new career', the target is not only one person, but a certain type of person.

Third, there is a **message**. Communication without meaning is not really communication. Language has meaning, music has meaning—a certain kind of music will convey a certain kind of message. Even colour can have meaning; if I give someone a bouquet of red roses it means something and it conveys a certain message. If the traffic light shows green it means something and tells the road user something.

Fourth, there is a certain **coding**. We use certain codes to convey our messages. I may say: 'Hello'. Someone else may say: 'Good morning'. A third person may say: 'Hi'. The message in all three cases is similar, but the coding differs vastly. Coding is also made up of non-verbal communication. Non-verbal actions (also called immediacy behaviour) include smiling, touching, eye contact, open body positions, closer distances and more vocal animation (Andersen et al, 2002:90). A smile whilst talking means something and a frown means something else.

Fifth, there is a **medium** of communication. The most common medium is the word of mouth, where people speak to one another, but writing is another medium and so is music or pictures or even body language.

Sixth, there are various **channels** that can be used. I can make use of a direct channel by talking to someone, as the Americans say 'eyeball to eyeball', I can write the person a letter, I can send the person a message via someone else, or I can send an e-mail message or an SMS to the person.

This whole process of communication always takes place in a certain **context**. Communication in the cafeteria is different from communication in the boardroom. Communication between friends is different from communication between business rivals. Communication, while we watch a football match, is different from communication while we attend a funeral service.

Now that we have all the ingredients, we know what communication consists of, but we still do not have communication. It is now necessary to mix all these ingredients, as we would mix the ingredients in a stew. Communication may consist of a sender, a receiver and a message, but that does not really tell us how communication takes place. If I say to you: 'It is very hot today', I am the sender, you are the receiver and the message is that it is very hot today. But then you may respond by saying: 'Isn't it?', while you wipe your brow. Now you are the sender, using a different code and I become the receiver, decoding your code so that it means to me: 'Yes, it is very hot'. Now both of us are senders and receivers, using different codes. The process of communication is also unpredictable. You could have responded by saying: 'It is not really very hot', or 'Are you mad! It isn't hot! Have you got a fever?'. Every time my response will be different. Imagine the communication process at a party where four friends talk to one another while loud music is playing. Every now and then some other person passes the group of friends and may say hello or make some remark to one or more members of the group, to which one or more of them may respond. In this scenario senders to one target may at the same time be receivers from another source. Different codes may be used even by the same source or sender. It makes for a very untidy situation, but also a very complex one in which communication becomes very difficult. Most of the communication situations resemble this untidy scene where it becomes difficult to identify sender, receiver, message and codes.

All this simply means that communication is not linear. That means it does not take place in a straight line: from sender to receiver. Rather, it is cyclic, which means after the receiver has received the message he/she becomes the sender and the sender becomes the receiver. These roles change all the time and at the same time different messages may be transferred between the participants and different forms of coding may be used.

## 10.3   BARRIERS TO COMMUNICATION

Because communication is complex, because it is unpredictable and because different participants use different codes, there are barriers in the way of successful communication. (This section is based on Swanepoel & De Beer, 1996.) We can group these barriers together and say that there are barriers to receiving a message, to understanding a message, and to accepting a message. These barriers are very serious because in any situation the sender of a message wants the receiver to receive the message, understand it and accept it. Communication is only successful if that happens.

### 10.3.1   Barriers to reception

Barriers to reception can include delays, a total breakdown of communication or influences causing distortion. The following barriers can result in the receiver not receiving the message, even though the sender has sent it:

▶ The receiver may have anxieties. The receiver may be scared of the sender or the message. The receiver may feel himself/herself in the corner and at the mercy of the sender. In such a situation the receiver does not really listen to the message and therefore does not really receive it.

▶ The receiver may have expectations. The receiver may think that the communication will lead to further good things and then pre-empt the message, therefore he/she does not listen properly and misses out some detail of the message.

▶ The receiver may be preoccupied. If you read a book on quantum physics, but your mind is really with the soccer match that will take place later today, you will not know what you are reading. Few people can really mentally concentrate on more than one thing at a time. But people's lives can be filled with something at a certain stage that preoccupies them and makes them poor receivers. If your child is seriously ill and there is no improvement, you are preoccupied and will find listening to something that is not related to the illness very difficult.

▶ The receiver may have a physical disability. He/she may be feeling sick. A severe headache makes concentration very difficult so that a message cannot be decoded properly. A common disability is of course that the receiver is deaf or his/her hearing is impaired.

▶ The sender may have a physical disability. He/she may stutter or have a very soft voice. Then the receiver does not really receive the message even if he/she tries.

▶ There may be environmental disturbances. Circumstances such as noise or competing messages, for example, the news being read on the radio at the same time that another message is conveyed may hinder reception.

These barriers make the receiver hear or read the sender wrongly, in other words, get the wrong message, or receive only part or very little of the message. It is clear that if communication stumbles over this first barrier, there is no hope that the message will overcome the other two barriers, in other words, that the message will be understood and accepted. Receiving the message is therefore absolutely necessary and that does not mean snippets of it, but as much as possible if not the total message.

## 10.3.2   Barriers to understanding

Barriers to understanding are common among people of different cultures and/or languages or of different ages or between professional and lay people.

▶ The receiver may not understand the language used. In a multilingual country such as South Africa it can easily happen that the receiver understands nothing or very little of the language that the sender uses.

▶ The receiver may not understand the jargon used. Jargon or official terminology permeates all languages more and more. Take for example the jargon attached to computers and their use. For somebody who does not have a computer or never uses one, it is very difficult to understand a message regarding computers. Examples of jargon are the words teenagers like to use (to the consternation and mystification of their parents), for example: vague up (make less clear); mootville (irrelevant); A world of no! (definitely not); carbon-dated (very out of date) and all-dat (everything).

▶ The receiver may have a problem listening intelligently. People differ in intelligence and in concentration span. If a message comes to a receiver in a language that he/she does not use everyday and if the message is also complex, it is very difficult to really understand the message.

▶ The receiver may have a poor knowledge of the subject of communication. If someone talks to you about something that you know very little about, chances are that you will understand nothing or very little of the message. Any subject has its own jargon and if you are not familiar with it, you will not be able to understand. Each subject also has its own causality and if you do not know that causality, it can be difficult for you to understand. The meteorologist knows what causes rain, but the receiver of his message may not know that and therefore may find it difficult to understand.

▶ The communication may be too lengthy. A long message runs the risk of not being understood simply because the receiver cannot concentrate for a longish period of time. Very few people can really concentrate for more than about 18 minutes and therefore one can state that the longer the message, the less it will be understood.

▶ The message may be garbled or coded. The message may be presented in such a way that the receiver finds it difficult to decode. Again, this happens when the subject of the message is not known by the receiver and he/she therefore does not know the meaning of jargon or does not know the causality typical of that subject.

▶ Again, the receiver may be anxious or preoccupied, which makes it difficult to listen intelligently.

These barriers result in the receiver hearing or reading the message, the message is received, but the receiver does not understand everything or understands wrongly or does not understand at all.

### 10.3.3 Barriers to acceptance

Barriers to acceptance occur when political, social, cultural, religious, moral and even biological differences between communicating parties are marked. The following factors usually cause these barriers:

▶ The receiver may have prejudices. In fact, we can say that the receiver will have prejudices because it is human to have them. It is hoped that the prejudices will not form a barrier, but quite often it does.

▶ There may be emotional conflict between the sender and the receiver. Because we are human we have emotions and quite often those emotions can conflict with those of the other person.

▶ The way the sender communicates may make the message unacceptable. For example, the sender may be bombastic. Good manners and civility can go a long way in simplifying communication.

▶ There may be a status clash or a marked status difference between sender and receiver. In severe patriarchal situations older men may find it offensive if younger women communicate with them. So-called 'hlonipa rules' in most of the traditional black communities in Southern Africa create a situation which can make communication difficult and can often lead to communication failure. These rules regulate relationships between, for example, young women and older men, teenagers and grown-ups, daughters-in-law and fathers-in-law and ordinary folk and tribal chiefs. In residential areas with marked social differences, one might find the same problem.

▶ The values and mores of the sender and receiver may be in conflict. This usually happens because of a difference in age or culture or simply because of a difference of opinion. People tend to think that their values and mores are universally acceptable and this can lead to a situation where the sender resents the receiver and the receiver resents the sender.

▶ The message may be in conflict with the receiver's interests. In this case the receiver is hardly going to accept it just like that. People are opportunistic. The common good is always subordinate to the individual interest. So, a message with a positive outcome for the society may still be unacceptable for the individual if it seems in conflict with his/her interests.

In these cases the receiver receives the message and understands it, but rejects it on one or more grounds. There are various reasons why barriers exist. Various situations put up barriers that make communication ineffective. Some of these are as follows:

▶ Different perceptions exist among communicating parties. Because every human being is unique, our perceptions of things tend to be unique too. We see things differently from one another. This results in our giving different meaning to verbal and non-verbal communication.

▶ Communicating parties quite often come from different situations. They live under different circumstances and experience different inputs. Thus, communicating parties may have different realities that may differ slightly or vastly and may even be in conflict with one another.

▶ Communication has got to compete with a lot of noise. By noise we do not mean only physical noise so that we cannot hear communication. We also include psychological 'noise' such as fear, social 'noise' such as prejudice, cultural 'noise' such as superstition, and political 'noise' such as opportunism.

▶ Much of our communication has emotional content. In such cases we tend to respond to the emotion and not to the content of the message. By this we do not say that communication should be void of emotion, but that we should be careful of how much emotion we allow in our communication and how we respond to emotion. We must also accept that communication can hardly be without some emotion.

▶ Very few of us are prepared to trust another person unconditionally. Distrust is really the poison for communication because, in communication, one does not only give a message, one gives something of oneself. One opens oneself through communication, but if we do not trust the receiver of our message, we are loathe to open up, to give or even reveal something of ourselves. As long as communication is less than spontaneous because of distrust it is facing a plethora of pitfalls that can cause its demise.

▶ Apathy is not very helpful to communication. One can have apathy towards the message. That means that one is not perturbed about the message and does not regard it as important. When one is apathetic towards the other communicating party, then one is not interested in the other person's feelings, interests or well-being. If you do not care for the message or for the sender, it is impossible for communication to be successful.

▶ It is human to feel apprehensive about change and even to resist it. If a message contains a hint of impending change or emphasises the need to change, many receivers will close out the message. The situation becomes worse if the receiver is confronted with change, if it becomes a matter of change or bust. It is easy to see why this is one of the most prolific barriers in development communication.

▶ Culture determines the meaning of the world we live in. It rationalises what we do and how we do it. It also causes a feeling of 'us and them'. The meaning that people from other cultures attach to things such as life, circumstances and situations, may not look rational to the receiver and this often leads to cultural snobbishness and prejudice. Communication on an equal footing where there is respect for the other person and his/her views becomes really difficult. According to Servaes and Lie (2003:11) culture does not only provide context but is becoming text. As text it constitutes the common, shared interest around which a community project evolves.

## 10.4 OVERCOMING BARRIERS TO COMMUNICATION

In community development work it is important to be a good communicator, in other words, to overcome the various barriers to communication. The first thing on the way to overcoming the barriers is to admit that they exist, also within you, and to decide to do something about it. This is a sincere way of addressing the problem and an important starting point that must lead to tackling the problem at two levels: first, at a psychological level and second, at a technical, mechanistic level.

### 10.4.1 The psychological level

The first step towards effective communication with others is successful communication with oneself. Intra-personal communication means messages sent and received within the same individual. It takes place whenever we evaluate and respond to internal and external stimuli. It reflects our physical, emotional, intellectual and social self. In other words, it reflects our self-concept.

As we increase our self-awareness we also tend to be willing to share that awareness with others. If we have reached this stage, we are on the brink of becoming a successful communicator because self-disclosure lies at the heart of communication. It is the vehicle by which others know what is going on inside us; our thoughts and feelings and what we care about. Self-disclosure opens a window through which others can look into one's soul. Self-disclosure is also the key to any long-term relationship, and most importantly, it leads to greater self-awareness because it works directly against the very negative natural tendency to hide feelings of incompetence, loneliness, guilt, fear and anxiety. See Massie and Douglas (1981:362) for a discussion of the Johari Window.

The less we feel threatened by communication, the easier it will be to trust the other party. If we succeed in trusting someone else, we can really look forward to fruitful and productive communication because without that trust very little communication can really take place. Trust is seldom instantaneous. It takes a while to get to trust someone, simply because it takes time to get to know him/her. Trust in a person therefore develops over time and can be accomplished only with a genuine effort to get to trust the other person. As this trust grows, it becomes reciprocal in most cases, in other words, the more we trust someone, the more that person trusts us. Only if that mutual trust develops can there be real communication between two people.

This process of real communication is boosted tremendously by feedback. If silence is the only feedback we get as a result of our communication; if we respond to communication directed to us with apathy, the communication stops right there. Feedback takes place internally and externally. Internally we conform or correct our understanding of a message or our feeling about a message by external feedback such as asking questions and responding with feeling. Such feedback comes in the form of a message to the other party who will again react externally by perhaps asking further questions or agreeing and internally by shaping his/her behaviour or perspective accordingly.

### 10.4.2 The technical level

At the more practical or technical level there are a lot of things that we can do to overcome the barriers. As a starting point one should follow a few standard guidelines:

▶ Acknowledge barriers. That means that we admit that barriers exist. This admission shows our honesty without which we will never overcome any barriers.

▶ Bring it out into the open. We should even admit to the other party that there are barriers and try to persuade the other person to help us to overcome them.

▶ Develop counteracting strategies to the barriers. Admitting to their existence is not enough. We are then still in a negative mode. We must also do something positive to overcome them.

▶ Be aware of the context of your communication. Take note of the circumstances and the situation because the context determines what barriers are present and how to overcome them. This context is both concrete or physical and abstract. It is a noisy room where people are coming and going all the time (physical) and it takes place between two people who do not know each other well (abstract).

▶ Be honest. That means that we should not lie to a person. Honesty will be the first step in breaking down barriers.

▶ Be sincere. Sincerity means that we mean what we say. It invites a positive response from the receiver that makes it easier to overcome the barriers.

Let us now look at a number of specific aspects; the everyday things, that one should do in order to overcome barriers and to make communication successful.

▶ Be aware of the importance of perceptions and take special care in ensuring that perceptions are clear and correct. Start with yourself. Are you clear on the issue at hand and is your perception thereof generally acceptable? Then look at the other person. Is there consensus between your understanding and his/hers?

▶ Consider the other person's point of view or frame of reference. About most issues in life there can be more than one point of view. The point of view of the other person is not necessarily incorrect because it differs from yours. The other person may have an altogether different frame of reference than you have.

▶ Use face-to-face communication if the communication situation is problematic or difficult. Feedback and responses are direct and can be responded to directly, which obviates many potential problems. The only advantage of written communication is that you can take care with the phrasing of the message, but on-the-spot monitoring of the communication process can only take place in a face-to-face situation. In order to have the best of both worlds you can put the message in writing where you take care with the phraseology and then work through it with the other party in a face-to-face process.

▶ Be sensitive to the other person's background and adapt to that background, culture and the person's circumstances. If you are a good communicator you will not regard the other party as an antagonist, but you will have empathy that will manifest in sensitivity for and an appreciation of the other person's background and circumstances.

▶ Use direct, clear and simple language. The clearer and less abstract the message, the better it will be received and considered. Symbolic meanings of words must be carefully explained so that there is no confusion as a result of cultural or background differences.

▶ Use frequent repetitions to make sure that the message sinks in. Repetition is a tried and trusted method used by educators. The rhetorical speaker such as the preacher or the politician does it too and usually with great effect.

▶ Be supportive to counteract defensiveness. Let a person be comfortable in your presence and ensure that your communication is objective and descriptive rather than subjective and prescriptive.

- Don't use racist or sexist terms. It can only have negative reactions and can even start conflict. It also shows your disdain for other people rather than your respect for them. Even if it is meant as a joke or a tongue-in-cheek remark you better do it only if you know the other party very well.

- Concentrate on the common grounds and aims and avoid differences. This does not mean that we should be blind to or ignore differences, but one should also not be blind to the common ground and the things that we agree about.

- Encourage a climate and atmosphere conducive to communication. The best way to do this is to be friendly, honest and sincere.

- Try to establish a rapport between you and the receiver. Having a rapport means to accept one another's bona fides; accept that the other person will be civil, decent, honest and sincere.

- Don't give a person the idea that you want something, but rather that you are willing to contribute and to make a sacrifice. This is the secret of the successful tradesperson who makes you feel that you are the receiver of something good. The fact that you pay money for whatever you receive does not figure strongly.

- Make sure that your body language corresponds with what you are saying. If it does not, you are guilty of lying. Inconsistency between verbal and non-verbal communication is picked up quite easily and has a necessarily negative reaction from the other party. On the other hand, if the verbal message and the body language agree, it is a sign of sincerity.

- Be wide awake to the other person's body language. Use that as a frame of reference for your participation in the communication process. In other words, observe the other person's body language, interpret it and adapt accordingly.

- Avoid politics and religion because there are too many tricky nuances that can get you into trouble. But if these topics do crop up, don't give the impression that you are wary about discussing them.

- Be prepared to admit your own mistakes and to take responsibility for them. People appreciate it when you make yourself vulnerable and usually respond kindly to it. It also makes you more human, something that can only be beneficial in a communication situation. It does also open yourself for outside scrutiny and shows some trust from your side.

- Prepare yourself thoroughly if you have to explain a difficult or foreign concept and make sure that it is pitched at the right level—not too high, but not too low either. Then let your sympathy for the other person's weaker position guide you so that you can move at his/her pace and remain at his/her level.

- Communicate with confidence. This is of course only possible if you are well prepared and sure of your facts. Then it is also necessary to accept responsibility for the message that you convey.

- Don't force the other person to communicate with you. It is every person's right to choose with whom he/she wants to communicate. To force a person to listen to you will border on aggressiveness that you should never have. You should be assertive because otherwise you are no better than a lame duck. Therefore, you should state your case and explain your opinion, but coercion should not be part of your argument; then it means bringing the horse to the water and forcing it to drink.

▶ Keep your information lean, in other words, give optimal information, not maximal. An information famine is just as bad as an information overload. So, the appropriate information and the correct amount of information are very important.

▶ A participant in communication should never feel threatened, therefore, don't put a person on the spot. Don't be overbearing, don't talk down to a person and don't make jokes at the expense of a person.

▶ Never gossip because the receiver will, rightfully, have anxiety that you will gossip about him/her too. Remember the importance of trust. Remember also that gossip breaks down trust.

▶ Talking of trust, be trustworthy and reliable, consistent and honest. Show your good intentions and illustrate your integrity to the other party.

▶ Regard yourself as a trainee communicator, therefore assess every activity of communication and learn from such an assessment.

▶ Finally, it is important to persevere. Communication is not easy and we will encounter obstacles that hinder communication. But obstacles are never insurmountable. They only provide huge challenges to our originality, our sincerity and our perseverance.

To a large extent these suggestions are meant for the sender, the initiator of communication. It will be wrong not to include the importance of listening. Remember that the sender becomes the receiver once the receiver responds to the initial input and then the sender must apply listening skills to ensure successful communication. We can say that you must be an active listener. This includes the following:

▶ Listen to fully understand a speaker's remark before criticising or evaluating it.
▶ Listen to evaluate a message only after you know what has really been said.
▶ Listen to the complete message. Do not listen and then assume that you know the rest of the message.
▶ Listen to provide support for the speaker. In other words, identify whatever it is in the message with which you wholeheartedly agree.

## 10.5  DEVELOPMENT COMMUNICATION

Personal communication and personal skills impact directly on what is known today as development communication. Development communication can be described as a process by which people become leading actors in their own development, which allows people to go from being beneficiaries of external development interventions to generators of their own development (Barker, 2001:4). The main aim of the concept of development communication incorporates:

▶ the need for an exchange of information to contribute to the resolution of a development problem;
▶ improvement of the quality of life of a specific target group; and
▶ implementation needs analysis and the evaluation mechanisms within the communication process.

Communication development models emphasise two-way communication to disseminate messages and to transmit information or to motivate people. These models also allow for horizontal communication among people rather than traditional vertical transmission from the expert to an audience. Steyn and Nunes (2001:35) go so far as to suggest that the communication roles of the various stakeholders should be plotted and if necessary communication training should be given. Emphasis is not on the use of the media but the process and strategies for participatory grassroots communication and an exchange of information through two-way media. Today communication models not characterised by participation and the need of the community and aimed at information transmission away from and not in harmony with community processes, are doomed to failure (Mersham et al, 1995).

The community development worker (CDW) should prompt the community to initiate the messages about their development needs. Individual circumstances must also be taken into consideration. In spite of the commonalities that link us into the social structure, no two lives are ever the same in terms of personal experience (Barker, 2001:7).

Development communication is aimed at and includes the following applications (Barker, 2001:8):

▶ an understanding of user needs through contact with target groups;
▶ target group analysis and message development;
▶ beneficial two-way communication relationship between participants;
▶ messages initiated and facilitated by the community;
▶ messages that are decidable because of simplicity and clarity;
▶ participants as co-managers of communication;
▶ skills among all participants in communication technology and techniques;
▶ a healthy internal culture and climate conducive to the dynamic flow of information;
▶ communication with meaning that depends on personal interpretation and collective agreement;
▶ internalisation and externalisation of the message;
▶ formulation of new ideas and directions through participatory action;
▶ messages relevant to inputs from the community;
▶ environmentally-sensitive message;
▶ carefully chosen communication channels;
▶ a well-planned and strategically motivated communication plan; and
▶ objective-achieving communication (See Chapter 11).

## 10.6 CONCLUSION

By learning more about what communication is, we have also learnt about the obstacles or barriers in the way of successful communication. It is clear that communication is the life of community mobilisation and facilitation, that it runs through a project and that it determines the vitality and success of groups, but it is also clear that it does not come by itself. We have to work hard to become skilled and successful communicators.

Without this skill we can hardly do our job successfully. Communication is such an important ingredient of our everyday task. It is therefore imperative that we give it top priority.

# CHAPTER 11

# LEADERSHIP DEVELOPMENT AND GROUP FACILITATION

## 11.1 INTRODUCTION

The participants in community development projects work together in groups. For this reason group wellbeing is of the utmost importance. Group wellbeing is dependent on the community development worker (CDW) knowing how a group operates, understanding group dynamics and being able to facilitate groups. This chapter therefore deals with these aspects in order to enable CDWs to facilitate groups. One of the most important aspects of group life is communication. It is of the utmost importance that communication inside a group is healthy and vibrant. The leadership of a group is per definition responsible for healthy communication and, for that reason, we will also look at leadership of groups.

## 11.2 THE ROLE OF LEADERSHIP IN COMMUNITY DEVELOPMENT

Leadership occurs when one person induces others to work toward some predetermined objective. Although this definition is very close to that of management, it emphasises the personal relationship through the use of the word *induce*. Another distinction between the words is made by viewing leadership as the influential increment activity that goes beyond routine acts of supervision. Leadership is the value added to the organisation or project by having an individual assume a role. This goes for all types of leaders, including managers of organisations from the private and public sector, the group leaders in a project and the CDW. Yes, even the CDW, though not formally, is a leader because he/she manages a process, not the project, be it behind the scenes.

The wellbeing of structures such as forums, project groups and committees is very dependent on their leadership. By leadership we do not refer only to a single leader such as a chairperson, but rather to a leadership corps such as an executive committee or governing body. The leadership of a group determines to a large extent the amount and calibre of communication, and the amount and calibre of communication similarly determine the success of the leadership. We therefore have two interdependent items—leadership and communication.

Communication can only be successful in an open situation. This is especially relevant for heterogeneous groups. The openness of a group is determined by its leadership. Therefore, one of leadership's more important responsibilities is to see that there is an open situation in which communication flows freely. One can also say that a leadership with a balance between task orientation and relationship, or group orientation, brings maturity among both leadership and followers and this maturity leads directly to motivation. Maturity is seen as:

▶ The ability to set high, but achievable goals. Maturity is obtained when goals will require effort, but not unduly so.

▶ The willingness to accept responsibility. Leadership must accept a leadership responsibility and the rest of the group must accept a participant responsibility.

▶ Education and experience applicable to a specific task. This is the outcome of the learning process that is foremost a capacity building activity.

▶ Work maturity and psychological adulthood, or, in plain language, the ability to do a job and the will and confidence to do it.

### 11.2.1 The importance of leadership

Are all these leaderships really necessary? To this question Massie and Douglas (1981:320) argue as follows:

> There are at least four inescapable facts of organisational life that demand leadership. First, no matter how superior the planning, procedures and design, there is a fundamental incompleteness in organisations. Gaps appear, overlaps emerge and the segments would come apart if it were not for someone functioning as a leader. A second fact of life is environmental change. Few firms can isolate themselves from the external environment with its changes. Organisations need people to interpret these changes. The internal dynamics of organisations represent a third fact that requires someone in leadership. Organisations are composed of many parts or subsystems If left to their own movement and energy, subunits may never become functional for the whole organisation. The last fact of life is that the nature of human membership in organisations is somewhat unpredictable. Human behaviour and subsequent responses vary so greatly that individual leadership is needed for adjustment and adaptation.

When we read this we realise that a manager should be more than a non-personal arranger of organisational functions. Leadership is interpersonal and a leader, be it the manager, the CDW or the group leader of a project, must realise that leadership has its essence with people.

Personality characteristics of people involved in the leadership act contribute a great deal to the effectiveness or ineffectiveness of the act itself. In the same way that personality characteristics of the leader are critical for effectiveness, the personality characteristics of those surrounding the leader must also be recognised and understood.

People in organisations carry different values, aspirations and expectations. A leader must be aware that these differences will affect any leadership attempt. To fully understand leadership the person factor must be acknowledged. This factor, including items like values and personality, appears in both leaders and followers.

Every person has some kind of an image of the way to act in a given position, and this image is called the role concept. Those who must come into contact with the position also have an image about how the person should act in the position, and this is called the role expectation. Both these images are important to the understanding of the human behaviour that flows from the position factor of leadership.

There are at least three sources of role expectations.

▶ **Personal expectations**. These are the ways in which people expect the leader to behave. In every group there is a pattern of expectations—the group expects the leader to do certain things and to refrain from doing others. The group expects certain patterns of behaviour from the formal leader. This goes especially in regard to the CDW and the leader of the project action group.

▶ **Organisational expectations**. Many organisations have definite and specific expectations about the behaviour of their managers and leaders. These expectations are frequently written into formal position guides and job descriptions.

▶ **Cultural expectations**. In addition to the specific personal and organisational patterns of role expectation that contribute to the shaping of the leadership role, there are also cultural expectations of many types.

There is no magic formula for becoming an effective leader. Management and leadership are not easy jobs, and the leadership function of a manager frequently requires many difficult decisions. The same goes for the CDW and the project leader. Not all people, obviously, have the physiological, psychological and sociological make-up to be leaders. Yet, there is a need and challenge for leaders.

### 11.2.2 Improving leadership behaviour

We can make a few suggestions how to improve leadership.

**Believe the best about others**. The leader's behaviour and the response to his behaviour depend upon beliefs about the nature of human beings. The Theory X philosophy states that if you believe that people are lazy, hate work, do not want responsibility, work as little as possible, are motivated by money and fear and are basically uncreative, you will tend to expect this behaviour from them. The leader who believes this and behaves accordingly will create just such behaviour in others. Again it is clear that there is no place for such an attitude in CDWs or any other person with leadership duties in community development. We should rather substitute this theory with Theory Y. According to this theory the nature of people would suggest that they are intelligent, creative, want to work, to achieve and to solve problems, and will initiate actions if given the opportunity (Massie & Douglas, 1981:339). With this attitude leadership can be successful.

**Be yourself**. If you can find yourself and know yourself, the behaviour will take care of itself. It is true for communication too as we have seen in Chapter 10. The good communicator, also the communicating leader, is the one who is at peace with him/herself.

**Meet the needs of your fellows**. This is not so easy. What do you do with those whose needs do not seem to find satisfaction? The leader must at least, show empathy regarding those unfulfilled needs. The leader can never come over as if he/she is uncaring about such things.

**Use what is available**. Use personal experiences to form a simple, concrete, day-to-day working model. A simple, logical and 'quiet' model is better than something grandiose and 'noisy'.

**Employ an integration approach**.

▶ Create support. This behaviour will let others feel that they are of worth and importance to the leader.

▶ Facilitate interaction. This will encourage members of the group to develop close, positive, warm, satisfying relationships.
▶ Emphasise goals. It will stimulate an enthusiasm among people to meet the performance goals of the group.
▶ Facilitate work. This behaviour is related to goal attainment and includes scheduling, co-ordination and planning.

These suggestions fall fairly and squarely on the shoulders of the CDWs, who must adhere to the attitude portrayed by the suggestions for their own 'leadership' style, but they must also enable the project leadership to do the same.

Capacity building is meant for all participants, but the leadership should especially enjoy this activity to enable them to manage projects better. In order to allow participants to take on responsibility, responsibility has to be given to them. Capacity building is vital in this regard, particularly because—in the field where we all work together—there are enormous differences in education, status, wealth and self-esteem.

Capacity building is often understood as a discrete period such as a 10-day training course. This understanding of capacity building is a limited one, and has limited results. Capacity building must be understood as an integral part of every effort to run a community development project. Capacity has to be developed in context, not in the offering of general once-off training courses in isolation from any other support, that are of little use in the long run.

Capacity building is embedded in various growth points, for example, in the issue of needs. Capacity building enables participants to recognise and express their needs. Without this foundation, there can be no constructive work towards a forum that truly reflects participants' needs. Other areas where capacity building is integral are: creating autonomy, facing and dealing with conflict, engendering the ability to deal with change, working with diversity, growing trust and respect, encouraging responsibility, celebrating success, integrating local participants, creating strategies, and encouraging flexibility. In every instance, the growth of these abilities and the capacity that makes them possible, occurs as an evolution.

## 11.2.3  Leadership and communication

A central aim of capacity building is to enable participants to enter into a range of situations with stable abilities and self-confidence, allowing them to actively engage in seeking agreements and solutions which work for them and allowing them to enjoy maturity.

If the leadership takes action without informing or involving the group members, or makes decisions without the knowledge of the other members, and if the members do not know what the leadership is doing, we have a closed situation. It is obvious that there can be no healthy, dynamic communication in such a situation. Here there is little or no sharing of ideas, little or no sensitivity for the feelings or the opinions of others, little or no transparency, and little or no concern from the leadership for group wellbeing.

This type of situation may often be the result of the leadership being overly task oriented. The result of this is an ever-widening gap between the leadership and the other members, and a loss of enthusiasm among the ordinary members who rightly do not feel themselves part of the action. This also leads to a drop in the numbers of ordinary members so that, over time, the executive becomes the group and the group as such disappears.

When communication is healthy and vibrant in an open situation, a certain cyclical dynamism is established between the leadership and the rest of the group. In this situation the leadership maintains a balance between task and group orientation. The leadership receives inputs from the group and responds to these inputs by making decisions. The group that is aware of the decisions being made because of continuous communication responds to the decisions and this response is then the next input for the leadership to respond to. This process goes on and on and the whole group becomes part of the decision-making because everyone can influence decision-making directly. In this situation the leadership knows the needs and sentiments of the group so that it can respond to these, and the group knows what the leadership is doing about its needs and sentiments. This is sympathetic leadership and participatory management. This leads to a vibrant group that builds confidence and self-reliance, which strengthens the leadership.

If the leadership of development-relevant institutions is open and the cyclical input-output model works, we will reach our goal. But do stakeholder groups and leaders of these groups know how important this open model is? If they do not, it seems as if capacity building should take place on this matter, not only for the group leadership, but for all members of groups so that whole groups can become aware of the ideal situation that will ensure participatory decision-making. Poor or ineffective participatory decision-making is not always the fault of the leadership. Ordinary members and supporters are often unwilling to participate in decision-making because they are unwilling to share the responsibility with the leadership or they are just too lazy to add to their responsibilities.

## 11.3 GROUPS

The groups that are busy with community development in various projects are the second role-player that we can identify in this chapter. Civil duty, civil responsibility and civil action are usually the domain of groups, not individuals. These groups are relatively small. They can number as few as ten people and never have more than 100 members. The small group is extremely important and it is necessary to know something about group dynamics and how to facilitate these groups. In order to fulfil their civil duty successfully, small groups must be kept healthy and active. Communication in these small groups is very important in keeping them healthy and active. It is interesting that the definition of small groups describes communication as the central ingredient of these groups. It describes a group as: a number of persons who communicates with one another often over a span of time and who are few enough so that each person is able to communicate with all the others, not at second hand, through other people, but face-to-face. The central place of communication is indisputable and that is why one cannot discuss group dynamics without looking at communication. That is also the reason why the topic of group dynamics is running hand in hand with the topic of communication.

### 11.3.1 Types of small groups

We are mainly concerned with the following types of small groups:

- **Governmental organisations**. Here we refer to councils and their committees. In metropolitan and other structures there are policy committees and liaison committees and all sorts of other committees such as organisational and action committees. All these take part in civil action and are very important.

- **Non-governmental organisations, also known as NGOs**. They are organisations outside the sphere of government that were created to serve some civil duty, for example the Red Cross, to fulfil a welfare task. We must be careful not to see the Red Cross with its many members across the world as a small group, but the local branch consisting perhaps of 30 members will constitute a small group.

- **Community-based organisations, or CBOs**. They can be divided into two types. The first is less formal. Burial societies, women's clubs, rate payers' associations and youth clubs fall in this category. The more formal types are school committees, clinic committees, water committees, project-steering committees, committees emanating from economic and other forums, and so on. We may be tempted to classify these last groups as governmental, but that would be wrong because they have autonomy to carry out specific tasks, quite often to advise and inform government organisations. There are of course also large CBOs such as mass movements, political parties and the like. Because of their size they cannot go through as small groups except if they are divided into branches. A branch will then constitute a small group in our view of the concept.

- **Ad hoc groups**. Ad hoc groups are tied to community development projects where a group of concerned citizens come together to address a need or problem common to all those members. A good example of this type of group can be found in Case Studies 17 and 18.

### 11.3.2 Group dynamics

Every individual person thinks differently from all other people and sees life differently and therefore he/she does things differently. There may even be big differences in perceptions and beliefs, even if the people live in the same society. A group consists of a number of such individuals and therefore a group becomes a melting pot with different ways of thinking, doing, perceiving and believing all thrown together. The one thing that we can be sure of is that this melting pot will bubble and boil. A lot of activity and energy is generated within a group because people respond differently to one another and these responses may change from one minute to the next. Conflict comes and goes, tensions rise and then dissipate, moments of happiness are followed by moments of unhappiness, laughter makes way for seriousness that makes way for laughter again, and hectic moments become serene.

The ups and downs of a group, the active and the restful parts of the life of a group and the differing and sometimes clashing personalities are all normal and part of a very normal group dynamics. The important thing is to understand the dynamics in order to work with groups successfully. It is also important to define and stay aware of the role of communication in this dynamism. We tend to think that group activities should go smoothly, that harmony must exist at all times and that everything must be done in concert. Not so! That is not how a group normally works. On the contrary, if group members always agree on everything and always work in harmony with one another, we would have reason to be concerned because then that group may be experiencing 'group think'. This is detrimental to the health and wellbeing of the group. In such a situation members do not contribute their individual ideas, perhaps because they are not encouraged to do so. The other reason is simply that the more a group develops mutual trust and a sense of togetherness, the less individual members are inclined to 'rock the boat'. People do not want to disagree on anything because they are worried that it will harm the feeling of oneness. Further, as a group grows together it develops a common set of beliefs. 'The values of each person, the values of the group, and the values of the leader are all moving toward a balance and agreement' (Massie & Douglas, 1981:140). Anyone who challenges that set of beliefs may be regarded as a rebel and disrupter. We can understand this trend in groups, but while it is good for the group cohesion, it makes a group less inventive and innovative and the group then forfeits the energy, wisdom, enterprise and uniqueness of the individual. A group must always be busy investigating itself, seeking better ways of doing things, and looking for alternatives that may work better.

### 11.3.3 Group psychology

Group activities and dynamics are informed by group psychology. Originally a group of people come together with different psychological backgrounds, different psychological outputs, and different psychological workings. One of the main characteristics of groups is that over time there is a tendency for the group to develop a group psychology. Members of a group tend to develop similar psychological processes, at least while they are together. They tend to feel happy about the same things, and sad about the same things and certain things and situations tend to bring about the same response from them. However, this does not mean that individual members lose their personal psychological make-up. It simply means that the individual psyches move closer to one another and form a harmonious entity in group relations. Again, while this is a natural process and while it is good to get a group to function properly, it can carry the danger of group think and it can stifle synergy.

### 11.3.4 Group wellbeing

A group must be kept healthy and well. If it is not healthy its functioning will also be poor, it will not reach its objectives and eventually it will be a great disappointment for itself and everyone else. The factors that can ensure group wellbeing are given below.

**Group identity**

A group must have an identity. This is obtained through regular meetings, if at all possible, at the same venue, agreement among its members on their objectives, an acceptance of one another in the group and a common belief in the capability of the members of the group to stand on their own feet. There are also more formal aspects giving identity to a group. These are a name for the group, a group emblem and/or logo, a constitution, and a vision and mission. Some groups form an identity by a uniform or colour or a piece of clothing such as a distinctive headscarf, tie, shirt or dress.

**Purposeful activities**

If a group is not purposefully busy the very reason for its existence falls away. In this case members will each follow their own fancy: meetings will be poorly attended and will ultimately not be regularly held. The moment that poor attendance at meetings and gaps in the meeting cycle happen without some sort of sanction against it, the reason for attending meetings or holding meetings for that matter falls away. It is clear that such a group has only one way to go and that is down to its ultimate death. Therefore, a group must have an objective to achieve, must have a strategy to obtain their objective and must be busy doing that. Even personal growth-oriented groups must attain that personal growth through task execution. The women's club will not continue to exist simply because all its members are of the same sex. They must have an objective and must have some project activity to reach that objective in order to remain a healthy group.

### Objective achievement

A group without an objective, or without acceptable progress towards an objective, will suffer and may even eventually die. Therefore, a group must have an objective that is reasonable and attainable and that falls within the group's line of function and within its reach. The best approach is for each group to have one objective so that each group can have a single aim that drives it forward. This objective will be the reason for the group's existence. This objective must be concrete and easily definable so that the group and the individual members can identify themselves with the objective. The more the members identify themselves with this objective, the healthier the group would be. That is why it is better to have committees for sanitation, water and what other service delivery item rather than to have a committee for service delivery. A focused view and activity are always better than a broad view and activities.

### Group maintenance

Just as a motor car or machine must be maintained to remain functional, a group also needs maintenance. Therefore, if something goes wrong in a group it must be put right. If the group lacks energy the cause must be identified and put right. If the group lacks cohesion the cause must be identified and put right. Conflict cannot go on unattended. Clique forming cannot be tolerated and free riders cannot be allowed to parasitise the group. Regular group evaluation may help to timeously identify things that are not right in a group. See Chapter 21 about group evaluation. Case Study 13: *The club with two committees* illustrates how easily something can go wrong in a group.

### Group leadership

The type of leadership determines the calibre of communication, as we have mentioned earlier. Leadership should therefore not only be strengthened, but, more importantly, the right kind of leadership should be established and the members of a group should be conditioned not to accept anything else. An open leadership style makes for open communication that means that all members participate in and are responsible for decision-making. No other leadership model is acceptable.

### Group strengthening

A group must become cohesive. It must be strong enough to withstand attacks on its integrity and identity. There is no better way to ensure this than to enable a group to achieve something. A CDW should encourage a group and help it to develop standards for its performance and then a CDW should support individual members to abide by those standards and to be proud of them. The setting of high but reachable standards in itself leads to group strengthening. Success is the surest way to strengthen a group and if that success is measured by the group's own standards it acts like a dose of vitamins to the group. Through success a group also gains recognition which will help in the strengthening of the group.

## Boundary maintenance

A group must have some boundaries that will keep it together and set it slightly apart from other groups. For this reason a group must have some exclusivity. It must not be open for a constant stream of new members. Members must feel that they have earned their membership and must be proud of it. In the case of committees membership is usually already closed. But the problem with committees can be when members are permitted to a delegate or secundus to represent them when they cannot attend meetings. Eventually, while the membership stays the same, the actual personnel changes all the time and very few boundaries remain and little exclusivity exists. There is very little evidence of any group life in this instance and one should rather talk of events (meetings) than of a group.

Eventually a group busy with a community development project should grow in ability and should improve the following aspects of the group's life:

*Awareness, ability to reflect and taking action*: At the initial stage, 'awareness' arises on the need to solve the common problems faced, to overcome the feelings of exploitation and alienation, and to meet the felt common needs.

*Capacity to exercise own abilities*: Normally, at the beginning of establishing a group or initiating an activity only one or two individuals may be involved. They are the local activists and group or project leaders who have demonstrated their leadership capabilities to mobilise, organise, facilitate and influence their friends to participate in a group to achieve group goals.

*Gaining control over their lives*: The people's capabilities to think about their problems and needs and to act upon them by establishing various types of community groups, conducting and sustaining group activities, pressuring and negotiating with the relevant authorities in order to solve their problems and meet their needs is part of the process by which people come to gain control over their lives.

*Developing and enhancing confidence, skills and knowledge*: In the process of participation, individuals learn. This leads to increase in confidence, skills and knowledge, which in turn further enhances existing abilities to organise, solve problems, initiate action, and manage group activities.

*Gaining and exercising power over another party*: An examination of people's empowerment should not be viewed only as individuals' abilities to put forward their effort by working together in a self-help fashion to meet their goals within the sphere where they live. People living in one community, at the micro level, also interact with the outside system, at the macro level, in the development process. The linkage between the two levels lies in the context of their living environment itself, for example in a planned village settlement, a state-sponsored community development scheme, which directly brings the community into the state patronising structure.

*Self-evaluation*: Empowerment does not end when people achieve their group goals. Motivated individuals who possessed the characteristics of empowerment begin to evaluate their activities. This self-evaluation process, facilitated by an empowering research approach, enables individuals to reconsider changing the dynamics of their group process in order to maximise benefits. They are able to see possibilities to improve the activity, the group and the whole working process that can promote members' involvement (Abu Samah & Aref, 2009).

## 11.4   SUPPORT AND ENABLEMENT OF LEADERS AND GROUPS

We now come to the third role-player in this chapter and this is the CDW who is entirely charged with the enablement and facilitation of the first two role-players.

### 11.4.1   Leadership support

When it comes to the support of the CDW for the leadership we should be very clear in saying: do what you do for the project. Play your roles as guide, adviser, advocate, enabler and facilitator just as you would do it for a project. Support the leadership with the same attitude necessary when working in a project. Remember that your goals and the goals of the leadership are not the same. They want a successful project and you want them to grow and develop into fine leaders. You have already been told to be humble and to regard yourself as the people's servant (Chapter 8), so just be it for the leadership too.

There is only one thing more that the CDW should do and that is such an important task that he/she can regard it as one of his/her prime tasks. That is to facilitate the input-output model between leadership and members. Make sure that this communication flows richly and swiftly.

### 11.4.2   Group support

The CDW has a very important task when it comes to the support and enablement of groups. We are using a framework that fits the social work group and its activities (CEFA, 2007), but it also says a lot about the activity of the CDW in the groups he/she facilitates. This 'to do' list is as follows:

▶ **Clarifying**: Ensure that there is clarity on the  purpose of the group.
▶ **Contracting**: Facilitate a mutual agreement between the group and you, specifying expectations, obligations and duties.
▶ **Motivating**: Facilitate members' motivation and ability to work in the group and  put their expectations regarding the CDW's role in perspective.
▶ **Addressing ambivalence**: Ensure clarity so that there are no mixed or contradicting ideas about the whole venture.
▶ **Anticipating obstacles**: Possible obstacles in the group's way towards its objective must be identified.
▶ **Structuring**: The work of the group need to be structured through the use of planned, systematic, time-limited activities.
▶ **Facilitating**: The final activity for the CDW is to help group members to participate fully in the process.

The CDW can do the following to facilitate participation and empower group members:

- Demonstrate faith and trust in the strength and ability of group members.
- Emphasise the group members' ownership and right to self-determination relating to the group and the group process.
- Acknowledge group members for reaching out to achieve their goals.
- Encourage group members to experiment with their project.
- Select activities that will enhance the learning process.
- Monitor and evaluate the group's progress. An excellent way of doing this is by the participatory self-evaluation method that is explained in Chapter 21. See also Addendum 1.

## 11.5    THREATS TO GROUP AND LEADERSHIP SUCCESS

The CDW must be aware of any possible threats to the wellbeing of groups. The following are a few that must be dealt with:

### 11.5.1   Domination

A dominating individual demands attention, controls the discussion, keeps others from being heard, prevents the group from concentrating on its task, and frequently creates resentment and power struggles within the group. However, this person is not necessarily a bad egg that must be thrown out. This person may care about the group and its goals and be frustrated if the work is not progressing smoothly. The dominator may have something important to contribute, and may bring energy and enthusiasm to the team process, but it must be channelled in order to be a very prolific resource.

### 11.5.2   Distraction

It is clear that distractions can become obstacles for group progress. On the other hand once in a while, distracting the group is a genuine service. Humour at the right moment or a slight side trip to break tension, can be a healthy contribution to transactional and task processes. But sometimes people dedicate themselves to distracting the group from its work. They may be playful distracters, like adorable puppies — or aggressive distracters, more like vicious attack dogs. One is more fun than the other, but both keep the group from its tasks.

### 11.5.3   Non-participation

People, who consistently stare out a window, doodle, mutter monosyllabic responses to questions, and say 'whatever' to any suggestion may not seem to constitute a major problem, but they certainly reflect and create one. Non-participation reveals a problem in that the group's processes obviously do not involve every group member.  It creates a problem because full participation is needed to facilitate the group's development and task.

### 11.5.4   Irresponsibility

People who do not show up, show up late, and/or do not do their share of the work constitute the most serious threat to the group.  Sometimes irresponsible behaviour results from other issues, so one might think about the irresponsibility of a group member in the same vein as what has been indicated in relation to non-participatory group members experiencing legitimate problems.

### 11.5.5   Reprehensibility

Reprehensible behaviour implies consistent unethical action, dishonesty, conniving, sexism, racisms, bigotry, nastiness; someone who enjoys making other people miserable; who has no conscience and prefers to take the immoral road. This individual constantly twists conversation into a negative rope with which he or she tries to 'hang' the group. The best way to solve this problem is to have the group to sanction that person and if need be, cut him/her from the group.

## 11.6   GROUP FACILITATION SKILLS

Facilitating a group where the members are not used to meeting procedures, where the chairperson is unsure of him/herself and where the secretary is slow in making notes of the activities of the group, is not an easy task. The CDW needs skills for this task.

**Active listening**
The CDW attends to the verbal and non-verbal aspects of the communication without judging or evaluating.

**Clarifying**
The CDW grasps the essence of a message at both thinking and feeling levels; simplifying the person's statement by focussing on the core of the message.

**Summarising**
Connecting the important elements of an interaction or session the CDW makes sure that all members have a grasp of the activities and thereby ensuring as little misunderstanding as possible.

**Questioning**
The CDW asks open-ended questions that lead to self-exploration of the 'what' and 'how'.

**Interpreting**
By offering possible explanations for situations and behaviour and activities within, the CDW helps the groups to understand the context.

**Supporting**
The CDW creates an atmosphere that encourages members to continue with their work, especially if members experience difficulties. It should also create trust.

**Empathising**
The CDW is not aloof from the group. Through empathising, the CDW fosters trust among members that enhances communication (Corey in Gladding:1995; Kadushin (1983)).

The CDW's most important skill is to know when to apply his/her skills and what not to do in groups and then not doing it. Being aware of pitfalls (what not to do) can thus assist the CDW to avoid potential problems that could damage or end the relationship between the CDW and group members.

Groups usually start off as weak and flimsy structures without cohesion and with little identity that must be supported and enabled by the CDW, among others, to:

- hold meaningful meetings by getting and learning the basic rules and procedures of meetings;
- make enlightened decisions by receiving appropriate information;
- implement their decisions by receiving aid to interpret their plans in a practical way;
- evaluate their actions by receiving simple and practical guidelines on evaluation;
- resolve conflict in their ranks by getting support for problem-solving communication;
- hold their own against outside threats by being supported by advocacy; and
- grow in confidence and self-esteem by enjoying a climate in which they can prosper.

## 11.7 CONCLUSION

A project is usually as strong and successful as the group that runs it. Problems in a project can inevitably be traced back to the group. It is therefore obvious that CDWs should concentrate on the groups running projects and assist them to reach their objectives and enjoy wellbeing. To a large extent the life of a group is a reflection of the communication taking place within the group and it is therefore important that communication should figure high on the CDW's priority list.

**CHAPTER 12**

# CONFLICT RESOLUTION, MEDIATION AND NEGOTIATION

## 12.1 INTRODUCTION

Conflict is often brought about by poor communication. Once conflict exists in a given situation it ruins all communication that may still have been present. Conflict is therefore the enemy of communication and—as such—it must be resolved. Very few of us know how to resolve conflict. In fact, we are usually scared of conflict and try to stay away from a conflict situation. However, our natural tendency to avoid a conflict situation makes us miss the very interesting truth; that poor communication causes conflict, but conflict is resolved by good communication. This good communication normally takes place through negotiation.

## 12.2 CAUSES OF CONFLICT

There are a number of causes of conflict. These causes are invariably the result of poor communication or they result in poor communication, causing conflict to develop. These causes are as follows:

▶ **Unclear boundaries**. If role definitions are not clear, it is difficult to know what to expect from various stakeholders. In a situation where these stakeholders influence each other and operate within the same set of boundaries, unclear role definitions make for unclear role boundaries which are bound to cause misunderstanding, friction and—eventually—conflict. In a situation that is already cluttered by the many stakeholders, those responsible for development projects should be wide awake to the threat held by unclear boundaries. One way to address the issue is by co-ordinating as many of these stakeholders as possible and to ensure a vibrant network of communication among them.

▶ **Clashing interests**. It is unfortunate that all interests of all parties cannot be served at the same time. However, if the potential for conflict in this situation is identified timeously, good communication can go a long way in preventing conflict. Good communication is present when a communication network exists. A communication network does not only point to a structure that may or may not be used, but it rather points to the functional structure, in other words, a working structure that can be used to negotiate interests and set participants' minds at rest. Case Study 13: *The club with two committees*, is a good illustration of conflict flowing out of clashing interests.

- **Clashing personalities**. Leaders of various role-playing organisations can have conflicting personalities, or—inside one organisation—clashing personalities can cause conflict. It can even happen that, inside a steering committee for a project, two or more clashing personalities are present. Usually this happens between senior people, or people with strong personalities, with the result that each opposing party will immediately have his/her followers, which increases the potential for devastating conflict. Clashing personalities can therefore cause conflict that can spread far beyond the confines of two conflicting persons. Conflicting personalities invariably result in conflicting interests. Conflicting parties would scarcely admit that the conflict is the result of the fact that they do not like one another. They will look for a reason at a higher level, such as clashing interests, viewpoints, opinions or agendas.

- **Dependency situation**. If one role-player is dependent on another for playing its role, it is obvious that a conflict potential exists. This is especially true of horizontal dependency as is found in a firm or organisation. Horizontal dependency can also occur in a development project or, more correctly, in a project steering committee. It is during the planning activity that these dependencies must be identified and it is at this stage that some checks and balances must be provided to obviate the possibility of conflict as a result of horizontal dependency. This does not only apply to persons, but also to institutions. If, for example, one committee cannot do its work before another committee has voted money for it, the potential for conflict is present. In this instance it is at the co-ordination level that these situations must be anticipated and dealt with. Dependency on a vertical scale is much more acceptable, perhaps because we are so used to a boss/underling situation.

- **Need for consensus**. In a situation where consensus must be obtained before action can be taken, the potential for conflict is greater because no party can go it alone without regard for anyone else. The effort to try and obtain consensus can then lead to conflict especially if communication is poor. Consensus decision-making accepts good communication as a given. If, however, the situation is different, the potential for conflict is very high. Decision-making in development projects are usually meant to be by consensus and for this reason community development workers (CDWs) must be awake to the potential for conflict.

- **Misunderstanding**. Misunderstanding is a direct result of poor communication. Misunderstanding leads to a situation where the different parties each have a particular perception that makes the other party suspicious. It is natural for distrust to grow between the parties and that is bound to bedevil good communication, which is followed by accusations and so on—each new development making communication more difficult and bringing the situation nearer to conflict. All the barriers to successful communication discussed in a previous chapter are present and everyone who is involved should be aware of it and should apply the suggestions made there for successful communication.

- **Unresolved prior conflicts**. A conflict must be resolved, not covered up, postponed or suppressed. If conflict is not resolved it has the tendency to go underground, only to pop up as soon as an opportunity favours it. Conflict resolution becomes extremely difficult in the case of old, unresolved conflicts, because the resolution does not lie only in the here and now, but also in the history. If one must revisit the past over and over again in order to make some headway in the present, the situation becomes very difficult.

## 12.3   PREVENTION OF CONFLICT

Prevention is better than cure and, therefore, it is better to anticipate conflict and remove timeously the cause, so that conflict does not erupt. This management of the conflict potential consists of the following:

▶ **Identifying potential clashing interests within an institution such as a project.**
Based on an evaluation of mandates, areas of activity, interest and needs of stakeholders, it is possible and desirable to identify stakeholders who will have clashing interests, to identify these interests and to manage the whole situation. In other words, the situation with its potential for conflict cannot be avoided, but it can be managed so that conflict does not occur.

▶ **Identifying potential clashing personalities.**
Clashing personality types can make management of an institution, especially a small one such as a project action group, particularly difficult and can impact severely on reaching consensus. Destructive conflict can often be avoided by depersonalising points of disagreement. Chapter 22 contains a number of ways to depersonalise inputs so that points of disagreement are also depersonalised.

▶ **Identifying potential high conflict situations in advance.**
One very seldom experiences sudden and unexpected conflict. There is always a smouldering fuse that, if unattended, will reach the powder keg with devastating results. Knowing the stakeholders and the situation with the identification of potential conflict well in advance and for such situations to be avoided or managed. In such situations it is essential that good communication prevails to defuse as much of the situation as possible.

▶ **Setting clear mandates for role-players.**
There should be no unclear boundaries. Each role-player should have its place and role clearly demarcated.

▶ **Improving communication skills.**
If the communication skills of role-players are strengthened, opportunities for misunderstanding will be minimised. The better the communication, the less misunderstanding there will be and the less misunderstanding there is, the less conflict will erupt.

▶ **Organising the activities of different role-players.**
Activities of role-players must be organised in such a fashion that dependency on one another is reduced as much as possible. This can be done with good programming and strategising and will definitely diminish the potential for conflict.

▶ **Setting clear 'Rules of Order'.**
It is advisable to have a standard set of agreed-upon rules of conduct for meetings and discussions. These may include 'rules of good manners' and 'rules of conflict avoidance'. While a goal-directed facilitative approach is most productive within an institutional context, it is essential that participants agree and adhere to very clearly set rules and boundaries. In this way the individual will be safeguarded against personal abuse and violent conflict. Apart

from the fact that it will diminish the potential for conflict, it will also give individuals and even groups greater confidence to participate in the activities.

▶ **Encouraging and promoting tolerance in a potential conflict situation.**
The message must be loud and clear that the project is bigger than any of us and that we should be prepared to take a slight without wanting to retaliate.

## 12.4 NEGOTIATION AS CONFLICT RESOLUTION

Negotiation is a way to resolve conflict in which all parties come out as winners. The objective is to bring conflicting or opposing parties nearer to each other until they can declare common ground and resolve their conflict within the parameters of their common ground. In this way no party is the loser, because each has gained something and is relatively satisfied with the outcome. Negotiation need not be a formal and drawn-out affair.

Then, because it is the policy not to vote on issues, a discussion takes place which can just as well be called negotiation, in which the differing parties try and resolve the issue to everyone's satisfaction. Negotiation can therefore be instantaneous and can last one minute or it can be a long drawn-out activity that can last months and where a lot of paper work is generated. Luckily in development projects negotiation is usually short and less formal and often takes place to prevent rather than to resolve conflict. In development projects the role of mediator can be laid on the CDW. The mediator is the person who facilitates a process of negotiation. This would be when the negotiation is more formal and takes place to resolve some existing conflict. If negotiation is necessary during a meeting, it is naturally the task of the chairperson to facilitate discussion.

The CDW must know and understand the position of mediator. Most important is that mediator is not arbitrator although the latter is there to settle a dispute between parties. An arbitrator, however, has the task to decide who is right and who is wrong in a dispute, and that the mediator never does. The mediator is entirely committed to bringing the opposing parties nearer and nearer to each other until they find common ground. Thus, no one is right and no one is wrong and no one is a lone winner and no one is a complete loser. The process strives towards a win-win solution where all parties will be relatively satisfied with the outcome. The mediator must be well prepared for negotiation. The following are five steps that should be taken before and during the negotiations:

**Step 1**: Review the specific environment and conditions in which the conflict and communication take place, for example spatial arrangements, group size and leadership structures.

**Step 2**: Review the existing attitudes and perceptions of the parties by looking at, among others, personality traits, different needs and self-esteem.

**Step 3**: Define the problem. This includes determining the basic issues, stating the problem as a goal and depersonalising the problem.

**Step 4**: Facilitate a joint search for alternatives. This can be done through the nominal group technique, brainstorming and discussion groups.

**Step 5**: Facilitate the evaluation of alternatives and the reaching of a consensus decision by narrowing the range of solutions, evaluating them in terms of both quality and acceptability according to criteria previously agreed upon and through various means such as sub-groups and sub-problems.

The mediator must also know what the negotiators' tasks and obligations are. The mediator must know what makes a good negotiator because that will inevitably impact on the negotiation process as such. The following so-called ABC of successful outcomes gives a good idea of the necessities of negotiation.

## 12.5 THE ABC OF SUCCESSFUL OUTCOMES

The ABC of successful outcomes is a synopsis of the most important aspects of negotiation. They are:

- **Aim for a specific result**. Negotiation that does not aim for a specific, concrete result will flounder and discussions will tend to go round and round without moving in a specific direction. This means that to merely talk about a disagreement will not achieve much. Discussions must be aimed at coming to a conclusion that will be satisfactory for all.
- **Be positive**. If one wants negotiation to move forward towards a decisive conclusion, one must be positive. It serves no purpose to dwell on the negative aspects. Criticising the other party for not seeing things the way you do will never bring an outcome.
- **Concentrate (see, hear, feel) on sensory data**. In a negotiation situation all the barriers to communication that can possibly exist are present. To compound the situation, communication does not take place only through the spoken word. One must therefore be wide awake to both verbal and non-verbal communication so as to identify all the possible barriers, remove them timeously and respond to positive responses and negative reactions from the other parties.
- **Dovetail desires**. Dovetailing is the opposite of manipulating. Dovetailing desired outcomes ensures your integrity because it shows respect for the other parties' integrity. While you cannot decide on outcomes for the other parties, you can aid them in attaining what they desire. Dovetailing is the intelligent way to ensure your own outcomes.
- **Entertain long- and short-term objectives**. Negotiation is not only to bring harmony for the present. A win/win solution is also necessary for the long term otherwise you will soon have to gather around the negotiation table again.
- **Find rapport as soon as possible**. Rapport is the most important ingredient of negotiation. Without it negotiation can never be positive. Rapport is present when you experience a level of comfort and a sense of shared understanding. Only when rapport is present can you proceed towards the outcome. So the first objective is to establish rapport. Once rapport has been established, it will develop and grow as the negotiation progresses.
- **Get as much information as you can**. Information on the other parties and their positions will help you to know with whom and with what you are dealing.
- **Have extra alternative options ready**. If your options are not accepted or if the situation changes, you will know that your options are no longer applicable.

- **Identify and keep outside influences in mind**. This usually constitutes pressure from outside, either to come to an agreement or not to sacrifice certain interests.
- **Join the other party if they make suggestions or state viewpoints with which you agree**. The whole objective is to move closer to one another, so if consensus or common ground is found, acknowledge it.
- **Know exactly what your maneuverability is**. Know how far you can go and what you can sacrifice. This helps you to be sure of yourself and makes a good impression on the other parties.
- **Leave space in which you can move**. In other words, do not move all you can the first time. If other parties are not satisfied, you cannot move any further or you may move so far the first time that there is very little for you to win and little for the other parties to forfeit.
- **Make sure that you are negotiating with someone who has decision-making powers**. These decision-making powers should be at least at the same level as yours.
- **Never be insulting or accusing**. This will put distance between you and the other parties instead of bringing you closer and it will also lead to accusations from the other parties. All this will just delay a solution and may even jeopardise a genuine seeking of solutions.
- **Obtain agreement from the other parties**. Find out whether there is a basis for negotiation.
- **Prepare yourself properly**. Decide on what you want the outcome to be with a best-case scenario (ideal outcome) and a worst-case scenario (the minimum that you will settle for).
- **Qualify your viewpoints and suggestions**. State the reason for a proposal before you make it. The other parties must know why you say something and if your qualification holds water it will be so much more difficult just to reject your viewpoint.
- **Remain flexible about sequence and options**. Negotiation is by definition flexible and hard base lines just do not work in such a situation.
- **Stand on your principles**. Do this by all means, but make sure that they are in fact principles and not unnecessary rigid base lines.
- **Think carefully about anything that is said**. Take time out if you need to think about some new option. Rather spend some time in the first place to think about things than to rush it at first only to come back on your word later on.
- **Untie the knots**. That means that things must be straightened out. Arguments must be clear, facts must be on the table and verified and the standpoints of the different parties must be clear. One just cannot negotiate if there is still a muddle.
- **Validate (confirm your understanding of) any proposal**. You need to understand the other party's proposal before analysing and criticising it.
- **Work towards consensus**. It is no use to try and keep your original position. That is not negotiation. Try to stay as near to your original position as possible (best-case scenario), but use the space between that and what you can settle for (worst-case scenario).
- **X represents the other parties who may be foreign to you or just unknown**. Just remember, though, that they are human beings with the same emotions and fears as you; with the same belief in their position as you have in yours; and with the same sense of being right that you have.

> ❱ **Yes is a better word than no in negotiation**. However, let your yes be yes and your no be no. In other words, be objective and trustworthy.
> ❱ **Zero in**. Concentrate on the problem from the beginning and do all you can to solve it.

The next list gives a good idea of the attitude of a good negotiator and can be used by the CDW to give the negotiators some parameters for the attitude with which they come to the negotiation table. A good negotiator:

❱ is a problem solver;
❱ separates the person from the problem;
❱ is soft on the person but hard on the problem;
❱ is more concerned with his/her interest than his/her position;
❱ obtains and maintains objectivity;
❱ gives in to reason but not to pressure;
❱ develops several options for later choice;
❱ avoids a rigid base line;
❱ investigates common areas of trust; and
❱ portrays an image of trust.

## 12.6 CONCLUSION

We have looked at conflict for the simple reason that development projects have the potential to generate conflict. We have also looked specifically at how to resolve conflict through good communication by way of negotiation. It is clear that we must be very careful because conflict can develop very quickly. Yet, we should not run away from conflict. There are ways to deal with it and solve it to everyone's satisfaction. CDWs have an obligation to help others, especially leaders—such as chairpersons of steering committees—to become knowledgeable about the potential for conflict and the methods to resolve it. They, as well as the leaders, should be prepared to use them in order to solve conflict situations.

# CHAPTER 13

# MOBILISATION AND MOTIVATION

## 13.1  INTRODUCTION

We communicate with people for various reasons. One of the most important reasons is that we want to motivate people. We want to motivate people for various reasons. We want them to do something, or we want them to continue doing something they have decided to do, or we want to change their minds for them. When we work within the civic milieu the importance of communication as motivational tool is clear. Commitment and enthusiasm are important ingredients in civic action. They must therefore be established among people. They must also be kept alive. Commitment and enthusiasm usually start to dwindle after a while. Councillors and members of committees and interest groups very easily slip into the everyday routine of such organisations and then their activities are no longer motivated. It is then that motivational efforts must be stepped up, because a loss in motivation can be disastrous. Community groups that lose their motivation, commitment and enthusiasm, usually fail to reach their objectives. Motivation as mobilisation tool is therefore of the utmost importance and that is the reason why we spend time on it.

## 13.2  CHARACTERISTICS OF MOTIVATION

Motivation can be a message from one person or persons to another person or persons. This message will convey certain meanings that will motivate the receivers thereof. It may contain hope or a very positive outlook on things. It can convey a message of belief in the capabilities of people. It can carry the feeling of enthusiasm and eagerness to tackle a task or problem. It can also convey the gravity of a problem and the necessity to do something about it. If this message can cross the various barriers confronting communication, it can become the property of those who have received it. If this happens and it becomes the property of the receivers, it will lead to a feeling of motivation, an enthusiasm coming from within.

Motivation can also be an influence that changes people's attitudes. This influence can emanate from a person or a situation. It can convey a very positive picture: other people had similar problems, but have been successful in removing them. Their before and after situations show that they are much better off now than they were before, so it is worth following their example. The picture can also illustrate a negative situation: just look how bad things are; something must be done to change it. This influence then leads to action.

The influence can also carry such a negative message that it angers people and this anger then becomes motivational: it is a disgrace that we must suffer in this fashion while others are much better off.

No one will deny that motivation is an inner strength. If the message really gets accepted and if the influence really works, a seed is planted in people that will grow so that people will motivate themselves. This is the objective of motivational communication, that is, people will not always need external motivation, but that, through intra-personal communication they will motivate themselves. This will also mean that even through difficult times people will be carried by this inner strength without being motivated externally every day.

Motivation creates energising forces within human beings that are invisible and impossible to measure. We are all different and therefore the motives energising us will be different for every person. It is, therefore, difficult to really know what motivates and what does not and to what extent motivation is accomplished. In the end it is advisable to observe the behaviour of a human being and, from that, to work backwards to find a possible motive for the behaviour.

## 13.3  RELATIONSHIP BETWEEN BEHAVIOUR AND MOTIVATION

It is clear that there is a close relationship between behaviour and motivation. It requires community development workers (CDWs) to be awake to individual and group psychology. We can take note of the following aspects concerning this relationship (Massie & Douglas, 1981:86, 87).

▶ **One motive may result in many different types of behaviour**. For example, a person's desire for prestige may lead that person to run for political office or give money away or get additional educational training or steal or join a gang. It depends on other situational aspects, other realities, which of the behaviours will result from this motive. In other words, a person's desire for prestige (motive) will result in different behaviours if that person is in gaol, or in the boardroom or in the swimming pool.

▶ **The same behaviour in different people may come from various different motives**. Just think of the many motives in different people for buying a motor car! For the one person it may be to appear respectable, for the other to be accepted by his/her peers and for a third because he/she wants to travel in relative comfort. One should therefore be careful not to read too much into a person's behaviour. One cannot say for certain what the motive behind the behaviour is. At best one can say what possible motives can be behind a certain behaviour.

▶ **Behaviour can be used to estimate a person's motive**. This may sound contradictory to what has been said previously. However, it is possible after repeated observations of one person's behaviour to make an estimate of the cause of that behaviour. For example, some people always seem to feel insecure and thus behave continuously in a manner reflecting that feeling of insecurity. The key to this observation is that this estimation of a person's motive can only come over time when a continuous and recurrent behaviour takes place.

▶ **Motives may operate in harmony or in conflict**. Behaviour is frequently the result of the interplay of several motives. These motives may push a person in one direction or in a number of directions, for example, a person may have to decide between a job that he/ she would enjoy and a job that offered a higher salary.

▶ **Motives come and go**. It is very rare that a motive has the same energy over a long period of time. This is very important for organisational managers to remember because what motivates personnel today may not necessarily motivate them in two months' time. Good meetings may motivate an action group in the beginning of a project, but later meetings lose their motivational power and now the group will be motivated by the attainment of their objectives. CDWs will be wise to keep this in mind.

▶ **The environment influences motives**. The situation at a particular time triggers or suppresses the action of a motive, for example, you don't realise how hungry you are until you smell food cooking. In the same way sociological needs or preferences become stimulated when you are in a situation filled with sociological factors that will lead to stimulation.

## 13.4 THE TWO-FACTOR THEORY OF MOTIVATION

The Two-Factor Theory of motivation devised by Frederick Herzberg (Massie & Douglas, 1981:93) says that people are usually motivated and demotivated at the same time. Some situational aspects satisfy people and that then usually leads to motivation, while some aspects lead to dissatisfaction which demotivates people. It is a CDW's task to have as many satisfiers present as possible and as few dissatisfiers as possible. This theory was meant for the workplace, the factory where certain things dissatisfy and certain things satisfy employees. It is, however, just as appropriate for other situations such as members in a group or committee or council or people participating in some civic action, such as a project. CDWs must therefore realise that they are the orchestrators of this mix of satisfiers and dissatisfiers with the golden rule uppermost in their minds, ie as few dissatisfiers as possible and as many satisfiers as possible.

### 13.4.1 Satisfiers

Let us first look at satisfiers that usually motivate the participants or members. They are as follows:

▶ **A sense of achievement**. People participating in an activity or belonging to a group would want to feel that they are achieving something. They must feel that there is movement forward. If they feel that their action results in forward movement, they may be more easily satisfied and motivated to continue with their efforts. People in the deprivation trap doubt themselves and their circumstances and need to obtain this sense in order to get further motivation for the road ahead. If this sense of achievement is absent, the participants follow a natural road towards demotivation and, consequently, towards dissatisfaction.

▶ **A job worth doing well**. People want to think that their efforts will lead to something better for them. The sacrifices that they make and the hard work that they put in must be worthwhile to them. At some stage they want to pick the fruits of their labours. This means that people will sacrifice their time, effort and money, only if they think that their actions and their sacrifices will, in the end, be worthwhile. It also gives them a sense of pride in what they are doing. They are not just bungling along, but follow a programme that will bring them somewhere. Case Study 18: *Food garden in Mapayeni*, is a perfect example of participants thinking that the job they are doing is worth doing well.

▶ **Being entrusted with responsibility**. People with responsibility want to carry that responsibility to successful conclusion. So, their responsibility obliges them to be motivated. Being entrusted with only menial tasks will not motivate people. Having responsibility for something makes them more than mere participants. They are not the guests at someone else's efforts but are owners of whatever it is they are responsible for. Ownership opens up new possibilities and vistas that act as strong motivators, to such an extent that they become masters of their own destination and decision-makers on their own future. In Case Study 6: *The parson who became a painter*, the minister failed to entrust the participants with responsibility with very negative effects. In the case of Case Study 18, however, the participants were entrusted with responsibility with very positive results.

▶ **Being recognised for achievements**. People naturally want to be recognised for what they achieve; it gives them a sense of worth and of dignity. Two of the most important motivators come into play, namely the sense of achievement and the sense of dignity. Recognition also stimulates the sense of achievement that, as we have said already, is a great satisfier.

▶ **Being afforded the opportunity to advance**. People are naturally progressive. They want to move forward from a position with which they are dissatisfied or which they feel could be better to one that they are convinced will be better. When people get this scope or opportunity to advance, they become motivated and therefore make use of their opportunities. But being afforded the opportunity does not only mean that they are allowed to do it. It is not a matter of swim or sink. It rather means that they are facilitated in their advancement, among others by supplying them with information and, in general, enhancing the learning process in which they participate.

### 13.4.2  Dissatisfiers

Unfortunately, every situation also has its dissatisfiers, and these dissatisfiers demotivate. The aim is therefore to remove all the dissatisfiers in order to ensure maximum motivation. The dissatisfiers that we must get rid of are as follows:

▶ **Adverse policies**. We include the policies of government at all levels: national, provincial and local, as well as policies of an organisation or even a committee. These policies need not be very formal statements, but can be the way a certain organisation or committee sees its task and its goals. When people feel that any kind of policy of whatever organisation prevents them from achieving something, from taking up responsibility for their own future, for making their efforts worth the trouble, they will become demotivated. If people who want to be successful in projects regularly come up against an organisation whose policy and rules do not allow the factors, aspects or situations the people desire, they will become demoralised because they will see this as a deliberate effort to keep them in the deprivation trap. If adverse policies create or maintain monolithic bureaucracies who in turn strengthen the adverse policies, you have a situation that makes community development impossible. Participants will regard these obstacles as insurmountable. Case Study 10: *The project that had its fences brought down*, illustrates how policy is not conducive towards self-help actions.

▶ **Poor operational conditions**. People are usually prepared to make sacrifices if they think, or hope, that it will help them in achieving certain goals. But there is a limit to their willingness to sacrifice. When the work necessary to achieve something is hard and the returns are few and far between, people become disheartened. Because people are naturally progressive, they do not want to toil for no apparent progress. That demotivates them. If people work under poor conditions and they come up against demotivators such as adverse policies or any of the other dissatisfiers that are discussed here, the demotivation will just be that much more pronounced. Case Study 15: *The inspector whose help was dumped*, illustrates that poor operational conditions can be demotivating. The other problem with this situation is that as people withdraw from the venture because of poor operational conditions, the participants who remain find themselves under worsening conditions because of the fewer hands to do the work.

▶ **Poor guidance**. When people are prepared to take the responsibility for certain things and want to work towards certain goals, but they do not receive the information that will enable them to fulfil their obligation, they become demotivated. Participation, ownership, empowerment, and self-help are hollow notions if information, advice, guidance and support do not accompany them. In fact, the one without the other leads to immense frustration that demotivates people. Eventually, wrong decisions, choices and actions because of a lack of support torpedo the project.

▶ **Lack of status**. People do not want to be mere pawns in someone else's plans and efforts. At least they want to be co-responsible for decisions made and deeds done. This again has a lot to do with human dignity. Without acknowledgement of the people's important place and role there can be little motivation for them to give their all. Case Study 6: *The parson who became a painter*, is again a case in point.

▶ **Deficient interpersonal relations**. Good communication fosters good relations and good relations are responsible for motivating people. The cement for any concerted effort of a group of people to reach certain goals is good interpersonal relationships. Without good interpersonal relations, efforts become haphazard and individualised. It is bad when good relations are absent, but usually deficient interpersonal relations take their place and that is worse. They act as powerful demotivators and result in activities grinding to a halt or becoming counterproductive. Case Study 7: *A community hall with no purpose*, illustrates the validity of this statement.

▶ **Poor financial returns**. People will make sacrifices if they know that they will gain tangible results and the best tangible results are financial returns. Without it or without some promise of it, people become demotivated. Very few individual human beings are prepared to give their all for the sake of humanity or for the good of society. Yes, they would not mind if these are the results of their labours, but then they want to gain in a tangible way otherwise they would be demotivated. In most of the projects mentioned in Case Study 17: *Mothers of the mountain community*, participants gained something tangible.

## 13.5 ANOTHER EXPLANATION – MOTIVATIONAL SOURCE FIELDS

Motivation can be seen as source fields making a direct input into the individual's behaviour. We say fields because there are more than one. In fact there are three, each with a number of aspects (Massie & Douglas, 1981:84).

▶ **External source field**. This includes equipment, climate, peers, organisational goals, policies, rules, structures and rewards. While these aspects differ vastly, they belong in the same source field because they are all external to the individual. You will recognise quite a few that we have dealt with under satisfiers and dissatisfiers.

▶ **Internal source field**. This includes ability, needs, aspirations, perceptions, mental set, personal goals and expectations. These aspects are all internal to the individual although the individual is not born with them. They become the individual's property through a process of informal education, or better known as growing up, not in a vacuum, but in a certain milieu and culture.

▶ **Genetic source field**. This includes genes, upbringing, parents, experience, size of family, socio-economic situation of family and early childhood. You will see the relationship between many of these aspects and those under internal source field.

We must realise that all three source fields are present in every individual and therefore that the motivation of every member of a group will be influenced by all three source fields. The CDW can do a lot to influence and change the external source field. This will definitely be the major focus of any CDW who wants to motivate participants. The CDW can also do something about the internal source field. Ability can be improved, for example, and aspects such as aspirations and expectations can be influenced positively to enhance motivation. It is clear that the CDW cannot really do anything about the genetic source field because most of it lies in the past in any case. But that does not mean that the CDW can ignore it.

## 13.6 LEADERSHIP AND MOTIVATION

Chapter 11 gave more information on leadership and therefore it is merely touched upon here. Leadership is influenced by communication and in its turn influences communication. We can also say that the leadership of a group or organisation or council or committee determines the calibre and amount of communication, and the calibre and amount of communication similarly determine the success of the leadership. We can therefore say that communication and leadership are interdependent and when we bear in mind that motivation is caused by good communication, we can easily make the tie between leadership and motivation.

One of the more important responsibilities of leadership is to ensure that there is an open situation in which communication flows freely. See Chapter 11 in this regard. One can also say that a leadership with a balance between task orientation and relationship or group orientation brings maturity among both leadership and followers, and this maturity leads directly to motivation.

## 13.7 MOBILISATION THROUGH INFORMATION

A community is part of a greater whole. It is part of a larger environment because of the information that flows to and through that community. An isolated community would be one where little or no information is reaching that community, either through official channels such as government structures or unofficial channels such as word of mouth or mass media. A normal community is the target of all sorts of information flowing through all sorts of channels. Further, this information flow is not only in one direction. Even if the flow to the community is larger, there is also a flow from the community, first to the wide world, but second to specific targets. CDWs have a specific job in relation to information flow. They must sometimes open existing, but non-functional channels. Sometimes they must establish new channels for a specific objective and all the time they themselves must act as information channels.

## 13.7.1  Information channels

Any community is serviced by a number of information channels. An ordinary community will have, for example, teachers who will bring a specific kind of information to the school children; health personnel who will provide information on health, sanitation and nutrition; a public or school library with a librarian offering general information to all who want to avail themselves of it; representatives of service units such as roads, public services, water, parks and traffic with very specific and sometimes very technical information; and political representatives with information with political content and meaning. We can also mention the mass media such as newspapers, the radio and television and the very informal and personal channels consisting of friends and family from outside the community bringing information from outside into the community.

All communication reaching a community is not 'raw' information. Much of it is interpreted information. In other words, someone has already interpreted the raw information and this interpreted version is now disseminated. Most educational information falls in this category. Information can also be of an interpretative nature. In other words, the information explains or interprets something, for example, information on why service fees must be paid. Information can also be of a motivational nature, where the receiver is called upon to do something or support something. Political information is usually of a nature where the objective of information is to solicit support. The same goes for advertisements that want a positive reaction in buying or doing something. Information disseminated through a campaign also has this objective. Examples are the information on Aids, anti-tobacco information and the campaign against crime.

Mobilisers and facilitators of communities, such as CDWs, are interested in and need specific information. It is necessary to convey certain types or sets of information in order to ensure the success of the mobilisation. First, they want to convey motivational information. Information should not speak only to the minds of people, but also to their hearts. In fact, it is wise to start with the heart and then to move to the mind. Second, the information is about organisation. Mobilisation and facilitation are targeted to get people so far that they will organise themselves. They must therefore know how to organise successfully and for that they need certain specific information. The third set is about the management of projects. People must get organised for a specific objective, namely to start projects that will address their problems and/or needs. They must therefore know how to run or manage projects. The final set of information is of a professional nature. It depends on the type of project that is launched. If the project is launched to address the sanitation problem, the information will be on sanitation, if they want to improve their homes, naturally the information will specifically address that issue, and so forth.

### 13.7.2  Information sources

Information channels are very important and without them communities will be isolated. However, it is very important that information channels are connected to vibrant and trustworthy information sources. Just as a tap can only give water as long as it is connected to a reservoir, community facilitators and mobilisers can only give information if they are connected to the source of information.

Many poor communities, however, are so isolated that they are starved of information. This isolation from information is an important cause of disempowerment of communities because without the relevant information they cannot become part of the modern world and they cannot fulfil their obligations as autonomous entities. Two things can go wrong with a water source. It can get polluted and it can dry up. The same can happen to an information source, and, different than in the case of water, information can also become dated. It is therefore very important to make sure of the following:

▶ **The information should not be polluted.** People need information to be able to govern and free themselves from the chains of poverty. A lot of information directed to communities contains very little useful information on how to govern and how to fight poverty. Unfortunately the information is 'polluted' with a great deal of political rhetoric, with easy recipes for development and with emotional banalities on self-help. This type of information and the way it is given to people raise expectations. Later people are bitterly disappointed and become apathetic towards all efforts to help them address their problems. So, not all information is good information!

▶ **The information should not dry up.** Communities struggling against poverty need information for a long time. Their fight for freedom against poverty is long and drawn out and therefore their facilitators must ensure that the information will be forthcoming for an extended period. They must make sure that the information reservoirs are full and vibrant and that they will supply the necessary information for a long time to come. At the same time they must ensure that the information channels are open and sturdy so as to convey the information for as long as it is supplied.

▶ **The information must be fresh.** Outdated information is just as bad as no information at all. Science and technology make progress so quickly that the danger exists that our information is outdated. Facilitators and mobilisers of communities can never be satisfied with what they know and with the information they have. They must always look for the latest verified information and provide that to the communities. In this regard a reliable, well-equipped resource centre is very valuable.

### 13.7.3  Information dissemination

Channels are important and information is vital, but the most important is the process of communication.

Much has been written about the best ways to spread information. In recent years we have tended to think that the mass media are ideal for this task. In a way they are, but they are not the only way and often not the best way either. To a large extent the circumstances of a community will decide which method of dissemination is preferred. We will look at broad guidelines, but we must keep in mind that the specifics of the situation will be the final deciding factor.

People or organisations that must spread information in a community tend to favour the public meeting for the task. Public meetings are not the only way to get information to the community.

The problem with public meetings is that they can be big and unruly. While they are usually good for giving out information, they tend to run their own course since people have minds of their own. A mass of people does not easily keep to an agenda with the result that such meetings can become more than only information dissemination meetings. In fact, other business can overshadow the information dissemination part to such an extent that eventually very little of the information is remembered. On the other hand, such meetings can accommodate two-way communication where the people respond to information received. So, we can see that the mass meeting has got negative as well as positive possibilities in this regard.

Apart from mass media and mass meetings there are other ways of spreading information in a community. These are through small groups organised by CDWs or through existing structures and institutions such as schools, clinics, or women's or youth clubs.

Small groups of concerned people can be formed to start projects or to assist existing interest groups to start projects. They usually come into being as a result of the activities of a CDW or other professional, and are usually concerned with one type of problem, for example sanitation, housing or agriculture. Because of their narrow focus they will also receive and spread more focused information. A small group concerned with sanitation will receive and disseminate information on sanitation, not on agriculture or energy provision. Because of this narrower focus it is unnecessary to bombard these groups with masses of information of a general nature in the hope that some of it will find the target. Because a small group is interested in something specific, say sanitation, it will gladly receive and disseminate information on sanitation. Small groups can play a very important role, even if they do nothing else than receiving and spreading certain important information. But they can do more. They can provide the feedback that is so necessary in development communication.

We must remember that any community is an organised society with various structures already in existence. Such structures can and should be used for the purpose of information dissemination. We will look at a few such structures, but actually the possibilities are limitless. About 80 per cent of all households or families are represented on the school grounds; therefore the school can be a very good place to deliver information. Children representing many households will receive the information and hopefully many of these children will also deliver this information to their parents. Children therefore become the targets of the information, but they also become the messengers or information channels.

Another state institution that can be used is the clinic. Women frequent clinics and they can be the targets as well as the bearers of information to their homes and their families. One would expect that information disseminated at the clinics would be about health, but it need not be so. Information on just about anything can be spread in this way.

There are other less formal organisations in any society that can also be used for information dissemination. Church services take place once a week and in between there are also prayer meetings. These gatherings can be used to provide information and to ask those present to spread the information to other people. The same goes for women's clubs, youth clubs, sports clubs, choirs, burial societies, stokvels and other interest groups such as agricultural, horticultural or music groups. If the information is interesting and important enough, people who receive it in this manner will pass it on.

We must remember that all these structures, whether they are more or less formal, are tied to each other by people. The school and the church, for example, share the same members. Their children tie families to the school. The members of the women's club are also the members of the church and also visit the clinic from time to time.

If one places information at strategic places within this set of structures, that information is sure to spread through the whole community. This is what we mean by horizontal communication, a very important ingredient of development communication.

People are mobilised to take responsibility for their own development. This development action usually takes place through various kinds of community groups. One should be very careful that the dissemination of information does not overlook and bypass these groups. In fact, they are the coalface participants in development communication. Therefore one should be intent on spreading some information through these groups. Information of a general nature can be disseminated through mass meetings and the mass media. Eventually, though, the spreading of information should be very specific in order to spread information of a specific kind. The groups of concerned people that are formed as a result of the initiatives of CDWs should take responsibility for the dissemination of the more specific information in a way and through the media that they decide, and for feedback to the point of origin of the information.

This is an important reason why it is better that small groups disseminate information. The spreading of information through the mass media and by way of large structures, such as the school, solicits relatively little feedback, while the more limited and direct spreading of information has a much greater response factor.

We give out masses of information and hope that a small percentage will be received, understood and accepted. Our hopes are just on a small percentage because experience has taught us that only a small percentage will respond. We therefore have a small return on a relatively big investment. It is perhaps economically wiser to rather make limited investments that are directed and targeted very specifically and that bring returns that are comparable to the returns of the mass investments.

## 13.8 CONCLUSION

One of the prominent characteristics of human beings is that they are motivated and demotivated all the time. Motivation is like an energy booster to them, but demotivation leads to lethargy. Managers of human resources must therefore be aware of the motivating and demotivating factors in their situation so that they can attend to both and ensure that the human resources under their care are motivated more than they are demotivated.

It is quite clear that group decision-making and group action are dependent on motivation. Motivation makes groups vibrant and eager to accomplish. Unfortunately, every situation has demotivators present. One must try very hard to get rid of as many demotivators in any situation as is possible. A situation must develop wherein motivation will be an inner strength of the people, not something that must be fed to the people on a regular basis to keep them going. Perhaps we should pay more attention to the importance of leadership in motivating people towards action and sacrifice.

We cannot even begin to think of the mobilisation of communities without the use of information. It is the oxygen of any mobilisation effort. But we cannot just throw information in the wind and hope that it will land somewhere where it will do something good. We must choose our information channels and sources and then we must plan the dissemination of the information carefully so that it gives us the optimal return. We must establish a development communication structure in which small groups play a very important role.

# CHAPTER 14

# OPERATIONAL WRITING

## 14.1 INTRODUCTION

A composition ready for action; that is what operational writing is about. Various types of operational writing can be distinguished. Keeping minutes of a meeting is one of the most important types of operational writing (see Chapter 15). The composition of curriculum vitae (a life history) is another type of operational writing. In this chapter we are, however, mainly concerned with:

❱ report and proposal writing;
❱ composition of a business plan or proposal;
❱ some problems associated with fundraising (as an objective of a business plan); and
❱ taking minutes.

A report is a vehicle or a tool with which to transfer information. In Section 14.2 we ask some of the questions an author of a report needs to ask and answer before and during the composition of a report. Section 14.3 describes some of the main features of a proposal or a business plan. You will notice that in describing the business plan we present it as a typical example of a fundraising request. The business plan in this context is therefore an example for a request for funding of an organisation or project.

## 14.2 REPORT AND PROPOSAL WRITING

Report writing must serve a purpose. Its main purpose is to inform people who are not directly involved in what is going on in a project. The aim of the report is therefore not only to provide information about the outcome of a project (product) but also what takes place during a project (process).

Before writing a report, four types of questions must be answered: why (the purpose of the report), what (the topic of the report) for whom (the message you want to convey) and how (style and format).

### 14.2.1 'Why' questions

Determine the purpose of the report. Is your report aimed at informing the community about progress or problems? Are you writing a submission to influence policy-makers?

Is your report a historical record of a specific action that took place? Are you evaluating a process or product and have to write a research report? Some reports such as minutes are recurring writing tasks. Others, such as information reports to the community may not be 'compulsory', but your committee may decide on it as a good communication medium.

### 14.2.2 'What' questions

Determine the type of report you should write. Once the 'why' question has been answered, you will know what type of report to write. It might be a historical record, a research report in which a problem is addressed, a discussion paper in which a new idea or strategy is introduced for reflection or a proposal with definite recommendations on something of importance to you or your organisation.

### 14.2.3 'For whom' questions

Identify the issue or situation on which you want to report. You must be very careful and specific in your choice. Remember, the golden rule is to address only one main topic in a report. If the report is on a comprehensive issue, make sure that individual aspects are addressed separately and clearly indicated as such. If you know the individual or group for whom the report is intended, you will use language and phrases that you know will be clearly understood. If not, your report must be in neutral language and as brief as possible.

### 14.2.4 'How' questions

Decide on the procedure to follow. What is the best way of presenting your message? Readers usually look for an introduction, a body, conclusion or summary and recommendations.
Select all the relevant material. You may need minutes of previous meetings, information brochures or even verbal accounts from witnesses or participants in a project. Organise the material logically in the form of the report. Answers to the 'why', 'what' and 'for whom' questions will dictate the form of your report. Do you see how interrelated the 'why', 'what', 'for whom' and 'how' questions are?

### 14.2.5 Presentation of a report

When someone picks up a report and looks at it for the first time, it must make a good impression, therefore it should be neatly set out. Headings must stand out, subsections must be logically numbered and the sheets should not be too full.

When someone begins reading the report, it must also make a good impression. Therefore sentences should be well-formulated, and what you have written must be clear, specific, easy to read and easy to understand. The style must be suitable, sometimes more formal and sometimes more informal, depending on the type of report and who is going to read it.

When someone has finished reading a report, the good impression that it made earlier, must continue, therefore the contents must be concise (don't tire your reader with a long-drawn-out report), but at the same time it must be complete (don't leave your reader hanging in the air). A lasting good impression is only possible if the structure of the report is correct.

A report must consist of at least:

- a title;
- an introduction;
- a main body divided into easily digestible and logically arranged chunks; and
- a conclusion.

Research proposals, research reports and discussion papers are all specialised reports and they contain all the above. Yet, because of their specialised nature they need more than ordinary reports. In addition to the above they need a discussion of the problem statement, objectives, literature study, research methodology, findings and recommendations to be added. The elements of a report are itemised below.

- **A title**: The title must be carefully formulated because it must in a few words summarise the essence of the report. A title should also not be ambiguous. The reader must know exactly what the report is dealing with by just looking at the title.
- **An introduction**: This is where you state why the report is being written and what you want to achieve by it. No argument is proffered yet, that will come in the main body
- **Background**: It is often necessary to provide the reader with some background to the report, for example socio-economic information of an area; typical problems experienced and types of resources and assets available. This information explains the context within which the problem occurs.
- **Problem statement**: A clearly formulated problem, issue or challenge helps to focus the mind of the author and the attention of the reader.
- **List of objectives**: Once the problem is formulated the author of the report should indicate the objectives of the report, in other words what he/she intends to achieve in the report with reference to the problem statement.
- **Literature study**: Books and journal articles are consulted to gain a broader understanding of issues, models approaches and historical information. Here relevant publications are discussed to provide a historical and theoretical background to the problem.
- **A main body**: The scope of the body will be determined by the complexity of the issue and this will influence the number of sub-headings used. Sub-headings are used to subdivide text into smaller, logical units that makes reading, understanding and remembering easier.
- **Findings and recommendations**: This section provides the answers to the objectives stated in the beginning and makes recommendations, in relation to the objectives and findings, on the way forward. Recommendations are the culmination in a logical conclusion of the argument developed in the main body and it answers the questions that have been asked.
- **A conclusion**: The whole report is finally summarised in a few paragraphs. The conclusion should show how the report addresses the problem and achieves the objectives. Never leave it to your reader to make the deductions, but guide him/her to accept your conclusions.

Don't forget to sign and date your report and make a copy for your records.

## 14.3  BUSINESS PLAN

A business plan is a well thought out finance proposal or financial plan for a business or project. A business plan shows what the enterprise wants to do and how it plans to achieve the goals. It can be used for micro- or small-business ventures and for development projects. In the case of development projects it cannot be a detailed planning document. It can provide for detailed planning later on but it cannot be used as a project blueprint for all the reasons that will be discussed in Chapter 20. It should show what amount of money is necessary to start the business or project and/or to ensure success. The way in which a business plan is written can have either a positive or negative effect on the receiver, that is, usually the banker, donor or funder. Remember the following important points:

▶ A business plan should be written in a formal manner.
▶ It should have a clear subject line.
▶ It should be factual and clear.
▶ It should not be a begging letter.
▶ It should reflect need, yes, but always in a positive manner.

A business plan should indicate:

▶ what kind of business or project you want to start;
▶ how you are going to do it; and
▶ how you will pay back the loan or fund.

A well thought out, well documented business plan shows that you know what you want, how you are going to achieve it, and by showing this, provides credibility to your potential funder. Apart from its funding purpose a business plan can also:

▶ be used to force yourself to take an objective, critical and unemotional look at your business or project in its entirety while putting the plan together;
▶ become your operational tool that, if properly used, will help you manage your business or project towards its success; and
▶ become a means of communicating your ideas to others and provide a basis for a financing proposal.

### 14.3.1  Proposed business plan format

The following indicates the most important categories to be addressed in a business plan:

**Project name**
Give the business or project an appropriate name that will reflect the nature of its business or activity.

**Project management**
The contact details of the organisation and person championing the project is needed. State the name, address and all other contacting details of the organisation that will be responsible for the overall management of the business or project.

## Implementing agency

State the name and address of the organisation or organisations that will be responsible for the physical implementation of various aspects. You also need to indicate the legal status of the organisation: is it a Section 21 company, does it have a constitution and what are the dates of registration? Bank details must also be provided: when is the financial year-end of the project, the name of bank and contact details and account number.

## Governing and membership

Donors need to know who are involved in the governance of the organisation (board members or directors or project participants) and who are the members of the management team. They also usually require a list of members of the organisation or project. If the beneficiaries of a project differ from its membership, a separate name list may be required. Sometimes the donor may ask whether the project is made up of family members and will ask for a list of names.

## Project description

The project description or funding request is the core component of the business plan. Describe exactly what you want to achieve and your plan to achieve it by starting with a problem statement. The more detail you give the better. This will show the donor that you really know what you need for the project to succeed.
The project description can be divided into three themes: training, equipment and material. For each of these a separate budget can be provided (see cost estimates below).

To make a favourable impression the project description should explain what the available expertise is. A donor may, for instance, require information about the technical and business skills available and the rate of literacy and numeracy of those involved in the organisation or specific project.

## Location

Describe the geographic area, as well as the political, social and economic area in which the project will take place or the business will operate, making specific reference to the target groups.

It may also be important to show in the project description the extent to which the organisation/ project networks in the community. Does the wider community know of your existence and do you have a relationship with and support from the local government, traditional authority, other stakeholders in the community and community development forums?

## Objectives

Objectives are the measurable results that an organisation aims to achieve within the timeframe of a specific project. They are those goals that you need to reach in order to realise your mission.

## Scope of work

Explain how you are going to reach your objectives. Give a strategic plan and the implementation process with indicators to be used for monitoring and evaluation purposes.

## Budget (cost estimate)

A budget is a planning instrument: it shows the expected income and expenditure of an organisation. A donor wants to see this document, at least the current one of your organisation, or they want a copy of the project's budget if this is separate from that of the organisation. Sometimes they also require a bank statement and a report from the auditor or bookkeeper for the past year.

The budget must provide the would-be donor with as much detail as possible and make sure that estimates are realistic and verifiable (see project description above). This section must indicate the seriousness of your financial commitment. It should not only indicate what and when the would-be donor should contribute, but should show the use of other available or own funds.

## Cash-flow plan

This section is of importance for two reasons. First, it shows when the donor should make finance available. Second, it concretises the plans and ensures that money will be available when needed.

## Time schedule

Indicate when you plan to start and end the different phases of the project. If at all possible, make use of a graphic timetable.

## Evaluation and reporting

Thanking and showing recognition are basic values in all cultures. It is common-sense good manners.

But to know who to thank and what for, information is needed. This is information gathered through regular monitoring and evaluation. Obviously when a business plan is prepared as a fundraising document, we want to evaluate our success in raising funds. But to do this one needs standards or benchmarks against which to do the evaluation. Though some guidelines exist, a firm set of benchmarks is not available. Through trial and error you will have to develop your own set.

Reporting is a vital component of effective donor management as it keeps the donor informed about your activities and whether you are succeeding in what you have set out to do. In other words, it ensures responsibility regarding the use of funds. Because of its importance, reporting should be covered in the business plan where at least an outline of the reporting procedure must be given.

## Beneficiaries reached

In this section you should provide proof that the business or project is satisfying or will satisfy the needs of the people who you intend to help. Under this heading can also be included human resource development, specifically capacity building (training), the use of small local enterprises and affirmative action (see also governing and membership described above).

## Documentation

The following documents should accompany the business plan:

- a *map* to indicate the physical location of the project;
- the *constitution* of the organisation;
- if registered, a copy of the *registration certificate;*
- the *annual report* or a copy of a progress report or minutes of a meeting;
- a recent bank statement; and
- supporting letters that will reinforce your application.

### 14.3.2  Fundraising: a special type of report and some pitfalls to avoid

One of the most important forms of operational writing is the preparation of a business plan to raise funds for the organisation or a project. Windell (1988) identifies ten pitfalls that seriously hamper or even contribute to failure of fundraising attempts:

- **Time schedules totally absent or not adhered to**. Not only will the organisation be unable to meet its financial and other commitments, but people will lose interest in the programme.
- **No clear strategy**. Everyone involved in the NGO and CBO sectors knows that donor funding is needed to meet budgetary needs. Sometimes it happens that the chairperson announces that they now need a specific amount to fulfil a specific obligation. He/she may even propose a specific donor to be approached. Everybody agrees and leaves the meeting, satisfied that the financial need will be addressed by means of fundraising. But, without a clear strategy, without a sub-committee or person made responsible for carrying out the fundraising, nothing will happen. At the next meeting the chairperson will most probably announce a serious shortage in funds needed to complete the project.
- **A lack of enthusiasm**. Not being enthusiastic about raising funds is a sure recipe for failure. However, the fundraiser can be enthusiastic only if he/she approaches the matter with clear objectives, in a planned way that fits into an overall fundraising strategy.
- **Dependence on the telephone and correspondence**. There are thousands of NGOs pursuing good causes, but the potential pool of donors is limited. The reply to a telephonic request for support may be a friendly (or unfriendly) NO! It is very easy to respond negatively over the phone because the eye-to-eye contact—presence of the fundraiser is not felt so intensely. Likewise, a 'begging' letter can be easily disposed of in the wastepaper basket.
- **Lack of orientation and co-ordination of voluntary workers**. As indicated above, fundraising must be driven by a committee or preferably an individual. The tasks of this person with regard to the voluntary workers are threefold: to orientate (train) them with regard to fundraising; to motivate them — they may feel isolated and become despondent when the public responds negatively; and to monitor progress and co-ordinate the action of volunteers.
- **An attitudinal problem**. An attitude of 'I have already lost the battle' means that you have already lost the battle. The attitude of the fundraiser must be friendly, open, sharing and willing to engage, as an equal, with a potential donor.
- **Inability to ask**. This is the essence of fundraising. The potential donor cannot read your mind. He/she will not know that your request, for example, 10 per cent of the total cost from his/her organisation, and not the full budget of R500 000,00! If you do not ask, you will not get.
- **No targets**. Fundraising targets must be clear and above all realistic. Macro-environmental factors and personal factors determine what people can or will give. The need is bigger than the amount available in society for contribution to NGO and CBO funds.
- **Inefficient and clumsy administration**. You do not need an expensive and sophisticated computer system to have an efficient administration. A card or filing system will do. Efficient administration is necessary in order to: monitor progress; know when to

remind contributors of their donations; know when to send birthday cards or other important 'thank you' gestures; keep a record of contributions and; compare it with the targets referred to above.

▶ **Unrealistic expectations**. We only have to find 10 people to donate R1 000,00 each then our target is met! This is quite an unrealistic expectation. It will only succeed in making fundraisers despondent and unmotivated.

We are sure that more sins can be added from practical experience. Nevertheless, this list can be used as a checklist to measure the performance of the organisation, to identify shortcomings and to plan solutions to problems. With this list as a guideline, writing a business plan can be better planned and executed. It can also help the organisation to set realistic goals and achieve small, interim successes in fundraising.

## 14.4  TAKING MINUTES

Minutes are the formal record of a meeting. During a meeting the secretary or recording clerk will take notes of the proceedings and will then afterwards formalise these notes into minutes. For the sake of accuracy use of a tape recorder should be considered but this must be approved beforehand by the meeting.  Minutes should:

▶ accurately reflect the proceedings of the meeting (transcribe the notes taken at the meeting as soon as possible after completion of the meeting);
▶ be brief and factual (long proposals or submissions should where possible be included as annexures and not be made part of the minutes/report of the meeting);
▶ be written with the agenda of the meeting as background document;
▶ be written in a formal manner;
▶ be written in the active voice;
▶ have numbered headings;
▶ consist of short sentences;
▶ have clear paragraphs;
▶ indicate what action should be taken and who is responsible for taking that action. When a decision is made it should be prefaced in the minutes with 'RESOLVED THAT ...'; and
▶ capture the proceedings correctly and avoid including subjective opinion.

The type of meeting will have an impact on the contents and composition of the minutes. Generally minutes should reflect the following:

▶ a clear subject line, in other words, what the meeting is about;
▶ the date on which the meeting was held;
▶ the venue where the meeting was held;
▶ the starting and closing times of the meeting;
▶ the organisation/institution conducting the meeting;
▶ the chairperson; and
▶ the list of attendees.

Generally, the following headings are used:

- Opening and welcome.
- Attendance and apologies.
- Approval of minutes of previous meeting.
- Specific items carried over from the previous minutes.
- Way forward.
- New matters.
- Date of next meeting.
- Closure.
- Attendance list.

## 14.5 CONCLUSION

Community development never takes place in a vacuum. That is why reports and proposals are necessary. While projects may be quite simple and their planning based on trial and error, these reports and proposals must have a professional look about them. It is clear that the community development worker (CDW) will have to play a major role in the writing of these documents. That does not mean that the CDW should 'take over the job'. It simply means that ordinary people not used to this type of writing should not be thrown into the deep end. The guidance role of the community development worker should ensure that no one will sink when they must swim.

Cuthbert (1995:141) makes the following very important statement: 'Thanking and recognition are the most important first steps in assuring a continuing and fruitful relationship with your donors'.

# CHAPTER 15

# MEETINGS

## 15.1 INTRODUCTION

A meeting takes place when a group of people come together in one place at the same time to discuss and, if needs be, decide on a mutual issue or issues. Groups, committees and organisations exist by the meetings they hold. Imagine any of these bodies without ever holding meetings. They will lose their identity and cease to exist in their current form. We can therefore say that meetings are extremely important. But it is also true that meetings waste a lot of time and energy. Meetings are often quite unproductive and are even counterproductive.

## 15.2 THE MEETING CYCLE

A meeting does not stand on its own. It is connected to the previous meeting and it leads to the next one. Meetings form a pattern or cycle that consists of three phases. The first is the preparatory phase where the secretary has a specific task, but other members also have a certain amount of preparation to do. The basic documents used as guidelines for the preparation are the minutes of the previous meeting and the agenda of the next meeting. The second is the meeting phase when the preparation comes to fruition. The third is the follow-up phase when decisions during the meeting must be put into effect. This phase dovetails with the preparation phase for the next meeting.

## 15.3 TYPES OF MEETINGS

Meetings differ in type and in size. There can be executive meetings with only a few people present, small group meetings with a limited number of people, and mass meetings with many people attending. Second, meetings differ in character. There can be information meetings where certain information is conveyed to those present. These are usually mass meetings where constituents are informed about matters. These meetings are sometimes called report-back meetings. There are also decision-making meetings where various items are dealt with and decisions are made on each item. Decision-making meetings can also be problem-solving meetings because many of the items on the agenda represent problems that must be solved. Problem-solving meetings usually take place on a lower level of decision-making where subcommittees or committees must thrash out matters and make recommendations to higher councils.

## 15.4  COMMON PROBLEMS ENCOUNTERED IN MEETINGS

Why are meetings often a waste of time? Why are they so unproductive? Why does it seem that they will never end? The answer is that common problems are experienced in meetings of all kinds. It is amazing to see how different people in different places and at different types of meetings experience the same problems. We look at this list of common problems with only one objective and that is to remove as much as possible of them in real life. This section makes use of Doyle & Straus, (1976).

### 15.4.1  The multi-direction syndrome

Everybody goes off in different directions at the same time. The meeting lacks focus and no one tries to let the participants move in tandem in the same direction. This is obviously a problem lying with the chairperson. Focus and order are two of the most important ingredients of a successful meeting. If they are absent, a meeting has problems.

### 15.4.2  Confusion about procedure

The participants have not sorted out what procedure is to be used in the meeting with the result that every now and then while discussing the items on the agenda, questions about procedure are likely to crop up or differences on the procedure to be followed will lead to an impasse. Again this is an indication that the chairperson is failing. The best is to have standing procedures that are known to everyone and that can be followed at every meeting.

### 15.4.3  Personal attacks

Individuals are verbally attacked when they say something that is not acceptable to all. The ideas of people are not the central focus, but rather the characters of people who dare to voice an own opinion. This is deadly for any organisation or group when their members are abused for having their own opinion. There is either conflict or the discussion dies down.

### 15.4.4  Traffic problems

In many cases it is difficult to leap into the conversational flow and get a chance to participate. This can lead to more than one conversation going on at the same time or it can lead to some members not participating, paving the way for a few individuals later on to dominate the proceedings.

### 15.4.5  Unclear roles and responsibilities

In some contexts, it is difficult to know what roles various participants are to play in the meeting and afterwards. Their status and power is also unclear. There is no clarity on who is responsible for what. Roles must be established, perhaps over some time, but eventually these things must be clear to everyone.

### 15.4.6  Manipulation by the chairperson

The chairperson may use meetings to rubber-stamp his/her decisions. Meetings become monologues by the chairperson where the rest of the members merely nod their consent or agreement now and then. This is surely the worst problem a meeting can have because the very purpose of meetings, that is, to solve problems through debate, falls away.

### 15.4.7  Data overload

We receive so much written and oral information that we cannot remember it all and may become confused. It is usually easier for a secretary to just put a lot of documents together than to sort out the really relevant portions. It is then left to the members to decide what should be read and what not. Unfortunately very few of them have the ability to do that.

### 15.4.8  Repetition and wheel spinning

Often a meeting cannot gain momentum. It is stuck at the same place and every speaker repeats the same old ideas. No new arguments are offered and no progress towards a decision is made. This usually happens when a meeting lacks focus. Then the members are not sure where they are and what has been decided. The result is repetition and lack of progress.

### 15.4.9  Win/lose approach

In such a situation, it is taken for granted that every time that there is difference of opinion one party must win and the other must lose. Instead of discussing matters thoroughly, everything is put to the vote as soon as possible. This is a way to save time and to progress quickly, but it introduces a sense of strife and competition into a meeting that makes open debate impossible. It also means that there are winners and losers, a division that may be continued after the meeting.

### 15.4.10  Expectations and questions of power

Sometimes there is confusion about the purpose of the meeting and what authority the meeting has. Is it only an information meeting or are the participants supposed to make decisions? Has the meeting the power to approve things or must it recommend approval by another body? Quite often it is the fault of the chairperson when this confusion is present, simply because it is nice to pretend that a meeting has certain powers and it boosts the image of the chairperson.

### 15.4.11  Problem avoidance

At times people may be so afraid of conflict that issues that can lead to a difference of opinion are avoided. This attitude is not conducive to problem-solving. One should warn against unbridled conflict, but it can go too far so that conflict is avoided at any cost. A difference of opinion, debate and talking 'against' someone's ideas or views are not necessarily conflict. It rather shows maturity among the participants if they can speak their mind freely without falling into conflict situations.

### 15.4.12  Poor meeting environment

If the room is too small, stuffy, noisy, draughty, dark or many other things a meeting becomes unpleasant and even unproductive. This problem is of course relative. The person used to modern and sophisticated facilities may find the meeting environment poor while other people are quite satisfied.

### 15.4.13 Pre-set ideas and assumptions

Sometimes the result of the deliberations is a foregone conclusion. The meeting can only decide in favour of this side. Everything that goes on before a decision is made is just window-dressing. This is the result of a lot of talking and caucusing among members before a meeting. Their ideas and perceptions are then formed before the meeting and nothing can happen to change it.

## 15.5 BASIC CRITERIA FOR A GOOD MEETING

The following criteria contribute to the chance of a successful meeting:

▶ There must be a common focus on content.
▶ There must be a common focus on process.
▶ The chairperson must ensure that there is an open and balanced conversational flow.
▶ The chairperson must protect individuals from personal attack.
▶ The meeting must agree on the basic principle that a win/win solution will be sought.
▶ Everyone's role and responsibility in the meeting must be clearly defined and agreed upon.
▶ The meeting must be governed by a set of rules to which all participants subscribe and which all participants know.

A meeting is successful when its business is conducted within a reasonable time, discussion takes place in an unhurried but business like fashion and the objectives of the meeting are being met, for example, decisions made or information disseminated.

## 15.6 MEETING PROCEDURES

Meetings are guided by a number of important procedural aspects.

### Opening

A meeting must be formally opened. The fact that a meeting is formally opened distinguishes it from a general unstructured discussion. At a discussion people talk about whatever they want and come and go as they please. In a meeting, however, certain rules of procedure govern the proceedings, the meeting is structured and focused, and has a legal status in the sense that decisions can be taken at the meeting which are or can be binding. A meeting therefore starts the moment that the chairperson has declared it open. The meeting cannot be declared open if there is not a quorum of members present. If it is clear that a quorum is not going to be present, one of three things can be done. Firstly, some of the absent members can be contacted and requested to come to the meeting as a matter of urgency so that the proceedings can start. Secondly, the meeting can be postponed to a later date. Thirdly, those present can decide to continue with the meeting, but without taking any binding decisions. All decisions taken at such a meeting will have to be ratified or condoned at a later meeting.

## Application for leave of absence or apology for absence

When members of a committee cannot attend a specific meeting they should send their formal apologies, or, more correctly, should request the meeting to be granted leave of absence. This should be in writing and should reach the secretary before the meeting commences. If a person is absent without application or apology it should be recorded in the minutes that such a person is absent without permission.

## Reading of previous minutes

The minutes of the previous meeting must be read and approved, preferably early on in the meeting. If all the members have received copies of the draft minutes well in advance of the meeting, the meeting can decide to take it that the minutes have been read. The attendants at the meeting can then suggest and recommend necessary changes to the draft minutes to ensure that the minutes reflect the proceedings of the previous meeting accurately. Minutes cannot be changed because someone does not like or does not agree with what has taken place. It can only be changed in order to reflect better what actually happened. The meeting must approve all such suggestions of change and finally the minutes as amended must be put to the meeting for approval. The minutes are then adopted formally as correct and the chairperson signs it. It is now the official record of that specific meeting.

## Matters arising from the minutes

All matters are not necessarily completed and closed at a meeting. It is sometimes necessary to look for more information or to make an inquiry. Sometimes a matter cannot be resolved and the meeting can then decide to refer the matter to a sub-committee for recommendation at the next meeting. All such cases must be identified by the secretary from the minutes and must be placed on the agenda under the heading: Matters from the previous minutes. These matters are not discussed *in toto* again, but are looked at in terms of the new information obtained or the recommendation made by a sub-committee.

## New matters or motions

New matters come to the attention of a meeting through correspondence, reports and requests via the secretary or sometimes the chairperson. Members can also table fresh motions for the deliberation of the meeting. All such new matters must be reflected in the agenda and preferably the agenda must contain appendices with more information on the new matters. Members should therefore also present their motions in writing to the secretary so that it can still be placed on the agenda. If members want to table a motion orally at a meeting the meeting will only take note of it and will rule that it be placed on the agenda of the next meeting.

## General

Most meetings have an item under the heading of general. This item on the agenda is not an opportunity to place new matters for discussion and decision on the table. It is a chance for general announcements to be made and sometimes it is also used for *personalia*, in other words, to table motions of condolences, congratulations and best wishes that are not for discussion, but only for general acceptance.

## Date of next meeting

The date for the next meeting must be set and announced. In certain instances meetings take place regularly, for example, every third Friday evening at 19h00. In such cases the chairperson can refer to the actual date of the next scheduled meeting and the secretary can take it up in the minutes.

**Closure**

Just as the meeting had to be formally opened, so must it be formally closed. What happens between the formal opening and the formal closure has other meaning than what happens outside of this period. Therefore, no decisions can be taken by a meeting after it has been declared closed.

## 15.7 ROLE-PLAYERS IN A MEETING

Meetings cannot carry unnecessary passengers. No person can merely be a silent co-traveller. Every person present at a meeting must play a meaningful role. There are basically three important roles at a meeting. They are those of the chairperson, the secretary and the members.

### 15.7.1 Chairperson

The chairperson is the most important role-player, not necessarily because this position holds the power to dictate, but because without a chairperson a meeting would erupt into chaos. A good chairperson is someone who acts as a referee or traffic officer. The chairperson must ensure fair play in a meeting. This includes giving everyone a fair chance to speak, guarding against undue interruptions, summarising the debate from time to time just to focus the meeting again, ensuring that a decision is taken on a matter and that everybody knows what the decision entails, managing the time allocated to the meeting, and generally, seeing that the rules of the meeting and the agreed upon procedure are followed without blowing the whistle like a real referee every time that rules are broken.

#### 15.7.1.1 Checklists for chairperson

The following checklists can help a chairperson in the execution of his/her task. A chairperson should strive towards the point where he/she can answer yes to every question in the checklists.

**Checklist for the beginning of a meeting**

- Is the objective of the meeting clear to everyone?
- Is everyone present aware of his/her important role?
- Is everyone aware of the rules and procedures governing the meeting?
- Is the chairperson well prepared for the meeting?
- Does everyone know that the goal during this meeting is a win/win solution?
- Does everyone know the contents of the agenda?
- Are the people present aware of constraints such as time?
- Does the chairperson have eye contact with everyone present?

**Checklist for during the meeting**

▶ Is there an easy conversational flow?

▶ Does everyone get a fair chance to make a contribution?

▶ Is progress being made in the discussion?

▶ Is the chairperson neutral and unbiased?

▶ Is there order in the meeting?

▶ Is the secretary keeping up with note taking of the decisions made?

▶ Is the chairperson dealing well with problem people?

**Checklist for after the meeting**

▶ Has the chairperson discussed the minutes with the secretary?

▶ Has the chairperson seen to it that the minutes are being despatched timeously?

▶ Has the chairperson followed up the tasks that he/she was given during the meeting?

▶ Has the chairperson made sure that the secretary has done the tasks given to him/her during the meeting?

### 15.7.1.2 Problem people with whom a chairperson has to deal

Unfortunately it is the chairperson's task to deal with problem people in a meeting because they are the potential disrupters of meetings. In good meetings the influence of problem people is minimised. The following are some of the problem people (broadly based on Doyle & Straus, 1976):

**The latecomer** always arrives late at the meeting and causes some kind of commotion, from greeting everyone by hand and enquiring about their health, to bumping and shuffling to get to a seat. When the latecomer has eventually settled in, he/she wants to be brought up to date on the progress of the meeting. The handling of this problem person will be dealt with together with the next one.

**The early leaver** drains the energy of the meeting by leaving early. Early leaving is often accompanied by clock-watching, finger-tapping, paper-gathering, apologising in various directions, and goodbye-saying to all and sundry, eventually exiting in a crouching manner. It is very important to settle the matter of punctuality among a group who have regular and frequent meetings. It should also be noted in the minutes when someone arrives late or leaves early. In any case, common meeting rules require that the early leaver obtain the approval of the whole meeting before leaving early.

**The broken record** keeps bringing up the same point over and over again. This person may not act in this way by choice, but because no one would listen to him/her or because he/she really needs more explanation before understanding. The chairperson should make sure that everyone present knows what the discussion is all about and, once a decision has been made, see to it that it is recorded. It is a good idea if the chairperson or the secretary reads a decision before the meeting moves on to the next item.

**The head-shaker** non-verbally disagrees or agrees in a dramatic and disruptive manner. Head-shakers shake heads, roll eyes, pull faces, throw hands in the air as if in despair, and laugh soundlessly. The head-shaker is either a very animated person, in which case he/she will probably not realise what he/she is doing, or has a low opinion of the rest of the participants and watches them as if they play in a comedy. The best way to deal with the head-shaker is to force him/her to translate his/her body language into words. Every time the head-shaker makes a gesture the chairperson should ask him/her to comment. In that way he/she will become aware of the mannerism and will have to defend his/her reaction to the rest of the meeting.

**The dropout** sits at the back of the room, does not say anything, never looks up, appears to be reading something or doodles. The dropout is especially disturbing to the chairperson. It is the chairperson's task as facilitator to get the whole group to participate freely and the dropout is living proof that the chairperson is failing. Firstly, the seating arrangement can encourage or discourage dropout. There should be no 'back of the room' seating. No person should be able to hide behind anybody else. Secondly, the dropout must be brought into the discussion by being asked for his/her opinion.

**The silent observer** is not a dropout, but he/she never says anything although he/she follows the discussion and may even nod now and then. The silent observer is usually the shy person who is unsure of him/herself. The chairperson should assure this person that his/her contribution is also important and should help him/her to gain courage.

**The Doubting Thomas** constantly puts down everything. He/she is always negative. You are wrong until you prove yourself right. No solution will ever work. It is good to be critical, but there is a difference between being critical and being aggressively negative. The Doubting Thomas must be kept honest. Every time he/she reacts negatively, he/she must be requested to substantiate the reaction.

**The whisperer** is constantly whispering to the person next to him/her. Eye contact with a whisperer may cause him/her to stop, or else physical movement towards him/her may stop the whispering. To ask the whisperer to repeat to the whole meeting what has been whispered may also quieten him/her down.

**The clown** is a potential disrupter of a meeting. He/she usually tells jokes or makes funny remarks in an aside that is only heard by the people sitting close by. The clown enjoys the attention of at least part of the group. His/her remarks cause peals of laughter from the people nearby. A bit of humour in a serious discussion is good, but the problem with the clown is that his/her humour is meant only for the people nearest to him/her. This can lead to the beginning of a subculture in the vicinity of the clown. Establishing eye contact and forcing him/her to be serious by asking his/her opinion may change the mood.

**The loudmouth** talks too much and too loudly, dominates the meeting and is seemingly impossible to shut up. In many cases the loudmouth is more senior than the rest. He/she then regards it as his/her right to dominate. The loudmouth usually makes it difficult for other people to participate so that a meeting quickly degenerates into a dialogue between the loudmouth and the chairperson. The chairperson should simply say at some stage that he/she is not interested in contributions from only one person, thus forcing the loudmouth to keep quiet while other people have the floor.

**The orator** makes a speech instead of an input. A speech is time consuming and tends to deal with various matters that are not totally relevant. A speech also tends to stifle lively discussion. The chairperson has a very difficult task in finding the opportune moment to interrupt the orator and quickly give someone else a chance to speak. In any case, the rules of the meeting should stipulate that a contribution should not be longer than a prescribed period of time.

**The attacker** launches personal attacks on other members in the meeting. This person is aggressive by nature and may even like conflict. Such attacks cause anger, shock and even fear. The attacker must be stopped and it is best if the chairperson can get the whole meeting to censure him/her. The rules of the meeting should also stipulate that no personal attacks may be made.

**The gun jumper** does not wait until the chairperson gives him/her a chance to speak. When a discussion is really going well, it is inevitable that a few people would have indicated to the chairperson that they would like to make a contribution. The chairperson must keep a waiting list in his/her head so that everyone can have a fair chance to speak. The gun jumper ruins this orderly proceeding and the chairperson must be very strict and not allow him/her to rob someone else from making a contribution.

## 15.7.2  Secretary

It is said that the secretary makes a good chairperson and it is also true that the secretary makes a good meeting. The secretary is the scribe and the assistant to the chairperson. He/she must help the chairperson to keep track of the proceedings, as well as keep to the agenda. The secretary in particular is the source of information for the meeting and must supply all relevant and needed information. The secretary must also note important points of debate and must record decisions so that true minutes can be written later. The following are the tasks of the secretary:

### Before the meeting

- Draw up the agenda in consultation with the chairperson.
- Arrange for a venue where the meeting is to be held.
- Send out notice of the meeting and include the agenda.
- Gather all necessary information regarding the items on the agenda.
- Discuss the agenda, item for item with the chairperson so that he/she can be fully prepared.
- Bring all the necessary documentation plus some clean writing paper to the meeting.
- Arrive an hour early in order to get everything ready for the meeting.

**During the meeting**

▶ Get everyone present to complete and sign the attendance register.

▶ Supply the meeting with the necessary information for each item.

▶ Advise the chairperson on an ongoing basis throughout the meeting.

▶ Take notes of all decisions made during the meeting.

▶ Ensure that every decision has a what, when, who and how item.

**After the meeting**

▶ Discuss the outcome of the meeting with the chairperson.

▶ Write the minutes as soon as possible after the meeting.

▶ Despatch the minutes timeously.

▶ Follow up all tasks directed to him/her.

▶ Advise the chairperson of all tasks directed to him/her.

▶ Start collecting items for the agenda of the next meeting.

### 15.7.3 Members

The ordinary members of a meeting are not spectators, but active participants with a great responsibility. They must:

▶ come prepared for the meeting;
▶ contribute to the common knowledge and insight of a meeting;
▶ help the meeting to run its course productively and in an orderly manner;
▶ help the meeting to make good decisions;
▶ carry out the tasks assigned to them; and
▶ be loyal to the decisions taken by the meeting.

## 15.8 CONCLUSION

Meetings are so often very unproductive. That is why we have looked at the problems with and problem people in meetings and have discussed ways and means to improve meetings. It is so important that meetings are productive; that they do not waste a lot of time. The beauty of it is that if meetings are productive and orderly they can be a tremendous boost for a group or a committee. They become showcases for its members. They can act as milestones for the group and can go a long way in motivating the group to reach its objectives.

Meetings are communication exercises where conflict resolution and negotiation take place regularly, where group dynamics and group psychology play a determining role and where problem-solving is done. Many of the communication functions are thus put to the test in meetings.

CHAPTER 16

# PUBLIC SPEAKING

## 16.1 INTRODUCTION

Public speaking remains one of the most difficult forms of communication and yet, it is something that community development workers (CDWs) must often do. It is easy to see why if one thinks of the communication model of sender—message—coding—receiver—feedback and multiply it to suit a situation where the sender addresses his/her message to a number of receivers who may all decode the message differently and respond to it differently. This, while all the barriers that we discussed in Chapter 10 are also present. For this reason there are a number of things that one should keep in mind with public speaking and there are a lot of things to do and not to do. The fact of the matter is that one should be very practical about it. Apart from the fact that it is a difficult form of communication, very few people find it easy to address an audience and few people have a natural talent to do it. Whether or not we have the talent, it is important sticking to a number of basic principles and doing thorough preparation.

## 16.2 BASIC CHARACTERISTICS OF EFFECTIVE VERBAL COMMUNICATION

There are a number of characteristics that make verbal communication effective. These go for all verbal communication, but are even more important for the situation of public speaking. These characteristics are described below.

### 16.2.1 Clarity

Clarity has to do with the way a message is encoded by the sender and decoded by the receiver. The encoding must be done in such a way that decoding will not be too difficult and will not give a new meaning to the message that was not originally attached to it. This means that the public speaker must be careful of:

▶ sentences that are too long;
▶ complex abstract and philosophical ideas;
▶ jargon;
▶ a muddled line of argument;

▶ byways and extras that are not really part of the message; and
▶ physical deterrents, such as a voice that is too-soft.

The best way to describe communication clarity is to liken it to a clear pane of glass. Effective communication is so clear that it allows the receiver/s to look into the sender's mind and to see and interpret messages from the sender's viewpoint.

### 16.2.2  Accuracy

Accuracy is the ability to verbally represent things as they are. Words have different meanings. Combinations of words change the meaning of the individual words. 'Love' is a word with many meanings; it could, for instance, describe something like sexual attraction, but used in the sentence: 'I love fruit', it has a totally different meaning. Different accents can also change the meaning of a phrase, for example 'I am sick' has a different connotation than 'I *am* sick'. So, one must be extremely careful to present a message as accurately as possible. Words and combinations of words also carry emotions and feelings and one should make sure that the right emotion or feeling is transmitted. In this regard, one should use adjectives and adverbs carefully and even sparingly. Sloppiness in speaking leads to a lot of misunderstanding, especially if the language used is not the mother tongue of those receiving the message. How often do we hear that somebody claims that he/she was misquoted? Be consistent in the use of terminology and make sure that the first time a term is used the audience understands it in the same way as the speaker does. Don't call an apple a pineapple and then next time a pear. In other words, use the same term, not 'development' now and later 'progress' and a little later 'change'. The audience does not know whether these are three things or one.

### 16.2.3  Completeness

Speakers cheat their audiences by not giving them the whole message simply because they assume the audience has the same set of information that they have. This is a dangerous assumption because it takes for granted that all members of an audience are as well informed as the speaker. It is better to include all possible information in a message than to starve it of information so that the audience cannot make the same mental progress as the speaker. Don't take it for granted that all members of an audience read the newspapers regularly or listen to the news bulletins on the radio. You may think something is common knowledge, but that is a dangerous assumption. Speakers also weaken their messages by giving incomplete messages. If their audience does not know that they base what they say on fact, simply because the fact is withheld from the audience, the latter cannot be blamed for underrating the message. When we deliver 'to do' messages, in other words, if we must give guidance on a sequence of steps and we use the wrong sequence or we do not complete the process or we give actions different names from what the audience knows them to be, we cannot expect that our message will be successful.

### 16.2.4  Conviction

The first three characteristics were characteristics of the message itself. This and the next characteristic have to do with the way in which the message is brought. The audience must always feel that the speaker regards it as worthwhile to bring the message. In other words, the audience must feel that the speaker is interested in the message, believes in the message and is enthusiastic about the message. This is done, not only through words, but is also shown through body language. The public speaker therefore, must make sure that his/her body conveys the same message as his/her words. Nine times out of ten a public address has a motivational function and the motivational message must be right in order for the audience to accept it and to make the motivation their own, so that the motivation becomes internalised. If the speaker uses emotive words like destiny, power, compassion and freedom, but his body is slumped over the lectern, the audience will very easily regard his speech as rhetorical nonsense. It is important that the speaker conveys to the audience that he/she is convinced that the message is right.

### 16.2.5 Tastefulness

Even if people do not accept your message, they must accept the way in which you have brought the message. A public speaker must, therefore, never insult or offend the audience and never hurt their feelings and never belittle them or that which they hold in respect. Always respect human dignity. This means that we should not try to make fools of them, talk down to them or be paternalistic in our address. We should also never underestimate their intellect.

## 16.3 PREPARATION

Even talented and experienced speakers will admit that good preparation is the key to successful public speaking. It ensures confidence, and a confident speaker is someone who can bring the message with conviction in a tasteful manner and can see to it that the message is clear, accurate and complete. The following are important aspects relating to the preparation:

**Theme or message**. One cannot start to prepare if one does not know what the theme, message or subject of the address is to be. If you are invited to address a group, make sure about the subject from those who invited you. They can be very vague about a subject because they are not familiar with it. If you are asked to choose your own topic, choose one that you can handle and one that will fit the group of people and the occasion. Remember that, in the final instance, you do not want to amuse a group of people, but you want to bring them a message that they should hear and which you want them to accept.

**Objective**. After you have established the theme or message, you must decide what you want to achieve. It is important to decide early what you want to achieve because that, together with the theme, will decide the contents of your speech. Your objective can be to convey information or to explain something. It can go further by wanting to convince people of something, in other words, to get people to accept something. Your objective will not only be important for the contents of your address, but also for the way in which you bring it across. Never lose sight of the objective. Every word of a public address must be one step forward in order to get to the objective. It must therefore be logical and it must be well structured. It must be well thought through. A speech that does not do this is no more than garbling and it is usually a waste of time and very tedious for the audience.

**Preparatory reading**. You must know what you are talking about. A speaker who portrays ignorance or a lack of understanding of a topic will not be very convincing. It is therefore necessary to make sure that you can talk with authority and that you understand the topic. This may necessitate reading documents, files, pamphlets, directives and books or websites. Before you can read the material you will first have to search for it and that may take some time, so do not wait too long before you get started. It is not necessary to know everything about a topic but just make sure that you have your facts right for the address and that you know and understand enough to speak to people on the topic.

**Writing it down**. While a speech is all about talking, it actually starts as something in writing. Remember, however, that eventually you will deliver the speech, not read it; therefore you must write it down as if you are speaking it. There is a written language and a spoken one and you want to write your speech down in the spoken form otherwise, later, when you deliver it, it will sound as if you are reading it. It is not necessary to write down every word that you are going to say. The first draft may be in that form, yes, but your final text that you will take with you will only contain main ideas. Your written text must help you when you deliver the speech. Your eyes will move from your audience to your text all the time and every time that you come back to the text, your sight must land at the exact spot. Therefore the letters or print must be large enough for you to see the text easily while you are delivering the speech. A font size of 14 is usually sufficient. The writing should not overflow a page, because you are going to get lost. Let space separate different ideas from each other. Underline headings or use a larger print, but let them stand out. Number your pages so that they cannot get mixed up while you are busy and staple them together in one corner so that the wind cannot blow them off the table or lectern. The secret of success is that you stay in command of the situation right through your speech and for that you must be organised, such as having a text outline or framework that you can follow easily.

When you write it down, make sure that you have it right from the start. An address must have a certain framework and you should write it down within this framework. It starts with an introduction where the theme of the speech is announced, sometimes in the form of a problem statement, and the objective of the speech is made known to the audience. The audience is now tuned in. They know what you are going to talk about and where you are heading.

After the introduction you should start on the main body of the address. Try to mould your speech in the form of an argument and everything you say must then substantiate that argument. Try to keep your speech lean, in other words, no frills or little extras to take the attention away from the main argument. Try to see your speech as a trip from point A to point B (the place you want to reach at the end or your objective). Try to reach point B in the shortest possible way. If you follow a 'highway' of logical argumentation, your audience will find it easy to follow you, but if you use little twisting and turning off roads to get there, you are going to lose at least some of your audience.

Divide your speech into sections. Each section must form a logical entity and the sections must follow in a logical sequence on the road to point B, your conclusion.

The conclusion should be the high point of your address. Your conclusion has to be the culmination of your argument. It must be strong and short, bringing together all the ideas expressed during the address. Some speakers use the conclusion to wind down their speech. That is wrong because it will cause the audience to switch off. Your conclusion should therefore be brief, but full of impact and must stop at such a high note that your last words will echo in the minds of your audience. When you travel from point A to point B, the best moment of your trip is when you arrive at point B. Your speech should be exactly the same.

**Preparing visual aids**. Visual aids should be aids to your speech and to your audience, not stumbling blocks. If you do not prepare your visual aids well and practise using them, they can easily become stumbling blocks. Visual aids, such as transparencies, cannot contain your whole speech. They should only show main ideas and rounded figures. Transparencies or charts should never be cluttered. The more you put on a transparency or chart, the longer it takes for your audience to read it, which will cause pauses in your speech while you wait for them to finish reading. In this way you lose momentum and you lose the rapport you have established with your audience. Further, the more you put on, the smaller the print gets so that the audience cannot read it properly and then your visual aids have become meaningless. In order to remain organised, number your transparencies, slides or charts and indicate in the text when to use each of them.

**Practising**. You cannot go out and deliver a speech without prior practice. If you are an inexperienced speaker this becomes even more important. Only after a few practice rounds will you have the confidence to speak in front of an audience. Time yourself when you run through your speech because it must fit within the allocated time. Make sure that it fits into the allocated time because it is very annoying when you go over your allotted time and perhaps use someone else's time for your speech. A speech should, in any case, never exceed twenty minutes because that is about the attention span of the average person. A twenty minute speech will fill about eight pages with 1.5 line spacing and a 14 font size.

## 16.4 DELIVERY

All the preparation in the world cannot ensure that you deliver the address successfully. It can only help to make it easier and to have a better chance of success. There are specific aspects that require attention to ensure success:

**Text dependency**. If you are too dependent on the text in front of you, you are going to read the speech instead of delivering it. The main problem with this is that you will not be able to make and maintain eye contact with your audience because you will have your nose in the text all the time in order to not lose your place. If you do not have eye contact with your audience you do not really communicate with them. Rather, you transmit or broadcast and you have no way of ensuring that your message overcomes all the barriers that exist. If you read to your audience there is always a gap between you and them, but if you deliver your speech the interaction is close and alive and the whole situation becomes dynamic. However, if you deliver your speech without being independent of the written text, you can pick up serious trouble if you forget what you wanted to say or if you leave out important aspects so that your argument becomes difficult to follow. So, you can only deliver your speech and stay afloat if you have prepared yourself very well.

**Dress**. Your dress must be appropriate for the occasion. If it is not, you will feel out of place and the audience may pay more attention to your dress than to your address. Your clothes can put you apart from the audience that can impede lively communication and the audience may even feel that you do not respect their dignity if you are inappropriately dressed. Your dress must, therefore, be appropriate to the occasion and to the audience. Therefore, make sure beforehand what function it is and what kind of people will be present.

**Stance**. Remember that non-verbal communication is just as important as verbal communication. Therefore the way you stand or sit in front of an audience will tell the audience something of how you feel and how you approach the occasion. Your stance should therefore never portray nervousness, arrogance or boredom, three totally different portraits, but equally devastating to a successful speech. It must exude confidence, eagerness and enthusiasm. Most importantly, your body language must be in line with your verbal communication, otherwise you will not get a willing and sympathetic ear. The audience will also follow the example your body portrays. If your body looks tired or bored, the audience's bodies will portray the same, but if you look vibrant and energetic, the audience will also look vibrant and energetic. The problem is that people always believe body language rather than verbal language. If your words are enthusiastic, but your body language portrays disinterest and boredom, the audience will believe your body language.

**Confidence**. You cannot be successful if you do not believe in your own ability. Never start your speech with an apology. Do not apologise or not knowing very much about the subject. If you apologise for your little knowledge the audience will regard it as not worthwhile listening to you. If you apologise for being inexperienced the audience will wait for you to make mistakes rather than listen to what you have to say. Do not apologise for having had only little time to prepare the speech. If you apologise for the little time you had to prepare, the audience might feel that you do not regard them as important enough and therefore have a negative feeling towards you. Instead, try to start with a few strong and well-spoken sentences. It will give you confidence and will impress your audience so that they will pay attention. Choose at least three short and strong sentences and learn them by heart so that your start can be fluent and impressive.

**Enthusiasm**. If you are not enthusiastic about your message you cannot expect any one else to be. Remember that enthusiasm is experienced in verbal and non-verbal communication. Your message has a much greater chance to be accepted if you are enthusiastic about it. There are words conveying enthusiasm and if you want to win your audience over, you can use them. Here are a few of them: shall, can, success/succeed, message, believe, dedicate, hope, utmost.

**Rapport**. The secret of successful communication between people is that there is rapport between them. Rapport means that people have positive feelings for one another. As a public speaker, you must therefore show that you understand the situation of your audience, that you have respect for them, that you share their concerns and their hopes, and that you have their interests at heart. They must have positive feelings towards you for what you are saying and for the way that you are saying it. Try to encourage, even create a feeling of 'us' between you and your audience because then communication becomes so much easier and, more importantly, more amicable and friendly. We are focussing here on your audience, because when you have established rapport between you and the audience, you have captured them and they are then truly your audience.

**Voice intonation**. When we sing we use different notes. We should do the same when we speak. If you want to take your audience with you, if you want to keep their attention, you must use your voice to do it. A lower key denotes seriousness or gravity, while a higher key gives a feeling of lightness and happiness. Emphasis on certain words shows that they are important. Repeating a sentence or phrase, perhaps slightly slower and louder, shows that you regard it as very important and that you want the audience to remember it. So you can underline a word or phrase also in speech. A longer than usual pause after a sentence tells the audience that you want them to think about it and let it sink in. While you can say certain things louder, it is not good to shout at your audience. They may consider you rude. Also, be careful of speaking too softly so that your audience cannot hear you properly. Remember, if they cannot hear you properly you have not crossed even the first barrier in the way of communication. (See Chapter 10.) Another problem, especially with inexperienced speakers who are nervous, is that they tend to speak too fast. This makes it difficult for the audience to follow and it makes it difficult for the speaker to use intonation to keep the audience captured. A voice is not just there to convey a message. It should also be used to maintain interest and attention and to tell the audience of enthusiasm, importance and seriousness. When a voice is used as a mechanical means of conveying a message, it usually lulls an audience to sleep. But if it is used as an instrument that can play beautiful melodies, you have a captive audience.

**Eye contact**. Normally, when you speak to someone you try to maintain eye contact. You should try to do the same with an audience. If you have eye contact with someone it is like a channel that you have built, which you can use for communication. Without it communication becomes that much more difficult. In the case of a large audience it may be difficult to maintain eye contact with all members all the time, but at least try to stand in such a position that you can see all the faces and that every member of the audience can see your face.

**Mannerisms**. Be careful of mannerisms because they annoy audiences and/or they act as distractions. Annoying mannerisms may be to scratch yourself or to stand with your hands in your pockets, or to play with money or keys in your pocket. Another annoying mannerism is to take your glasses off and put them on repeatedly, or to lift your waterglass and to put it down continuously without drinking from it. Distracting mannerisms may be to move from the one leg to the other in the same rhythm all the time. Such a movement has a hypnotic effect on the audience. Mannerisms in speech can also distract or annoy. Be careful not to punctuate every sentence with an 'eeh' or a guttural throat cleaning. Avoid phrases like 'you know', 'sort of', 'on the other hand', 'seemingly', 'therefore', and 'etcetera'. Remember, you are on the highway between point A and B and these mannerisms are potholes in the road that slow you down.

**Visual aids**. Visual aids can be very helpful, but then you must know when you are going to use them and how you are going to do it. Visual aids should never bring your speech to a stop. This breaks the logical line and flow of your argument and disturbs the concentration of the audience. In this way visual aids can have the exact opposite effect than what they were intended for. Visual aids and the verbal message should become one, should become integrated so that the one never plays second fiddle to the other, or hinders the other's message. This you can only accomplish if you have practised your address with your visual aids. You must also be very clear in your mind what role the visual aids will play. One often sees a speaker following a text until the first slide is shown and then he/she starts to talk off the slide, only to later look through several pages of text to try and find the correct place when the slides have run out.

**Outside influences**. There are always some external influences that usually act as disturbances. You should identify these quickly and try to counteract them. Noise from outside is usually one of the most serious external influences. If you cannot counteract it like closing a door or window, it will be better to stop altogether and first remove the source of the noise before you continue. Outside influences can also manifest themselves inside the hall or room where you are delivering your speech. Cellular phones, loud coughing, the creaking and clanging of chairs, the buzz of an air conditioner and the movement of people all belong to this category. Outside influences need not be so disruptive if your audience is captured by your presentation and if you use all the tools available to you.

**Response from audience**. If your audience does not react to your speech, your efforts are fruitless. An audience responds with laughter, a buzz after you have said something, interjections such as 'yes!' or 'right!' or just a nod of affirmation from a few people. You should respond to those responses because then you have true and natural communication going. You must be wide awake to pick up these responses and then to respond to them by emphasis or repetition or by saying something in a different way.

## 16.5 CONCLUSION

Some people are better speakers than others. Therefore, we can say that public speaking is an art and some people are born with the talent to do it. While this is true, it does not mean that those with fewer talents cannot be successful speakers. It simply means that they must try harder and concentrate on all the pitfalls and use as many of the tools as possible to make their public speaking successful.

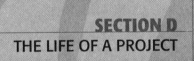

# SECTION D
## THE LIFE OF A PROJECT

## CHAPTER 17
# CONTACT-MAKING

## 17.1 INTRODUCTION

Contact-making is community development's most important phase, even though, at this stage, development has not taken place yet. The community development worker's (CDW's) initial contact with a community will make or break a development effort. It is of the utmost importance that it be done correctly. In a previous chapter we covered the CDW's attitude. It is at the initial contact-making stage that attitude is all-important. If the CDW appears to be a know-it-all or a 'superhuman', people may react in several ways; all of which are bad for community development. The community may develop a grudge against the CDW for disrupting their everyday lives or they may resent a know-it-all attitude and withhold their co-operation and support. Alternatively, they may be so impressed with the CDW's knowledge and contacts that they may assume that they have no place in finding solutions to their own problems. Initial enthusiasm will result from the great impression made by the CDW. But it is misdirected, applauding the CDW's presumed excellence instead of the people's innate abilities. The attitude that generates unrealistic expectations is the most damaging of all, leading to inevitable disappointment and the demise of all enthusiasm.

The contact-making phase has three objectives. First, the people must get to know and accept the CDW; second, the CDW must get to know and understand the people and their circumstances; and third, the people and the CDW must get to the point where they can identify a need that they can address through a project.

In this chapter we are going to use a case study to illustrate how these three goals can be reached during the contact-making phase.

## 17.2 CASE STUDY

In the excerpt from the case study below (King, 1965) the dilemmas faced by the professional are well illustrated. We will call the case study 'The Story of Miss Najafi', which took place 50 years ago in the then Persia, now Iran. Miss Najmej Najafi was a young woman of a well-to-do family in Teheran. After studying in America she returned to Teheran determined to help the villagers of her native Persia (Iran) realise a better existence within the pattern of their ancient culture. The Ford Foundation granted her a small scholarship and complete independence of action. This is her account of how she gained the confidence of the village of Sarbandan where she decided to work.

## CASE STUDY

## THE STORY OF MISS NAJAFI

I clambered out of the ancient automobile that had brought me fifty-six miles from Teheran ... I looked over the rooftops of the village to the apricot and cherry orchards fanning up over the foothills; my eyes followed the clear stream of mountain water which we Persians called the jube as it flowed through the centre of the village. Along this stream, I could see people going and coming. My people. My heart shook for a moment! Perhaps, I thought, perhaps this is the place.

Very near, there was a tea house ... In a moment the owner stood before me. 'I would like tea', I told him. 'Bring one for yourself too so that we may talk together.' As we drank tea he told me that he was called Mash'hadi Mokhtar and that he was the owner of the place. ...

'You own a very fine tea house. But who owns the village?'

'Many own land here.'

'No landlords?'

'Some landlords. A few big ones. I am one of these.'

'You are a man of importance,' I told him.

The man had taken my sincere words for dangerous flattery. Again his eyes were veiled.

'Another tea, my lady?'

'Another tea. A tea for each of us, please.' Again he came with tea. I curtained my eyes, too, and we were strangers.

'Well, Mashdi Mokhtar, what about the population of Sarbandan?'

'Almost two thousand – in the summer.'

'And in the winter?'

'They do not stay in this place ... they do work in the rice fields of Mazandaran. Only women and children and old men are left here.'

We talked for a time and I asked if the people had a bath.

'Bath? How could we have? Our forefathers made one about a hundred years ago but it is ruined now. Its pool is so unclean that no one has the desire to go into it.' Then he looked at me with a flash of anger. 'My lady, why do you ask these questions of me? Why?'

At this moment I loved Mash'hadi Mokhtar. I loved him because I saw the fear leap into his eyes, and I understood this fear. My people are proud and they have much to be proud of. How can they be happy when so many want to change them?

'Because I think I may want to make my home here, Mashdi Mokhtar,' I said very quietly. 'I think perhaps Sarbandan is the place for me.'

He left me and returned with his clopogh, a sort of long pipe. He drew on it two or three times. Then, wiping the mouthpiece first with his fingers then against his cheek, he handed it to me. I drew two or three suffocating breaths and returned it to him. 'Do you have a school, Mash'hadi Mokhtar?'

He smiled ... 'Indeed we do. Four years ago we built the school. We turned it over to the Ministry of Education. We have grades one, two, three, and four. Next year, perhaps, we will have five and six. If not next year, at least some year.'

'And is there a school for the girls?'

'What are you talking about, my lady? A school for girls?'

I changed the subject. 'Tell me, does Sarbandan have a clinic?'

'Clinic? What is a clinic?'

> 'A place of care for the sick.'
> 'How would we have such a place when we have no doctor?'
> 'I am hungry, Mashdi Mokhtar. What can we eat?'

The CDW needs to establish rapport between him/her and the people because with rapport communication is so much easier and meaningful. This rapport is established while the CDW learns more about the people and their area, and they learn to know him/her. Ms Najafi, not knowing the community, immediately started probing into the issues she knew to be important among developing people: a bath for hygiene, a school for education, especially the girls, and a clinic for treating the sick. But Mashdi Mokhtar, an important man in the village, listened to her questions with suspicion. And for that you cannot blame him, in fact, Ms Najafi appreciated this attitude and detected her people's pride in it. Her attitude towards the individual she was talking to, the people of the little village she was visiting and the poor of her country in general can be admired and followed.

> I wanted to work 'heart to heart', not in the mechanised way of organisations. Besides, I did not want to make a little America in the mountains of Persia (Iran). I wanted my people to stay as they were, keeping the feeling of security that goes with doing things the sweet, almost sacred way. I wanted to see if a better life could be built on a foundation of native customs and mores. For my people, I wanted happiness rather than that colder goal that is sometimes called progress (development).

Knowledge by CDWs of the poverty context is an important prerequisite to developing an empathetic approach towards assisting in the development of people. The ability to use such knowledge is, however, tested when the professional meets the poor face to face. Outsiders such as professionals seldom meet the poor '... when they are met, they often do not speak; when they do speak they are often cautious and deferential; and what they say is often either not listened to, or brushed aside, or interpreted in a bad light' (Chambers, 1983:104).

> When Mash'hadi Mokhtar returned ... I asked, 'Do you have a village council?'
> 'Yes, we have. But the members seldom see each other. When they meet there is nothing but quarrelling at the tea house.'
> 'Tell me, why do the old men quarrel?'
> 'My lady, in Sarbandan the people are divided into two factions. We even have two Kadkhodas.'
> 'Two Kadkhodas?' A Kadkhoda is a responsible man selected by the large landholders to keep order in the village. ... 'Two Kadkhodas? That is incredible.'
> 'But we have. You see, we are two tribes and our landholders...'
> The walls of the clinic and the school that I had just built in my mind crumbled away. Two factions. Two tribes. Cooperation, which is always hard to achieve with people as individualistic as my people, might be impossible. I would have to spend time and energy avoiding petty jealousies, ironing out petty disputes. I could not afford to waste myself that way. I was defeated before I began.
> 'Come,' he said, standing. 'Allow me to show you the village, my lady.'
> Half reluctantly, I followed him along the banks of the jube. Women were washing clothes along both sides.

> The crying of a lamb drew my eyes upstream.
>
> Two men were killing the little creature, and its blood was flowing into the water. Between the men and the women bent over their washing, a half-grown girl dipped a jug into the stream and lifted it, dripping, to her shoulders.
>
> Sarbandan needs me, I thought. I looked at the faces of the women and the children. Their skin was transparent; their cheeks like spring petals. Again my heart shook me.

Through talking and listening, a CDW can really get to know the community. Ms Najafi discovered very important aspects about the people and their area when she started to listen to one of the people, a leader from the community where she intended to work.

Let us return to the story of Ms Najafi. She moved to Sarbandan and rented a room to stay. First she had convinced the elders that she was not from a development agency or from a government department but a volunteer willing to teach at a school. She successfully introduced the idea of building a school but proposed that the council discuss it first. After settling in she set out to meet the households and do a survey in an informal fashion.

> I knew that I had much to learn and that I had to learn as I worked, but I was determined to start out in an orderly way. Although I did not know the strange sea I had embarked on, nevertheless I needed to chart my course and decide upon my destination. Carefully I drew a map of the village. On it I placed every home. Starting from the west and moving to the east, street by street, alley by alley, house by house, I would visit every home. Sometime, and that very soon, I would know the names of everyone in the village, I would know which families were rich, which ones were poor, which ones owned land ...

Ms Najafi used the contact-making period to get to know the people and their circumstances. In fact, while she had the idea of starting a school for girls, at this stage it was not uppermost in her mind. Her primary concern at this stage was to get acquainted. She was also concerned about her acceptance by the people as the following excerpt will show.

> Shortly after dusk I set out the things for supper: tea, rice, cheese, sugar. In the villages a cone of sugar ... is considered the most desirable possession in the world ... Three women, wrapped in their chadors, each carrying a lantern, were coming to call on me. They stood outside the doorway until I said, 'Won't you come in and have tea with me?' Glancing covertly about them, they came in and stood awkwardly just inside my house. 'I am breaking sugar,' I told them, not because they could not see me do it but because I must say something and could not speak the questions that were in my head Who are you? What names do you have? Are your children healthy? Why do you not keep them clean? How much money do you have for food in a year? ... I thought of some of the ... social workers asking people who were almost starving for a handful of rice if they were serving their families the seven basic foods every day. So I might have asked, What do you know about nutrition? I could ask none of these questions. Some would never be answered. Some would be answered later – much later. I said 'I am breaking sugar.' 'May I help?' the youngest of the three, a woman of about thirty, asked. ' I would be so grateful. Now I can prepare the tea.' I turned the cone over to her.
>
> Many times I have knelt in a mosque at the closing month of Ramazan; but never in a simple mosque like this ... After the service I stood in the doorway with a reed basket filled with halva which I offered to the

> women as they left ... I heard one of them say as she turned away from me 'She's young but she is a good Moslem.'
>
> I dressed carefully for my visits. I did not wear the dress of the women of Sarbandan; that would have been effrontery. The dress belonged to them and I was a stranger. I put on a full long skirt of bright print, a long-sleeved, high-necked blouse that matched it. Over my hair I put a kerchief. I suspect that one must have a feeling for matters of this kind and cannot follow a fixed rule. The only guide is probably a sincere sensitivity to the feeling of others.

Ms Najafi is extremely careful not to act with disrespect towards the people and the way they socialise, their religion and how they perform it, and their dress.

No community is a homogeneous entity living in idealistic, caring harmony. The people are also not ignorant — they have survived without much help for generations — and they have cultural practices that assisted in their survival. Not all people will respond positively to professionals, or any other outsider entering a community. And not all responses will be equally honest. In situations of continued deprivation any outsider can be viewed as a potential resource of goods, money or job opportunities. Therefore the professional entering a poor community should guard against creating expectations or viewing him/herself as a redeemer, a superhuman who will save the community. In Ms Najafi's case she found the people decent towards her, but definitely not overenthusiastic or very friendly, for that matter.

In the excerpt above, Ms Najafi began to understand the pitfalls of getting acquainted with the community. Of course, the flipside of the coin is even more important: allowing the community to get acquainted with her. Ms Najafi realised that speaking to the leaders only would not make her fully acquainted with the community. She also needed to talk to the women, the children and men: at the river, in the market and other places.

While doing the survey she came to the house of Fatemeh ...

> ... I could hear the mewing of a sick child. I went around the back. A slender young woman, dressed in a bright cotton print, holding a whimpering child in her arms, was bent over a black kettle hanging above an open fire.
>
> 'Salaam,' I said quietly. She didn't turn, just kept stirring.
>
> 'May I help you?'
>
> She turned her face towards me. There was a look of complete despair in her red-rimmed eyes and I could trace the tracks of tears down her smoke-grayed face. I took the child from her arms and looked down into his yellowing face. He was six months old perhaps, but unbelievably thin and dry-skinned.
>
> 'He isn't going to die. Six I have that died, but Ali will live!' There was hysteria in her voice. 'I won't let him die!'
>
> 'What are you making?' I watched her rough hand, white-knuckled around the shapeless iron spoon.
>
> Her glance at me said, 'Why, you stupid woman! How is it that you don't know?' Her lips said defiantly, 'Medicine.'
>
> 'And what is this medicine?'
>
> 'The blood of a living raven boiled with crushed beetles.' Her eyes, wide with fear, came to my face for a minute. 'It is a good medicine?'

'No, no, no!' I wanted to cry out. 'It is not a good medicine!' Instead I said, as calmly as I could, 'It is a strange medicine for one so small, so helpless.'

I did not know how to answer her. All I knew was that I must save this little one from that horrible brew. I moved to overturn the kettle, but I stopped myself. What right had I to do this? The baby's father had probably spent hours in snaring a living raven so that the blood could drip from it while it still lived.

I reached for the child and the mother put him in my arms. Think of something, think of something, I told myself as I hushed him against my breast.

In the tiny village of Japon, about five or six kilometres from Sarbandan, the government had opened a small, well-stocked clinic. I did not know who was in charge there. I didn't even know that I knew there was a clinic, but I trusted this moment of inspiration. 'Come,' I said. 'You hold the baby and I will go rent a donkey. We will take him to a doctor.' ...

I described the cough. 'Croup,' he said, 'with a respiratory infection.' He studied the yellow face, the yellow eyeballs of the child. 'Give plenty of boiled water and as much milk as he will take.' The mother put her hands on her shrunken breasts, a mute gesture that said the milk had left her breasts and she could not feed the child.

The doctor put a package of dried milk into my hands. 'You'll know what to do with this,' he said. Then he gave the mother a small bottle of medicine. 'When the child coughs, give him a dose of this every few minutes until he vomits,' he said.

'Vomits?' she questioned.

'Yes, that will clear his throat for breathing.'

When I returned, my home was full of women with their children in their arms. 'You helped Fatemeh's child,' they told me. 'My child, too, needs help.'

So now God had answered my question. I had asked Him where I should begin. Was it to be with education, with industry, with sanitation? Now I knew. Unprepared as I was in the field of medicine, I must begin with a clinic.

And so Ms Najafi came to understand what the real need in the community was. She also realised that in spite of a good education and knowledge about developmental issues, she could not proceed without first gaining the confidence of those whom she passionately wanted to help. If we look at the other case study dealing with the contact-making (Case Study 14: *The case of the community worker who met his match*), we detect quite a different attitude and a different way of going about it. The objective of that contact-making differs from that of Ms Najafi's case. The CDW is much more in the foreground, much more hands on, taking the initiative and accepting his superiority to those he works with.

## 17.3 PREPARATION FOR ENTRY

A CDW cannot just wade into a community and, from then on, act on the spur of the moment. CDWs need an operational strategy to guide their actions. One should not think that Ms Najafi just plunged willy-nilly into the community. She made careful preparations, such as getting an organisation to support her, obtaining funds for the venture and deciding the way she wanted to approach the matter. She was not even sure whether she will work in Sarbandan.

The CDW must plot a strategy, leaving room for a good-, a bad- and a worse-case scenario. The CDW should discuss this draft strategy with his/her supervisor and colleagues and, taking their feedback into account, change and improve it where necessary. In fact, a team of CDWs with their supervisor can sit together and devise the operational strategy. Only after this has been done, can the CDW enter an area with the view to facilitate a project.

If the CDW uses the guidelines discussed above, his/her operational strategy will be an adaptive and milieu-sensitive tool. In compiling the strategy the CDW should consider the following questions:

First, it must consider the position of the CDW's organisation. What are the organisation's mission and objectives? What is the CDW's brief? What resources can the organisation provide?

Second, the CDW's own position must be considered. What is his/her objective? How should he/she set about reaching that objective? What time constraints must be kept in mind? How much time can the CDW spend in the community?

Third, the community's position must be considered. How large is the community? What type of leadership does it have? What are the political, social, cultural, economic and psychological environments? What aspects of the natural environment need special consideration? Who will be the target group? What resources will come from the community itself? All these aspects must be considered and moulded within a structure containing the following:

▶ CDW's goals: What do you want to achieve?
▶ CDW's plans: How are you going to achieve your goals?
▶ Time frame: In what order and within what length of time are you going to work towards achieving your goals?
▶ Side issues: How are you going to approach the various steps you are planning? What resources will you need? Where are you going to find those resources? (Note: this does not refer to sources needed by the community/organisation to achieve their aims.)

Important things to remember:

▶ Be realistic in setting goals for yourself and in planning to achieve them. Don't aim too high because this will put you under pressure and if you cannot carry out your strategy, you will become frustrated.
▶ Write your strategy down so that you can refer to it regularly.
▶ Evaluate your actions in terms of your strategy regularly (preferably once a week).
▶ Discuss your strategy and your evaluation of your own actions with your colleagues or anyone with knowledge and experience. In fact, it would be better if the CDWs of one organisation could form a team who work out their operational strategy together and even with their supervisor present.

CDWs should remember that their operational strategy is not a blueprint that cannot be changed. It is an opportunity for them to learn how to devise and implement their plans better next time. CDWs should use their operational strategy as a guide for their own actions. This is the only way in which they are also going to be part of and benefit from the learning process.

## 17.4   ENTRY

The contact-making phase starts with the CDW's entry into the area. Entrance into a well-defined community is the exception, not the rule, although in the case study the village was rather well-defined although they had the trouble of two tribes sharing the same area. Usually the CDW enters an area inhabited by a mass of people belonging to more than one community, representing various institutions and groupings, and subject to all the stratifications  that a layered political, social and economic environment can provide, see Chapters 2 and 7.

The CDW enters a rational social life experience. People naturally regard their daily activities as being the most appropriate to their circumstances. Therefore, the society's members regard the activities taking place as normal. People are also suspicious of change. This holds true for people trapped in poverty. Even when they suffer deprivation, they tend to adapt to it, becoming complacent rather than upsetting everything by effecting change. Galbraith (1979) calls it the culture of poverty. The CDW, therefore should enter an area without broadcasting that he/she wants to bring about change. It is better and safer to display empathy with and interest in the people's situation, like Ms Najafi did. The people must come to a point where they realise that change is needed, usually through a process of awareness creation. It is not something that they should be told by a CDW who has just entered the area, as in Case Study 14: *The case of the community worker who met his match.*

It is clear that the principle of learning is important in this situation. The many pitfalls facing a CDW can best be obviated by following the learning process approach. This approach stipulates that the CDW should enter an area without a preconceived objective or programme for the people to adopt and follow. Yes, he/she should have an operational strategy, but that only covers what the CDW's approach should be, not what the people should do. The CDW should keep an open agenda that he/she and the community will fill gradually as they get to know one another better and after they have completed a process of analysing their situation (Korten, 1980). This is the most natural way of coming to a point of needs identification. Ms Najafi was in danger of negating the learning process approach when she pre-empted the realities of the community by announcing to the council that she wanted to open a girls' school (not recorded above). However, the way she made contact from that point on helped her to become aware of the most important need in a natural way.

The unnatural way, which is most definitely not recommended, is for the CDW to establish contact with the community by way of a public meeting. Apart from it being unnatural, a public meeting showcases the CDW and he/she should only take a small step to become the community's redeemer. Case Study 14 illustrates this point nicely. No community development can and will take place if the CDW is cast in such a light. Buildings can be erected, facilities provided, but the community will not gain any of the human objectives (the first principle) of community development and they will remain stuck in the deprivation trap regardless of the physical results (the principle of release) of the project.

## 17.5   GOALS OF CONTACT-MAKING

We named the three goals of contact-making earlier on. Let us now see what they contain.

### 17.5.1    Getting to know the CDW

The people must get to know and accept the CDW for what he/she is and has come to do. The CDW should remember that people are not obliged to be accepting. People are autonomous and they can therefore accept or reject a CDW. The community's acceptance must be earned. There are CDWs who think that people must and will accept them because of their position in government structures. Such CDWs will find that it is easy for people to say that they accept without any real commitment. Ms Najafi is an excellent example of earning acceptance. It was only when she took the seriously ill baby from its mother and told herself to do something that she had started to earn acceptance. CDWs also cannot obtain acceptance through marketing themselves. This part of the contact-making should also not be rushed. Later it may be necessary to pick up speed, but at this stage enough time should be available so that people can accept the CDW's bona fides over a period of time. Ms Najafi took her time with her house to house visits. She wanted people to get used to her being among them. This may also be a good time to make sure that there is no misunderstanding about the CDW's goal, his/her position and his/her role. Ms Najafi made sure that there was no misunderstanding about her position. She was not from the government, she was not from a multi-national NGO, she had no logistical or financial backup other than the small bursary. In other words, acceptance must be based on the correct understanding of the situation.

The people will not be receptive to development before they have become fully acquainted with the CDW. The CDW can help the process along by informal talks, friendliness, a keen interest in the people and their circumstances, and by just being present. These are the things that Ms Najafi did. A brief visit by the CDW once or twice a month will not win the people's acceptance. Regular and longer presence is needed to establish a strong relationship with the people. The CDW in Case Study 14: *The case of the community worker who met his match* gave himself no chance for this. This also means that one CDW should not serve too many communities.

It is important that the CDW acknowledges the leaders in the area, especially the formally elected ones. The CDW must visit them and explain his/her role to them. Circumstances will dictate whether formal leaders will later participate in a community development project. At this contact-making stage it is necessary only to acknowledge their position and to ensure that they know why a CDW is working in their area. Ms Najafi did the right thing to meet with the leaders on only her second visit to the village (not recorded above). It established her position and role formally there and then. The CDW in Case Study 14, however, never got to the headman before it was too late.

A CDW should not pick champions early on in the contact-making phase. A person may act and look like a leader and may convince a stranger of his/her credentials as an accepted leader, but at the same time they could be mistrusted by many of the ordinary folk. If the CDW is associated with such a person, the mistrust and animosity directed towards that person can easily rub off on the CDW, making acceptance by the people nearly impossible. In this instance Ms Najafi could have made a serious blunder by associating with the tea house owner from the first moment of entry, but luckily he was apparently accepted as at least one of the leaders. In the other Case Study 14 the CDW picked someone who was not on a good footing with the headman, something that immediately made the CDW the headman's opponent – the last thing he wanted to be. Again, good observation skills are called for. A CDW must remain vigilant to avoid being associated with false or unpopular leaders by the community.

CDWs must be open about their position with everyone they meet. Their bona fides will suffer grave setbacks if misunderstanding surrounds their role. If they are intentionally misleading from the outset and are later found out, it is even worse.

The argument may be put forward that because of this potential pitfall, it would be better to use a public meeting to introduce the CDW and inform the meeting of his/her role in the community. While there is merit in this suggestion, it is still fraught with danger. A political leader may try to make the most of the occasion and have the CDW in front or on the stage with the other leaders. Immediately, the association is wrong. The CDW should never be seen as a leader. Further, the leader may use the opportunity to impress those present that he/she has organised that the CDW now works in their area. Again the association is wrong. The CDW is not in the service of the leader. The leader may even go further and try to show how many good things will flow from this arrangement and by doing so he/she makes the CDW a superhuman and raises the expectations of all those present that the CDW is going to save them from their problems. So, while a public meeting may be an opportune moment to inform the community of the presence and work of a CDW, there are just too many dangers attached to it to make it worthwhile.

It is good if the people regard a CDW from the outset as a compassionate person. It is amazing how easily people are affected by enthusiasm and motivated by compassion and how keen they are to return the friendliness – to the extent that they are prepared to forgive the occasional blunder from the CDW. Compassion from the CDW leads to a deeper and more sincere relationship with the people and it makes community development so much easier. Ms Najafi's hospitality towards the women who visited her, her kindness at the mosque, and her total commitment to save the sick child's life, are indications of her compassion. On the other hand, if the CDW is aloof and acts as an important government officer, people will accept his/her status and access to important people. That is not where a CDW wants to be. It creates a lot of expectations and places the CDW in a formal position where compassion will be slightly out of place.

### 17.5.2 Getting to know the people

The contact-making phase is the ideal time for the CDW to get to know the people and their circumstances. He/she must get to know the environment and all the social groupings sharing the environment. He/she must therefore make a demographic and sociological study of the area. In Chapter 18 we discuss ways to do studies and surveys in a fashion that is well suited to the principles of community development.

The CDW must augment information gained locally with information stored in government and agency offices. Statistical information, which may be difficult to compile, may be readily available in some government office. Information from government offices should, however, never replace the local survey completely, because, as we will see in Chapter 18, the local survey is much more than only gleaning information.

This is the time to start identifying resources and obstacles to their use. Not only is the physical environment important, but all those environments discussed in Chapter 2. The CDW must know and understand the possibilities and constraints of these environments.

During this stage, the CDW must make contact with formal and informal groupings. These groups, more than individuals, will be interested in the CDW's presence and they might also harbour some reservations about the envisaged task. The CDW must allay their fears, but must also analyse them with a view to earmark one or more groupings as project action groups.

### 17.5.3 Analysing the needs

During the contact-making phase a CDW cannot but notice the people's needs. Through observation, through listening what the people say and through some survey, a fairly clear picture emerges. In the case of Ms Najafi the picture emerges quite clearly. In her mind a clinic was not primary, simply because she was not medically trained. Her heart was on a school for girls. But because she has not pushed her ideas and let the situation rather dictate, it became quite clear where the need lay and what the people thought of it. It is also possible that previous research identified needs. This then, is the time for the CDW to find out how the people perceive their needs. It is also an important time to start changing any negative feelings the people may have about their circumstances and their capacity to do something about them. In other words, the CDW must suggest to them that they can do something to meet at least some of their needs. Identifying needs can be a very negative activity; it can even be hypochondriacal. In itself, there is nothing positive about needs identification. It is necessary, therefore, that people be led to understand that they should not accept their abjection, but should start thinking positively of using their abilities to do something about them. We will come back to this aspect in Chapter 19. Community development cannot start until at least some people have a positive attitude. They may still have doubts, but they must be prepared to try alleviating their own poverty. This has a lot to do with mobilisation and motivation, discussed in Chapter 13.

The needs coming to the fore, people's perception of them, and groups identifying themselves with the needs will give the CDW a clear indication of who is going to comprise the action group once a development project develops out of the contact-making phase. Either an existing group (an interest group or club) will identify a specific need as its main concern, or a number of individuals will voice their concern about a certain matter. In the former case the interest group will become an action group for project purposes and in the latter case, the individuals and others influenced by them will form the action group. It can also happen that a large part of a community at a public or mass meeting identifies a need and decides to launch a project to address it. They may then select a project steering committee that will be the action group for their purposes.

Obviously, if there is a need for child care, the group that will concern itself with it will comprise, not senior citizens or teenagers, but mothers or parents of small children. A farming problem will be addressed by people concerned with farming and an education problem will be investigated and tackled by parents of children of school-going age. Yet, even if the need identification is done as described in this chapter, the CDW can experience difficulties. In Case Study 10: *The project that had its fences brought down*, it is shown how a CDW can break down initiative among grassroots people, in this case because of the mindset of his organisation.

## 17.6 CONCLUSION

As it has been described here, the contact-making phase is a natural progression from entry to project. All too often a CDW will enter an area with express orders to get a specific project going in the shortest possible time. Such projects never become the property of the people. They are agency efforts and, if there is some participation, it is only by casual participants, and, more often than not, 'free riders'. What has been described in this chapter is a process that evolves naturally as it is beautifully described in the case study. For that reason, many of the grave concerns about needs identification and group institution simply fall away. Figure 17.1 illustrates this process.

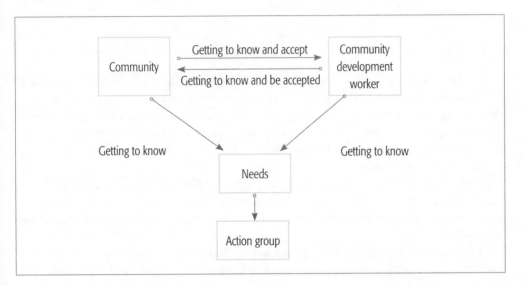

Figure 17.1 **The contact-making process**

It is clear that the contact-making phase is not a waste of time. Besides obtaining all the knowledge that must be acquired, it is a crucial relationship-building period. It is a time in which the people get to know the CDW for what he/she is: not a miracle worker, an enforcer of innovations, but a concerned person who wants to help. It is an important time to start breaking down the attitudinal constraints of feelings of inferiority, fear of the unknown and apathy. It is a time of team building; a team consisting of the CDW on the one side and a group of concerned people on the other – a group of people with enough interest, concern and willingness to do something about their needs. During this phase, the stage is set for community development to proceed.

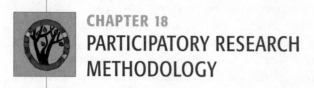

**CHAPTER 18**
# PARTICIPATORY RESEARCH METHODOLOGY

## 18.1 INTRODUCTION

In this chapter we discuss a qualitative method of research called Participatory Rapid Appraisal and Planning (PRAP). The method is characterised as qualitative because it is based on the perceptions, opinion and insight of people, and not on formulas working with figures and counting (quantifying) items. It is also characterised by participation because there is not a researcher vis-à-vis respondents, but all participants are researchers and respondents at the same time.

PRAP can be used for most facets of community development research: identification of community needs; surveying of resources in a community; recording of a history; measuring perceptions and so forth. It is also a useful tool to do assessment of progress with community development.

The purpose of this chapter is to provide an overview of the methodology and techniques associated with PRAP. The reader may use this information to apply and experiment with PRAP in community development. Please note, however: in community development we work with people. Their emotions, knowledge and humanness need to be respected at all times. So do not make guinea pigs of them, especially not without their knowledge and permission. The aim of doing social research, especially in and with a community should be:

> about creating a mutually respectful, win-win relationship in which participants are pleased to respond candidly, valid results are obtained, and the community considers the conclusions constructive (Mcauley, 2003:95).

When engaging the community in PRAP, the community development worker (CDW) should be guided by at least the following ethical principles:

- obtain the voluntary and informed consent (to be given by the research participant/community);
- ensure anonymity and confidentiality of the participant and information shared; and
- ensure that the research will do no harm to participants.

**Informed and voluntary consent**: Before starting a study, a researcher (in this case the CDW) must obtain informed voluntary consent from members of the community. This means that the participants are given all the relevant information about the research. The researcher must ensure that the participant understands the purpose and possible risks/benefits of participation. The participant must be free to choose, decline or withdraw from the research at any stage.

**Anonymity and confidentiality**: During a study, members of the community may reveal sensitive information, which, if linked to them, could cause harm. The researcher must ensure that they are protected, data and information remain confidential and anonymity is protected. Confidentiality is defined as 'a researcher undertaking not to publicly link a specific response or behaviour with a particular research participant' (Du Plooy, 2000:112).

**Do no harm**: Members of the community must be treated with respect and consideration. In a study, people may be exposed to physical danger, emotional discomfort, emotional stress, embarrassment and humiliation. Researchers should be particularly sensitive when working with children or disadvantaged and vulnerable people. Du Plooy (2000:109) recommends that researchers deal with the issue of 'doing no harm' by 'reviewing our perceptions, values and judgements as researchers – and ensuring that all these are open to public review'.

Participatory research always takes place with the wellbeing of the community as its goal. Therefore we agree with White and Pettit (2004:23) when they state: '… the key issue in participatory research is not so much the techniques used as the way in which the research is conducted and the relationships established between researchers and research participants'.

## 18.2 IDENTIFYING COMMUNITY NEEDS

The following list of do's and don'ts in need identification needs careful consideration. We place it here because we will show that these do's and don'ts conform perfectly with PRAP:

- Don't call a public meeting when you enter an area to do a needs identification exercise.
- Don't ask the people what their needs are.
- Don't tell the people what their needs are.
- Don't take the lead in the identification of needs.
- Don't regard your perception of needs as more important than theirs.
- Do just move among the people and their needs will be identified and discussed naturally.
- Do help the people to believe that they can do something about their needs.
- Do show the people that you believe in their ability to do something about their needs.

Having identified the needs of the people means that the CDW fulfils his/her role as a development generalist: but it does not mean it is his/her job to address all the needs. It means, however, that he/she must use the information and bring the community into contact with people with relevant knowledge and interest to address the need. For instance, if a need for a food garden is expressed by the community, the role of the CDW should be to bring the community in contact with the agricultural extension officer responsible for the area. An official from the education department should be brought into contact with the community in the case of a need related to skills development and education. The CDW can therefore act as broker in certain situations.

To return to our topic of PRAP, there are, of course, participatory tools that can be utilised to gain a better understanding of the community, determine and assess needs and plan, with community participation, development projects relevant to their needs.

In the social sciences new concepts and methodologies are created continuously. The methodology discussed here is participatory rural appraisal and planning (PRAP) (Selener et al, 1999). The origin of this methodology can be traced to academic disciplines such as Anthropology, Development Studies and Agricultural Extension. It has close relation with development approaches, such as the basic needs approach and community development with its more recent permutations of participatory development, adaptive administration and empowerment. According to De Beer and Swanepoel (1998:27), empowerment takes place in a milieu that emphasises: 'community knowledge, resources, self-reliance, initiative and decision making'.

The research techniques utilised clearly qualify PRAP as qualitative methodology number one using action research techniques. PRAP evolved from the earlier rapid rural appraisal (RRA) and its successors rapid and participatory rural action (RRA and PRA) (Chambers 1992:6 et seq). Bhatia (1995) refers to Empowering Rural Appraisal. Participatory Learning and Action (PLA) is one of the more recently evolved interpretations within the broader 'participatory research' school of thought. It is indeed said that: 'Participatory Learning and Action are closer to what many practitioners of PRA believe in and are doing, but PRA remains the usual label' (IDS, 1997:1). The ultimate form of participation in PLA is self-mobilisation where people take initiative independent of outside agencies to change systems (Pretty et al, 1995:61).

## 18.3 PRINCIPLES AND CHARACTERISTICS OF PRAP

To summarise, this 'basket' of related and overlapping approaches consists of the following approaches:

- Rapid Rural Appraisal (RRA);
- Participatory Rural Appraisal (PRA);
- Participatory Learning and Action (PLA); and
- Participatory Rural Appraisal and Planning (PRAP).

From all the permutations it becomes clear that these approaches (hereafter referred to as PRAP) are aimed at participation by the 'target group' in the action and appraisal, where learning and planning around the development issue that concerns the group, should be a result of the process. The approach allows outsiders to learn from the people and make use of indigenous technical knowledge.

Chambers (1992:7) identifies the following principles of RRA:

- **Optimising trade-offs.** This principle has a dual meaning: that of optimal ignorance — knowing what is not worth knowing, and appropriate imprecision — not measuring more precisely than is needed.
- **Offsetting biases.** By being relaxed and not rushing, listening not lecturing, being unimposing and by learning about the concerns and priorities of the poorer people, biases are neutralised.

- **Learning from and with rural people.** Having first-hand access to technical, physical and social knowledge of a community will give a clear insight into local perceptions.
- **Learning rapidly and progressively.** This means to not follow a blueprint programme but rather a learning and adaptive approach.
- **Triangulation.** This means verifying data by cross-checking.
- **Planning with the people.** The advantages of community participation are many, among them strengthened collaboration with outside agencies and an affirmation of community ownership of a project.

## 18.4 ADVANTAGES OF PRAP

Selener et al (1999:4–5) identify the following twelve advantages of PRAP:

- **Community mobilisation.** This empowers communities to solve those problems identified by them.
- **Use of visual techniques.** The techniques used, assist in information gathering in a way that activates and gives control to the community.
- **Participatory community analysis.** This includes identifying problems and potential solutions.
- **Promoting grass-roots development.** This would ensure that development takes place among the neediest.
- **Strengthening collaboration between the community and external organisations.** The resultant strategic partnerships contribute to sustained problem solving and community ownership of the project.
- **Realistic proposals.** The formulation of realistic proposals must be allowed for.
- **Promoting integration.** Diverse groups, including women and children, become part of the process.
- **Speed and low cost.** Once the initial contact has been made with the local power structures and their co-operation ensured, the fieldwork can be done in three to four days per group, with insignificant resources. Prior training of the facilitator-researcher is probably the most expensive part of the exercise.
- **CDWs 'wake up' to a new reality.** First-hand, community-based information is gathered that reduces the risk of 'desk-based' designs and increases the workability of the designed project.
- **The community has control over project definition.** This contributes to community ownership of the project.
- **First-hand information.** Since it is carried out in and with the community, it is based on first-hand information.
- **It encourages a systemisation process.** The collective memory and oral tradition of the community is used as source of information that can be systemised for future reference.

## 18.5 SOME PRAP TECHNIQUES

Selecting the most appropriate techniques from a long list is perhaps a bigger problem than applying it. Chambers (1992:8) identifies the following techniques:

- direct observation;
- secondary data review;
- transect and group walks;
- do-it-yourselves;
- key informants;
- semi-structured interviews;
- group interviews and discussions;
- chains (sequences) of interviews;
- key indicators;
- workshops and brainstorming;
- sketch mapping;
- aerial photographs;
- diagramming;
- wealth ranking;
- other ranking and scoring;
- measurement and quantification;
- ethno-histories and trend analysis;
- time lines (chronologies of events);
- stories, portraits and case studies;
- team management and interactions;
- key probes;
- calendaring;
- short, simple questionnaires; and
- rapid report writing in the field.

The list above is not complete but gives an indication of techniques that can be used. In the next few pages we discuss some of the techniques we found most useful in doing PRAP. When using these techniques one should go prepared and be certain what you want to know, which technique will bring the best results and how to record information. In direct observation, for instance, you will use a diary or make a summary for later use. With transect walks participants must note or report and this information needs to be discussed to make sure that all understand what is meant. The CDW may also need to make notes for own use and to later remind the group of its findings. The important thing to remember is to keep notes or summaries of information obtained in using the techniques or the exercise will be futile. The discussion below is based on Chambers (1997:187–190) and Chambers (2004:1–13).

### Secondary data review
Published and unpublished material, maps and aerial photographs give an overview of an area or community. Before entering a community or starting a PRAP exercise, a secondary data review should be conducted. This will help the CDW to become familiar with the community. It can also be done as part of PRAP and then it will not be an activity of the CDW alone and it will include also discussing and interpreting.

### Direct observation
This entails personal visits over time to areas to observe and identify dynamics and changes in the community. An observation checklist is a useful tool to keep track of observations.

Direct observation is useful in getting to know the community and for the community to get to know you (see Chapter 17). Observation over time also helps to turn the snapshot effect of a single observation act around.

### Transect and group walks
Walking through an area with and by local people frequently reveals resources and problems in an area. It provides an opportunity for first-hand observation of the micro-environment. It means meeting people, listening, asking, discovering, and identifying problems, resources, dynamics and many other issues. Participating community members are very important in this exercise because this gives them an opportunity to reveal local knowledge. Transect walks can also be undertaken to verify information on a map or model. Apart from its verifying function, it can also be used as an assessment tool to observe changes in infrastructure and changes in life patterns.

### Venn diagrams
A Venn diagram is useful to classify various objects into categories. It can be used to compare two or more objects or to identify and show links between a number of objects, for example, stakeholders can be identified and their link to each other and/or the community can be visibly illustrated. This helps to form a picture of who is involved and how they relate to one another in a community.

### Semi-structured interviews
These are conducted with the aid of checklists but not a formal survey questionnaire. It is an open-ended technique which allows for probing and for participants to voluntarily provide relevant information. Interviews should be conducted with those key informants identified by earlier research.

### Group interviews and discussions
These may be casual in the work place or in a shebeen or it may be structured allowing representation of concerned stakeholders. While group interviews and discussions should be conducted in an informal and relaxed manner, it should be structured in some way. A checklist is a useful tool in doing this exercise. The group doing the research will often change hats and become the respondents in a group session where they will discuss what they have gleaned and try to make sense of it. The 'threat' of exposure can very easily be waylaid by the use of techniques such as the nominal group technique and brainstorming.

### Sketch mapping
Maps are based on local observation and knowledge. They can be used to reveal physical as well as social information. In a project in Nicaragua (in Latin America) social mapping was used to show information on gender differences in mobility, wealth and wellbeing. In a land claims project in North-West province, South Africa, in which the authors were involved, the community used mapping to firstly identify resources on the land. Once this exercise was completed they did mapping to plan future use and development of the land. Eventually, through these processes the participants give life to the image so that it can become the basis of the community development project emanating from this exercise.

### Time lines (chronologies of events)

A time line records the sequence in which history played out in a community. Remembered history provides 'anchors' to recall events. For example: The drought was just before the release of Mr Mandela. The Chief got married a week after the train crash between Johannesburg and Durban. By using a time line with 'big' national or international events as anchors, histories and events in communities can be reconstructed.

### Stories, portraits and case studies

In communities with a strong oral tradition, stories and case studies can reveal much about the history, practices and dynamics of a community. Likewise, portraits or sketches bring out information that may otherwise not be revealed. Stories and case studies reveal histories of a family; crises in farming; environmental impacts and issues such as droughts and many other relevant themes.

### Seasonal calendars

By major season or by month to show seasonal changes such as days and distribution of rain, food consumption, types of sickness and prices, incomes and expenditure are useful records. Just think how long traditional research can take to obtain this information and how arduous a task it is. The information gleaned in this PRAP method may not be that accurate, but it is reliable and shows trends so that we can make our own judgement.

In Table 18.1 an indication is given in the first column of some of the types of information that will be gathered. In the second column some of the techniques to be utilised are indicated, and the third column shows some of the results to be obtained.

## 18.6  APPLICATION OF PRAP

Action research through methods such as PRAP is used in various types of projects. In southern Botswana the Kuru Development Trust uses this approach to establish a rural micro-finance scheme under the participant San communities (Dekker personal communication, 2000). Lightfoot et al, (1994:22) write about 'dramatic results' achieved in a rural biological resource recycling exercise in the Philippines. In a Ugandan primary healthcare project, the utilisation of PRA resulted, among other positive lessons in: '... the local people (being) ... capable of assessing their own situation and mapping out strategies for improvement' (Osuga & Mutayisa, 1995). The importance of action research such as PRAP is illustrated by a case study from Somalia. Research was undertaken into the reasons for the failure of an immunisation programme aimed at infants. One of the findings of the research was that no effort was made throughout the implementation of the programme to assess community needs or attitudes towards immunisation. The community has participated in the programme '... as the 'object' rather than the 'subject' of development efforts' (La Fond, 1992:22–26).

Table 18.1  **Types of information and techniques to be used**

| TYPES OF INFORMATION | TECHNIQUES | PRODUCTS |
|---|---|---|
| General background of the community | Brainstorming in groups Observation Interviews | Matrix of basic characteristics |
| Spatial information | Mapping | Community map (a graphical representation of the community) |
| Time – history and trends | Time line Ethno-history Trend analysis | Community history (a chronological description of important events in the history of the community) |
| Socio-economic data | Venn diagram Trend diagram Income and expenditure matrix Migration diagram Ranking | ▶ Institutional relationships in the community<br>▶ Trend analysis (eg malaria-related illness over time)<br>▶ Types of livelihood, income generating activities and expenditure<br>▶ Impact of migration on community<br>▶ Identification of levels of wellbeing in the families |
| Production and technical information | Transects Flow diagram (of production system) Farming calendar | Information on the resources, technical aspects in the community |
| Identification of problems and solutions | Preference matrixes Problem trees Ranking | List and describe issues of importance to community |
| Project planning | SWOT analysis Programming matrix | Identification of strengths, weaknesses, opportunities and threats of proposed solutions Design a project |

Many more documented case studies can be quoted. The point is that where sustained empowering development is the objective, PRAP has a proven record over many years in various types of projects. What remains for implementing agencies to make the approach succeed, is to demonstrate a willingness to accept the integrity of this approach and devote time and energy to its implementation.

## 18.7  SOME PROBLEMS WITH AND LIMITATIONS TO PRAP

In the PRAP process the role of the implementing agency or the researcher should be: '... that of catalyst for social change as well as co-learner with the people. He or she does not pretend to be detached, as does the traditional researcher, in the name of objectivity and neutrality' (Selener, 1997:12).

This very noble view on the role of the 'outsider' using action research such as PRAP is, however, difficult to attain.

Development agencies have to deliver, spend donor money according to agreed programmes so that new donor funds can be applied for. They have their mandate to which their constituency holds them accountable. In this situation it is hard to avoid agency-led development projects (Van Diessen, 1998:46–47).

The client—a community—where PRAP is applied is usually caught in the deprivation trap characterised by poverty, powerlessness (including illiteracy), vulnerability, isolation and physical weakness (see Chapter 1). The implementing agency, on the other hand, is a government department, an NGO or private consultancy that has a political mandate and responsibility, is donor-dependent or pursues profit. All these agencies are to some extent task oriented and need to achieve certain benchmarks in pursuit of their goals. The implementing agencies make use of professionals and therefore presume superior knowledge and/or insight. If the management and staff of implementing agencies are not aware of the difficulties inherent in bridging the gap between these two worlds, and actively pursue solutions to it, the following limitations to PRAP will soon become apparent and may mean the termination of a project. In Table 18.2 below the limitations are indicated, as well as the remedies that may be followed in a project. The limitations are listed by Selener et al, (1999: 6–7).

Table 18.2  **Limitations to PRAP and its remedies**

| LIMITATIONS | REMEDIES |
|---|---|
| 1. Raising of false expectations in communities, especially concerning financial aid. | Be open with the power structures and community members from the outset on the aims and limitations of the implementing agency. |
| 2. Correct identification of problems and the design of feasible solutions do not automatically guarantee successful action. | The implementing agency must provide dedicated and well-trained staff that can provide the motivation through proper communication with participants. |

3. Some information gained can be superficial and even false.

A variety of PRAP techniques must be used in order to validate information. Prior knowledge can also be used as a benchmark.

4. The speed of the PRAP process may leave insufficient time for establishing the necessary trust between the facilitator–researcher and the community.

Openness and honesty from the implementing agency generating goodwill and political commitment from the power structures must be aimed at from the start.

5. Individual interpretations and analysis may be lost during group discussions.

A selected number of open-ended interviews with key members of the community will overcome this limitation.

6. Lack of experience by the facilitator–researcher may result in him/her doing the PRAP for, and not with the group.

Selection of staff with the correct empathetic attitude and intensive training.

7. Very little experience exists in replicating the success achieved at community level at regional and provincial level.

Phased implementation, starting with a pilot project.

8. Language and cultural differences can result in communication problems.

Facilitators will be from the area, understanding the language and culture. Trainers of the facilitators will include individuals with knowledge of local language and culture.

9. Speed of the process can affect the quality of participation and inputs from the community.

Qualified and experienced facilitators will know when to halt the process and review proceedings to catch up any 'losses' in quality.

10. Some communities are simply not interested or have other more pressing issues to address.

The 'target' communities have something to gain from success. This will be communicated to them in clear terms.

11. An 'outsider' (agency or person) may 'steal' the information and use it for their benefit (eg for writing a thesis).

The implementing agency must make a specific decision on this issue and negotiate the need for further use of the information with the power structures.

12. Uneven representation or lack of representation of some groups in the community may occur.

The facilitator will actively endeavour to include all identified groups.

13. Using several methods of analysis or indicators may confuse the understanding by community members of the issues at stake.

The issues are clearly focused and should not contribute to misunderstanding. The facilitator will be sensitive to the group's reaction and 'body language'.

It is clear from this list that many of the limitations are true for all or most research methodologies, also those originating in a more traditional school. Its limitations therefore, do not put it in a bad position vis-à-vis these more traditional methods.

## 18.8    CONCLUSION

The objective of PRAP is to gather field data in a simple yet reliable manner and to analyse it by using local indigenous knowledge and perceptions of reality. But it goes a big step further in that it wants to start something, it has a mobilising effect and it leads to further action. This fits in perfectly with our own idea of a contact-making period during which the CDW and the community get to know one another and identify the community needs. PRAP is part of the contact-making phase. The decision to launch a project is a natural outflow of what has been learnt through PRAP methodology. See Chapter 17 for detail on contact making. We have merely introduced this subject.

# CHAPTER 19

# THE START OF A PROJECT

## 19.1 INTRODUCTION

All community development projects are built around needs and resources. The starting point of any project is a resource or a need.

A community development project can be approached from a 'problem solving' or an 'asset building' angle. In the past much emphasis was placed on identifying problems in communities and solving them. As a corrective to this somewhat negative approach (as we warn against elsewhere in this book) an asset-based approach emerged. The asset-based approach to community development (ABCD) wants to focus on what communities have, instead of what they need. The idea is to build from within and focussing less on what can be added from outside. According to Kretzmann and McKnight (1993:6) communities can 'begin to assemble their strengths into new combinations, new structures of opportunity, new sources of income and control, and new possibilities for production'. An asset according to this approach is not only physical objects or money but also include 'personal attributes and skills [and]... the relationships among people through social, kinship, or associational networks' (Mathie and Cunningham, 2002:5). ABDC is, according to Mathie and Cunningham, (2002:6):

> a strategy for sustainable community-driven development—Beyond the mobilization of a particular community, ABCD is concerned with how to link micro-assets to the macro environment.

We agree in general with the sentiment to identify what people have and build upon it, rather than focusing on what they do not have and try to supply it. Yet it is important to distinguish between resources and assets in a community. A resource is something that can be used to create an asset. Human resources, capital and infrastructure, land and entrepreneurship (or business and organisational skills) are resources. All communities possess some or all of these in varying degrees. Below we identify and list potential resources in communities.

Turning resources into assets—something that will produce a benefit of some kind (social relations, income, better services)—is what asset-based community development is about. In an economic sense an asset is a resource controlled by a person or group (an entity) 'from which future economic benefits are expected to flow to the entity' (Advisory Expert Group,

2006). Another view on an asset is to define it as an economic resource that 'has the ability to generate favourable cash flows to the entity' (International Accounting Standards Board, 2006:3).

In communities we also find social and other resources that may generate favourable social and other gains. A stokvel, for instance, is a social grouping that represents some of the characteristics of a resource. Using this social resource can lead to the development of an economic asset (a savings club, for instance) or may have a demonstration effect for others in the community to follow and become organised in a similar way (a social asset). A resource thus holds potential to become an asset to the community and to individuals.

## 19.2  RESOURCE IDENTIFICATION

Resource identification takes place before a project is started. It should be part of the PRAP exercise so that needs and objectives will be handled in terms of the available resources. A PRAP exercise or any survey for that matter, should not only concentrate on the negative; on the needs and problems, but should have a positive side. The identification of resources will adequately fill this positive side. Because the identification of resources is a positive step, it influences people positively. If we define available resources in terms of the needs, those resources point to an outcome, a solution. Resource identification encourages people to pay attention to their objective and, by doing so, lays the foundations for a community development project.

No community development project can function without resources. It is ironic that the need addressed by a project is invariably the lack of some resource. One must, on the other hand, be careful not to see a poor community as without resources. However poor the people may be, they are never entirely without resources. There is a tendency to look for resources outside the community. People are very much aware of their needs and they can identify many when they are asked to do so. Yet, when asked to identify their resources, they find it difficult to identify more than a handful. One can also argue that it is terrible to use the few resources people have while there are abundant resources outside the community. Should one not use the abundant resources rather than the meagre ones? It is easy to sympathise with these tendencies. The community resources are in any case seldom enough to run projects.

The big problem with external resources is that they usually come with strings attached. Donors of resources may have their own agenda and their own reasons for funding development. They may attach provisos to the use of their resources that are not in line with the principles that we have discussed in an earlier chapter. Communities may also increase their dependency on these external donors; something that will work against their obtaining self-reliance and accepting ownership of projects. People can be manipulated by resource grants. They can be made to do things they do not want to do, or do not usually do. Donor dependency can be as bad a trap as the deprivation trap and it can keep people in perpetual bondage. When decisions must be made regarding the use of resources, the community development workers (CDWs), their organisations and all levels of government service should keep this danger in mind.

## 19.3 TYPES OF RESOURCES

There are four types of resources of importance for community development projects.

### 19.3.1 Natural resources

Natural resources are those provided by Mother Nature, such as water, a temperate climate, a good soil, rainfall, vegetation such as trees, and minerals. These natural resources are especially important in rural areas. Harsh climates, low rainfall and poor soil types are serious obstacles to development.

It is important to remember that natural resources must usually be shared with other communities and with other generations. A river that flows through a community is a natural resource and may be used by that community, but without unnecessarily depleting it and polluting it because it also flows through other communities who also have the right to use it. We also share natural resources with people still to be born. Many of the natural resources, such as water and vegetation, are finite and must be used responsibly and very carefully so that future generations can also use them.

A community development project that leads to the abuse of natural resources is a worse-than-futile exercise. Development cannot be sustained if a project harms the environment. It can, at best, bring short-term relief and long-term damage. The long-term disadvantages of such 'developments' are usually permanent and make nonsense of any short-term benefits. People and their environment are integrated and harm to the one means harm to the other one. Instead of abusing the environment, community development projects must enhance natural resources. In order to do this, CDWs should make use of expert advice. CDWs may think that a proposed project will not harm the environment, but may be unaware of indirect or covert results that may be harmful to nature. It is a fact that the world's poorest people live in the most fragile environments (Elliott, 1994:21). CDWs cannot be too sensitive about this and must guard against good intentions leading to environmental degradation or even disaster.

### 19.3.2 Manufactured resources

Manufactured resources are all those that are artificially made and include roads, water reticulation, communication networks, shops, markets, electricity, buildings and sanitary systems. These are collectively called infrastructure and projects are dependent on at least some of them, but may also develop or improve them.

The existence of infrastructure does not necessarily mean that it is available and that it can be used for community development. Various questions must first be asked because the use of infrastructure is usually accompanied by some provisions. These questions are, among others: For who are the resources open? How must the resources be shared? What will they cost? Who has authority over them? CDWs must seek answers to these and other questions regarding the use of infrastructure. It is important to establish who manages and maintains a certain infrastructural item. It is also important to know whose permission must be sought for the use of infrastructure. In this instance a bit of bargaining is also in the offing because special cases can be made out for community development projects so that infrastructure can be used at lower cost or even free of charge.

One of the most important manufactured resources is money. All community development projects need money. The community, even with poverty prevalent, will generate some of the necessary funds for a project, but only if they think that it will be worthwhile and not too risky. However, most of the money will have to come from outside the community. It is very important that the action group knows the conditions under which they receive money for a project. Is it a loan or a grant? If it is a loan, what are the conditions for the repayment of the loan? Does the donor want some decision-making powers concerning the project? Does the donor know what community development is? Is it a once-off donation or is it a long-term financing of the project until completion? Will the action group be able to meet the terms of the financing?

Action groups are frail and vulnerable entities comprising poor people who must be assisted so that they do not fall prey to donors with ulterior motives or hidden agendas. On the other hand, action groups must also know what their obligations will be and what responsibility they must bear. They need to know the consequences if they commit themselves to a financial deal. They cannot make sound financial decisions if they don't have all the relevant and necessary information.

### 19.3.3  Human resources

We quite often regard people as the reason for certain needs. We see them as part of the problem and from there it is easy to treat them as if they are the problem. People become the beneficiaries of development efforts. External agencies start projects and the people who are the beneficiaries are supposed to be grateful. Because they are part of the problem and because they are the target, the people have no say in the matter of their development. If they are involved it is usually to fulfil soft options such as providing developers with wish lists and doing some manual work sometimes required in projects. The fact that people are also a vital resource is completely obscured. The fact that people can and should be a part of the solution is overlooked. Human faculties are important resources and most people are potential contributors to development. Human skills are extremely important resources. In poor communities there are always people who had mastered a skill when they were employed. They may be out of work and not practising their skills, but they still retain knowledge about them and can easily take up such a skill. The fact that people have knowledge and skills does not mean that they do not require further development as resources, among others through training (Massie & Douglas, 1981:309). To make better resources of people, in other words, to make assets out of them, is one of the objectives of community development. Community development is a learning process and far-from-perfect human resources will become better equipped if they are part of the process. The CDW must assist people to become better human resources by providing learning opportunities in the normal process of development projects.

The road to self-reliance and self-sufficiency is the same as the road along which people become increasingly better human resources.

We tend to think that human resource development belongs to formal education and training. Education and training help in the process, but are not the only means of developing human resources. Reflection, debate, decision-making, experimental implementation and evaluation – all ingredients of the community development project, are all part of resource development.

We can also regard norms and traditions as human resources. Again, one is more likely to see them as obstacles to development (which is quite often the case), but there are norms and traditions that can be used to tackle the poverty situation. Norms and traditions normally bring stability and harmony. This might be very valuable in a project. It also strengthens discipline, another important asset to a project.

Whether norms and traditions are a resource or an obstacle depends, to a large extent, on how they are handled. The CDW must handle norms and traditions very carefully. If people see a CDW as someone with little respect for their norms and traditions, they will seldom accept such a person's bona fides. The situation of the poor is often so bad that their norms and traditions are the only guardians of their remaining dignity. To treat their norms and traditions with disrespect is to treat them as badly.

### 19.3.4 Organisational (entrepreneurial) resources

No resource is of use if organisational resources are absent. That is why this fourth type of resource is so important. The societal structures and external structures influencing a society are very important organisational resources. They make the use of all other resources possible. The ability to organise is an inherent part of the human species. Even the most unsophisticated and isolated society uses its people's organisational ability to structure its existence. This extraordinary resource must be identified and used. It must also be developed because it is a resource that cannot be depleted through use. In fact, the more it is used, the better it becomes.

Interest groups that are community-based organisations (CBOs) are important organisational resources. Because we easily overlook them, they warrant specific mention. Every community has several interest groups; in fact, often they have a great number of such CBOs. Every community has its burial societies, stokvels, ratepayers' societies, women's clubs, youth clubs and sports clubs. These are all valuable organisational resources. Normally, they are fairly well organised with clear membership and leadership structures. Members of an interest group with some experience can form an action group for project purposes. One could therefore find a group of young people, all belonging to the same youth club, forming an action group to pursue a specific objective or address a specific need. The track record of these types of organisations is quite good. People's participation through such groups seems more intense and authentic (Salem, 1978:19), and they are able to mobilise the local people (Obaidullah Khan, 1980:75–76). However, the mere fact that such organisations are present is no guarantee that they will play their proper role (White, 1986:250). One must be careful not to overlook the fact that when interest groups feel a project to be prejudicial to their interests, or if they foresee a project's spin-offs affecting them negatively, they can become huge obstacles in the project's path.

## 19.4 CONSENSUS ON NEEDS

A need is not an unspoken wish or a vague feeling of discomfort. A need is much more concrete, more definable; otherwise a project can never be well planned. The people know their needs, but a project cannot address all or many of the people's needs at the same time. A project can only tackle one need at a time. A project will therefore evolve out of a problem, need or concern of a specific group of people. A project can only address a need if that need is properly identified, and if the people participating in the project can reach consensus on the definition of the need they are trying to address.

We have seen in a previous chapter that needs identification starts informally during the contact-making phase. We can therefore say that needs identification undergoes an informal phase during contact-making and a more formal phase when a project is instituted. In fact, we can say that there must be an informal phase for the formal phase to develop naturally. PRAP lies between these two phases and is therefore a link or bridge from the informal to the formal. It is difficult to describe PRAP as either informal or formal. We must admit that there is something of both present. It may start more informally when discussions and brainstorms are held around the situation in which the participants find themselves. It becomes more formal when those discussions are followed by PRAP methodologies for learning more about the situation such as transects, calendaring and ranking (see Table 18.1 for examples of the application of these techniques). If the informal phase of needs identification follows its natural course and is naturally followed by a more formal phase of needs identification (Wileden, 1970:165) according to PRAP principles and methodologies, then needs identification is complete before a project starts. By then the need will be quite obvious. Formal meetings in order to launch a project will then be more concerned with need formulation and not need identification.

During contact-making the CDW may realise that different groups of people are concerned about different needs or they may have different perceptions about the same need. It is quite obvious that all people will never agree on needs. It is natural that different groups of people will identify different needs for attention. A group of mothers of small children, a group of maize farmers and a group of pensioners will differ in what they regard as urgent needs. When CDWs realise the existence of these different groups with different needs, they have taken the first step in establishing different action groups capable of launching different projects catering to their different and peculiar needs. In this regard the only limitation is the capacity of the CDW who can facilitate only so many projects.

It is something else when people have different perceptions of the same need. It is obvious that conflicting views must be ironed out through informal and formal discussion before a project can be launched. The important thing is that the people comprising an action group charged to address a need within a project must enjoy full consensus on the definition of the need.

It is also important that a project is limited to a single need, especially if the action group and the CDW are unsure of themselves, or have a small base of skills or other capacities and capabilities. There is nothing wrong with admitting that there are several needs and to identify them. They must then be ranked in order of priority according to urgency or do-ability or whatever other criterion is chosen so that they can be tackled one at a time.

A public discussion of needs is fraught with danger because the outcome cannot be anticipated. We have already seen in the chapters on contact-making and PRAP what the proper way is to identify needs. It is most definitely not through a public meeting. We have established that needs identification should begin as an informal discussion progressing naturally to a more formal stage in which PRAP methodologies are followed. When this stage is reached, the participants will not be the public at large, but the people who have identified themselves with the specific concern; the action group in the making. The need will then not require formal identification. It will require formulation to bring more clarity to issues relevant to it, in other words, to contextualise the problem or need.

## 19.5 FORMULATING NEEDS

People often need assistance in formulating their felt needs correctly. A vaguely felt or broadly described or obscure need cannot successfully be tackled through a project. Obscurity is quite often the problem in coming to terms with the need. One needs to clarify the issue and for that a causality and linkage exercise might prove to be very valuable. It will help to streamline perceptions and it will put the needs in proper context so that a general understanding of the situation and milieu can be developed.

A causality and linkage exercise can be done with the help of a spider diagram, also known as a tree diagram. The best way of doing it is on a blackboard or flip chart where all present can concentrate on the same thing and experience the same visual effect. A causality and linkage exercise establishes the causes and the results of a felt need. It also establishes the linkages that exist between causes and results.

A causality and linkage exercise is not meant to identify a need. In logical framework exercises, one can start with problem areas and decide what the desired outcome should be if something is done about the problem areas. Between the problem area and the desired outcome a logical sequence must be sought and on this logical linkage a subject or need can then be identified as focus for a project. However, it is not something that will ensure success in the fluid and unsure situation of the poverty context and it is thus much better to start with an identified need that can be better and clearer formulated through such an exercise.

## 19.6 FEELING A NEED

It is imperative that the people forming the action group should feel the identified need to be their own. In the development graveyard there are many tombstones with the inscription 'Here lies a community development project whose need was not felt'. People will rally together and will be prepared to contribute labour, time, energy and money only if they feel a definite need and if the need is a matter of grave concern to them. The poverty situation does not allow luxuries, which means that people are not seeking to indulge in 'interesting' or 'worthwhile' activities. CDWs should be careful not to impose needs on people or to organise people for what they regard as a good cause. Nor should they regard community development as a hobby some people would like to pursue; as something pleasant and stimulating to do in one's free time. People in a crisis situation have very little inclination to do something 'nice' or 'pleasant' while their crisis persists and confronts them daily. Community development is a constructive process in which people involve themselves to eradicate a serious need or solve a serious problem. They participate not because they enjoy it, but because they regard it as a last resort, as the only alternative left to them. Case Study 18: *Food garden in Mapayeni*, is a case in point. Many a community development project has floundered because of basic misconceptions surrounding this issue.

A CDW may think that after one or two visits to an area he/she can identify the main needs and even put them in order of priority, but in the final instance it is the people's conception of what constitutes the most important identifiable need that is paramount and should therefore receive primary attention. The secret of success is found in a great deal of informal discussion of the need. Through that period of relaxed discussion people's views can be honed so that they grasp the problem correctly. This discussion can run over into a PRAP phase of more formal surveying where the group as a whole gets to grips with the problem or need. Eventually, the need will have gained such a prominent place in their minds that they can, better than anybody else, formulate that need clearly.

People will not easily be moved to action if they do not feel a need, irrespective of the reality and urgency of that need. For this reason the felt need must receive preference even if the CDW feels otherwise about the needs. It is necessary for the CDW to work through the felt need in order to bring the action group to the real need. When one considers that the eradication of a need is not the only objective of community development, but that it is also a learning process through which people's dignity is enhanced and self-reliance is strengthened, the time spent on a felt need that may not address the real problem cannot be regarded as wasted. See in this regard Case Study 16: *The felt and the real need.*

## 19.7 THE FIRST PROJECT MEETING

We have seen in a previous chapter that the contact-making phase must be a natural process. For that reason it must come to a natural conclusion. The contact-making phase results in the first project meeting. By this time the CDW must be sure that he/she knows the community and that they know him/her and have accepted his/her bona fides. He/she knows that the contact-making phase can come to a conclusion if he/she can identify a group of people, either individuals or an existing group that is concerned about the same problem or need and, very importantly, is keen to do something about it. This means that the first project meeting must be the direct result of a consensus among the group of concerned people that something must and probably can be done about the identified need. It is the logical outcome of a spontaneous reaction by the people. It is the next logical step to be taken in a process that started when the CDW entered the area and it brings the contact-making phase to a natural conclusion.

It is quite possible that the first project meeting will not really be the first time that many of those involved have met. If the people concerned about a certain matter were part of the survey, as a group in conversation with the CDW or as a PRAP team, they would have met before. Yet, the nature and the goals of the first project meeting are different from previous gatherings and it can, therefore, be regarded as the conclusion of one phase and the beginning of another.

Invitations to the first project meeting should be extended only to those people who have already shown a clear concern for or have aligned themselves with the problem. This is not a public meeting. It is not a good thing to get 200 or 300 people together to discuss a problem identified by a small group of people. The identified need grows immediately because it is now not only the concern of a small group of individuals, but has become a topic for general discussion. It catches the eye of the politicians and other leaders and is therefore open to manipulation or, if the venture is regarded by some influential stakeholder or stakeholders as a personal threat, it can be destroyed. The group of individuals who have aligned themselves with the need may be a group of poor women. In a public meeting where elite and leaders are present, the women will not be heard. They will not even speak and, eventually, their concern and their initiative will be taken away from them and others will decide the issue. The principle of simplicity requires that one begins small. If the group is really small (less than twenty), participants can be invited to bring along one or two other people who they know share the same concern and hold the same views on it.

This meeting does not have an open agenda. It is not a needs identification meeting. The need has already been identified. This meeting has a closed agenda with just one objective, which is to talk about a specific problem or need already identified by those concerned and to discuss what can be done about it.

### 19.7.1 The role of the CDW during the first meeting

At this first project meeting the CDW will, of necessity, play a prominent role. This poses a dilemma because the CDW does not want to play too prominent a role. Those present must realise from the start that it is their concern and that they must do something about it. If the group comprises members of the same interest group, the problem is not as acute because the existing leadership will also lead the meeting. The problem is more severe if an ad hoc group comes together. Who is going to set the ball rolling? Who is going to act as chairperson? Perhaps the CDW should start by stating the purpose of the meeting and by suggesting that a chairperson be chosen for that meeting. The role of the CDW will still be more prominent than is desirable because he/she will have to assist the chairperson who would not have had the opportunity to prepare for the job. The CDW must therefore be very careful not to be domineering during the meeting.

It might be necessary for the CDW to do the secretarial work during this first meeting, but he/she must stress that it will be for this first meeting only. If there is someone present who is able to fulfil the secretarial function, he/she should be nominated to do it. In this case the CDW can assist such a person.

The CDW must come to this meeting well prepared. He/she should:

▶ bring enough paper to write down the minutes of the meeting;
▶ arrange for a board or flip chart to do the causality exercise;
▶ be familiar with the presentation of the causality exercise;
▶ prepare a ceremony for the people giving their commitment (see later);
▶ prepare well for the first short-term planning meeting in case the group decides to go without a committee (see later);
▶ prepare for an election of committee members in case the group decides to elect one at this meeting; and
▶ have a pro-forma constitution ready that could be used by the group as a working document to draw up their own constitution.

### 19.7.2 Contents of the first project meeting

At the first project meeting the following should take place:

▶ The meeting should discuss the problem or need. This should be a free-for-all informal discussion with a view to formulating the need.

▶ The free-for-all discussion should culminate in a causality exercise.

▶ The outcome of the causality exercise should be a precise formulation of the need to be addressed.

▶ After the need has been formulated, the next step is to decide what is to be done about it. In other words, the meeting must decide on an objective.

▶ A discussion of the objective can only be meaningful if resources and obstacles to their use are also discussed.

▶ The next step is to do some long-term planning. This should comprise a scenario, drawn in broad terms and tied to roughly estimated dates and a roughly estimated budget. It serves no purpose to do detailed long-term planning as we will see later.

▶ Now, some logistical arrangements must be made. These include the number and frequency of meetings, the duties and obligations of the various role-players, the necessary registrations and approvals that must be sought and the working method that will be followed, for example the planning-cycle method and what methodology will be used to evaluate.

▶ An optional item at this stage, not earlier, is to get a personal commitment from every person present to join the group and the venture. This can even include a little ceremony. The CDW must obtain the names and contact details of all those who commit themselves.

▶ The group must discuss the possibility of a committee. It must decide whether one is necessary and (if yes) whether it wants to elect one immediately or postpone it to the next meeting. It must also discuss the functions and obligations of the proposed committee.

▶ If the group decides to elect the committee immediately, its election can take place.

▶ If the group decides to elect the committee later, they must decide on a date and place for the election to take place. Such a meeting should, preferably, take place within a week of the first meeting so that the momentum generated by the first meeting is not lost.

▶ If the group decides to go without a committee, the meeting can either constitute itself as a short-term planning meeting, or it can decide to hold such a meeting on a specific date in future.

## 19.8  THE COMMITTEE

It must be a rule not to have a committee elected before the group has decided on the need it wants to address. The felt need is the most important and fundamental aspect of any community development project. It is also the most important binding factor. It is better, therefore, to have the whole group involved in the identification and formulation of the need than to entrust it to a newly elected committee. If a committee is elected too early it may not know where to begin with the result that it may not start at all. This may lead to conflict between the committee and the group, but, more often it will lead to nothing, which is just as bad. The election of a committee is often followed by a protracted period of inactivity. The very early election of a committee can also undermine the principle of participation because usually the group will wait for the committee to start the ball rolling, and if it does, the chances are that it will roll it alone.

Another reason for not electing the committee too early is that most of the members of the group may have no idea of what a committee should do or may have the wrong impression about it. If the committee is elected before the project is underway, the group or some of its members will expect from the committee activities falling outside the ambit of the project.

When the committee is elected after the need has been identified and formulated, its task will be much clearer. It will have a basis from which to work. More importantly, though, if the group has been involved in these tasks and others leading up to the election of the committee it is doubtful that it will leave all subsequent actions to the committee. Because the action group already has an interest in the matter, it will maintain that interest and, in so doing, identify itself with the project. In such a situation the committee will fulfil a real leadership role. It will not do everything itself; the group will not allow it to. Rather, it will lead a committed and concerned group which is as much part of the project as the committee. It is clear that the CDW must guard against over eagerness to get a committee established. The committee exists to provide leadership; not to dominate a project.

A committee's election is also part of the learning process. Members of the committee will not necessarily start out as good leaders, but their participation in the learning process will make them better leaders. The CDW must encourage the climate and must continuously provide opportunities to learn.

The CDW can serve on the committee as an official adviser. Then the CDW is present in an advisory position only and the decision-making function lies with the committee. At the same time, the committee is not thrown into the deep end because the CDW is available as an adviser and a guide. It is obvious that this situation can easily go the wrong way. The CDW can become the wise oracle with everyone dependent on his/her wisdom. Then the committee no longer makes the decisions. It either offers suggestions which the CDW accepts or rejects, or it waits for his/her advice and promptly converts it into decisions. The best way to give advice is by offering the committee options and assisting it to work out the consequences of every option. With this as its background, the committee must then make the choices.

## 19.9 PROBLEM-SOLVING

Groups make decisions by solving problems. How this problem-solving is done can make a big difference to the wellbeing of a group. The wrong way of problem-solving can and will adversely affect relationships in the group. We must remember that problem-solving is the core business of most groups. If it is done wrongly, the whole group functions in a wrong way. Problem-solving can lead to the wrong conclusion, which will also have a bad influence on the group. In any case, the problem will still be there because the solution the group had chosen was not the correct one.

One should therefore try and follow a pattern divided into discrete phases so that everything is done correctly and the group prospers as a result. Such a pattern will consist of the following different discrete phases. (This section is based on Doyle & Straus, 1976.)

### 19.9.1 Problem perception

The problem-perception phase is the time for the problem-solving group to try and get closer to the problem. It is not a very well-disciplined phase because we are still trying to get a grip on the problem. It has therefore been called 'the sniffing, groping and grasping phase' where ideas about the problem are brainstormed. The group must ask themselves questions such as 'Is there a problem?', 'Whose problem is it?', 'Where is the problem?', 'What does the problem look like?', 'What does it feel like?' and 'How big is the problem?' This is all that is done in this phase. We only want to get a clearer picture of what we perceive as a problem. We want to make sure that we are all talking about the same thing.

### 19.9.2   Problem definition

Once you have perceived a problem, the next logical step is to define it. This is the phase where boundaries must be set around the problem. What is part of the problem and what is not? The problem must therefore be described – who, what, where, when and how. The importance of a definition is that it synchronises all the opinions about the problem so that all participants will describe the problem in the same way. It also determines the range of acceptable alternatives. One should, however, be careful that the problem is not defined in terms of the alternative. This is done when the problem is phrased as the lack of something, the something being the alternative, for example the lack of school toilets.

### 19.9.3   Problem analysis

In the analysis phase the objective is to break the problem down into component parts and to examine how they fit together. This is how you try to learn more about the problem. Group members should now think what questions need to be answered in order to build a complete and detailed picture of the problem. Any problem can be broken down into smaller sub-problems until you reach a size that you can handle. This exercise is very important if a problem is complex. As the problem is defined and analysed it is usually found to consist of a number of sub-problems. Eventually it will be good if the group could reach consensus on how to divide the entire problem.

### 19.9.4   Thinking of alternatives

Now that the problem has been looked at from all angles the first positive phase can commence. But this phase should start only after the previous three phases have been dealt with to the satisfaction of the whole group. If not, we may be doing more harm than good by letting the group charge on to generating alternatives. It is important that participants should come forward with creative ideas during this phase. Brainstorming is one of the best ways to solicit creativity and originality.

Part of this phase is to set criteria for alternatives. This is usually not done in a formal exercise. Reactions to ideas about alternatives will invariably contain criteria and if they do not, such criteria must be provided. 'That is not a practical idea because ...' 'That is an excellent idea because ...'. It is not permissible to only say that an idea is good or bad: the reasons for saying so (the criteria for alternatives) must also be given.

When thinking of alternatives, past experience is also drawn from. After all, it is not necessary to reinvent the wheel. 'So and so had the same problem and they did ..., 'Remember when we last had a similar problem, we did ...', and 'Last time that we had this problem we tried to ... but it didn't work'.

Any one or all of the sub-problems identified during the problem analysis phase can now be placed on the agenda. Remember that we have not yet come to the planning phase where we will have to concentrate more on the central aspects. We are still not talking about what we are going to do. We are simply suggesting alternatives to the situation as it exists now. During this exercise members must learn how to work with other people's ideas and to admit that their own ideas are not necessarily correct or the best.

It is important to work for agreement on common criteria before judging alternatives. The development of explicit criteria has important benefits:

- It forces all group members to externalise their values and to re-examine them.
- Being clear about your personal criteria helps others to understand how you make your decisions.
- The procedure of developing criteria for evaluation causes a useful interlude between generating alternatives and the evaluation of alternatives.
- It is much easier to reach consensus on criteria before alternatives are discussed than to try this afterwards.
- If you cannot reach consensus on criteria, it is not likely that you will reach agreement on an acceptable alternative.
- If you can reach consensus on criteria, future decisions concerning the problem should be greatly simplified.

### 19.9.5   Decision-making

During the previous phase possible alternatives would already have been screened. Some would have remained on the table and some would have been discarded. During this phase a choice must be made between those that remained. Decision-making is thus a making of a choice or choices. In order to do so, the consequences of each choice must be considered. This is an extremely important and necessary exercise and the people must realise why it is done. 'If we decide to do it this way, we will have to ...', 'If we decide on this or that option, just remember that this or that will happen ...', 'This option will cost us ...', 'This alternative will mean that ...'. It is not necessary that only one alternative be chosen. In certain situations two or more alternatives can be considered or there can be a plan A and a plan B. The important thing is that there must be consensus about the decision, and so, a bit of negotiation may be necessary. In fact, if this whole process is followed, nothing but consensus can be the end result. It is when problem-solving becomes a landslide instead of a well-thought out exercise that voting must be done to see which alternative carries a majority and that is definitely not recommended.

### 19.9.6   Planning

The alternative has now been chosen. During the planning phase it must be decided how the desired result will be obtained. Planning is task oriented. Action must be taken in order to eradicate the problem. Planning decides what is to be done, when it is to be done, how it is to be done, and who is to do it. But in the case of a community development project the planning cannot be done in detail and only once. We will see in the next chapter that planning should take place incrementally.

## 19.10 CONCLUSION

The first project meeting is the first positive manifestation that people want to do something about a need. As such, it is the culmination of a process that has started with the entry of the CDW into an area. A very important process has taken place during this period. Relationships have been sorted out and established. The CDW's bona fides have been accepted and he/she has found a niche for him/herself. A group of people have become aware of a situation that they cannot tolerate and therefore are going to address through a project. That group of people has also committed itself to an all out effort through a project. They have set themselves a target and they have mapped out a rough path of action. So, we can say that this is the launch of a project.

The CDW must realise that the meeting following this first one will really show who is committed to participating in the project. It is natural that, during the first project meeting, the curious and the free-riders will be present. People may even commit themselves during the first meeting not through conviction, but because of group pressure. Those who are really committed will attend the second meeting, and those who are not will fall by the wayside.

# CHAPTER 20

# PLANNING AND IMPLEMENTATION

## 20.1 INTRODUCTION TO PLANNING

Planning is a process in which an individual or group of people decide on what to do in the future. Planning points the way to what must be done, when it must be done, by whom it must be done, and how it must be done to reach a certain objective. When dealing with planning for development we must realise that there are serious differences in approaches. The two main and opposing approaches to planning can be identified as a rationalistic and synoptic approach versus an adaptive incrementalist approach.

## 20.2 THE RATIONALISTIC, SYNOPTIC APPROACH

As a tool for decision-making this approach assumes that:

- Decision-makers are authoritative and objective. They are professionally trained and judge everything without bias.
- Exhaustive analysis will define problems. All problems can be analysed so that they can be described in detail.
- Models of social change can be constructed to aid in defining the problem and formulating the policy. The rationalistic approach is a great believer of models.
- There is a direct relationship between government action and the solution of social problems. The rationalistic approach needs a strong, capable and benevolent government.
- Plans must be carried out through hierarchical structures of authority. A hierarchical organisation ensures that decision-making is situated where it should be.
- Deviations from preconceived plans are detrimental to achieving objectives. When you assume all the above, then this is obvious.
- Conflicts over goals or courses of action are adverse and irrational manifestations of politics. There is no place for this in rational planning.
- Planners and policy-makers determine correct action for others to follow. It is clear that the 'others' are only involved in carrying out the plans of professional planners.
- Analysis should be systematic regarding:

  - cost-benefit;
  - linear programming;

- network scheduling; and
- planning-programming-budgeting.

This last point needs further criticism because it forms the core of this approach. Systems analyses require a concise definition of goals and objectives, but it is impossible because they are expressions of social values. Concise definitions of goals are therefore the ideal, but very difficult to attain. This also goes for identifying and categorising inputs, outputs, costs and benefits because they are subjective and analysts and interest groups disagree on them.

A further strong consideration is that government agencies lack administrative capacity to do analysis effectively and further is it impossible to obtain adequate data on which to base systems analysis and synoptic planning. We can therefore say that systems analysis ignores and discounts complex processes of social interaction. Because of this it is quite clear why political leaders do not understand or are unwilling to accept results of systems analysis and comprehensive planning.

In the final instance systems analysis is not always suited to the job at hand. It is difficult to make comparisons between programmes and policy options, for example. Another problem is that systems analysis and comprehensive planning are episodic and time consuming whereas political decision-making is continuous and cyclical. Finally, systems analysis is concerned with how to maximise utilities, whereas policy-making is concerned with how to distribute public resources.

We can therefore conclude by saying that this approach:

▶ is difficult to operationalise;
▶ is incompatible with how political decisions are made; and
▶ discourages analysts from understanding the complexity and uncertainty of problems.

It is part of our culture to strive towards excellence. The way to obtain excellence, we believe, is to devise and to follow methodologies that bypass the human factor as much as possible. We regard people as subjective and irrational and therefore to be kept away from the planning process or to be severely limited in the planning process. We tend to think that the more planning emulates a machine or the computer, the better. We therefore regard planning as a technological process where variables and task paths are brought into harmony through a rational and logical process. Unfortunately reality tells us that this tendency is a fallacy, that planning simply cannot be done in that fashion considering the situation that we work with. If ordinary people with just a basic knowledge are responsible for the planning; the situation in which the planning takes place is fluid and therefore constantly changing; the planning process is to be a learning opportunity for those involved, then rationality and logic are of little consequence and excellence can only be obtained through trial and error. In this regard Rondinelli (1983:321) says:

> [...] methods of analysis, planning and management must be better suited to recognizing and dealing with uncertainty, detecting and correcting errors, generating and using knowledge as the experiments progress, and modifying actions as new opportunities and constraints appear.

Majone and Wildavsky (1978:106) point out another very important consideration when they argue that most constraints remain hidden in the planning phase and are only discovered in the implementation process. Also see Rondinelli (1993) in this regard.

## 20.3 THE ADAPTIVE INCREMENTALIST APPROACH

Incrementalism assumes uncertainty as a fact. The premises on which it is based are:

▶ More detailed planning should proceed incrementally. Planning must be viewed as an incremental process. It is also known as emergent planning (Collyer, et al, 2010).
▶ Complex social experiments can be partially guided but never controlled. Certain parameters can be set, but only as guides.
▶ Methods of analysis and procedures of implementation must be flexible and incremental. A trial and error process is all that can work.
▶ Analysis and implementation should facilitate social interaction. Analysis and implementation should facilitate continuous learning and interaction.
▶ Planning and implementation are mutually dependent activities. Experimentation with implementation reflects on the planning.
▶ Fundamental changes are necessary in the way governments plan and implement. The more the government becomes an enabler, the better. All role-players' dynamic capability is of great importance (Collyer, et al, 2010:110)
▶ It stresses that in the real world:

- Information is always partial and often faulty. Perfect information is not obtained through perfect analysis, so why waste time on perfect analysis.
- Goals must often be left vague. We have said before that objectives must be as precise as possible and that still holds, but it is easier said than done.
- Choices are highly constrained by prior commitments. There are a lot of role-players with various commitments among themselves. A perfect system of a clean slate is therefore not so easy.
- Consequences of action in a complex system are unpredictable. We are dealing with a very volatile substance because of the complexity of the situation.
- Interests are pluralistic and frequently contradictory. There are a lot of role-players in a complex situation and therefore it would be naive to think that interests will always fit and enhance one another.
- The situation changes so rapidly that the 'big picture' is out of date. It is a volatile system and therefore forever changing.
- Only weak control exists over the instruments of policy execution.

The perception of development policies as experimental activities implies that new forms of analysis, planning and administration must be devised that are better suited to experimentation and to uncovering and coping with uncertainties and risks attending policy implementation. The primary purpose of projects should be to build up gradually planning and administrative capabilities of people and organisations; to design and organise projects to reduce uncertainties and unknowns incrementally; to integrate planning and implementation;

and to use acquired knowledge to alter and modify courses of action. The strategies based on this adaptive incrementalist approach reflect more sophisticated understanding of the dynamics of development, the constraints on economic and social change, and the political and social forces that influence processes of change.

## 20.4 CONCLUSION ON THE APPROACHES

One should be careful not to view planning as a technological process done by planners. Community development is human-oriented and involves people with subjective notions of their needs and what they can do about them. People-oriented planning is therefore tinged with subjectivity, is incremental and takes place through a process of trial and error. It is a learning process, it is somewhat dirty, to use an expression of Chambers (1978), and can even be emotional. To force a rational planning mode onto an action group is not only impossible; it would effectively estrange the people from the process. The rational blueprint approach has serious flaws when used in community development. One of the most apparent flaws is the assumption that an institutional structure exists that will fit any current situation. Another flaw is the assumption that a fully operational institution exists that will be able to monitor all eventualities and address all needs. This simply is not so in the situation that we work. We have seen in a previous chapter that there are certain practical principles to adhere to. Those principles of learning, adaptiveness, compassion and simplicity come to bear in the planning process. It is therefore much more than just a preferred way of planning. In fact, there is no other way to plan for development.

This means that project planning must be viewed as an incremental process of testing propositions about the most effective means of coping with complex social problems. For this to be possible, planning must be incremental, and can only be short-term, objectives must be attainable in a fairly short period, planning must be simple and singular and must involve all possible role-players.

Planning and implementation must also be regarded as mutually reinforcing activities that refine and improve each other over time rather than as separate functions (Rondinelli, 1983:321). If planning is a participatory learning process, so is implementation. The two functions simply cannot be separated. Implementation is part of the experiment and makes evaluation possible. In fact, implementation can be regarded as the greatest test of planning. For this reason implementation cannot be regarded as the mechanical execution of a plan, in fact, implementation informs the plan and makes it necessary to go back to the drawing board (De Beer & Swanepoel, 1998:54). Because of this close relationship between the plan and its implementation, because a specific plan is implemented, the mode of implementation differs from project to project. Like planning, implementation is a situation-specific, step-by-step affair, unique to each project.

Let us give Rondinelli (1993:18–19) the final word:

> Attempts to plan in more detailed and precise fashion should proceed incrementally, as uncertainties or unknowns are reduced or clarified during implementation. Planning must be viewed as an incremental process that tests propositions about the most effective means of coping with social problems, reassessing and redefining both the problems and the components

of development projects as more is learned about their complexities and about the economic, social and political factors affecting the outcome of proposed courses of action. Complex social experiments can be partially guided but never fully controlled; thus, analysis and management procedures must be flexible and incremental, facilitating social interaction so that those groups most directly affected by a problem can search for and pursue mutually acceptable objectives. Rather than providing a blueprint for action, allowing policy-makers and managers to readjust and modify programs and projects as they learn more about the conditions with which they are trying to cope.

## 20.5 THE PLANNING PROCESS

Planning means bringing together three elements: the need, the resources, and the objective, and relating them to a fourth element, namely action. It is obvious that the planners must know the first three elements in order to decide on the fourth element of action

### 20.5.1 A rational planning method: The logical framework as a planning method

Logical framework analysis was developed in the United States of America during the 1960s and came into use in the early 1970s. The logframe, as it is popularly called, was not designed for use in development projects. However, its relative simplicity, its clarity and its rationality make it apparently a reliable device to make project kick-off possible. The logframe's main advantage is that its aim is to improve the way in which projects are prepared, planned, implemented and evaluated, therefore managed.

A logframe consists of a rectangular matrix that provides a full picture of the project. It consists of four columns, one each for project structure (narrative summary) or what is to be achieved, indicators of achievement, verification methods and assumptions (Wiggins & Shields, 1995:3).

| Project structure | Indicators | Means of verification | Assumptions |
|---|---|---|---|
| GOAL: What the project seeks to achieve | What are the qualitative and quantitative measures that indicate achievement of objective? | What sources of information can be used to be able to measure the goal? | What external factors are necessary to sustain the objectives? |
| PURPOSE: What are the intended immediate effects of the project? | What are the qualitative and quantitative indicators by which achievement of purpose can be judged? | What sources of information are available to make measurement of purpose achievement possible? | What external factors are necessary to ensure the purpose to contribute to the achievement of the goal? |

| OUTPUTS: What deliverables are to be produced to achieve the purpose? | Quantity, quality and time | What sources of information will verify the achievement of the outputs? | What factors outside project control may restrict the outputs? |
| ACTIVITIES: What activities are to be achieved to accomplish the outputs? | What kind and quality of activities and when will they be produced? | What are the sources of information to verify the achievement of the activities? | What factors will hinder the activities from creating outputs? |

The fact that there is a hierarchy of objectives tells us that there are causal linkages between the various items. If the means are provided, the ends will be achieved. If the necessary inputs are provided, specific outputs will result. This will lead to a purpose being achieved and this will lead to broader goals being met. We therefore have a column of purpose and intent with two rows or columns that give us the indicators and their sources that will be used for monitoring and evaluation. Finally there is a column for a set of assumptions which state the conditions that must apply before causal linkages can be realised.

The logframe methodology is very popular among project facilitators and project donors for the following reasons:

▶ The logframe model is rational with clean lines of causal moments. Because of this, it shows when a project lacks internal coherence and external plausibility. If we look at the narrative summary we can see whether the project is logical in terms of its stated objectives. It can also determine external plausibility by ensuring that the team responsible for project design clearly stipulate the assumptions that they take as their starting point.

▶ It helps project designers to define tasks and responsibilities and it clearly lists the indicators that will be used in monitoring and evaluation.

▶ It is a comprehensive document that obviates misunderstanding because of poor communication. One diagram provides an at-a-glance summary for everyone to understand (Cusworth & Franks, 1993).

The logframe methodology also has its shortcomings:

▶ The most important shortcoming is that it does not always fit into a situation run by adaptive measures. Rondinelli (1993) emphasises that community development projects are experiments with no rigid lines, no step by step causality. The very rigid nature of the logframe makes it difficult for it to fit and may lead to very important principles of development being left by the way.

▶ The logframe is an imposed procedure maintaining a relationship of control and domination that goes directly against the principles of participation and empowerment.

▶ The conceptual starting point for the logframe is western and therefore its parameters for planning and implementation are formal and thus fixed. It is culture specific and therefore it does not allow ownership of the logframe as an approach.

▶ Interestingly, the logframe is rigid in its approach, yet by itself it is not sufficient for management of a project. It cannot give guidance to the means of obtaining project objectives. It is therefore a tool to identify the what, but cannot answer the question of how.

▶ The creators of the logframe are usually a selective group, but without the participation of a broad community representation, the principles and priorities of each stake-holder will not be reflected. We can say that the different interests are concealed and therefore areas of conflict are ignored.

▶ The development environment that we have looked at previously is complex and unstable. This dynamism is not really accommodated by the logframe with its inflexible structure. It does leave space for assumptions, but it does not ensure that assumptions are realistic, nor does it offer alternatives in case they are not. The logframe is linear while the reality is not. It assumes that all contingencies can be foreseen and that the progress will be predictable. It sees a linear causality from activities to outputs to purpose to goal. Once this linearity is logframed, there is no chance of adaptability, reflection is not an option. Yet, the situation is so fluid that you do need continuous opportunity for rethink.

▶ The logframe seems concerned with quantitative indicators. It lacks qualitative measures of progress. It is also critical of the learning process approach because it is seen as something that takes place before a project, not during it. If the expected progress is not made, it means that someone is at fault. Policing and upward accountability are therefore at heart of the whole reporting system, not the opportunity to learn from the situation.

## 20.5.2 An adaptive incrementalist planning method: the planning cycle method

There are a number of important aspects to take into account in order for planning to be successful in a community development situation.

Planning must be incremental. Planning cannot be done only once because there are so many changing factors in most situations that precise planning is impossible. No committee or action group can have one planning meeting covering the whole process up to objective attainment. It must return to the drawing board. There are so many unknown and changing factors in most situations that precise planning for the long term is quite impossible. At most, broad guidelines can be drawn on how to reach a certain objective, but detailed planning can only take place on a step-by-step basis. Not only does the situation change frequently, but the people participating are unsure of themselves and unsure as to how to reach their objective. It therefore cannot be a blueprint, but is rather a learning process.

The fact that planning is incremental also tells us that it is a process of trial and error; of experimentation. Decisions on action are formulated in the light of an assessment of previous actions and in the light of an assessment of previous planning. Through the process of trial and error and experimentation a process of learning takes shape. Ackoff (1984:195) explains it as follows:

> Development is a product of learning, not of production; learning how to use oneself and one's environment to better meet one's needs and those of others. Because the development process is essentially a learning process, one person cannot develop another ... Now, how can

we plan for development understood in this way? The answer ... lies in who does the planning because the principal benefit of planning is not derived from consuming its products ... but from participating in the planning process ...

Planning must and can only be short term. It is suggested that the planning body meet monthly to plan for the period up to the next meeting. This planning is done in the light of an assessment of the actions taken since the previous meeting. Each planning meeting is therefore both a planning and an evaluation exercise.

In this way people will be in a position to judge their progress step by step and adjust their course from time to time. Only in this way can the community development process be a continuous learning experience for those participating. The added advantage of regular assessment and planning meetings is that a project will not easily run out of steam. Every meeting is, in a way, a milestone and fresh planning for another month helps to keep the enthusiasm alive. In this way the project generates its own rhythm.

Objectives must be attainable in a fairly short period. Objectives only have value if they are achievable, acceptable, measurable, motivating, understandable, and flexible enough to adapt to changing circumstances. Therefore it is almost impossible to work towards a goal that can only be reached in a fairly long time. If at all possible an objective should not lie further than one year down the line. If an objective cannot be reached in such a short time, it is necessary to set interim objectives. For example, if the objective is to have an own building for a crèche, it might be impossible to realise it within a year. An interim objective must then be formulated, for example, to get the crèche temporarily established in a house or another building.

Quick results, therefore minimise the risk factor. Quick results have a further advantage in that those outside the group who doubt the practicability of a project, will be confronted with proof that something can be done. This will make them more inclined to follow the example of one successful effort and it might even lead to the replication of the first effort throughout the larger community. Case study 17: *Mothers of the mountain community* is a case in point.

Planning must be simple with one objective at a time. It is always easier to plan for one project with one objective at a time. That objective should not tax the project to the extent that the project becomes complex. We should also guard against sophisticated projects. Their planning becomes so technical that it is difficult for ordinary people to participate meaningfully. We say that planning and implementation are participatory actions, but we must be aware of the fact that many projects are large and 'technical' and that these projects cannot be made participatory so easily. Gran (1983:288) says emphatically that large projects violate every premise of participatory development. He maintains that these types of projects deny the poor the possibility of developing their own creative skills, which is the process of development with the greatest long-term potential for human welfare (Gran, 1983:289). So, we are faced with a dilemma. What to do with the larger and more technical projects, especially when it comes to planning and implementation? We have already in a previous chapter contemplated this question and decided then that large, technical projects should be divided into doable chunks so that participation can still take place.

Planning must involve everyone. Planning is not the prerogative of the celebrated few. In a project where a group of participants is led by an executive committee, not even that committee can claim a sole right to planning. In one way or another, the whole group must be involved in planning. The reason for this is simple. It is the right of all members of the group to make decisions and carry the responsibility for those decisions, but the most important reason is that the planning process is a learning opportunity that should be attended by as many of the group as possible. See in this regard Cusworth and Franks (1993).

There is also a risk that the committee take over the project from the action group so that they become either uninvolved or involved only with doing physical labour while the committee makes the decisions. In this case a project's abstract aims will not be met because the group will not be strengthened and will not gain self-reliance. The whole action group must remain an intrinsic part of any action, including planning. Regular action group meetings should therefore be held. At these meetings the committee must inform the group of its actions and the larger group must have the opportunity to discuss them at length and even to reverse them or to send them back to the committee for a rethink. The action group must also have the right to task the committee with new matters. The committee's position in community development is slightly different from other executive committees. The committee does not act on behalf of the action group. It provides leadership, continuity, co-ordination and a certain measure of preparatory organisation to enable the action group to remain optimally involved. Community development workers (CDWs) should explain this situation to their groups and should facilitate them to make practical arrangements to accommodate this position. Action group meetings, for example, could follow close on committee meetings – on the same day if possible, so that the action group can discuss and approve the planning for the next month. If the whole action group is small (ie not more than 25 members) the committee can hold a preparatory 'caucus meeting' before the action group meeting and this latter meeting then becomes the primary planning exercise.

Planning must be written down. During the whole planning process everything must be recorded in writing. At meetings minutes must be kept which specify what must be done, how it must be done, when it must be done and who is responsible for each task. This must be distributed among all persons involved in the process to keep them up to date with the situation.

The planning cycle method is a simple way of ensuring a meaningful relationship between monitoring (evaluation) and planning. Planning meetings should take place once a month (it can even be twice a month if the ability of the group to plan and implement is still very weak). Every planning meeting should start by evaluating the actions of the previous month. The actions of the coming month are then planned using the previous month's actions as a frame of reference. In other words, the meeting evaluates its implementation in terms of its decisions. In this way it learns something of its ability to put plans into action, and it also learns something of its ability to plan – the failure to implement or operationalise plans can often be ascribed to incorrect planning. Only when this process of evaluation has been completed, does the meeting decide on the actions to be taken in the next month. Actions for the next month will be determined by what has taken place in the previous month. If a planned action for the previous month has not been done or completed, it must again appear on the planning for the next month, perhaps with a changed 'how' in the light of the evaluation and definitely with revised timeframes. See Figure 20.1 for a diagramatical illustration of the planning cycle.

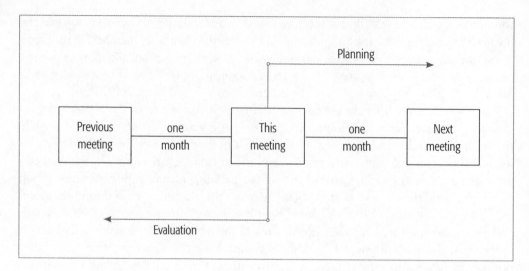

Figure 20.1 **The planning cycle**

The first objective of a planning meeting is to decide what action to take. It is very important that the '*what*' items should be separated from each other so that one '*what*' item will comprise only one action. It is therefore necessary to break down an action into its smallest component parts. Each '*what*' item is numbered separately.

The second phase asks when that action should take place. A timetable must be attached to planning. Action takes place sequentially because certain things cannot be done before others have been completed and certain actions enable others to commence. Attaching actions to dates helps maintain this sequence. In the minds of the planners it gives a clear picture of how the various tasks will follow each other. A timetable ensures that each action is meaningful in relation to other actions and it prevents duplication and repetition.

The reaching of a milestone within the planned time is proof that the action was effective and that the action group was, up to that point, successful in its efforts. It acts further as a confidence booster that generates enthusiasm, and it acts as a barometer of the project's success.

This is all true only if a timetable is not cut too fine. The action group should not be under continuous pressure to meet the next deadline. Dates in a timetable should never be seen as deadlines, but rather as goals or targets. If a timetable is cut too fine, it is inevitable that most goals will not be reached within the set time. This may dampen the action group's enthusiasm. The unpredictability of the whole situation must also be acknowledged (see Rondinelli, 1993, in this regard). It may even be wise to attach two dates to completion of each task; one in the event of everything going without a hitch (best-case scenario) and one taking unforeseen problems into account.

The third phase addresses who will be responsible for the planned action. Planning must tie every action to a person or group of persons who will be responsible for it. If this does not happen the chances are that nobody will attend to it. Either that or the secretary or even the CDW will have to do everything. Two people, the one not knowing about the other, may even undertake the same action and, apart from the duplication, it might also lead to quarrels and a host of other problems. Because every action in a project should be a learning opportunity, various people must be assigned to tasks affording them the opportunity to gain experience and knowledge.

Attaching actions to a specific person or persons enables the equal and fair distribution of the work. It helps to appoint people to tasks that they are equipped to do, thus using everyone's talents and skills optimally, or it appoints tasks to persons not skilled for those tasks, thus affording them the opportunity to gain first-hand experience. It usually also helps to identify those people who are really keen and those who tend to shy away from work. Finally, it shows who can go it alone and who needs assistance and guidance in carrying out tasks.

The fourth phase addresses how a certain action should be done. It is not enough to assign tasks to a person and tie them to dates for completion. The planning body must at least describe each task in more detail so that those tasked with it will know what the task entails and how much money can be spent on it. After a planning meeting a person assigned a task must have reasonable clarity on how to perform it. Tasks cannot be given only to those who know how to perform them. This would rob other people from learning through action. Although tasks must fit the persons who perform them as closely as possible, people must also be given tasks that they do not know how to perform. The problem is that, if a person does not know how to perform a task, he/she may be too shy to ask for clarification or assistance, and as a result not do the task or do it wrongly. If this person is 'found out' it might be humiliating and a very unpleasant experience. A discussion during the planning meeting detailing how a task is to be done will avoid this kind of problem. Even if the person assigned a task does know how to perform it, it might still be worthwhile discussing it, perhaps under the leadership of the designated person. Such a discussion can be a learning experience for the whole group and can bring new insights to the matter.

## 20.6  RECORDING PLANNING

Not only is the human memory amazingly short; it is also amazing how different people interpret different decisions differently. This can easily lead to conflict in a group and it can delay the whole process. For these reasons planning decisions must be recorded in writing. During planning meetings, minutes must be kept, especially of envisaged actions. They must indicate clearly what action has been decided, who is to be responsible for its execution, by when it should be performed, and how it should be done. If the planning cycle method is used, actions will obviously be undertaken between the current and the next planning meeting. Problems may arise if the decisions regarding those actions are recorded on a draft document that will only be ratified at the next meeting. Therefore, to have a correct and official written record from the outset, it is suggested that the minutes should be approved at the end of the meeting, rather than waiting to do so during the next meeting. Minutes can even be approved as a meeting progresses. Once a decision has been taken on a specific action, who should take responsibility for it, by when it should be performed and how it should be done, the minutes for that item can be read and approved and, at the end of the meeting, a decision can be taken to approve the minutes in their entirety. This method of looking at each decision via the minutes at that very same meeting can also help the secretary who is not sure of him/herself to correct mistakes and to do it better.

Table 20.1    The minutes of a planning meeting

| Action | Who | When | How | Evaluation |
|---|---|---|---|---|
| Item 2:<br>Buying of kitchen utensils | Mrs A | 10/8<br>15/8 | 15 bowls; 15 spoons;<br>1 large pot; 2 ladles;<br>2 trays; 1 bread knife;<br>2 knives.<br>Buy at Cash & Carry.<br>Don't spend more than R250.00.<br>Minutes of this item approved.<br>JC Rarles | Action on 12/8<br>Items bought at C&C.<br>Mrs A negotiated a special price – spent R175.<br>Utensils now kept at her house until needed. |
| Item 3: | | | | |

It is obvious that this cannot be done if minutes are written in 'story form', in other words, if the opening and welcoming are detailed and if the discussion leading up to a decision is recorded. One needs simplified minutes. First, the minutes should reflect only the decisions taken and the 'who', 'when', and 'how' of it. Second, minutes can be kept in the form of a decisions register. For this a sheet of paper with columns can be used instead of a minute book (see Table 20.1). The keeping of this type of record does not require many sophisticated skills or an education. Relatively unsophisticated groups with little schooling can handle this type of recording with minimal initial help.

## 20.7   INTRODUCTION TO IMPLEMENTATION

The second step of the management cycle is the implementation process. Implementation should take place according to a plan. It is a plan that is to be implemented. It is the operationalisation of the plan. If it is not done according to a plan, it cannot be called implementation. Without a plan all we have are ad-hoc actions or 'shots in the dark'. Implementation is a step-by-step process, addressing each separate task in the plan. Although the implementation process has a number of definite steps, the content is specific to each project and may vary greatly. Because a specific plan is implemented, the mode of implementation differs from project to project. Like planning, implementation is a situation-specific, step-by-step affair, unique to each project.

Because implementation reflects the plan, it is an important test of the plan. If implementation fails, it could be that the plan is incorrect. It could also mean that management is insufficient or that circumstances have changed so drastically since the plan has been formulated that it is not relevant to the situation anymore. In either case it means going back to the planning process. Alternative solutions must again be considered and the best option and implementation requirements must again be chosen. The participants in a project, including the CDW should accept this situation because projects are experiments and the planning process is a learning opportunity where we learn, among others, from our mistakes.

Circumstances do change between a plan and its implementation. For this reason implementation must come as soon as possible after the plan. This is an important reason why it was suggested earlier that planning should be done for not more than one month in advance. Implementation will follow immediately after planning because there is only a month to do what should be done.

Changing circumstances do not necessarily present grave problems, especially if planning and implementation are strictly short term. But, if circumstances do change drastically over a short period, the plan must inevitably be scrapped and reformulated. The longer the period between plan formulation and implementation, the greater the chance that drastic circumstantial change will take place.

## 20.8   IMPLEMENTATION WITH STRONG COMMUNITY PARTICIPATION

All participants in a project must take part in the implementation of the plans.

Implementation is not for the management team alone. The people affected by a specific issue and committed to act on it, must participate in the implementation process as far as possible. People from outside a specific project can also be involved; for example a driver with a tractor can be hired to plough a piece of land for a community garden. Some technical tasks needing specially trained people cannot be done by the ordinary participants, for example land surveying and soil sampling. It is important, though, that the tasks of such a person are prescribed in the action plan and that the prescriptions are adhered to. Such people or organisations must operate in accordance with a contractual relationship with the action group where the latter is the client and they are the suppliers of services. Such a relationship has less of a chance to harm the participants' independence or self-reliance. It is advisable that at least some of the participants are present when people do something in a project, for them to learn, to make sure that the plan is adhered to and to show that they are in charge of the project, not the person or persons from outside.

Even with contractual arrangements in place, involving too many external contractors in a project tends to change its character and relegate the action group to a less important and hands-on position. In such cases the action group's participation is eroded and the whole learning process comes under severe pressure. Case Study 10: *The project that had its fences brought down*, and Case Study 11: *The project that was taken over*, give an indication of how external participation can kill a project.

### Implementation checklist

There are a few critical questions we have to ask ourselves when we are implementing a project:

▶ Does the plan address the issues? We can just as well ask whether the plan will lead to the objective that will mean the end of the need or problem.

▶ Have tasks been identified and written down? Planning is about what to do and if this task is not done properly, implementation will meet with a lot of problems.

▶ Is there somebody responsible for each task? Neither the angels nor the fairies will do the implementation. Implementation is a human activity and from the members of the group people must take responsibility for the various tasks.

▶ Do the people understand the finer details of the plan? There is no question of being empowered if people do not understand what they are doing. Explaining the finer points of the plan is the task of the CDW.

▶ Is the implementation done step by step? There is no other way than taking small steps. One cannot take giant steps when implementing a plan. Either the implementation will go skewed or participants will miss out on the learning process.

▶ Have all tasks been completed? One cannot start with a new batch of implementation tasks before the previous tasks have been done. If this rule is not adhered to chaos will ensue and that is usually the end of the project.

### The conclusion of implementation

Some projects are never concluded because what has been established must be managed and maintained. Yet, there comes a time when the main action comes to an end and a different type of action is necessary. This phase of a project is truly a high point for the action group and the most should be made of it. This is also the time to decide whether it is necessary to continue with the project. If the necessary maintenance and management can be done without a project in place, then so be it.

If the objective of a project is a physical facility such as a crèche or communal hall, and if the group of participants have involved themselves fully in the planning and implementation, the facility should never be handed over at an inaugural function to the group whose efforts have brought it about. How can something that is your own be handed over to you? The group should hand it over to the larger community or the mayor or another appropriate dignitary acting as a trustee. The self-esteem gained by a group when it can hand over the key to a building that was erected through its efforts, instead of receiving a key to a facility placed there by external agents, is of immense value.

The successful conclusion of a project must be celebrated. A celebration strengthens relationships among those involved; it underlines the importance of the action group's achievement; it advertises to the world that that group achieved something through its own efforts; and it is a statement that the group can stand on its own feet. It is, therefore, a terrific confidence booster. And, after all, if a group has really worked hard to achieve something, it has earned a celebration! Jeppe (1985:51) is correct when he says:

> The holding of ceremonies to celebrate the successful completion of a CD project ... and ceremonies to honour and reward outstanding achievements of individuals and groups all have strong motivational value for those already involved and help to influence others to participate ...

## 20.9 THE ROLE OF THE COMMUNITY DEVELOPMENT WORKER IN PLANNING AND IMPLEMENTATION

The CDW should not regard it necessary to enforce blueprints onto the participating group to demonstrate a superior ability. A CDW cannot be judged by the time it takes an action group to reach its objectives, but rather to the extent that they have participated and have learnt from the project.

Interim, step-by-step and experimental planning is not the sign of a weak CDW, but instead the sign of a wise one, enabling the participants to learn as much as possible from their participation.

The most important task of the CDW in this experimental planning is to provide the planning group with relevant information. The group must make choices – that is what decision-making is all about. Its members must know what options are available to them and they must know what the consequences of each option will be. By providing relevant information, the CDW enables them to identify the options, discuss their pros and cons in the light of their probable consequences, and make the best choice under the circumstances. The CDW must always encourage broad participation in planning so as not to limit this fantastic learning opportunity to a privileged few.

The CDW's position in implementation is, at best, a delicate one, but usually also a very difficult one. If the CDW becomes too involved, he/she may be accused of not trusting the action group with the work. If the CDW does not become involved enough, he/she may be criticised for being aloof and 'above the ordinary people'. A CDW should not try to be ever present. Most CDWs are involved in more than one project with the result that they cannot spend all their available time at one project. The CDW's presence is more important during the planning meetings. His/her most important task during implementation is to help the group to translate decisions into action and then to orchestrate the action. But it does act as a morale booster if the CDW sometimes gets involved in physical action. It at least shows the group that the CDW believes that their plan is correct and can be implemented.

One thing a CDW should never do is to take over a job from someone who has been nominated by a planning meeting to do it. Apart from it giving people the opportunity to shirk their responsibilities, it may also be interpreted as a vote of no confidence in that person. It may be necessary that a certain job or task be demonstrated to a group or an individual. This can be done by the CDW or any other competent person, but then it must remain a demonstration. See Case Study 18: *Food garden in Mapayeni.*

It may be necessary to assist a person initially in a certain task until it is clear that the person can do it properly, for example helping someone with the secretarial duties. A CDW should be extremely careful not to show paternalism in this situation. He/she is not there to teach, but to assist. His/her competency level is not to be a yardstick for the group. He/she is not a quality controller, but a partner in an endeavour that is new to the person and the group.

CDWs often complain that, if they do not do most of the implementation work, nothing gets done. In such cases something is seriously wrong. Either the action group tends to take a backseat because the CDW was too prominent from the start (and therefore perceived to be the de facto leader); or the group lacks enthusiasm; or it does not realise that it owns the project and therefore also the responsibility to see it through to its successful conclusion. It is usually a sign that the approach from the start, especially during contact-making, was not right. To 'fix' such a project is extremely difficult because a pattern has evolved and has settled and this pattern has already solidified roles and positions.

## 20.10 CONCLUSION

Planning in community development is a very positive action. People who are the victims of deprivation are given the chance and opportunity to plan a route out of the deprivation trap. Planning should not be a mundane technical affair that most of the participants do not understand. The CDW should be open minded about planning. A few 'musts' were given in this chapter. As long as planning adheres to them, the rest of the planning action can be quite unorthodox. It must be a discovery. It must be adventurous. Why plan in a room around a table? Planning can just as well take place in situ – where the action takes place. Why follow strict meeting procedures during planning meetings? A bit of 'free-for-all' can be very productive and people not used to strict meeting procedures may feel more inclined to participate in an informal discussion. Why plan with paper and pen? Use other items to 'build' plans; just make sure that it gets recorded. Planning must be a monthly high point. It is the best way to maintain momentum and to generate an even greater enthusiasm.

Implementation should hang on to the planning and at the same time fulfil it. It is part of the learning process and just as planning it is out of the question to expect excellence. Mistakes are also going to be made during implementation, and they are to be treated as all mistakes in community development, as opportunities to learn. By treating implementation as a learning opportunity, it becomes more than just the operationalisation of the plan. It also serves to instil confidence in the participants; it is an object lesson to all who want to take note; and it is the basis for further action.

People who take their first steps in community development lose heart easily. For this reason they must realise results quickly, even if these results are small in the eyes of the CDW. Quick results act as incentives for the group to strive harder towards its next objective. Further, poor people are vulnerable to circumstance and a prolonged effort to reach an objective makes them even more vulnerable.

# CHAPTER 21

# EVALUATION AND CONTROL

## 21.1 INTRODUCTION

There are many good reasons for doing evaluation. One of the most important is that, without evaluation, community development cannot be a learning process. We can assume that mistakes will be made and that the identification and analysis of those mistakes will help make future efforts more effective. A mistake can perhaps be seen without delving too deeply for it, but it needs a deeper scrutiny to get clarity on the context in which the mistake occurred. Korten (1980) says that through the learning process, organisations become more effective, more efficient and learn to expand. They can only do that through evaluation.

Because community development is a learning process and because it strives towards clear concrete goals within a murky reality, it needs to make course adjustments during the project from time to time. This is the control part of project management. The principle of adaptiveness is of importance here. Community development usually takes place within an environment of uncertainty. It is usually not very clear what must be done to achieve the desired results. It is not clear what people's responses will be to a project. It is therefore inevitable that things will not always go as planned. Course adjustments as part of the control function will be necessary, but a course adjustment is impossible if the degree of course deviation is not established first. If evaluation is not a continuous part of the project, assuring that timely course adjustments can be made, the chances are good that the deviations will become so severe that nothing will bring the project back on course again.

The debate on the evaluation of community development is very much an ongoing one. This debate has run for many years and has resulted in a lot of soul-searching. Despite many years of discussion, debate and associated examination could not find comprehensive answers to the many problems experienced in evaluation (James et al, 1983:20). A lot of ground has been made since James and associates wrote their article in 1983, but there are still many unanswered questions relating to evaluation.

## 21.2 THE EVALUATION DEBATE

Traditionally evaluation sought to answer the question: Did this project accomplish what it set out to do? Evaluators began with the original goals and attempted to document the extent to which goals had been realised (Staudt, 1985:28). This type of examination was firmly based on providing a numerical value to project outcomes by quantifying the input-effort-output sequence. In other words, evaluation of community development worked on the premise that all projects should meet requirements of economy, efficiency and effectiveness. The evaluators had to find ways how to minimise costs and maximise benefits in the pursuit of profitability (Marsden & Oakley, 1991:317). Even now, the tendency remains to regard evaluation as a measurement, and literature on the subject is concerned with giving a numerical value to the supposed results of a project. The concern is with the effort expended, the effect of the project and efficiency of the use of resources. Evaluation therefore measures the economic performance of a project and even now this tends to be the sole criterion for judgement in many cases (Oakley, 1988:3). But if we are party to the general debate on development with its specifically human focus, we tend to develop some negative reaction to this situation.

We will agree with the concern that the social dimension of development efforts cannot properly be measured by the traditional tools used in evaluation. In fact, it is doubtful whether we are still interested in the traditional answers obtained through evaluation, that is, the effectiveness of project outcomes in terms of the input-effort-output sequence. Central issues for evaluation are participation, capacity-building, sustainability and empowerment (Marsden & Oakley, 1991:315). It is argued that it cannot be expected that all the effects of development projects could be given a numerical value. Oakley (1988:5) goes so far as to say:

> [...] indeed one could argue that the quantification of such effects is merely the tip of the iceberg which hides a whole range of unforeseen and non-material consequences of rural development projects.

This viewpoint on how evaluation should be done and what it should evaluate is embodied in the radical interpretative approach, which is based on the assumption that evaluation cannot be neutral, that evaluation is fundamentally about control over direction and resources, and that its main aim is to address the issue of power (Marsden & Oakley, 1991:321). It therefore questions the conventional view of evaluation, in the words of Marsden and Oakley (1991:328):

> For evaluations to become instruments for liberation and tools for empowerment ... they must transcend the old dichotomies which separate subjective from objective, and which consign insiders and outsiders to separate sides of the fence.

Another dimension of the interpretative approach, that is a logical continuation of the basic premise, is that evaluation must be participatory. Evaluation of projects should be a collaborative venture and the project beneficiaries should have a major role in describing the process, analysing the results and making a judgement upon the outcome of the activities of the project (Oakley, 1988:6). Participatory evaluation is given a solid foundation by the principle of learning. While this principle is as old as community development itself, this can be regarded as a genuine effort to concretise it in a way that will ensure that learning leads to empowerment. Evaluation then becomes part of an educational process, and, because the whole project is then an educational process, evaluation becomes part of the basic dynamic of the project. Then the motivation for evaluation becomes empowerment and learning from experience (Swanepoel, 1996:56). People involved in the project develop a methodology for reviewing their own experience and all conclusions are obtained from the collective reflection that is part of the learning process (Vargas, 1991:269). In this fashion a participatory evaluation approach is not only an evaluative, but also an educational approach (Feuerstein, 1988:24).

We thus arrive at a further dimension which we can call participatory communication and which can and should contribute significantly to the methodologies used in evaluation (Swanepoel, 1996:57). Through participatory communication people can gain a better perception of reality; a fundamental part of evaluation. By encouraging people to question and understand their reality, participatory communication is contributing to a more active role of the poor in projects and their evaluation. It is a process based on people's creative potential. 'The self-expression of the poor people, reflecting upon reality and creating their interpretation of it, is a key element in the Social Development evaluation' (Altafin, 1991:313).

We agree with the main ideas of the radical approach to evaluation. Evaluation must be part of a process of discovery in which the local people are entirely participating. Through this process of discovery, understanding is gained of reality and this understanding is the main impetus for the participants to enjoy a learning experience, to give them a further opportunity for capacity-building. Vargas (1991:269) is correct when she says that a process of this nature is necessarily an educational process because each step helps to bring more comprehension of 'what has been done, how and why'. Evaluation should be regarded as participatory research in which the people, the development agency and/or the donor and one or more researchers are involved. The features of the participatory research technique as identified by Anyanwu (1988:15) should be guiding principles for all involved in evaluation. They are:

▶ The notion of the subjective commitment of the researcher/development agency/donor to the people under study.
▶ The researcher/development agency/donor becomes a participatory social actor.
▶ An active endeavour to understand the conditions underlying community problems.
▶ An educational process for the researcher/development agency/donor together with the community.
▶ Respect for the people's capability to produce and analyse knowledge.

The rest of this chapter will try to fall in with this approach.

## 21.3 MONITORING AND EVALUATION

Evaluation is an integral part of a project. It forms part of the survey—it evaluates the reality or situation through the information obtained and it evaluates the information to ensure that it is legitimate and correct. It is also tied up with needs and resource identification by seeking the fit between needs and resources. It is an important part of planning—it tests the situation specificity and the feasibility of the planning. It is necessary during implementation—it assesses the action group's ability to operationalise the plan.

It is clear that a large portion of evaluation takes place throughout the life of a project and only a small part has to do with a final, after-the-fact evaluation. This larger continuous part can be regarded as keeping the finger on the pulse of a project and is called monitoring. The second type is an action performed at the end of a project. It is the final opportunity, with the benefit of hindsight, to identify weaknesses and mistakes made during the lifespan of a project. It seeks to establish whether the project was successful in terms of obtaining its objective and whether it was successful as a learning process; whether the action group gained more than only the physical results it was aiming for.

### 21.3.1   Criteria for monitoring and evaluation

Three main criteria are used in monitoring and evaluation. The first is that of appropriateness or 'fit'. Using this criterion it must be established whether the needs, objectives, plan of action and the action itself fit one another. The following questions must be asked:

▶   Will the attainment of the set objective satisfy the identified need? (Does the objective fit the need?)
▶   Do we identify the correct resources to reach the objective? (Do the resources fit the need?)
▶   Will the plan lead to the attainment of the objective? (Does the plan fit the objective?)

The second criterion is that of feasibility. It concerns itself with the claims a project will make on resources, including human resources. These questions must be asked:

▶   Is the objective within reach of the action group?
▶   Are there sufficient resources to reach the objective?
▶   Is the project completely dependent on external resources to reach the objective?
▶   Can human assets be developed during the project?

The community development worker (CDW) has a special duty regarding this part of the monitoring and evaluation process. He/she must be very honest with a group if it is apparent that they are aiming too high. Without telling the people bluntly that their objective is beyond their means, the CDW can help them to map out the consequences of their decisions. A CDW should never tell a group that something is beyond their means. It is much better to help the action group establish the costs in terms of time, money, experience and effort. It is also feasible to help the action group identify alternative choices and assist them in exploring the consequences. This method of confronting a group with choices, rather than telling them what to do, is a good way of letting them take the initiative and accept the responsibility. Eventually, it is a great opportunity of learning and must lead to greater self-reliance.

Questions using the criteria of appropriateness and feasibility must also be put in the past tense. In other words, these criteria must be used for monitoring and for evaluation. It is necessary in monitoring and in the final evaluation to establish whether decisions taken interpret(ed) feasibility and appropriateness correctly.

Eventually, the criteria of appropriateness and feasibility both point to the criterion of effectiveness. The action group wants to establish through evaluation whether its actions during the lifespan of a project were (are) effective. However, effectiveness in terms of the principles discussed earlier, must also be established. How effective was the project in fulfilling abstract human needs; in providing a learning process for the participants; in establishing ownership in the action group; in empowering the action group; and in releasing the people from the deprivation trap? These questions must be answered truthfully because the danger exists that the CDW and the committee may rush towards the objective with a lot of external help while the group of participants are left behind and find themselves mostly outside of the important activities. In terms of effectiveness a project may score highly because the principles were ignored. In order to obviate this possibility, effectiveness must therefore also be evaluated in terms of the principles.

Many questions can be suggested to evaluate effectiveness. Some of these assess effectiveness without taking community development principles into consideration. Others evaluate effectiveness only in terms of the principles. Both these types should be used. For ease of use, the two types appear in two separate lists of questions.

List 1: Questions to establish the effectiveness of objective attainment

- Was a survey done before a need was identified?
- Which research techniques were used in the survey?
- Was a need eventually identified?
- Was the need contextualised?
- Was the objective specified concretely?
- Was the objective within reach of the action group?
- Was the objective to alleviate the whole or only part of the identified need?
- Was the objective fully attained?
- Was the objective attained within the planned time?
- Did the attainment of the objective satisfy the identified need?
- Was a survey of resources undertaken?
- Were the right resources identified to reach the objective?
- How often were planning meetings held?
- Was a record kept of the planning?
- In what way was recording of planning done?
- In what way was the planning done?
- Did the planning specifically appoint certain people to certain tasks?
- Did the planning attach a timetable to action?
- Did the planning address how to do certain tasks?
- Was the planning appropriate to the identified need and the set objective?
- Was the project monitored?
- What monitoring techniques were used?
- Was money handled correctly?
- Was bookkeeping done correctly?
- Were measures taken to institutionalise and maintain the objective?

List 2: Questions to establish whether the objective was attained successfully in terms of the principles

- How was the action group for the project formed?
- Did the action group decide on the need?

- What was the role of the CDW in deciding the need?
- To what extent did the action group participate in the survey?
- Was the committee elected by the action group?
- What was the CDW's official position on the committee?
- How often were action group meetings held?
- Did the committee report back to action group meetings on its activities?
- What percentage of action group members attended the action group meetings?
- Was enough time allowed in meetings for action group members to participate in the discussion?
- Were members encouraged to participate in discussions during meetings?
- What part did members play in project planning?
- What part did the CDW play in project planning?
- What percentage of the action group members were involved in the implementation?
- In what way were persons/organisations from outside involved in the project?
- To what extent did members participate in monitoring and evaluation?
- To what extent was the CDW involved in monitoring and evaluation?
- Were the benefits of the project distributed equally among participants?
- To what extent was the larger community advantaged by the project?
- Did the CDW's role diminish as the project progressed?
- Was leadership strengthened during the project?
- Were new leaders identified and involved in leadership activities?
- Did the action group accept ownership of the project?
- Did the action group accept responsibility for the project?
- Did the action group take more initiative as the project progressed?
- Did attendance of action group meetings increase or decrease?
- Did the action group have the power of decision-making regarding the project?
- Did the project lead to the action group identifying further needs?
- Is the action group now better able to identify its needs?
- Is the action group now better able to plan?
- Is the action group now better able to organise itself?
- Is the action group now better able to tackle a project?
- Is the action group now desirous of tackling further projects?
- Is the action group now less dependent on external aid?
- Is there any notable change in the attitude of the action group regarding its situation?
- Is there evidence that the larger community wants to follow the action group's example?

Some of these questions can be asked during a project and some only at the end of a project. There are, therefore, monitoring questions and evaluative questions. Most can be dealt with by the participants, but some of the questions in the second list will have to be answered by the CDW.

## 21.4  PARTICIPATORY SELF-EVALUATION

Projects are as successful as the action groups running them. Therefore, if we evaluate what an action group is doing and how it is doing it, we can learn much about the project. Participatory self-evaluation is based on the assumption that if an action group is evaluated, it is as good as an evaluation of the project. The objective of this evaluation technique is to enable action groups to get a better idea of their weaknesses and strengths. (This whole section is based on the work of Uphoff, 1989, 1991.) When they have obtained this knowledge, they can take action to improve on their weaknesses and use their strengths to greater effect. This evaluation is interested mainly in the process of a project, but it also looks at the product of a project. The process is what happens in an action group: the way in which it communicates, plans, works, holds meetings and implements plans. The product is what the action group accomplishes: the objective it has reached, the maintenance of what it had achieved, the happiness and contentment of the members on reaching their objective.

### 21.4.1   The method used

The group must evaluate themselves on a regular basis throughout the project, for example every three months. The group must answer a number of questions. There are 42 process and 14 product questions from which the group must select several to answer. Preferably, not more than 20 questions should be chosen. Four possible answers are given for every question and the group must, after discussion, decide which one of the answers best describes them. The first possible answer represents a very good result and is worth 4 points. The second possible answer represents a fairly good result and is worth 3 points. The third possible answer represents a barely fair to poor result and is worth 2 points. The fourth possible answer represents a bad result and is worth 1 point. It is very important that the action group discuss each question thoroughly before they decide on the best answer. In fact, the discussion is the most important part of the exercise because it ensures a vigorous look into the processes that guide that group and it forces the group to use communication to come to some consensus about the group's standing. And this is the second important part of the exercise, that is, that consensus must be reached and that it is not allowed to vote on the best possible answer for the group. At the end of the exercise the group can see where it stands by adding up the points. More importantly, the group should take all the questions for which it has scored only 1 or 2 points and decide what is to be done to improve those aspects covered by the questions. They represent the action group's weaknesses. At the next evaluation exercise the group will be able to see where it has improved and where it has taken a step backwards.

### 21.4.2   The role of the CDW

It is very important that the group be facilitated in this exercise. The CDW can play the facilitating role. This will include explaining the meaning of each question and its 4 possible answers; to ensure that each question and its 4 possible answers are discussed in detail; to ensure that the discussion is honest and serious; to ensure that every individual has the freedom to speak his/her mind; and to help the action group decide what they are going to do with the results of the evaluation.

If the CDW wants to introduce this type of evaluation to an action group, there are certain steps that he/she should follow:

**Step 1:** Go through all the questions and their possible answers carefully. Take out all those that are irrelevant to the group or the project.

**Step 2:** Approach the group and tell them about this method of evaluation. Explain the method and the objectives of the evaluation. If they decide that they want to use it, continue with step 3.

**Step 3:** Present the questions that have not been removed from the list to the group. Read every question and explain it so that the members understand it correctly. Do not read the answers. Ask the group to make a selection from these questions and arrange a date for the exercise.

**Step 4:** Write each of the chosen questions with its possible answers on a separate card, but even better, on a transparency or large sheet so that every member of the meeting can see the questions and answers during the exercise.

**Step 5:** Explain the methodology and objectives once again at the evaluation meeting. Then present each question in turn. Read the question and possible answers and, if necessary, explain them. Ask the group to pick one answer. Remind the members that it is absolutely essential for them to be honest and that they must take their time in discussing each question before deciding on their answer. Each time the group has decided on an answer, mark that chosen answer on the card or transparency and write up the points value of the answer on a separate piece of paper.

**Step 6:** Give the score at the end of the exercise, but, more importantly, identify with the group the items where the group has scored only one or two points. Explain to the group that it must decide on a plan of action to improve these items. Also explain to the group that they can regard those questions where they got full points as their strengths which they can use.

**Step 7:** Remind the group in good time when the follow-up evaluation is due and then repeat the whole exercise. One of the advantages of this evaluation method is that the answers to the questions can be scaled up or down, depending on the strength and experience of the group. The high scoring answer can be levelled at 'very good' and the low scoring answer at 'not very good', in which case a high scale will be used. But the scale can easily be lowered so that the high scoring answer levels at 'good' and the low scoring answer at 'bad'.

### 21.4.3  Evaluating the CDW

This method of evaluation can also be used to evaluate the CDW. After all, the CDW is responsible to the action group and therefore they have the right to evaluate him/her. The CDW cannot facilitate this evaluation because the facilitator must be as uncompromising as possible. Thirteen questions are available for this evaluation.

Addendum 1 contains the set of process questions, the set of product questions and the questions for the evaluation of the CDW.

## 21.5  RECORD-KEEPING AND MONITORING/EVALUATION

One of the most glaring shortcomings of projects is that they are seldom systematically recorded. As a result extremely valuable information is lost and cannot be used to learn for future projects. Good record-keeping enriches the process of evaluation and, because evaluation is one of the cornerstones of the learning process, one can say that well-kept records enhance the learning process. There are several ways in which records can be kept. These do not include material usually placed in files such as letters and memorandums because it is obvious that these ordinary administrative outputs should be kept and perused when necessary. We will discuss some of these ways in this section.

### 21.5.1 Records of planning meetings

In a previous chapter we saw that planning meetings should also be an evaluating exercises. Every planning meeting should start with an assessment of the activities undertaken since the last meeting and then plan in the light of that evaluation. If records are kept of both the evaluation and planning sections of each meeting as was suggested in the previous chapter, a complete picture will evolve and be available by the time the final evaluation is reached. This record will start with some broad guidelines on how to reach the objective (decided on at the first meeting), followed by detailed planning for one month. This will be followed by an evaluation, first, of the implementation of that detailed planning and, second, of the 'implementability' of the detailed planning, in other words, an evaluation of the planning. This in turn, will be followed by detailed planning for the next month in the light of the evaluation of the previous month, and so on. We would therefore have a record of every step we decided on (the what), a time frame attached to it (the when), a person or persons responsible for that step (the who), the way we think that step should be carried out (the how) and what happened, reflected in the right most column of the minutes.

### 21.5.2 Reports

Another way of keeping records is to request full reports at planning meetings by key participants on all activities engaged in since the previous meeting. These reports can be written (in which case they can be attached to the minutes) or they can be oral (in which case detailed notes must be made of them in the minutes). The advantage of this method is that the correctness of the reports is verified when the minutes are approved, and the records are kept in a central place with other documents and correspondence. The disadvantage is that it places a heavy burden on the secretary if the reports are delivered orally. Further, participants may find it difficult to write reports on their activities and, lastly, the tabling of detailed reports may lengthen planning meetings considerably.

### 21.5.3 Event cards

In order to spread the burden of record-keeping more evenly, the key persons in a project may be given event cards.

Each of them completes an event card each time they are involved in some action pertaining to the project. The completed cards are then left at a central place or with someone such as the secretary or CDW. The advantage of this method is that the work of record keeping is shared by several people. Another advantage is that the event cards are completed immediately after the event. The reports are therefore fresher than an oral report at a meeting perhaps three weeks after the fact. A further advantage is that several reports may be received of the same event because several people are usually involved. It means that more than one person's perception and experience of the same event is recorded. A final advantage is that records are short and precise and will not take much time to make out or analyse. The disadvantage of this method is that no-one is really responsible for writing down the events, and it may happen that it is not done at all. If all or some of the key people are illiterate, this method cannot be used. The purpose of these event cards is not to table them at the next meeting. They form a separate and parallel record of the project. A comparison between this and the official record can be very interesting. See Figure 21.1 for an example of an event card.

DATE OF EVENT: _____

REPORTER: _____

DESCRIPTION OF EVENT: _____

_____

_____

ROLE OF REPORTER: _____

_____

REMARKS AND PRELIMINARY ASSESSMENT ON REVERSE

Figure 21.1  **Example of an event card**

## 21.6  DISCUSSION AND OBSERVATION AS MONITORING/ EVALUATION TECHNIQUES

For monitoring and evaluating purposes written records must be augmented by observation and discussion, mostly of the experience obtained through simply participating. The CDW must keep his/her eyes and ears open to observe, not only physical detail, but also the attitudes and perceptions of those participating in the project. This observation is not of an isolated event, but views over time so that progress and growth and attitude and approach can also be noted. Discussions can be formal or informal, between groups or individuals. There is not a best way. The circumstances and the situation will decide which method is best for the moment. The important aspect regarding this type of monitoring and evaluation is that we should not treat it as a sloppy way of research. It is not a second ranked or rated way of doing things; it is just another, equally trustworthy way. We should realise that there are both objectivity and subjectivity present in any given situation. The one is not more important than the other. Both are present and therefore both must be considered. Just as in any other 'scientific' research the CDW and the participants must use triangulation (see Chapter 18) to verify the information received. The other important aspect that must be adhered to is that the CDW, who is part of the monitoring and evaluating process, can never stand aloof of the situation and view matters from a bird's eye advantage point. The view is strictly lateral, sometimes even worm-like. We looked at the evaluative, interpretative approach to evaluation earlier on, therefore suffice it here to simply say that we must have extremely open minds geared towards adaptiveness (Chambers' new professionalism, 1983) when dealing with evaluation and monitoring.

CDWs must consider the possibility of holding a diary in which they can record from time to time (not necessarily every day) their observations and specifically subjective observations such as attitude, animosity, keenness, belief and self-reliance. All of these observations can be very valuable inputs in a final evaluation of a project, especially when dealing with the second list of questions above.

## 21.7 DO'S AND DON'TS REGARDING EVALUATION

Evaluation tends to have negative connotations. People do not like to be evaluated. In most people's minds it is like writing an examination—it is never pleasant. For this reason the CDW should handle evaluation carefully. The following aspects require special attention:

▶ Evaluation should never be presented as a test. It is not intended to establish whether a person or group has succeeded or failed. Evaluation tries to establish whether an action had the desired result and to determine the reasons for its outcome.

▶ Evaluation should never be personalised. It is not a person or even the group that is evaluated, but an action. If the 'how' aspect is thoroughly discussed in a planning meeting, the individual cannot, in any event, be blamed if an action fails or has a less spectacular outcome.

▶ Never tie evaluation to a penalty. A less than successful outcome is already a letdown. A penalty will only have negative results under these circumstances.

▶ Evaluation should be done openly. It is not the prerogative of the CDW or the executive of a group. When evaluation becomes something done by an individual or a few individuals after they have distanced themselves from the rest of the participants, all the negative perceptions will find fertile soils for them to proliferate.

▶ All participants must also participate in evaluation. No one is to be barred from it because apart from the elitism engendered by it, it also keeps certain people away from the learning opportunity offered by evaluation.

▶ Evaluation should be simple. Complex, so-called scientific methodologies require great skill that makes it impossible for most participants to participate or at least understand what they are doing. Such complexity and sophistication can only have negative reactions from the ordinary people, to the extent that they do not understand the data and even less the analysis of the data and that they therefore develop distrust in the activity of evaluation and the results it produces.

▶ Evaluation should always be presented as a learning opportunity. When evaluation shows a negative result, two questions must immediately be asked. What have we learnt from it? What should we now do? Every negative result must be turned into a positive learning experience. It must always be accompanied by planning or replanning, which is a positive expression.

▶ The CDW should not distance him/herself from a negative result. He/she should never be critical of a person's or the group's actions. If something goes wrong the CDW must accept with the group responsibility for it. Success must be ascribed to the action group, but for the mishaps the CDW must accept joint responsibility.

## 21.8   CONTROL

Control sounds a very important function and one would want to attach authority to it. Only those with authority can control a project. Because of a lifelong preoccupation with amorphous figures of authority, we also tend to turn away from the community, from ordinary people when we are seeking those figures of authority. Yet, when we speak of control as a management function in projects, we do not have other role-players in mind than those who we are familiar with. Those people who were participating in needs identification, who were present at the planning meetings and who are actively involved in implementation, are also the ones who control a project.

The control function is a very important one, but we should be careful not to tie it to supervision and executive discretion like that of organisational management. Yes, it has to do with supervision and discretion, but not that of one person over others. The supervision and discretion in our context lies with the participants who must supervise their own actions and exercise discretion over their own plans. If they realise through the learning process that a project needs adjustment, then they adjust accordingly and that is what is meant by control. Every planning meeting therefore, is also a mechanism of control and every evaluation activity informs the control function. We can therefore conclude by saying that control is an everyday function and it is situated in the project with the participants, not outside with some vague figure of authority.

## 21.9   CONCLUSION

Objective quantifiable evaluation is not the only good evaluation. Some things that must be learnt through evaluation cannot be established in an objective quantifiable way. Many of the questions in the two lists detailed earlier, as well as in the participatory self-evaluation, require a subjective evaluative assessment of the situation. The intention of monitoring and evaluation is to afford the CDW and the group an opportunity to learn. It is obvious that continuous evaluation will establish a critical disposition in the action group that will enhance the learning process. This type of evaluation relies on two factors for reliability and correctness. The first is honesty – dishonesty will lead to the evaluators bluffing themselves. The second is verification. No evaluation result stands on the say-so of one person. That is the reason for group evaluation rather than evaluation by a person. That is also the reason why PRAP (see Chapter 18) relies so heavily on triangulation.

It is important to accept that there is nothing wrong with qualitative interpretative evaluation. A lot of information necessary for community development cannot be gleaned in any other way. Such evaluation is not of a poorer quality than quantitative evaluation. In fact, Uphoff (1991:284) says:

> It can be argued that this method is more objective than when an outsider comes in with an interview schedule and asks questions of individuals, who do not have to compare and justify their views in front of one another. They have no obligation to speak truthfully or fully with this outsider whom they do not know and who probably knows little about the workings of the group anyway. Their misunderstanding of his questions and his misunderstanding of their answers are likely to add up to significant miscommunication.

Taylor (1991:8) adds that 'we should be less defensive about the role of personal values, convictions, impressions and opinions than is sometimes the case'. Marsden and Oakley (1991:325) come to the conclusion that 'the way forward lies in the construction of a practical evaluation that embodies many of the central concerns of an interpretative enquiry'.

The evaluation discussed in this chapter can be regarded as an alternative, even radical approach. (See Swanepoel, 1996.) It is in sympathy with and tries to give substance to Oakley's (1988:5) ideas on evaluation:

> We need an approach to M&E, therefore, which is not based exclusively on the measurement of material effects, but which is able also to explain what happens in a ... development project which seeks to promote participation. We will need to move away from a dependence upon measurement and equip ourselves with other techniques for understanding such concepts as participation.

In dealing with participation, we are not only concerned with results (which are quantitative). More importantly, we need to understand processes (which are qualitative). Evaluation must be a process of discovery through which an understanding of reality is attained or enhanced. This understanding allows the participants to enjoy a learning experience providing further opportunities for capacity-building—an absolute prerequisite for empowerment (Swanepoel, 1996:57).

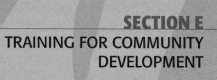

**SECTION E**

**TRAINING FOR COMMUNITY
DEVELOPMENT**

# CHAPTER 22

# THE TRAINING DIALOGUE

## 22.1 INTRODUCTION

The community development worker (CDW) has many tasks and roles. We have seen throughout this book how the CDW is involved in every part of development and poverty eradication. The last important task that we would like to discuss in this book is that of trainer because the CDW will have to train people to become motivators, mobilisers and advisors for people who want to take charge of their own lives (De Beer, 1995). 'Since the learning process is a vital aspect of community development, it is important that as many role-players as possible are exposed to, and share the same type of training input' (De Beer & Swanepoel, 1998:90).

This chapter and the next have been written with reference to De Beer (1995); De Beer & Swanepoel (1996); De Beer & Swanepoel (1998); and Swanepoel & De Beer (1994). The United Nations (1984:17) stated:

> Training requires special skills and talents that are not common, and competent persons with a good deal of practical experience are required. It is often difficult, however, to attract such persons to the job of training and to reward them sufficiently to keep them on the job and improve their performance.

The teaching model supported by the authors may be described as a model of 'teaching by discovery' or as capacity-building (workshop). This method of training, which the authors follow, is described in this book and should be used by the student trainers, such as CDWs who will undertake the training of people involved in the development of communities.

However, this workshop or capacity-building method is not easy. The advantages of this method and the disadvantages of the direct or lecture method are so obvious that the relatively difficult method is preferred. Opportunity for interaction is encouraged and a dialogue between trainer, trainee and material can be established to the extent that the trainer becomes a facilitator of a process of knowledge creation by the trainees. The trainer is required to accept the challenge with an open mind, a willingness to experiment, and above all openness to regard every training episode as an opportunity for him/her and the trainees to learn.

The trainer must become a 'dialogical man' as Freire (2006:90) puts it. This person must first of all have faith in humankind, in their ' ... power to make and remake, to create and recreate, faith in their vocation to be more fully human …'. The facilitator who enters into dialogue with the community must show humility, because without it dialogue cannot take place. 'How can I dialogue if I always project ignorance onto others and never perceive my own. … How can I dialogue if I am closed to—even offended by—the contribution of others?', Freire, 2006:90).

It may take time and practice for the facilitator, especially the person who starts anew, to handle the workshop method efficiently. The results, once the method is mastered, are very rewarding.

This chapter provides a broad framework; some ideas; and approaches that are proven successes that have proven successful in practice. Facilitators are advised to use them as guidelines and not as gospel. The reality and the challenges facilitators face will differ and will require adaptation and experimentation. Ideally, the guidelines should be used as part of a training package. However, student trainers can also use it as a manual for self-training. All CDWs will not necessarily be facilitators, but they should still take note of these two chapters because they will come across training packages for development projects. They will then have the opportunity to evaluate those in the light of these chapters.

## 22.2   TRAINING AS A DIALOGUE

### 22.2.1   Introduction- the concept explained

To be optimally successful, development training should be a dialogue between the three key elements in a training situation: material, trainer and the trainees.

The material may be a text book or journal article, a videotape, equipment for simulation games or ideas in the head of the trainer: usually it consists of a combination of the items mentioned.

The trainer may be an expert, and his/her task will be to transfer his/her knowledge to the trainees. He/she comes with knowledge, norms and attitudes and, because of his/her position, with authority, if not power. Sometimes the trainer is not an expert, but knows how to facilitate a group to create their own knowledge, or knows where to find and how to involve an expert when the subject is very technical.

Trainees are adults with some life experience and probably knowledge applicable to the theme they are about to be trained in. They also bring along norms and attitudes developed during their lives.

These elements—material, trainer and trainees—form the 'raw material' with which to carry out a training session.

The modes of training according to which the process can be conducted are action, discussion and presentation.

Action training is experiential in that it allows trainees to 'do' and therefore experience certain situations. From their experience they are able to discover knowledge, learn a skill or identify and improve attitudes. A diagram of action training is shown in Figure 22.1.

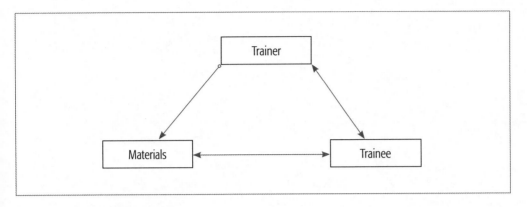

Figure 22.1 **Action training diagram**

The role of the trainer is to choose an activity or topic and then to manage the action; the trainees engage directly with the topic and explore, discover and solve problems through the experience afforded.

Discussion is a method of training also called reflective learning. In this method both the trainer and trainees engage in the 'dissecting' of material—be it a pre-read article or the material generated by the group in a workshop. They raise issues, analyse, and come to conclusions by participating in the discussion. The trainer has to decide on the topic or material and generally, 'regulates the traffic of discussion'. A diagram of discussion is shown in Figure 22.2.

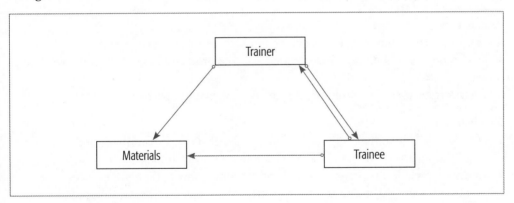

Figure 22.2 **Discussion diagram**

Presentation is a formal lecture in which the trainer relates the material to the trainees. He/she is a filter and in this situation the trainees have very little, if any, direct contact with the material. A diagram of presentation is shown in Figure 22.3 on the next page.

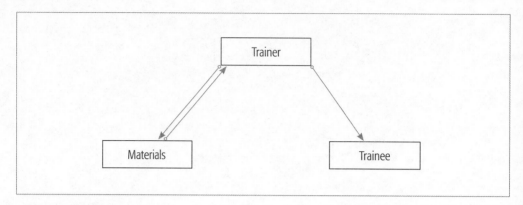

Figure 22.3 **Presentation diagram**

During a training episode often more than one, if not all three, of these methods are used. For optimal learning to take place the facilitator must plan a properly balanced learning episode in which, through action, discussion and presentation the facilitator, material and trainees are continuously in dialogue.

## 22.2.2  The meaning of participation in training

Can we talk of participation when trainees are only allowed to answer questions posed by the trainer? Certainly not, though it may be a small part of participation. Participation in training means, among others, that:

Trainees:
▶ are expected to and must be encouraged to help set the 'training agenda';
▶ must contribute their practical experience to the process taking place in the workshop; and
▶ must 'create' their own understanding of and solutions to problems.

Facilitators:
▶ must be flexible in their approach, willing to be challenged by trainees and able to deal with the situation without causing tension or animosity among the trainees;
▶ must be capable of integrating and interpreting contributions by trainees so that it contributes and becomes part of the process taking place in the workshop; and
▶ must accompany and guide trainees in the process of gaining understanding of and solutions to problems.

Participation in training means that the facilitator encourages an atmosphere in which the trainee, facilitator and material engage in a dialogue to find applicable answers. It is, in other words, not an ordinary classroom situation in which an 'expert' shares with passive students his/her wisdom. It is taxing on the facilitator and requires practical experience, knowledge of the subject and a non-threatening disposition. It also requires of the facilitator a maturity to handle difficult situations and adult people.

### 22.2.3  Setting the climate for learning

All people fear the unknown and all have expectations regarding specific situations they may experience. Fear and expectations are the two main issues to be addressed in order to set a relaxed and purposeful climate for learning.

In a classroom situation people fear the trainer because he/she has power stemming from knowledge and position; other participants for they may be better qualified to voice their opinions; their own inability to be assertive; the environment in which teaching takes place; and above all, they fear failure.

Facilitators should address the trainees' fear of the facilitator by making themselves vulnerable: acknowledge their shortcomings and emphasise the potential contribution of the trainees—the facilitator is not a know-all and the trainee not an empty slate; address the fear of other trainees by introducing them to one another informally, also talking about their background; address the fear of lack of assertiveness by treating each trainee as an individual, and providing an opportunity for each to make his/her viewpoint known; address the fear of the environment with applicable seating arrangements and by a relaxed attitude; address the fear of failure by emphasising the mutual learning experience and the approach that is not aimed at examination and 'passing a test'.

Expectations are often determined by factors that are not controlled by the facilitator. The community whom he/she represents may 'impose' their expectations on the trainee; the general political climate in the country may create high and unrealistic expectations; trainees themselves may view any kind of training as an opportunity for personal growth, and, often, as a guarantee of future employment opportunities; above all they may expect the training to empower them to move the world, or, conversely, they may expect that they would in any case fail. By allowing expectations to surface we will be in a better position to deal with them.

Address the expectations of trainees by explaining very clearly the composition and objectives of the course. Discuss the organisation of the training. Allow trainees to explain and discuss their problems, expectations and aims.

### 22.2.4  Ensuring participation

The capacity-building approach is extremely dependent on the full participation of the trainees. But participation does not come of itself. Those who are supposed to participate always have some reservations. The main reason for this is that participation increases vulnerability (remember the fear factor). It is safer to keep quiet and look interested than to participate and be challenged or even be criticised. The facilitator can also be fooled by a quasi-participation which in the end contributes nothing to the process. Head nodding and phrases such as 'I agree', 'yes, yes', 'that is so' fall under this category. It is acceptable for everyday conversation and makes it lively, but it is not participation in discussion.

Participation must be invited, made possible and made worthwhile. An important prerequisite for participation is an atmosphere conducive to participation and this ties in closely with the attitude and ability of the facilitator. The trainees must be convinced that the facilitator is dependent on their contributions; that he/she is interested in their contributions; that he/she regards their contributions as valuable; and that he/she views their contributions as giving momentum to the process. The facilitator must also have the ability to give every trainee a fair chance to participate; to regulate the discussions so that no one person will dominate; and to make sure that every trainee is safeguarded against personal attack.

It is very important that the discussions have relevancy and that they deal with practical aspects. Trainees will feel it unnecessary to contribute, or feel themselves incapable of contributing if the discussion does not affect them or their work situation directly. Many trainees also feel themselves incapable of contributing to theoretical discussions while they are quite competent to talk about practical issues. The feeling and attitude among the trainees may also work towards discouraging or encouraging participation. A few overly critical trainees may dampen the appetite for contributions to the discussions. If the training programme is for a multi-level group, the more junior members may feel incompetent to talk in front of more senior personnel. The facilitator must nullify these negative aspects by playing the role of catalyst and enabler. He/she must be a competent and fair traffic officer who will give everybody a fair chance to contribute. He/she will regard every contribution as important and will show it through his/her gratitude for every contribution. The trainees' understanding of the capacity-building approach is also very important. The trainees must realise and believe that no knowledge transfer is going to take place from the trainer to them; that they are responsible for finding solutions to their problems, and that it will not be rude to say what is on their mind.

They are used to the presentation (lecture) method. They had years of experience of lectures in school, college and university. In that context, participation is to ask at the end of the lecture if there is something that they do not understand. It may be difficult for them to make the leap to the type of participation required by the capacity-building approach.

A usually successful solicitor of contributions is a discussion on the needs of the trainees. A need orientation is therefore very important. People like to talk about their needs and problems and it is the task of the facilitator to steer the discussion from this topic to the possible solution to the needs and problems.

## 22.3   INTERACTIVE (WORKSHOP) TECHNIQUES

Many interactive training techniques exist and more are developed by facilitators as they gain experience and face new challenges.

### 22.3.1   Open session discussion

The inputs that the facilitator makes must never be regarded as gospel. The facilitator must submit it for the scrutiny of the trainees. Don't be satisfied with a simple reaction that they agree with the input. Ask the 'yes, but' questions if they don't do it. This scrutiny of the inputs takes place mostly through an open discussion by all the participants. The same applies to report-back sessions. Impress upon the trainees that reports from groups must also be scrutinised and therefore discussed.

### 22.3.2   Group work

It is often taken for granted that work in small groups is better than in plenary sessions, and that it is the best way to involve all trainees. This is not necessarily true. Small groups can have various disadvantages, among others, the following more important ones:

▶ It can lead to synergy loss. The facilitator's objective is to establish synergy, in other words, a combined energy that is greater than the sum total of the energy of the individuals. Fragmentation into smaller groups can work against this objective. Breaking into smaller groups entails a stop to proceedings in plenary session, movement of people to other rooms or another place in the same room, some people rushing off to the toilets or taking a quick cigarette, chats between people on any subject, sitting down for the small group discussion, and breaking the ice in order to start the work. In other words, the momentum of the workshop is lost and with it also the building up of synergy. Another cause of synergy loss is that groups do not finish their work at the same time. Some groups finish sooner and loiter while others are still busy.

▶ It can be duplicating. Group work can be so structured that groups do the same work and come to the same conclusions. At the report-back the one group repeats what the other group has already said and this can happen three or four times depending on the number of groups. This is not the most productive way to use limited time.

▶ It can be time-consuming. It takes time for groups to move to their places of work and to move back to the main centre for report-back. It can take as long as twenty minutes and breaks of thirty minutes are not uncommon. A report-back session can also be time-consuming. If there are three groups, it cannot be completed in less than twenty minutes.

▶ It can lead to competition. Groups tend to compete with each other. Basically, there is nothing wrong with this — a critical disposition towards each other can have good results — but a lot of energy can be spent on the competition, therefore spent on peripheral foci. Competition between groups can also work against the unity of the larger group. It can therefore spoil its dynamics. Competition can also waste time and misdirect attention when groups try to catch each other out during report-back.

▶ Group work does not ensure better involvement of the individual trainee. It is generally accepted that the shy, unsure of him/herself trainee will participate better in the small group. There is some merit in this belief, but it is not universally true. The leader of the small group may not be such a good facilitator as the facilitator and the very people who cause the trainee's shyness and reluctance to participate may be with him/her in the small group. This is not going to help his/her participation in the least. On the contrary, he/she will be in more of a face-to-face position with them than in the larger group.

▶ Facilitation is taken out of the facilitator's hands. One of the most serious disadvantages is that the success of the small group depends on its leader. The facilitator has very little control over who will be nominated as leaders and they can have all the flaws a group leader can possibly have. They can be steamrollers, not allowing the group to participate. They can be biased towards certain people. They can be incapable of maintaining a free flow of ideas or of getting a group going. Group work can therefore be a low point with not much going on. Animosities and bad blood in the small group can also be brought to the larger group.

All these weaknesses must be kept in mind and the facilitator must try to prevent them from weakening the workshop.

If group work is done, then:

▶ the task must be precisely described so that the group can operate within well-defined parameters;

- it must be ascertained whether the group understands its task before it is sent away;
- enough time must be allocated (less than 30 minutes for group work is counterproductive);
- groups must not be loaded down with a number of tasks for a single work session; and
- report-back must lead to discussion.

Group work can be of value if different groups give attention to different aspects to save the larger group's time. Not more than four groups should be operative because it taxes work space severely and because it makes report-back too long.

The division of the trainees into groups can follow one of two points of departure; that is to put together what belongs together or to make each group as diverse as the large group is. People belong together if they share the same work place, do the same job, and find themselves at the same level of the hierarchy or when they are friends. It is better if the small group reflects the composition of the large group. The best way to get this diversity in the small group is to simply give trainees a number in repetitive sequence, that is 1, 2, 3, 1, 2, 3, starting at one point and running through to the end. It ensures the break up of friends or colleagues from the same office who usually sit next to one another.

### 22.3.3 Buzz groups

Buzz groups may be a better option than larger groups although the one cannot replace the other. Buzz groups consist of two or three people sitting next to one another. The aims with buzz groups are not to let them work out things in detail and to report at length. Therefore, a buzz group session lasts a maximum of fifteen minutes. The idea is to get a few ideas from every buzz group on the table and then to work with that 'raw material' until some refined product is achieved. Buzz groups are also less formal than small groups.

It is not necessary for all buzz groups to report-back. The primary idea is to get a discussion going. Therefore the facilitator uses inputs to solicit reaction and then invites only inputs that will represent a counter reaction. Or he/she takes up a point from a buzz group and develops it up to a point and then invites inputs that will develop it further. It can be quite a hectic session with buzz groups clamouring for attention or violently opposed to one another's inputs. Later the inputs are not all from buzz groups, but individuals make inputs. This is fine, as long as the argument develops at a fast pace. The facilitator is therefore more than a chairperson who gives everyone a fair chance to report-back. He/she manipulates inputs to get a discussion going and even plays devil's advocate to make the discussion livelier.

### 22.3.4 The nominal group technique

The purpose of the nominal group technique is to ensure equal inputs from all trainees. The method is briefly as follows: A question is put to the trainees. This can emanate from the facilitator or can come out in discussion, for example:, What are the most serious problems you encounter in your work? What are the most serious constraints in your communication with the public? The questions need not only be pathological. One can also ask questions such as: What are the solutions to the credibility crisis you experience? How can communication between you and your supervisor be improved? Trainees must draw up a list individually, without consulting with anyone, in which answers or solutions to the question or problem are given. When all the trainees have done that, the facilitator starts at a point and each trainee gives the first item on his/her list which is then written down on a board or preferably on a flip chart. The contributor's name is not written next to his/her contribution. When every trainee has had a chance to contribute one item, the facilitator goes back to the starting point and gives every trainee a second chance to contribute an item. This he/she continues to do until no trainee has any item left.

A very important rule of this technique is that no item is discussed or criticised as it appears on the flip chart. After all contributions have been received and have been written down, the list is purified. This is done by discussing the different contributions one by one; not in relation to their importance, but to their truth and relevancy. Items that are related may be consolidated and wordings may be changed slightly to better bring out the meaning. A fresh list can be drawn up to reflect the purification and improvements.

This technique has two real advantages. The first is that every trainee is obliged to make a contribution without being held directly responsible for it. Because discussion is postponed to after the completion of the list, trainees are no longer sure who contributed which items. An item becomes removed from its contributor and is discussed without the contributor having to defend it, which he/she can do, of course, if he/she wants. The second advantage is that all possible answers are given to a question. Any question or problem can therefore be discussed with all viewpoints or suggestions or whatever on the table. In this way the trainees experience that they are creating knowledge: it is their own answer to an issue, not that of the trainer that they must accept.

The disadvantage of the technique is that it takes a great deal of time. It will be impossible to use the technique all the time, as it will simply take too much time. It is therefore also not very effective with large groups. If the group is too large, say more than 20, the trainees can be paired and then the two people must decide on their combined contribution; they are then regarded as one person.

The nominal group technique is ideally suited to get a group going. It is therefore especially good for early on in a training session. After the first contribution by a trainee the ice is broken for him/her and he/she will from then on participate easier.

The following are alternatives to the full exercise:

▶ The facilitator does only one complete round of trainees before the list is closed, irrespective of whether there are more contributions to be made.
▶ The facilitator requests the trainees to prioritise their contributions and to submit only the number one priority on their list.

## 22.3.5 Brainstorming

Brainstorming is an unstructured discussion that may seem confusing (especially at the start of the process) but which, if carefully conducted, will lead to a synergy of inputs into original and often new ideas. Brainstorming is used to break new ground, to overcome what seem like insurmountable stumbling blocks or to find a way out of a stalemate situation. This technique is also time-consuming, perhaps more than others because of the absence of structure. An added problem is that it can end in total confusion, causing bigger problems than those it intended to overcome. The facilitator must therefore be very attentive to what is said: he/she must pick up the positive contributions, integrate ideas and in an ongoing fashion structure the debate, without monopolising it.

The aim of brainstorming is to get a lot of ideas on the table and then to look for the 'rough diamonds' and to polish them until they can be used. It is a very creative exercise, but also very hectic because it is the group mind at work, not the minds of the individual trainees.

## 22.4  TEACHING AIDS

### 22.4.1  Introduction

The use of games, role-play and case studies as methods of experiential and participatory learning, fills a definite niche in the training of people involved in development at grassroots level. Among others, they have the following specific advantages:

▶ They can be used to convey facts, teach concepts, promote attitudes and foster ideas.
▶ They are extremely flexible both in time and content.
▶ They can be adapted easily to meet changing circumstances and needs.
▶ Learning is enhanced because it is fun and participation is maximised.
▶ They provide a safe environment within which to experiment, be exposed to new ideas and attitudes and take risks.
▶ High levels of literacy and numeracy are not prerequisites.

### 22.4.2  The rationale for using games, role-play and case studies

Before making the decision to use one of these teaching aids, one has to keep in mind that it represents only a single component in the learning process and can never convey all the knowledge on a particular topic. Ideally, this method should be supplemented with other adult and non-formal educational aids such as posters, film/video shows, informal discussions, and formal lectures.

The principal advantage of the teaching aids discussed here over other instructional methods is that it represents an optimal experiential and participatory learning activity in which participants take control of their own learning. It also ties in well, therefore, with current development theories and approaches, such as participatory development, human-centred development and the learning process approach.

Some of the most important benefits are listed below. As is the case with all other teaching/learning approaches, these teaching aids are not without limitations. These are listed in the second part of this section.

**Advantages** (Cornwell, 1996:9).
▶ Most people have been exposed to the formal classroom situation only and find the use of different teaching/learning experiences stimulating. This, in itself, enhances learning and the retention of information.
▶ Learning that has already occurred through other informal or non-formal methods is reinforced.

- People are active participants in processes and activities that reflect real-life situations and problems. Skills such as problem-identification, relating cause and effect, identifying alternative courses of action and problem-solving are in particular practised through these teaching aids.
- Active learning is more effective than passive learning.
- Empathy and increased awareness of and insight into major societal factors affecting the lives of participants are developed.
- It provides a safe learning environment because the actions and outcomes are fictitious. At the same time, it gives participants the chance to discuss and apply different courses of action and experience their outcomes.
- An excellent opportunity is provided for experiencing situations which, in real life, would be too time-consuming, costly or dangerous.
- It involves a move away from one-way communication between teacher and learner and becomes an interactive and mutual learning process.
- The result of actions is visible almost immediately. Feedback is provided in which information is given on the effectiveness and the cost of certain decisions. The environment is non-threatening and participants have the chance to try again, or to correct mistakes, within a short space of time.
- The content is flexible; a broad range of issues and concepts can be addressed.
- The duration is equally flexible. Games taking less than 30 minutes are available, others may last for three days. Some are played for one hour per week over a period of months.
- Some games (such as Exaction) enable one to see the different facets that make up the whole. Other games extract only one aspect of reality, enabling participants to study/ experience it in detail.
- The ideal mechanism is provided for compressing time, for example, several 'years' can be simulated within the course of a day. It is also possible to draw out time, or even suspend it.
- The facilitator is provided with an opportunity to use his/her initiative and design a role-play, game or a case study to illustrate a specific situation, or to choose a case study through which certain situations can be explained.
- Possibly the most important advantage is that it is fun and is normally an enjoyable experience for most people.

**Limitations** (Cornwell 1996:11).
The teaching aids discussed here may prove to be dysfunctional if it is not ascertained right at the outset that this is the best or most effective way to meet learning objectives. There are other limitations:

- Only some of the variables contained in reality are extracted—reality is edited or filtered.
- Some participants may regard the 'playing of games', or the adoption of roles, as beneath their dignity and may refuse to enter into the spirit of a simulation/game or a role-play.
- It is possible for the competitive element to dominate the learning experience. Games designed to develop empathy may be particularly susceptible to this.

▶ Participating in such exercises can be an emotional experience. This can even prove traumatic and have a lasting effect if not handled correctly by the manager or facilitator.

▶ Case studies used reflect only a condensed version of reality. Some influencing factors may not be accounted for, leaving an incomplete picture.

These are some of the limitations of games, role-play and case studies. There are others, for example, that the 'wrong' lessons may be learnt. Many limitations can be removed by a well-trained and sensitive facilitator. This will be covered below.

### 22.4.3 Case studies

A case study usually describes a facet of, or the process related to a particular phenomenon or action. The case study may be used to illustrate attitudes, to highlight problems or to point to solutions to particular problems. Case studies may be lengthy, but many are short and concise. In using a case study the facilitator must ascertain that the particular one used addresses the issue he/she has in mind, is clear and easy to understand and relates, to some extent, to life experiences of the trainees. Trainees with inadequate literacy skills need access to case studies that are short and written in a simplified style.

One of the most important advantages of the case study is that it allows trainees the opportunity of 'group learning'. Trainees from disadvantaged communities in particular benefit from discussion of cases in smaller groups.

### 22.4.4 Playing and facilitating role-play and games

Each role-play and game is different and even when only one exercise is used repeatedly; no two sessions are ever identical. All exercises start with a briefing session led by a manager or facilitator (the trainer) in which the rules, constraints and possible courses of action are explained to the participants. The role-play/game is then played for the stipulated time, or the period agreed upon by the participants. At the completion of the exercise itself, an extensive debriefing has to take place, led by the facilitator. This is one of the most important aspects of the entire exercise.

Because of the importance of the facilitator or manager in role-playing/gaming, who is usually also the trainer, this section is devoted to this person's position and prerequisites for fulfilling this role.

Facilitators have to be trained well in the uses and effects of role-playing/gaming. Apart from understanding the broad principles of gaming, they need knowledge of the specific game they are dealing with: they need to know its background and aims, and how participants may respond to the process portrayed in the exercise. Ideally, they themselves need to have been ordinary participants in the game and should also have practised managing it in a safe environment.

In a role-play the facilitator must clearly know what he/she wants to illustrate. Practical experience of a situation similar to that portrayed by the role-play will be to the benefit of the facilitator in his/her role of 'director' and in the debriefing period. To optimise the learning effect, he/she needs to be able to relate the lessons from the role-play or game to the real-life circumstances of the trainees (Cornwell, 1996:13).

Facilitators need to be flexible and able to adapt to different exercises and a wide range of participant responses. Most role-plays/games expect of facilitators to be neutral and totally divorced from proceedings. They should never be seen to take sides or become another variable in the learning process. Above all they must allow participants to make their own decisions, irrespective of whether the facilitators believe these to be wrong or unwise.

Depending on the nature of the exercise, they must have the courage to either let the role-play/game or the participants themselves dictate the pace. The point was made earlier that one of the advantages of role-playing/gaming is that participants take control of their own learning.

Because the debriefing is one of the most important aspects of the process, trainers (as the facilitators) should be proficient in leading and managing it. Facilitators need to practise skills required in debriefing, as they may, initially, experience the task as threatening.

In conclusion, they need to be able to handle the conflict, anxiety, frustration and anger that may result from gaming. It is important to realise that a role-playing/gaming experience may be extremely traumatic. Facilitators need to accept that this is one of the dangers of role-plays/games and that they need to provide sufficient time for people to 'unpack' much of what they have experienced. Only then will participants be confident and eager to experiment with other gaming exercises. (See also below.)

### 22.4.5 The relevance of role-play, games and case studies for training

Trainees come from developing communities which are often well organised and enthusiastic about improving their own situations and those of their fellow human beings. However, some of these communities, especially in newly settled informal areas, are characterised by a lack of community identification. Almost invariably the communities are poor and levels of literacy and numeracy are low. The potential for conflict between opposing groups or individuals is high.

The very flexible nature of role-play, games and case studies means that they are ideal in situations where resources are scarce. They need not be expensive or sophisticated as these are not the determinants of successful tools. Various inexpensive games are available in South Africa. Many of these have as their aim the fostering of a sense of belonging, of community, by stressing co-operation and collective action. Case studies abound and if one that fits the training episode specifically cannot be found, an experienced trainer can compile his/her own case study.

Poor communities are often wary of taking risks. Through role-playing, gaming and case studies people can be made aware of the possibilities involved in weighing up alternatives, calculating risks and doing assessments. This strengthens people's confidence and may make them willing to innovate in real-life situations as well.

## 22.5 CONCLUSION

CDWs who are tasked with the job of facilitating training, face a daunting challenge, yet, it can be one of the most stimulating jobs that they have to do. They must remember that empowerment of communities is the objective of people-centred development and training simply becomes a tool in that process (De Beer & Swanepoel, 1998:91). Although it may be relatively safe for them to follow the old, discredited lecture method, the rich rewards of capacity building training should convince them to walk the more difficult road. Commitment is necessary for success, so that none of the techniques briefly discussed in this chapter may be rushed over or totally ignored. For success it is also important to be creative, because the learning process going on here is a creative one.

# CHAPTER 23

# PLANNING AND FACILITATING A TRAINING WORKSHOP

## 23.1 INTRODUCTION

In the previous chapter we attended to the principles underlying facilitating training and the role of the facilitator in a training set-up. In this chapter the focus will shift to the more practical aspects of planning and facilitating a training workshop. It is also important to make the planning and presentation relevant to the contents of the training which will, in this case, be themes, such as getting to know the community and appraising resources, planning and project execution, organisation and communication and—finally—the meaning and process of community development (De Beer & Swanepoel, 1998:93).

## 23.2 TRAINING AS A WORKSHOP

### 23.2.1 Introduction

The approach that we recommend community development workers (CDWs) will use in training is that of capacity building. That means that CDWs are not going to deliver lectures, but that they are going to facilitate the trainees to participate fully and to create their own knowledge. This takes place in a workshop. We use 'trainee' for lack of a better word and not to suggest distance between the trainee and facilitator. In the true spirit of training or capacity building as a dialogue, trainee and facilitator become partners discovering knowledge, skills and attitudes relevant to their situation.

### 23.2.2 Workshop setting

The workshop setting is the ideal one to promote the dialogue between facilitator, material and trainees. 'Workshop' is a concept usually associated with the manufacturing of an article. In the workshop raw material is taken through a process which leads to an end product. In a training workshop the same elements are identified: *raw material*, a *process* and an *end product*.

The raw material comprises the learning material (guides, articles, videos) provided by the facilitator; experience, knowledge and ideas contributed by the trainees and facilitator.

The process is the action and interaction between facilitator, trainees and material taking place during the workshop: problem identification, discussion, argument and doing assignments.

Through the process specific problems are solved, definitions formulated or strategies developed. This is the end product.

To make a training workshop succeed as a place where raw material is processed into an end product, is a responsibility that requires the careful hand of a well-trained and experienced facilitator. The rest of this chapter is devoted to giving an idea of this facilitator's role.

## 23.3 RAISING ISSUES

### 23.3.1 Adult learners

When facilitating training of people involved in development, it must be kept in mind that the trainees are adults, that they are already in a sense practitioners and that they ought to be participants in the learning episode.

In teaching, the following three spheres of learning are important: knowledge, skills and attitudes.

These three spheres are interrelated: we want to increase knowledge, develop skills and influence attitudes. Knowledge may refer to concepts, ideas and explanations of phenomena which may be regarded as necessary for trainees to have in order to learn about a theme. Knowledge of the pathology of poverty is for instance needed to be able to identify development needs and solutions.

Skills refer to an ability to do things. The skills may include tangible abilities like writing reports or intangible skills like communication.

Attitudes that may need to be influenced are those related to and informed by the trainee's environment: the community, other role-players, him/herself. To some extent the attitude expressed by a trainee during the training session will be an indication of his/her ability to be involved in the development among the grassroots and of his/her ability to change his/her attitude if it affects his/her role negatively. The expectations with which a trainee arrives at the training session may cause an 'attitudinal problem'. The facilitator may encounter expectations of, for instance, an accredited diploma or immediate access to employment after completion of the course. Such an attitude must be corrected immediately, but preferably even before it starts, when trainees are invited to attend the training course.

Trainees bring along previously acquired knowledge and skills, pre-shaped attitudes and practical, everyday experience. Trainees also come to a training episode with their own source fields. See Chapter 13 for a discussion of motivational source fields.

For training to be a truly capacity-building experience, the facilitator must concentrate on making it possible for trainees to give their input to the fullest extent possible. This fact holds implications for the training situation regarding:

▶ perceptions;
▶ confidence;
▶ unlearning;
▶ experience as a learning source;
▶ varieties of experience; and
▶ learning styles.

**Perceptions**. Trainees (just as facilitators) will see all new material through the 'spectacles' of their existing experience. Constant feedback will be necessary to determine how the perceptions of trainees 'distort' or influence their understanding of the material.

**Confidence**. New learning must be linked to existing knowledge and experience in order to sensibly contribute to the acquisition of knowledge and skills and the adaptation of attitude. Often, however, trainees lack confidence regarding their own potential contribution, in spite of having acquired practical experience.

**Unlearning**. 'Unfreezing' trainees from a narrow and perhaps non-participation-oriented approach may be necessary – especially for trainees from a strict professional background or those with a strong ideological base to their beliefs and attitudes. Existing knowledge, skills and attitudes may therefore have to be 'unlearned'. Direct challenges exhorting trainees to change seldom succeed. Case studies probably offer the best opportunities for unlearning, providing an opportunity for trainees to come to their own conclusions and to realise the need to discard or adapt existing knowledge, skills and attitudes.

**Experience as a learning source**. Having indicated the need for unlearning, it is as important to remember that experience can be an important source of knowledge. Especially when 'theoretical' or 'academic' concepts are explained, the facilitator is well advised to link the discussion to previous experience of the trainees.

**Varieties of experience**. The 'packages' of experience trainees bring along, vary in depth, breadth and weight. The result is that the trainees are at different levels of experience. By using tried and trusted techniques and developing new ones as you go along, an opportunity must be provided to allow for learning from the existing variety of experience.

**Learning styles**. Limited exposure to learning (and even illiteracy) complicates the issue of learning. At school 'spoon feeding' is the learning style used. In a capacity-building approach the learning style is totally different and may require time for the adjustment of trainees. Here too the facilitator must experiment and adapt his/her approach to allow for the development or change of learning styles. 'Group learning', especially where trainees are semi-literate, is a learning style that needs to be experimented with. In small groups, case studies or relevant articles may be discussed with the aim to transfer knowledge or skills or to influence attitudes. In the small group, group learning allows for the fluent to read, the quick-witted to explain and the 'slower' trainees to benefit by asking questions and contributing practical examples in the safe environment of a smaller group.

### 23.3.2 Establishing a teaching agenda

Establishing and coping with a teaching agenda may be difficult to a facilitator new to the situation. With careful planning and a little experience, problems may, however, be overcome. The teaching agenda may have one or both of the following aims: to establish the expectations of the trainees and to establish the problems experienced by the trainees in carrying out their duties. A list of expectations will be useful to the facilitator to get to know the group better; if, however, you have made prior contact and know the trainees it may be a waste of time to do this exercise. A problems agenda can be compiled to determine training needs experienced by the group. As the training proceeds the facilitator ought to refer back to the problems agenda and link the training to it. The list of expectations and the problems agenda provide the opportunity for trainees at an early stage to contribute to the learning from their own experience.

In using either a list of expectations or a problems agenda the facilitator must take care to immediately 'weed out' unrealistic/unattainable expectations and problems that do not fall within the ambit of the course (for example expectations of employment, transport problems). The facilitator must carefully consider the situation before deciding on the type of agenda he/she wants to compile. Some prior knowledge of the trainees and their situation may help making the correct choice.

A list of expectations will assist the facilitator to understand something of the attitude with which trainees arrive: is it personal gain, is it community-oriented expectations, is it interest or curiosity that brought them together? Do they fear the learning episode or are they positive? The list of expectations gives the facilitator some prior 'warning' of what may be expected from the particular group of trainees.

Compiling a problems agenda may be a worthwhile exercise, but taxing on the facilitator. The perception trainees most often have of a problems agenda is that it is a list of problems (needs) experienced by the community. Thus items such as community needs for employment, schools and clinics are put forward as problems experienced by the trainee. Before compiling a problems agenda, the trainees must be well informed on its nature and place in the exercise. A few examples will illustrate to the trainees what is looked for: conflicting political groups; indecisive leadership; personal transport, and so on. These are examples of problems that a person involved in development experiences in doing his/her work.

Establishing a problems agenda is not merely a means to fill a time slot: it is a means of providing for the integration of the trainees' contribution into the workshop. The facilitator uses the agenda as a point of reference, referring back to it during discussions. This means that the agenda must be put up where it is visible to all; it also means that in between, while the trainees are busy with practical assignments, the facilitator must study the agenda and determine points to 'hook on' as the workshop progresses. As the facilitator becomes more expert, he/she will be able, during a discussion session, to 'hook on' to items on the agenda.

While the problems agenda can make a valuable contribution towards integrating the trainees' input, it holds the danger of creating expectations among the trainees. To avoid this, the facilitator must be absolutely clear on the place and role of the problems agenda in the workshop. Unrealistic expectations and problems (eg finding money for projects) clearly not fitting within the scope of the workshop, must be pointed out. Though not all expectations will be met, nor all problems solved, the trainees must be sensitised to the fact that with their input, some of it may be addressed during the workshop.

To balance the list of expectations and/or problems agenda, the facilitator must also make his/her objectives or agenda known to the trainees. By doing this, he/she starts out by encouraging a relaxed atmosphere, and can also indicate where his/her ideas and those of the trainees meet or complement one another.

Finally, in concluding the workshop, the problems agenda can be used as a tool of summary. The facilitator on his/her own, or with input from the trainees, can conclude the workshop by running through the problems agenda.

### 23.3.3  Drawing a picture of the milieu

Drawing a picture of the milieu and establishing problems and resources in the community may seem awkward when the trainees come from the community and supposedly know it. Milieu in this context means the particular people and society that surround you and that influence the way you behave. Yet this exercise has a number of advantages that cannot be overlooked, for example:

▶ It puts some distance between the trainee and the milieu.
▶ It allows the opportunity to illustrate the integrated nature of the problem.
▶ It allows trainees the opportunity to demonstrate their practical experience and knowledge.
▶ It allows trainees the opportunity to 'clear the throat' and vent their frustration.
▶ Finally, by also identifying resources available, it brings a positive note to the training episode and gives some hope to trainees who may be overwhelmed by the perceived hopelessness of the situation.

The aim of this exercise can be said to allow trainees to see their situation in a wider perspective, and to realise the integrated nature of the problem—and of the solution.
As an organising tool for drawing a picture of the milieu, the 'deprivation trap' as described by Robert Chambers (1983:103 et seq) is ideal. See Chapter 1.

The clusters of poverty, isolation, physical weakness, powerlessness and vulnerability—the deprivation trap—can be explained with reference to examples provided by trainees. How inadequate housing relates to poverty and to physical weakness can for example be explained by referring to examples given by trainees. The interrelationship between these clusters and its causal relationship is illustrated with examples from the milieu known to the trainees. In this way the trainees are assisted in understanding their work situation; they are also equipped to better analyse the situation and to find solutions. See De Beer & Swanepoel (1994) for an exposition of the urban poverty situation.

Time spent on raising issues is time well utilised. It allows trainees the opportunity to bring into the training session themes that are important to them and it makes it easier for them to relate to and participate in the training.

## 23.4  TRAINING AS COMMUNICATION

### 23.4.1  Introduction

Teaching skills revolve around the ability to communicate. The facilitator needs not only knowledge about communication, but also practice in applying it. It is only through applying knowledge that the skill of communication is developed. Once this skill is mastered, motivation of trainees, dealing with group dynamics and coping with problem-makers become manageable.

### 23.4.2  Communication

Communication is not simply sending and receiving messages. More things are at play than a speaker (sender), a message and a listener (receiver). It is therefore wrong to think of communication as linear. Communication is rather a circular process, with an in-built dynamism. The spoken language, body language, environmental influences (noise, climate), culture, the social position of the speaker and receiver, all interact to give meaning to the communication taking place. See Chapter 10 for a detailed discussion.

As a process, communication takes place in a circular fashion. This model, however, also has its limitations. It interprets communication as a closed-circuit process. In reality, when the communication circle is completed, it may set off another round of communication; it is perhaps best depicted as a spiral of communication.

It is common knowledge that communication entails more than the spoken word: non-verbal communication (or body language) is increasingly recognised as an important part of communication. People in a lift communicate—without having to say anything! Chapter 10 explains the communication model in detail.

Training poses an opportunity and a challenge for communication. Trainees from poor communities are often illiterate, unsure of themselves and suspicious of other people. Their illiteracy is compounded by poor language skills and often an inadequate knowledge of the language used by the facilitator. The facilitator's presence may on its own pose a threat to the trainee: being an official from government (or a professor from a university!) he/she has power; has proper training and may therefore appear to be too 'wise'; the trainee may be young and inexperienced, therefore not accepted as a person who speaks with authority. These are some of the challenges faced even before the facilitator has spoken a word.

In a training situation, the environment is a crucial, and sometimes a determining factor, for the success of communication. Noise of lawnmowers, people talking outside the room or music in the distance hampers communication. The climate may be too hot—making trainees sleepy or too cold—disturbing their concentration. Seats may be too soft or too hard, the distance between facilitator and trainee too far to facilitate proper communication. Outside observers may come and go, each time distracting the attention of trainees; worse, they may make an unsolicited contribution and then leave you as facilitator to win back the attention of the trainees.

Since this chapter is mainly about the skills and attitudes of facilitators, we deal only with direct communication between facilitator/trainees, in a one-to-one or a classroom (workshop) situation. 'Mass communication', reading, viewing and other forms of communication will not be dealt with.

The spoken word is the means by which to communicate, but may also be the stumbling block to communication. The message will not be heard if the facilitator speaks too softly or is unclear. The facilitator who occupies the floor and undertakes a one-way conversation will soon lose the attention of trainees. Successful communication requires active and creative listening, both by the trainer and trainee. It is, however, the duty of the trainer to create the atmosphere in which active and creative listening can take place.

Body language is a very important means of communication. Your body language will tell the trainees a lot about yourself and your attitude. It may, however, also be misinterpreted. Shyness may be 'received' as unfriendliness; an overbearing approach may be viewed as a know-all. Direct eye contact is very important to establish rapport between facilitator and trainee. By not looking trainees in the eye, you make them feel that you have something to hide or, perhaps worse, that you want to keep a distance. A hurried presentation will cause anxiousness, while a relaxed approach will make the trainees feel comfortable.

Culture and body language may cause confusion. Arabs use a backward jerk of the head to indicate 'no'; we may interpret it as a 'yes'. In the South African society the matter of greeting is sometimes a cause for miscommunication: some people waiting for the other person (eg a white person) to greet first and the white person expecting as a sign of submission to be greeted first. Where a facilitator meets trainees from a different culture (and social standing) he/she should acknowledge the pitfalls, discuss it with the trainees and elicit their help in teaching him/her when necessary!

Training-communication should take the form of a dialogue. If one follows Freire's vision of dialogue then the relationship required puts a great burden on the facilitator. 'Founding itself upon love, humility and faith, dialogue becomes a horizontal relationship of which mutual trust between the dialoguers is the logical consequence' (Freire, 2006:91). The facilitator is not a know-all and should not pretend to be one. He/she should rather be a conduit (or link), putting the trainees in touch with the training material. Remember, the trainees bring along some knowledge, some experience and if you allow the opportunity, some valuable wisdom will come from the group. Their own 'body of knowledge', the training material and the facilitator's input should be in constant dialogue in order to create their own knowledge. If we succeed in establishing this cycle of communication, the trainees would find their training episode a worthwhile experience and will learn much more than in a linear, one-way type of communication.

### 23.4.3 Motivation and group dynamics

The most important principle in motivation is recognition of the individual. This may take a number of forms. By simply remembering (and using) the name of a person in addressing him/her shows him/her that he/she is regarded as someone distinguished from other persons. Acknowledging the contribution made by an individual tells him/her that you (a powerful person) regard his/her input as important. Allowing individuals and the group as a whole to voice their fears, articulate their expectations and share their ideas, builds a foundation for motivation. Taking them and their inputs seriously, and showing your earnest interest, build mutual trust and contribute to motivation.

It is most important to provide opportunities for individuals and groups of trainees to taste a sense of achievement. Challenge them, give assignments and make it possible for them to experiment and solve problems or master skills; few things motivate better than a sense of achievement.

On a practical note, motivation is supported by the physical wellbeing of the individual: a hungry and thirsty person is demotivated; a person enduring an uncomfortable bed and cold water on a winter morning will find reason to complain; if the facilitator does not allow time for breaks in between and during training episodes, the trainees tend to lose concentration and become demotivated.

If the individual trainee does not have the capacity or mechanism for self-motivation, these peripherals will be of little value to get him/her motivated, however well the facilitator handles the factors that contribute to motivation. In exceptional cases individuals will be found without the capacity to motivate themselves. Such individuals often revert to 'trouble making' and can only be handled effectively by the group (see discussion below).

Group dynamics is influenced, and sometimes shaped by the type of characters present. In most groups one finds, among others, the clown, the snob and the know-it-all (see discussion on pages 245-247). These characters can make or break a training episode. The communication skills of the facilitator will be taxed to the full to avoid serious disruption. An important partner in handling these characters is the group. By harnessing the group to act as adjudicator, disciplinarian and memory, group dynamics is used positively in the communication situation. Some suggestions in this regard are provided below. See also Chapter 11 regarding groups. It is in the nature of groups that the potential for conflict always exists. A few rules of thumb to manage conflict are provided, but the facilitator will always have to explore new ones and use his/her initiative in finding solutions. Chapter 12 deals in more detail with conflict resolution, and below we provide a set of rules to manage conflict in the classroom. Rules of thumb in conflict management are:

▶ concentrate on the issue, not on the person;
▶ avoid personal accusations and the forming of opposing groups;
▶ avoid muddling the discussion by rhetoric and side issues;
▶ allow for difference of opinion, feelings (emotions) and ways of doing things;
▶ have self-respect, respect people and set the example;
▶ allow people to speak their minds but emphasise the importance to also listen to others; and
▶ do not apportion blame.

### 23.4.4 Discipline and coping with problem people

The capacity-building method of training is more prone to disruption by problem trainees than the lecture method. The discussion is very much a free for all and therefore problem trainees have a good opportunity to affect the process negatively. The capacity-building method is very dependent on a continuous discussion and therefore it is imperative that the negative effects of problem trainees be minimised. It is important that the facilitator's handling of problem trainees be experienced by the group as firm, fair, consistent and to the benefit of the whole group.

Doyle and Straus (1976) have identified a number of problem types at meetings. Their list has been used for discussion on discipline in meetings in Chapter 15. But we are again using it in this discussion for its appropriateness although a few more types have been added and the suggestions for handling the types do not necessarily follow Doyle and Straus. The typology of these problem trainees is perhaps an overstatement. One should keep in mind that problem types are manifested in various degrees. One should also remember that something of these types are present in most people. The original authors discussed this list in relation to meetings; we change the scenario somewhat to a training situation.

**The latecomer** always arrives at the discussion late, making some commotion, from greeting everyone with the hand, enquiring about their health, to bumping and shuffling to get to his/her place. The handling of this problem trainee will be dealt with together with the next type.

**The early leaver** drains the energy of the session by leaving early. It is very important to settle the whole matter of punctuality very early in a training session. The group should decide on starting and break up times and the facilitator and trainees must abide by this. The only way to start on time is by starting on time, whether one trainee or half of the trainees are still not at their places. One way of keeping discussions punctual, is to let the group appoint a person or persons to take responsibility for this aspect.

**The broken record** (sometimes he/she is simply a 'slow thinker') keeps bringing up the same point over and over again. The facilitator should make sure that the point has been noted and recorded. The broken record can act so, not by choice, but because no one would listen to him/her or because he/she really needs more explaining before understanding. The use of a group memory, transparencies and slides also helps to get rid of the broken record.

**The Doubting Thomas** constantly puts down everything. He/she is always negative. You are wrong until you prove yourself to be right. No solution will ever work. There is a difference between being critical and being aggressively negative. Criticism keeps a group on its toes, but aggressive negativism puts a damper on creativity. First, the Doubting Thomas must be kept honest. If he/she reacts negatively, he/she must substantiate his/her reaction. Second, exercises such as the nominal group technique and brainstorming where no comment or evaluation is at first allowed, may quiet him/her down and give an ideal time to gain support before it is attacked.

**The head-shaker** non-verbally disagrees in a dramatic and disruptive manner. He/she shakes his/her head, rolls his/her eyes, crosses and uncrosses his/her legs, pulls faces, throws his/her hands in the air and laughs soundlessly. The best way to deal with the head-shaker is to force him/her to translate his/her body language into words.

**The dropout** sits at the back of the room, does not say anything, never looks up, reads something or doodles. The dropout is especially disturbing to the facilitator. First, the seating arrangement can encourage or discourage the dropout. There should be no 'back of the room' seating. No person should be able to hide behind anyone else. If every person sits in a position where he/she is very much part of the group, it is very difficult to drop out. Second, the dropout must be brought into the discussion and that can only be done by the facilitator by asking the dropout specifically what his/her views are. He/she should be aware of the fact that the facilitator is aware of him/her and does not like his/her dropout act.

**The silent observer** is not a dropout, but he/she never says anything although he/she follows the discussion and may nod or shake a head now and then. The silent observer is usually the shy one in the group or the one not sure of him/herself. It is the task of the facilitator to show him/her that his/her contribution is also necessary by asking him/her to comment, perhaps at first on a fairly simple issue and then to congratulate him/her on his/her contribution. The silent observer must gain courage and the facilitator must help him/her to do it, also by talking informally to him/her during breaks.

**The whisperer** is constantly whispering to a neighbour. Eye contact with a whisperer may cause him/her to stop or else physical movement towards him/her may interrupt him/her.

**The clown** is also a potential leader of a sub-culture within the group. He/she usually tells jokes or makes funny remarks in asides only heard by the people sitting near to him/her. Again, eye contact and forcing him/her to be serious by asking him/her to contribute, may change the mood. Seating arrangement should also discourage anyone to take the role of clown.

**The loudmouth** (sometimes he/she is simply a manipulator) talks too much, is too loud, dominates the discussion and is seemingly impossible to shut up. His/her action can cause two negative results. First, he/she can establish a communication link between him/her and the facilitator to the exclusion of the other trainees. Second, because he/she tends to react to every input, he/she can take over the role of facilitator or at least take the initiative away from the facilitator. The nominal group exercises and brain storming exercises will go a long way to quiet the loudmouth and to ensure that the initiative remains with the facilitator.

**The orator** makes a speech instead of an input. A speech is time-consuming, contains clichés and peripheral matters and expresses various ideas strung together. For all three these reasons a speech is not conducive to lively discussion. The orator must be stopped, but how? One feels reluctant to interrupt in the middle of his/her speech because it is rude to interrupt. It takes an experienced facilitator to wait his/her chance to pounce, grab an idea expressed by the orator, comment on it with great interest, turn away from the orator, and throw the idea to the group as a delicate morsel to be savoured. The orator has been silenced, but also noted and the last fact should make up for the interruption.

**The attacker** launches personal attacks on other trainees or on someone in the organisation, usually someone in management. The attacker is aggressive by nature and can even be one of the rare breed of people who thrives on conflict. The attacker must be censored and the facilitator must get the group behind him/her. He/she is looking for group censure against such a person. For the sake of the group and the discussions, it is imperative that the attacker does not get away with it. Every trainee must know that he/she is safeguarded against personal attack.

**The know-it-all** uses credentials, age, length of service and professional status to argue a point. Usually the know-it-all is a more senior person and therefore more difficult to handle. A variation on this theme is the benevolent know-it-all or rescuer. His/her intention is pure, merely helping a fellow trainee whom he/she regards as being in need of assistance to make a contribution. The know-it-all and rescuer should be reminded that in spite of his/her superior knowledge, he/she is part of a learning process, just like the facilitator and that all inputs, also those from trainees without credentials, are important to keep the learning process going.

**The busy bee** is always ducking in and out of the discussions, constantly receiving messages or rushing out to take a phone call or deal with a crisis. Having the training session at a venue away from the office is about the best way to pin the busy body down.

**The interrupter** starts talking before others are finished. Interruption and double talking are quite normal in any discussion, but it can be tolerated only up to a point. The facilitator is responsible for a smooth flow of contributions and he/she must stop the interrupter if he/she starts making a habit of it. If a group memory is used, the facilitator has the good excuse that an idea which gets interrupted halfway cannot be recorded properly.

**The gun jumper** is worse than the interrupter. He/she does not wait until the facilitator acknowledges him/her. When a discussion is really going well, it is inevitable that a few people would have indicated to the facilitator that they wish to contribute. The facilitator must keep a waiting list in his/her mind so that he/she can acknowledge the next speaker in the sequence. The gun jumper must wait his/her turn like all the other trainees.

**The teacher's pet** spends more energy looking for approval from the facilitator than concentrating on the contents of the training. The teacher's pet should not be given the slightest notion of encouragement. The facilitator does not want anyone of the trainees to become dependent on him/her.

**The snob** is a rare species that regards him/herself as better educated and better informed than the other trainees. He/she will inform you and the group of his/her superiority. Deal with him/her by keeping him/her honest: let the group respond and show to him/her that his/her superior knowledge has shortcomings. Above all, remind him/her that this is a learning experience to the educated and well informed as much as to the uneducated and uninformed.

**Nibblers** are equally annoying. Their habits cause discomfort and distraction to both the facilitator and fellow trainees. Rules on eating during sessions should be determined at the outset and enforced by the group and the facilitator.

**The peace keeper** can play an important role when arguments get heated. Yet his/her anxiety to restore peace can interrupt a challenging and important debate. The facilitator should allow him/her to make a contribution, but nevertheless let the debate proceed.

**The invader** is either an official responsible for organising, or who has to report back to superiors on progress. Such a person may sit and read a newspaper, comes and goes as he/she likes and, generally disturbs the process. He/she may be made part of the workshop or asked by the facilitator to be unobtrusive and not to disturb the proceedings.

The most important precondition for successful capacity-building is a free-flowing discussion. All of the above problem trainees can cause a breakdown in this free flow. It is therefore imperative to deal with these people. The best possible position the facilitator can wish for is that these people will be censured by the group. He/she needs strong group cohesion for that and it is his/her task to promote group cohesion and to channel group dynamics.

## 23.5 PLANNING AND PRESENTATION

### 23.5.1 Introduction

No facilitator can walk into a training situation unprepared. You must plan for a training session. Planning consists of establishing the aims or goals of the unit. Write them down and after you have completed your preparation, check if you have kept to those goals.

The best is to have a written plan of your presentation of a unit. This must include contents, timing, techniques and tools. The facilitator must make sure that he/she knows the plan by heart and must take it along to the classroom. He/she must put it at a special place on the front table or podium so that he/she can refer to it when necessary.

Take note: A facilitator with a cluttered table or podium will have cluttered training sessions. It also makes a bad impression if a facilitator must stop everything and hunt for some document on his/her table while the trainees look on. The unit plan must be in a specific place where it will not be covered by other papers. The transparencies must be in sequence and there must be a place to put down the transparencies already used. The facilitator must have his/her notes (notes of inputs they must make without the help of a transparency) in such a position that he/she can easily read what he/she has written. The flip chart must be clean and the pens close to it. The overhead projector must be switched on at the wall socket and focused.

### 23.5.2  Timing and time management

The facilitator has previously established time frames and time limits within which he/she must complete his/her work. It is therefore necessary to plan the presentation within a time frame. It is better to plan time liberally. Rather have time free than find yourself hopelessly behind schedule.

As the facilitator progresses through the programme, it is his/her task to always check the time. According to these regular time assessments he/she will make changes in the programme in advance. Use plenary session breaks to assess time use and to adapt the further programme. Remember that certain breaks, such as for tea and lunch, are previously arranged and cannot be altered. The facilitator must plan the programme with these compulsory breaks in mind.

The time issue should not, however, be in the forefront during the training. The trainees should not be constantly aware of the fact that the facilitator is trying to fit everything into a previously decided time frame. It is good to refer to the time issue now and then. That reminds the trainees that they cannot continue discussions unlimited. However, the ever-present time constraints in most of these training situations should not be uppermost in the minds of the trainees. The programme is in service of the workshop, not the other way around.

### 23.5.3  The venue and seating arrangements

The facilitator very seldom finds a really suitable room for his/her training sessions. He/she invariably finds rooms that are too large, too small, too noisy, too hot, too cold, too draughty or too far from other facilities.

It is important that the room can be used for both plenary discussions and group work. If smaller rooms for group work are not available adjacent to the training room, the latter must be large enough to accommodate at least three groups at work at the same time. It must also have enough space for simulation exercises.

Keeping in mind the size of the group, an auditorium is not suitable for training purposes. Sound tends to disappear or reverberate in such a large room. The smallness of the training group amidst the vastness of the hall tends to have a negative psychological effect on the group. On the other hand, a room must not be so small as to only allow the necessary tables and chairs with no space to move about. Such a situation can become claustrophobic and the inevitable stuffiness leads to drowsiness and consequently to an energy loss.

The seating arrangement is of crucial importance. A few general rules can be stated:

▶ The facilitator must be able to communicate with the group and with individual trainees.
▶ Each trainee must be able to communicate with the group, with the individual trainees and with the facilitator.
▶ The facilitator and the trainees must be able to move around easily.
▶ The facilitator must be able to look every trainee in the eye.

- The facilitator must be able to see the whole group without having to move his/her head more than 20 degrees in any direction.
- Trainees must be able to see the screen and the flip chart without turning their bodies in their chairs, or straining their neck muscles, and without playing a dodging game with a head in front of them.
- Trainees must have a table in front of them for their note paper and they must be able to write without difficulty.
- The seating arrangement should never make obvious divisions in the group.

With these general rules in mind, a few arrangements are clearly preferable and a few are decidedly not. The more preferable ones are as follows:

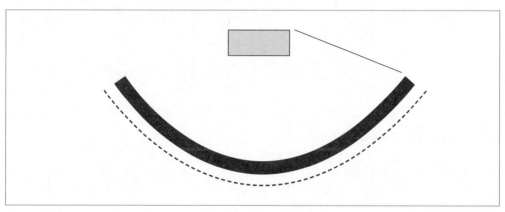

Figure 23.1 **The flat horseshoe**

The flat horseshoe. This is one of the most appropriate seating arrangements. Trainees can see and communicate with one another. The facilitator can move about on the inside of the horseshoe. No trainee is too far from the screen and flip chart stand.

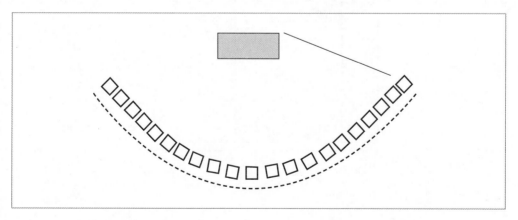

Figure 23.2 **The semicircle**

The semicircle is definitely the best seating arrangement. Unfortunately, not many trainees can be accommodated.

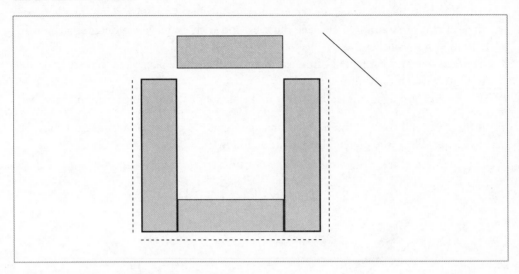

Figure 23.3 **The open U with outside seating**

The open U with outside seating is also one of the better arrangements. The trainees at the bottom side of the U may, however, be too far from the screen and the flip chart stand.

The less than satisfactory arrangements are the following:

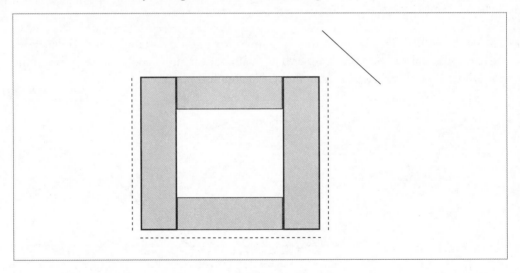

Figure 23.4 **The closed U**

The main problem with the closed U arrangement is that the facilitator can only move about behind the trainees. In fact, the whole space in the centre is wasted.

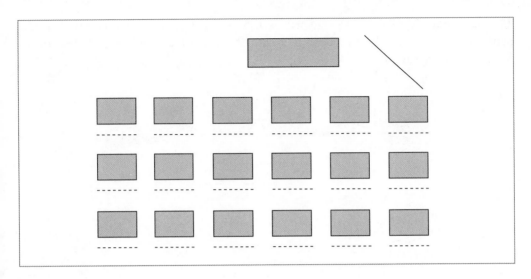

Figure 23.5 **The classroom**

The classroom seating arrangement is totally unacceptable for a number of reasons. Communication except with the person next to you is virtually impossible. A trainee in a row behind may address a trainee in front of him/her who will turn around and in so doing will sever all contact with the facilitator and the screen and flip chart stand. Trainees in back rows have a problem seeing the facilitator, screen and flip chart stand, and will be dodging heads in front of them all the time. The back row syndrome is bound to be present. That is that the trainees in the back row will either drop out or form a subculture. The movement of the facilitator is also restricted and so is that of the trainees in the inside rows.

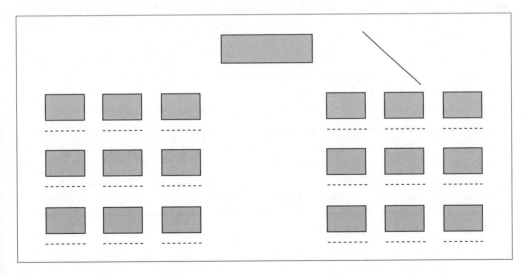

Figure 23.6 **The classroom with division**

The classroom with division arrangement is also unacceptable for the same reason as the previous one with the added problem of a natural division that will inevitably lead to the formation of two subgroups.

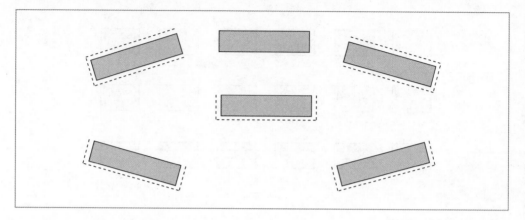

Figure 23.7 **The random tables**

The random tables arrangement is popular but is unacceptable. The facilitator finds it extremely difficult to maintain eye contact with all the trainees; many of the trainees have their backs to the facilitator, screen and flip chart stand. Free communication between the trainees is impossible. Subcultures will tend to form around each table.

There are other aspects of the training room that merit attention.
Room temperature is one of the most frequent and annoying problems. Part of this problem can never be solved. People experience temperature differently. What is hot for one may be chilly for another. However, a too hot or stuffy room saps the energy of the group and makes them sleepy. Air-conditioning has a very negative effect on some people apart from the noise it makes.

Stuffy rooms can be aerated by opening the windows, but often outside noise or a strong wind makes this impossible. In such cases more breaks should be taken.

It is imperative that training takes place with the minimum disturbances from outside. If the door of the training room is constantly opened by people looking for an office or a person, it is not only annoying, but counterproductive too. Therefore, a note must be pinned to the door with the words: Training session in progress. Don't disturb.

A tea facility too far removed from a training room is a time waster. A group of people move much slower than an individual. It takes a group of people a minimum time of 20 minutes to drink a cup of tea. Another ten minutes can be added if the toilets are not on the same route or adjacent to the training room. So, a total of 30 minutes are necessary if the tea facility is not very near the training room.

### 23.5.4 Study and relaxation

A training session of five days' duration needs a balanced pattern of study and relaxation. Even if the trainees are very eager, the subject of training extremely interesting and the facilitator excellent, trainees can concentrate and work for limited periods of time only.

A day session should last from 08h00 to 16h00 (08h30 to 16h30; 09h00 to 17h00). During a day session there must be a tea break in the morning of 15 to 30 minutes, a lunch break of 45 minutes and an optional tea break in the afternoon of 15 to 30 minutes plus a few short leg-stretch-breaks. In all about an hour and a half per day is necessary for relaxation.

Leg-stretch-breaks are essential, especially when it is hot or when the room is stuffy. But leg-stretch-breaks have the tendency to stretch. A three minute break will always end two or three minutes later than it should (it takes about six minutes to smoke a cigarette). If the toilets are some distance from the training room, no break can be shorter than ten minutes.

There should be discipline in a group regarding the time. It must be stressed during the ice break session that starting times and break times will be strictly adhered to and this must then be carried out.

Relaxation can also come from certain activities other than the ordinary breaks. A simulation exercise usually provides some relaxation. The same is true of group work where something must be created. Even an amusing case study can provide a break from the more disciplined way of concentration and work.

### 23.5.5 Visual aids

Of all the many visual aids the best are still the overhead projector, with a screen and a long extension cord, and a flip chart with pens. A flip chart is preferred to a white or black board because it is not necessary to destroy the record when a sheet is full. Filled sheets must be numbered to ensure that they remain in sequence, removed and stuck to the wall so that everybody can refer back to them.

PowerPoint presentations can also be used in addition to or as replacement for transparencies. A PowerPoint presentation can work well for a short lecture or giving information in an uninterrupted way. The facilitator should plan the use of this tool carefully. It is more structured and rigid and makes cross- and back reference to other slides more difficult than transparencies. You must also be well-trained and used to this tool, or have an assistant to 'page' back and forward or else you may lose track and the presentation may become confusing to the facilitator and the trainee. The do's and don'ts for transparencies listed below and on the next page equally applies to the preparation of a PowerPoint presentation.

Videos can be used, but a 51 cm or even a 67 cm screen for a group larger than 20 people misses its purpose completely. A video can never stand on its own. It must be followed by a discussion or must be interrupted for discussions. When standing on its own, a video assumes the character of a lecture or of entertainment and that is not the purpose.

Transparencies and PowerPoint slides are excellent visual aids, but there are a lot of do's and don'ts:

- A transparency should only reflect the main idea or information regarding a matter
- Words, phrases, brief sentences or simple diagrams are used. It does not carry the whole text.
- The writing on a transparency must be large enough so that all trainees can read it easily.
- Illustrations on transparencies must be as simple and clear as possible.
- A transparency must look professional. Freehand writing looks sloppy and amateurish.

There are also a few do's and don'ts regarding the use of transparencies:

▶ A transparency is always put on an overhead projector that is switched off and before the transparency is removed, the overhead projector is first switched off.
▶ While explaining the contents of a transparency, a thin pointer can be used, not a thick flip chart pen or your finger which does not point to anything and usually obscures words.
▶ The sheet used to cover part of the transparency must be of a thin white paper so that the wording underneath it is legible to the facilitator. Then he/she will know what is coming next.

## 23.6  ASSESSMENT

### 23.6.1  Introduction

Assessment and monitoring are two of the most crucial yet often neglected aspects in a training situation. What is meant by these terms? Assessment is used to refer to the 'testing' at the end of a definable module or training episode (eg a learning outcome or objective). Monitoring takes the form of a process – it is continuous and needs not be formalised. For the facilitator monitoring means to 'keep an eye' on the trainees, to see that all have an opportunity to participate, to detect when a trainee falls behind, to know when a trainee does not follow the discussion or does not understand concepts, ideas or phenomena under discussion. With monitoring goes remedial action: to elicit participation, to repeat and explain concepts, ideas and phenomena.

It is not only the facilitator who does assessment and monitoring. In an interactive, capacity-building training exercise the trainee should be allowed an equal opportunity to monitor and assess. The trainee should assess and monitor his/her own progress and also the input and performance of the facilitator. By allowing for self-assessment and facilitator assessment the capacity-building experience is enhanced and strengthened.

### 23.6.2  The role of assessment in training

Assessment must be conducted according to a kind of relationship—an ethos—which reflects the spirit of participation. This means:

▶ That not only the facilitator is responsible for assessment. He/she is, in dialogue with the trainees and assesses the training.
▶ It is not only the product that is assessed but also the process.
▶ The product is not only assessed through the conventional examination method. The portfolio, test or examination as a reflection of the amount of knowledge and skills successfully transferred, forms only a small part of assessment. How the trainees assess their progress is equally important.
▶ It is also necessary to assess the training process: what the aspirations and expectations of the trainees are, how they progress towards fulfilling them and how the input of the facilitator relates to addressing their aspirations and expectations. The most important aspect of process assessment is that it engages the trainee in self-assessment.

▶ The trainee assesses the course contents, its presentation and the attainment of his/her goals against the objectives set for the course.

### 23.6.3 Monitoring and assessment of progress

As with all things in life, training is also subject to monitoring and assessment, measurement and setting of standards. In an ordinary educational setting (schools, universities) the paradigm used is standard tests, examinations and perhaps also orals and portfolios. In interactive or capacity-building training we operate in a different paradigm; a paradigm in which simple 'wrongs' and 'rights' cannot determine levels of competency. We deal in this type of training, as you will remember, with knowledge, skills and attitudes of adults who may be illiterate or semi-literate but who in many instances have acquired skills through experience. In this instance tests and examinations may be of use but it can definitely not be used as the sole mechanism for monitoring and assessing progress. The facilitator, in planning a training episode, must also determine his/her learning objective and ways and means of measuring success.

Knowledge can be determined through essays, written tests and examinations. Yet, the trainee with knowledge but no or underdeveloped writing skills will most certainly fail. It is up to the facilitator to be inventive and apply other methods of monitoring and assessment. In discussion, small groups and practical assignments, trainees can demonstrate their knowledge. The facilitator must be sensitive to it and somehow devise a mechanism to keep record of such informal evidence of knowledge.

How does one monitor and assess the acquisition of skills? Skills cannot really be tested in a written test or examination. Depending on the type of skills, an appropriate mechanism—a game, case study or role-play—should be used or developed. Once again the ingenuity of the facilitator will be tested severely.

To monitor and assess attitudinal changes is perhaps the most difficult of all. Change or influence of attitudes is in any case seldom an overtly expressed aim or learning objective in training. Yet in development training it is most often a crucial ingredient to the success of the exercise! Monitoring and assessment of attitudinal change should start with the facilitator. What is his/her attitude towards the trainees? Is it paternalistic, know-all or dominating? Or is it inviting, reassuring and relaxed? His/her attitude will create an atmosphere in which attitudinal change is possible or will be smothered. Observation by the facilitator is one, yet subjective, way of monitoring and assessing attitudinal change. A more accurate measure is perhaps to use the group as barometer. In all groups one finds the trouble-maker, the know-all or the clown. It is hoped that, as the training progresses, his/her attitude will change. If it does not, the group reaction to his/her antics will tell. If it does, it will be noticeable in the way which the group deals with and accepts the person. Attitudinal change can also be monitored in subtleties such as enthusiasm, concern and dedication. The way a person responds to an input can also be an indication of attitudinal change.

### 23.6.4 Product and process assessment

For an assessment to be thorough, both the product and the process must be evaluated.

Product assessment means to determine what has been learned. Is there a change in behaviour of the trainees? Have the learning outcomes or objectives been met? Product evaluation can be for the sake of the trainees – to monitor their own progress; it can be for the sake of the facilitator to determine the success in achieving the set outcomes or objectives; or it can be for the sake of the agency to ascertain a basis for accreditation.

In short courses such as we are dealing with, assessment of the first two kinds mentioned above is of particular importance. By involving trainees in assessment, an additional learning opportunity is provided. Being subjective, their self-assessment is bound to be more rigid than that of the facilitator. The facilitator needs, however, to know how successful he/she was in achieving his/her objectives; it is after all also a learning opportunity for him/her and an opportunity to improve his/her next presentation.

In almost every training episode an opportunity exists for product assessment through trainee involvement. Writing case studies, conducting surveys, doing simulation exercises and presenting (group) reports, all provide opportunities for participatory assessment. It is, however, very important to carefully structure the assessment, work within clearly defined parameters and let the trainees fully understand what their role is and why it is important.

Process assessment relates to (1) how the learning has been facilitated (to what extent can the design and implementation (teaching) of the training account for the degree to which learning objectives have been met?), and (2) how the trainees have made use of the training. To what extent have the trainees understood the material, availed themselves of the opportunity to gain knowledge and insight, and made use of the interactive method to create knowledge?

In assessing the process, trainees act as a 'sound board' for the facilitator. They are given the opportunity to share their experience and perception of a particular training episode: the contents, the presentation and the training techniques used. Their assessment may initially be polite and reserved, for fear of antagonising the facilitator. If, however, the 'ice break' session is successful and through proper communication a welcoming atmosphere is created, soon the response will become open and unrestricted. Throughout the training the facilitator should stress (and make possible) assessment as a co-operative venture between him/her and the trainees; their input, as his/hers, is for the common good, to jointly find flaws, strong points and improve the training experience. At the same time and without the trainees even being aware of it, the facilitator can ascertain the second point, that is, how the trainees have made use of the training.

If this type of understanding and relationship is not established, some trainees may interpret the assessment as an opportunity to 'get back' at the facilitator, and he/she may experience the assessment very personally and very negatively.

### 23.6.5 Feedback

All people are curious about their performance. They have, in any case, the right to know the results of their evaluation. Assessment is not only meant as an opportunity to score marks; it should above all be treated as yet another learning opportunity. Therefore it is vital for the facilitator to provide trainees with feedback on their assessment. Continuous feedback not only underscores the learning process, it also reinforces a relationship of trust and openness in the group. Feedback is the final and ultimate product of a training session. It should never be ignored or neglected.

## 23.7 CONTENTS AND RELEVANCY

The most important aspect of training for development is that the contents must be relevant. If the CDW acts as a facilitator he/she should have a good idea of what information the different role-players in projects need by way of training. With this internalised knowledge the CDW can discuss the various training needs with the various role-players and try to marry his/her knowledge of training needs with their perceptions of what is needed in their armoury. What follows here is only a framework divided into three 'modules'. What the detail of these fields of study or training should be and where the emphasis should lie, is something to be sorted out with the role-players.

### Introductory training course for beginners

**Module 1: Community capacity-building**

- Poverty–the problem to be addressed
- The development environment
- The basic principles of community development
- The role of the CDW
- An operational strategy
- The community development project
- Evaluation

**Module 2: Community-based development management**

- Principles of management
- Mobilisation of community-based structures
- Basic recordkeeping
- Basic bookkeeping

**Module 3: Communication for development**

- Communication and its importance for development
- The characteristics of motivation for community development
- Conflict resolution and negotiation
- Problem-solving mechanisms for development projects
- Group dynamics and group work
- Public speaking
- Operational writing
- The dynamics of meetings–making them more productive

We also suggest an advanced course although we realise that perhaps one needs more experienced facilitators than CDWs for this.

---

### Advanced course for role-players in community development

**Module 1:  Development context**

▶ Sustainable development
▶ The politics of development
▶ The economics of development

**Module 2:  Advanced skills**

▶ Advanced management techniques
▶ Advanced negotiation techniques
▶ Advanced problem-solving techniques
▶ Advanced planning techniques
▶ Advanced evaluation techniques
▶ Advanced office management and bookkeeping

---

## 23.8  CONCLUSION

Facilitating training for community development is directed at project staff, community facilitators, at communities or CBOs or at combinations of these (De Beer & Swanepoel, 1998:89). The single most serious problem, though, is the scarcity of training facilitators. For this reason it is necessary to view the CDW as a potential facilitator. This potential is extremely vital and reachable because the work done by CDWs in their communities and the type of training that has been espoused here have a lot in common. The training discussed in the previous pages is part of the whole process of learning and adaptation towards the breaking of the deprivation trap.

# CASE STUDIES

## CASE STUDY 1

### THE STORY OF SIPHO

To illustrate how a family can be enmeshed in the deprivation trap.
(Taken from De Beer, F. & Swanepoel, H. 1996. *Training for development—A manual for student trainers*. Halfway House: International Thomson)

Sipho is the son of a small farmer in the deep rural area. He can remember that as a small boy he had to look after their two cows, that is until the drought came and the cows died. That drought broke his father's spirit too. It was only about a year later that his father died of TB.

After his father's death his uncle was supposed to help the family, but his uncle was so poor that he could hardly look after his own family. Sipho's mother then went to the nearest town to look for a job and he had to look after his younger sister and the baby boy.

Sipho couldn't make any progress in school. So when he was thirteen years old and in standard two he left the school to look for a job. He never got a decent job. He had to do piece jobs for small amounts of money.

His baby brother was always sick and his mother was mostly away in town with her job. Sipho remembers how the baby always cried at night until one night when the crying stopped and his aunt told him that the baby had died.

Then the big rains came. Their house was very dilapidated because there was no money to repair it. With the big rains their house just collapsed and they lost everything they had. There was no food on the land left and he and his sister really had nothing to eat. His mother would bring home a little food once a week from town, but it was not enough for them and his mother also didn't eat enough. So when she became ill she lost her job and the family then depended on him.

His sister was only twelve years old when she moved to the town to look for work, but she never got a good job and only brought a baby back that had to be fed from their meagre supplies. The father of the baby is the son of a rich trader, but he just laughed at Sipho when he went to ask for money to care for the baby. This rich man just said that he won't mix with the likes of them and that they must look for the father elsewhere.

Sipho doesn't know what is to become of them. His mother needs medical treatment, but they don't have the money. He is still trying to get their house fixed, but the job he has pays so poorly that it is difficult to afford anything but a bit of food.

## CASE STUDY 2
### FRANCISCO'S STORY

To illustrate the effect of poverty on more than one generation.

(Taken from Harrison, P. 1984. *Inside the Third World. The anatomy of poverty*. Second Edition, Harmondsworth: Penguin.)

Francisco's mother Fatima is small for her age. She is visibly weak, distant, yet easily irritated by the children. Years of pregnancy and menstruation, along with an iron-poor diet of maize, have made her chronically anaemic. Her husband Jaime is a landless labourer, with a low, erratic income barely enough to keep them all alive and clothed. No one eats enough, and when there's not enough to go round Fatima goes without, even when she's pregnant. And that is frequently, as the couple use no form of contraception. They have had ten children, six of whom survived to adulthood.

Fatima went through several periods of undernourishment while Francisco was in her womb. There were times when Jaime could not get regular work and everyone went hungry. Fatima also had several attacks of stress and anxiety when Jaime beat her. Francisco probably suffered his first bout of growth retardation, both mental and physical, before he even saw the light of day.

He was born underweight, and his brain was already smaller than normal size. For the first few months he was breast-fed and suffered few infections, as he was partly protected by the antibodies in his mother's milk. Then he was weaned onto thin gruels and soups, taken off the breast and put onto tinned evaporated milk, thinned down with polluted water from the well. His diet, in itself, was inadequate. Then he started to get more and more infections, fever, bronchitis, measles and regular bouts of gastro-enteritis. With well fed children these pass within a few days, but in his case they went on for weeks and sometimes a month or more. In these periods he could tolerate no milk and few solids, and so was given weak broths, tea or sugar water. By now he was 25 per cent underweight. Because of poor nutrition, he was even more susceptible to infection, and each time he was ill, he lost appetite and ate even less. Then he got bronchitis which developed into pneumonia. But Fatima borrowed money from a relative, went to town and got antibiotics for him.

So he survived. But malnutrition made him withdrawn and apathetic. His mother got no reward from playing with him, so he received little of the stimulation his brain needed to develop properly. As he grew older, infections grew less frequent, but by the time he went to school, aged eight, he was already a year behind normal physical development and two years behind mentally. The school, in any case, was a poor one, with only three classes, no equipment, and a poorly qualified teacher. As Francisco was continually worried about whether and what he was going to eat that day, he was distracted, unable to concentrate, and seemed to show little interest in schoolwork. The teacher confirmed that he was a slow learner, and could not seem to get the hang of maths or reading and writing. As the family was poor, they did not want to keep him on at school. He was doing so badly anyway that there seemed no point. He did a year, then was away for three years helping an uncle who had a farm, then did another year, then left for good, barely able to read or write more than a few letters. He soon forgot what little he had learned. So, like his father, he began tramping round the local ranches asking for work. Without any educational qualifications or skills, that was all he could ever hope for. And because so many were in the same boat, pay was low. When he was twenty-two he married a local girl, Graciela, aged only fifteen. She too had been undernourished and was illiterate. She soon became pregnant and had to feed another organism inside her before she herself had fully developed. Graciela had heard about family planning from a friend, but Francisco would not let her use it and anyway she was not sure she wanted to. So, by the age of only twenty-five, Graciela already had five children and had lost two. The children had every prospect of growing up much as Francisco and Graciela did, overpopulating, underfed, in poor health and illiterate.

## CASE STUDY 3
### A DESPERATE WOMAN

To illustrate the depths of misery for one poor household.

(Taken from Wilson, F. & Ramphele, M. 1989. *Uprooting poverty: The South African challenge*. Cape Town: David Philip.)

'My husband lost his job about five months ago ... then two months ago I lost my job. We were desperate. There was no money coming in now ... Now they've cut off the electricity and we're two months in arrears with rent. They're going to evict us, I'm sure, we just can't pay though. My husband decided to go to Jo'burg ... I don't know where he is ... Sometimes (the children) lie awake at night crying. I know they are crying because they are hungry. I feel like feeding them Rattex. When your children cry hunger-cry, your heart wants to break. It will be better if they were dead. When I think things like that I feel worse ... I'm sick ... I can't take my children to the doctor when they're sick because there's no money ... What can one do? You must start looking. You can also pray to God that he will keep you from killing your children'.

## CASE STUDY 4
### THE STORY OF THEMBALIHLE

To show that a very bad situation can be turned round.

Thembalihle with her six children was brought from the rural areas to a squatter camp by her husband. However, she wasn't there long before her husband abandoned her, leaving her with her children without any support. She lived in a single shack made out of old flattened water drums which leaked in several places on rainy days, thus soaking the muddy floor which made their sleeping most uncomfortable. The squatter settlement had very little infrastructure and Thembalihle had to walk quite a distance to fetch water. Sanitation was very poor and definitely the worse aspect of living in the squatter camp.

In an attempt to better her situation she teamed up with her neighbour who had been surviving for some time by hawking in town. This was the only avenue opened to her since she had very little basic education. She left her children in the care of her neighbour's eldest daughter while she was hawking. What she didn't know was that her children were not well looked after. One of them contracted a serious disease as a result of food poisoning from food taken from rubbish bins. To worsen the situation, the eldest child was struck by a motor car and seriously injured.

This situation forced Thembalihle to abandon her hawking effort so that she could look after her children herself. Her only way now open was to take in more children from other hawker women who paid her something if they made a little money. Obviously, there were no real facilities for these children. They played outside whether it was hot or cold and had to hide under plastic sheets if it rained.

One day a social worker noticed all the children playing around Thembalihle's shack. She enquired from Thembalihle what the situation was. Through the assistance of the social worker Thembalihle received a social grant to set up a proper day care centre. She worked very hard at this and with further assistance enlarged the facilities. When women realised the improvement in the facilities of their children's care, more of them wanted Thembalihle to take in their children. The result was that she started to employ people to help her. At present she has five employees working in the day care centre now named Thembalihle's Day Care Centre. This venture was so successful that it is now used as a pilot for similar projects elsewhere in squatter and informal areas. Thembalihle herself today lives in a properly built and modern house with all the necessary facilities.

## CASE STUDY 5
### A DAM CAN BRING HARDSHIP

To illustrate how so-called development can work against the first principle of community development. (Taken from De Beer, F. & Swanepoel, H. 1996. *Training for development–A manual for student trainers*. Halfway House: International Thomson.)

Our area was completely changed when the government announced some time ago that it was going to build a dam in the river. We were very surprised because it is not such a big river. Our chief was worried about this project and wanted to know why the government was planning this dam if the people had not even asked for it. The government people explained to him, and later to all of us, that the dam was needed to provide irrigation for the farming areas some kilometres from here. They also said that we would be assured of a regular water supply for our household needs. The people thought the idea was a really good one when we were told that the government would need many labourers to build the dam and that we could all get jobs.

In the end the company that built the dam brought a lot of workers from elsewhere and only some of us could get work. Some of the labourers who were brought in from other areas had very bad ways. They taught our young people to drink and quite a few of our daughters were made pregnant. We were very glad when the work was done and the workers left again.

In the meantime, the water started to rise and a number of our small farmers were threatened by this. We were very upset about it because we were never told that such a thing could happen. However, the government people said that they had told us that some of us would have to be relocated. Eventually, about twenty families had to be moved to higher ground about five kilometres from here. It was really a sad day when they had to leave. The worst part of it, though, is that where they are living now the soil is very poor and they are so far from the dam that they can't make use of all this water.

## CASE STUDY 6
### THE PARSON WHO BECAME A PAINTER

To illustrate what can happen if people do not really participate in a project.

Mr Robinson was the minister of a church adjacent to a former mission hospital in a densely populated rural area.

One day he decided that the church building would look much better with a garden and a new coat of paint. He asked his wife to sound out the women of the congregation about the matter at the weekly prayer meeting. She reported back that they agreed that it would make the church look better.

During the morning service the following Sunday, Mr Robinson announced that the congregation was to smarten up the church premises by laying out a garden and painting the building. He invited everyone to be at the church the following Saturday when the work would commence.

On the day a considerable crowd turned out. They were clearly disappointed when Mr Robinson announced that the garden would be tackled first. They were all obviously keen on helping to paint the church building and there was even a suggestion that the matter be put to the vote. However, Mr Robinson pressed on with his plan and the work on the garden began. Very little progress was made and less than half of the work was done by the end of the day. Mr Robinson, who had worked very hard all day, announced, grim faced, that the work on the garden would continue the next Saturday, and the next, if it was necessary and that the church would be painted only when

>>

the garden was complete. On the appointed day, only two ladies arrived. Mr Robinson decided that there were not enough people to continue work on the garden and they could start painting.

After the morning service on the Sunday, Mr Robinson was confronted by a group of dissatisfied members of the congregation. They accused him of not sticking to his original plans. They reminded him of his decision to finish the garden and to then start painting.

The result of the confrontation was that nobody turned up to work after that. The garden remained unfinished and Mr and Mrs Robinson spent several weeks painting the church building.

## CASE STUDY 7
### A COMMUNITY HALL WITH NO PURPOSE

To illustrate what can happen if the people are ignored in development projects.

A community hall was built in Freedom Village by a private contractor hired by the provincial government. Expectations in the community were raised when the project was launched and eventually completed. The community was under the impression that they would be in charge of the hall and that community members would be hired to do various jobs at the hall. However, the provincial government instructed community workers in its service to take charge of the hall. This upset the local community immensely. The result was that the hall operated for one day before it was damaged. The damage went on until the hall could not be used for anything.

The provincial government decided to do something about the situation by involving the local community. A community meeting was held. It was decided to renovate the hall and to put a fence around it. It was recommended that a local private contractor be used to erect the fence. This recommendation was met with loud applause. The representatives of the local government present noted this request. Yet, an outside private contractor was hired to erect the fence. This was immediately damaged and the renovations to the hall were never done. Today the dilapidated hall serves no other purpose but to remind the people that their wishes regarding the hall were not considered.

## CASE STUDY 8
### SMALL IS BETTER

To illustrate the principle of simplicity.
(Taken from De Beer, F. & Swanepoel, H. 1996. *Training for development—A manual for student trainers*. Halfway House: International Thomson.)

We have a very progressive civic organisation in this town. They decided some time ago that something had to be done about the housing situation. So they called us together one day and announced that we were all going to launch a house improvement scheme. Some of us were very glad to hear this and were keen on the plan, but others had their doubts and said that they had no money for such schemes.

The civic organisation started to make big plans for this project. They brought in some experts from outside and we were told to call at the office so that we could say what improvements we wanted done to our houses. This was a big affair. We stood in queues for long hours, waiting our turn, but when the people heard that they would have to make some payments, they just walked away and some said bad things about the executive members of the civic organisation.

>>

Eventually the civic organisation realised that this whole affair was getting out of hand. It was too big for them and most of the people didn't understand it properly, either. They changed their plans completely. They announced that those people who were interested in house improvement and who were prepared to contribute towards the costs, should meet. Only fifty people attended this meeting, but the civic people were not disheartened by the small number. They divided us into ten small groups of neighbours. Now only five of us are working together to improve our houses. This is very good because we help one another and, in the meantime, we have become good friends. We also learn from one another, so much so that when we are finished with our own houses, we are going to start a business to improve other people's houses.

## CASE STUDY 9
### THE DAUGHTER OF HOPE

To illustrate the right attitude, place and role of the community development worker.
(Taken from De Beer, F. & Swanepoel, H. 1996. *Training for development—A manual for student trainers*. Halfway House: International Thomson.)

Nomsa is a daughter of this village. She was born here and she grew up here. But then she left for school in the city. When she returned, she was very concerned about many things in the village. She befriended the clinic sister and you could often see them talking with each other or with other women. Eventually, Nomsa convinced a small group of women that they should start a vegetable garden. We men told one another that only a woman could be so stupid as to work so hard for so little.

The garden project went quite well. Poor Nomsa had to find out many things so that she could guide the women in their endeavours. Then other women started to be interested in what this group of women were doing and, often, you would see one or more go to Nomsa's house for some advice about something they wanted to do. Nomsa really gained the respect of the women when she went to the chief on their behalf to ask for more land for gardening and for his support in getting the school upgraded. What the people really liked about her was that she never tried to tell them what to do. She never tried to take the place of the natural and traditional leaders in our village. She was always in the background, as if she new her place.

Nomsa's most important contribution to this village is not all the things that she has done. Rather, it is her enthusiasm. People say that when she speaks to them it makes them feel as if they are able to do things that they had thought impossible before. Even we men are becoming interested. Our wives tell us that we must start doing things for ourselves and when we don't know how to, they say we must put our pride in our pockets and ask Nomsa to help us. But we don't only hear it from our wives. We can see with our own eyes that this woman wants to and can help us without trying to make us feel that she knows more than we do.

The people like Nomsa very much. They say she knows her place and yet she gives them new things to think about. In the women's prayer meetings, they pray for the daughter of hope and, in the shebeens, this very same name is mentioned with smiles and fondness.

## CASE STUDY 10
### THE PROJECT THAT HAD ITS FENCES BROUGHT DOWN

To show how a government organisation can break down initiative among grassroots people.

Mr Dube, a sports organiser in an urban area, was approached by the chairman of a soccer club about the poor condition of the local soccer field. The field was level and well grassed, but there were no other amenities. Mr Dube, who had just finished reading a book on community development, saw the potential to build a community development project around the need for better amenities. He explained to the chairman, Mr Radebe, that the town council could not upgrade the field because of a lack of money. It could contribute something, but the club had to take responsibility for the effort. They discussed the matter further. Eventually they decided to approach the other two clubs that also made use of the field to solicit their support for a project.

Mr Dube and Mr Radebe each visited the chairman of one of the other clubs. After some time a meeting was arranged between the executives of the three soccer clubs. At this meeting Mr Dube explained that it was apparent that all three soccer clubs saw there was a need to update the soccer field and its facilities. He set out the position of the town council and urged the clubs to do something for themselves.

The representatives of all three clubs seemed keen to start on a project to upgrade the facility. Mr Dube suggested that they make a list of their needs. Various needs were identified, such as new goal posts, cloakrooms, a pavilion and a fence around the grounds. They decided to take the matter to their clubs and report back at a second meeting.

At the second meeting, two clubs clearly showed their support for a fence around the grounds. That would mean, they argued, that people would have to pay to see matches which would boost the coffers of the clubs. Mr Dube explained that the town council would take a large slice of the gate money, but that the clubs would also benefit financially. The other club was not so keen on the fence. They were the smallest of the three and felt they would not be able to afford it. The matter was discussed at length and it was finally decided that they would go for a corrugated iron fence. Mr Dube was asked to get information on prices and to find out what the town council would be prepared to contribute.

Mr Dube was not very keen on a corrugated iron fence. He was afraid that it would not look so good. Nevertheless, he enquired from a senior official in the town council about the whole matter. He was informed by the official that the town council would never subsidise a corrugated iron fence. He said, however, that it might be possible that the town council would pay in full for a precast concrete wall. He undertook to submit an application and promised that Mr Dube would know the outcome within six weeks.

At the next meeting of the club representatives, Mr Dube informed the meeting of the possibility that the town council would fund the whole operation of erecting a precast wall. It was decided that the clubs would, in the meantime, get organised for the erection of the fence. It was also decided to combine the erection of the fence with a dedication ceremony and soccer matches between teams of the three clubs.

It took three months before the town council decided that the fence should be erected. When Mr Dube enquired from the senior official about the date on which he should organise the clubs to erect the fence, the official informed him that the town council had contractors doing that type of work.

Mr Dube called the representatives of the clubs together to inform them that their work would not be required. Seeing that the town council had taken over the fence issue, he suggested that they think of another need that they could address. However, the meeting felt that they should wait until after the erection of the fence. They also decided not to continue planning the dedication ceremony because, as Mr Radebe put it, 'They first want to see if the town council will ever get so far'.

>>

In the meantime, the town council experienced a rent crisis. It had to make some cuts in expenditure. The fence around the soccer grounds was one of the first items to fall by the way. After this, all attempts by Mr Dube to organise the clubs around another need met with very little enthusiasm. At long last Mr Dube decided to concentrate on soccer and to forget about community development.

## CASE STUDY 11
### THE PROJECT THAT WAS TAKEN OVER

To show how an insensitive government agency can ruin a very promising venture.

Mr Kekana was a teacher in a rural village. He was born in the area and when he was posted there as a teacher, he requested from the chief a piece of land on which he erected his home. Mr Kekana decided to plant the traditional crops on his land, but to use fertiliser and modern farming methods. The result was that his crops were markedly better than those of the other small farmers. They started to talk about it, but Mr Kekana, who was expecting it, quickly forestalled any hint of sorcery or any other supernatural means of getting beautiful crops by telling the farmers simply and plainly what he did to get better crops. He also offered to help them do the same.

Over a period of two seasons, more and more farmers used Mr Kekana's advice and the crops showed a marked difference. By that stage the farmers had organised themselves into an association and they farmed co-operatively to ensure cheaper inputs and lower running costs, for example the marketing of their produce. They were so successful that the regional government got word of their work. Regional representatives visited the area so that they could see for themselves what could be done to improve agriculture. They were so impressed that they decided to help the farmers.

At the beginning of the next season, the government sent a number of tractors to the area and started to plough the farmers' lands. They then brought in the planters and started to plant. The farmers were bewildered. Everything was taken out of their hands. Mr Kekana pleaded with the government to leave the farmers to their own devices. He was told that the area had been earmarked for demonstrating agricultural methods to farmers from other areas and that the highest possible yields had to be ensured.

Suddenly, the farmers had little to do. The decisions had been taken out of their hands and even the hard work was being done by the government with its implements. The result was quite devastating. Within a season there was nothing left of the farmers' initiatives. When the government decided to hand the lands back to the farmers, they were met with disinterest.

## CASE STUDY 12
### THE DIVIDED COMMUNITY

To illustrate how politics can put paid to any effort at development.

Green Village is a squatter settlement now being upgraded. It had a village committee, but most of the people demanded the committee's resignation. The members of the village committee refused to oblige and, since then, there has been bitter animosity and rivalry between two groups, one supporting the incumbent leaders and the other one very much against them. Provincial government officials find themselves in the middle of this squabble. All their efforts to resolve the matter had so far failed. As a result, the whole community is prone to intimidation and lives in fear of itself.

Because of the open animosity it is impossible to establish any development action. The youth, sport and cultural day that was organised by officials of the provincial government, and was supposed to take place in the community hall, is a good example. Everything started peacefully enough. After a while, though, some people marched into the hall and told those present to disperse. They said that the village committee were going to hold a meeting. The officials of the provincial government pleaded with them, arguing that nobody had known anything about a meeting. But it was to no avail. The crowd were intimidated and forced to leave the hall or to attend the village committee's meeting. This was the end of the youth, sport and cultural day.

## CASE STUDY 13
### THE CLUB WITH TWO COMMITTEES

To remind us that conflict and animosity are always just below the surface.

The Hlangani women's club was asked to do the catering at a seminar that was to be held in the township. The local government paid R600 for this service and the community worker pointed out that the club could do the catering for less and then have something left to spend on themselves. The club agreed to the request and did the catering. It went very well and the club showed a profit of R185. The community worker suggested that a bank account be opened and that the money be deposited. The club agreed and chose people for the task. These people were not part of the committee, but the chairperson and the other members of the committee had no qualms about this. However, at the same meeting, it was suggested that a new committee be elected as the incumbent committee's term of office had expired. At the suggestion of one member it was decided, without discussion, that those people who were chosen to see to the banking account would be the new committee.

A few months later the community worker visited the club again. She was surprised by the small attendance. The members of the previous committee were all absent. She learnt that the bank account had still not been opened and that the money was still with the new chairperson. The reason for the delay, the community worker was told, lay with some members talking behind the backs of the new committee and this had made them cross.

## CASE STUDY 14
### THE CASE OF THE COMMUNITY WORKER WHO MET HIS MATCH

To illustrate how contact should not be made.

Mr Dladla was a newly appointed agricultural extension officer to a rural tribal area. He was taught at college that an extension officer should get the local people to participate and that he should identify leaders to pull the rest of the people along.

His first task as extension officer was to visit each farmer and to invite him to a public meeting the following Sunday to discuss farming matters in the area. Mr Dladla was exceptionally impressed with one young farmer, a Mr Kubheka, who farmed very progressively and was very keen to befriend Mr Dladla.

A large number of farmers attended the meeting. Mr Dladla was glad to see that Mr Kubheka had quite a following and he decided that he had already done one part of his job, that is to identify a leader.

Mr Dladla addressed the meeting. He told those present that it was clear to him as a professional that they had very low yields and that their farming methods were to be blamed for that. He emphasised how glad he was to be given the opportunity to help them to become wealthy farmers. He also stressed the fact that he could not farm for them. Whilst he had the knowledge and contacts at the government, they had the ability to learn and to work. He sketched a picture of maize fields standing high in the cob and of broad leaved tobacco plants earning the farmers a lot of money. He implored them not to think that such progress is impossible. If they all pulled together they would reach their goal very soon.

Mr Dladla continued by suggesting that they make their first objective a doubling of their maize crop and each farmer to plant at least half a hectare with tobacco to be reached by the end of the next season. This speech drew very warm applause. The whole meeting was buzzing and it was apparent that Mr Dladla had made a great impression.

Mr Kubheka took the floor and thanked Mr Dladla profusely for his inspiring speech. He ended by asking what the next step should be. Mr Dladla ticked the various steps off on his fingers. One, they should form a farmers' association; two, they should elect a committee; three, the committee should go to the regional office of the Department of Agriculture to state their plan; four, they should hold another meeting so that the committee could report on their plans for the following season.

An elderly man then stood up and explained that they already had a farmers' association that was established some years ago. Mr Dladla interjected that he was glad to hear that an association was established, but that the committee was not doing its work and should therefore be sacked.

Mr Kubheka replied in a sneering way that the old headman was the chairman of this dormant committee. Mr Dladla immediately sensed that he was now on dangerous ground. He enquired politely where the headman was, but was told he was not present. Mr Dladla thought that he had saved the situation when he suggested that they proceed with electing a new committee and that the chairman and vice-chairman would then pay the headman a visit to discuss their further plans with him.

The meeting thought it a good idea and promptly elected Mr Dladla chairman and Mr Kubheka vice-chairman. In his acceptance speech Mr Dladla said that he would gladly lead this new effort, but that he would resign in favour of Mr Kubheka as soon as he saw that the association was well on its feet.

After the meeting Mr Dladla and Mr Kubheka talked at length about their plans for the association. When Mr Dladla said that they had better visit the headman as soon as possible, Mr Kubheka pleaded a very busy week and suggested that Mr Dladla go alone to the headman.

>>

Mr Dladla visited the headman the following week. He was greeted by the headman saying that he heard that Dladla and Kubheka had kicked him out of the committee. Mr Dladla tried to explain that that was not the case, but that it was unfortunate that the headman was not present at the meeting. The headman replied that he was not informed of the meeting and that the meeting was therefore illegal. It took Mr Dladla more than an hour to come to an agreement with the headman that they would hold a second meeting, this time at the headman's homestead where they could iron out the differences.

The second meeting was again attended by a large group of farmers. After the headman had solemnly welcomed all present, a man stood up and proposed that they again elect a committee. Mr Dladla replied that that was not necessary. They could easily include the headman on the committee. A long debate ensued in which it was eventually decided that seeing that the previous meeting was illegal the committee was illegal too and for that reason a new committee should be chosen.

The headman immediately called for nominations for a chairman and his name was suggested by a chorus of voices. No other name came up. Then the headman asked for nominations for a vice-chairman. Mr Dladla and Mr Kubheka were nominated. Mr Dladla did not want to be in opposition to Mr Kubheka and he therefore withdrew, saying that he would rather serve on the committee ex officio as adviser.

The meeting decided that the committee should meet as soon as possible. Three weeks passed before Mr Dladla enquired from Mr Kubheka when the committee is going to meet. He said that he had not heard from the headman yet. After another three weeks Mr Dladla enquired from the headman when he planned to call a meeting. He was told by the headman that a committee meeting had been held but that there was nothing of importance to report.

## CASE STUDY 15
### THE INSPECTOR WHOSE HELP WAS DUMPED

To learn from the mistakes of a community development worker.

Mr Williams was a health inspector in an urban area situated close to the city centre and in a state of decline. When he visited the cafés and butcheries on his inspection rounds he was struck by the presence of large numbers of idle children.

Mr Williams noticed a boy sitting on the same café veranda every day, surrounded by followers. He made a point of regularly greeting and occasionally exchanging a friendly word with the boy. He soon realised that this boy, Gary, was regarded as a leader by many of the children.

Next to the café was a vacant lot that had originally been zoned as a park, but was now overgrown with grass and strewn with car wrecks and other scrap. Mr Williams decided that the lot could be put to good use and obtained the city council's permission to clean up the site for the children's use.

Soon after, Mr Williams asked Gary whether they would like to have a place where they could kick a ball. Gary and his friends were appreciative, but said that there was no such place. Mr Williams pointed to the adjacent lot and invited them to follow him. He explained to them that, if they could clear the site, they might use it. Gary and his friends did not look too keen, but Mr Williams suggested that they organise the children in the vicinity and then try to clean up the site over a few days. He promised that he would arrange a lorry to cart away the rubbish.

>>

On the appointed day, a considerable number of children arrived, but most of them were rather small. Gary and his friends were the only big children. But they were not really working. They were 'supervising' the smaller children. They worked until dark and Mr Williams then realised that it would take quite a few days of hard work to get the place clean. He arranged with the children to resume work during the afternoon of the next day and encouraged them to bring more children to help them.

The next day there were quite a few new faces, but many from the previous day were absent, including Gary and his friends. Again, they worked until dark and agreed to come back the next Saturday to try to finish their work.

A few days later, Mr Williams was called by his superior who told him that parents had complained that he had used their children to remove scrap, that they had returned to their homes after dark, and that some had had their clothes torn as a result of the work.

Mr Williams visited the café adjoining the site and pleaded with the owner to tell parents who visited the café the purpose of the clean-up. He asked Gary and his friends, who were at their usual place on the veranda to gather as many children as possible for the following Saturday so that they could finish the work.

On that Saturday, only Gary and his friends were there, kicking a ball on the cleared part of the site. Mr Williams asked them where the other children were and was told that they found the work too hard and that, at any rate, the parents were not pleased with the idea.

Mr Williams decided to take a short cut. He asked the municipality to clean up the site. It took him three days to unravel all the red tape, but, ultimately, the municipality agreed and, within a week, the site was clean and the grass cut. A proud Mr Williams handed the clean site over to Gary and his friends and urged them to get the children to play ball games.

Two weeks later, Mr Williams visited the area again. He was surprised to see children idling everywhere. He arrived at the cleaned-up site and was very upset to see not a single child, but a new car wreck with several loads of rubbish next to it!

## CASE STUDY 16
### THE FELT AND THE REAL NEED

To illustrate that community development is a learning process through which we can also learn about our needs.

Mrs Mathebula, a social worker, had been stationed only a few months in a large, rural town when she attended a seminar on community development.

After the seminar, she was very keen to launch at least one community development project. Up to that moment, most of her cases came from a hilly area far from the main road where the people were markedly poorer than elsewhere. Nearly all the cases Mrs Mathebula had handled from this area had to do with child neglect and poverty-related problems affecting children. She identified this area as the place where people really needed help. She decided to get a community development project going among the mothers to improve their children's diet.

Mrs Mathebula first spoke to the wife of the local headman, who had a shop on the fringe of this area. From this conversation, she learnt that the mothers might be more keen to get a sewing class going so that they could make most of their children's clothes themselves.

>>

Mrs Mathebula was disheartened by this news. She was hoping that a poor society such as this would give preference to their children's health and diet. However, she decided to talk to the women themselves. It took her the best part of two weekends to visit the women at their homes or to talk to them at the communal washing place or water pump. She was disappointed to learn that very few women were interested in improving their children's diet. Just as the headman's wife predicted, most of them were keen to start a sewing club. Mrs Mathebula had to make a decision. Either she would look for other women interested in starting a food garden, or she would start a project addressing these women's felt need. After some soul searching, she opted for the latter. From one of the women she had talked to, she had learnt that a teacher at the nearby primary school had a knowledge of sewing and could teach the women basic skills.

Mrs Mathebula went to see the teacher, Miss Makhanye. She was quite willing to give weekly sewing classes to the women. They decided to call a meeting at the school to launch the sewing club. Mrs Mathebula tried to contact as many women as she could to tell them of the meeting.

The meeting was attended by seventeen women who were very keen to start the classes. They wanted to know from Mrs Mathebula and Miss Makhanye what it would cost to buy two second hand sewing machines and some material. The two ladies were unprepared for such questions. They had not thought of finding such information. The women expressed their disappointment because they wanted to start as soon as possible. Mrs Mathebula undertook to find out the costs and to let the women know over the weekend. She then suggested that the women elect a committee to take up leadership positions. The women thought it a good idea and promptly nominated Mrs Mathebula as chairperson. She declined, however, explaining that she may be transferred at any time and that, as a social worker, she had many other tasks to perform. They then elected a person not known to Mrs Mathebula, with Miss Makhanye as vice-chairperson and a young woman, who had several years of schooling, as secretary. They wanted to elect Mrs Mathebula as treasurer, but she declined again in favour of someone else.

It took Mrs Mathebula a few days of hard work to find out the cost of the sewing machines and the material. Eventually she found two second hand sewing machines in a shop in town. She calculated that the seventeen persons involved would each have to pay R10 to cover the cost of the machines and the material. Again, Mrs Mathebula spent most of the weekend conveying this information to the women. Mrs Mathebula and Miss Makhanye bought the two sewing machines and the material out of their own pockets, hoping that the women would each contribute their R10.

At the first class, twelve women were present. Mrs Mathebula explained that she and Miss Makhanye had bought the sewing machines and material and that the club would have to pay them back. Ten women had brought their money. They wanted to give their contributions directly to the two ladies, but Mrs Mathebula explained that they had to pay it to the treasurer, who would open an account in the post office before paying them from that account.

After three weeks, only five women showed a continued interest in the sewing lessons. These five enjoyed it greatly and two of them made quick progress. Mrs Mathebula and Miss Makhanye were not properly refunded. After the first ten contributions no others were made. The treasurer explained that two of the women who had dropped the classes had claimed their money back. Another had borrowed R10 from the fund but, shortly afterwards, had taken a job in town and had not been seen since. The treasurer should therefore have had R70 in the account, but it held only R50. She really could not tell what had happened to the rest. The two ladies decided to take R20 each, leaving R10 in the account.

>>

271

Mrs Mathebula was unhappy that, after her initial effort, only five women were benefiting. She decided to visit the twelve women who had dropped out since the first meeting. She learnt that most of these women had found the classes too difficult. They would rather do something not requiring many lessons. Mrs Mathebula then suggested a communal vegetable garden and ten women showed interest. She arranged for them to go to the headman as a group to ask for a piece of land. On their way to the headman, they called on his wife at her shop. She told them that the clinic sister was also organising a communal garden, but that she had had trouble in getting enough women to participate.

There and then the group decided to pay the clinic sister a visit. From her they learnt that all the clinic's grounds, which were already fenced and had running water, were available for vegetable gardening. She had already obtained the help of one of the extension officers who was prepared to give the project professional advice. Her problem was that she could only get five women who were prepared to participate in the venture. That same day, Mrs Mathebula, her group and the clinic sister decided to join hands in an effort to get a garden project going.

The garden is really prospering. The garden club's membership has risen to twenty-five and it has had to obtain land adjacent to the clinic grounds to accommodate all the participants.

The sewing club has disintegrated. Miss Makhanye was transferred out of the area. Two of the women who made good progress are now fulltime seamstresses. The other three will never master the art of sewing. Two of them have since joined the garden club. The other one, the treasurer, has R10 to show for her efforts, the R10 Mrs Mathebula and Miss Makhanye left in the sewing club's account.

## CASE STUDY 17
### MOTHERS OF THE MOUNTAIN COMMUNITY

To illustrate that community development projects can be spectacularly successful.

The superintendent of a hospital in a rural area in the foot hills of a mountainous area realised that the same women would bring their children with kwashiorkor to the hospital for treatment. The child would be hospitalised for two weeks and the mother would receive information on a balanced and healthy diet for her child. However, within a month or two she would be back with the same child needing treatment again. The superintendent decided to speak to these women about the feeding of their children. He identified the monthly clinic day when these women could collect some powder milk for their children as an opportune time.

In his discussions with these women he soon realised that they knew what constitutes a healthy diet, but that they simply did not have the means to provide the right food to their children. This discovery of the superintendent started a discussion between him and the mothers about a food garden to supplement their children's diet. After a while a group of twenty mothers declared themselves willing to start a garden. They acquired a piece of land in the hospital grounds with ample water. Their garden was an instant success, so much so, that more mothers wanted to join them. When this one project just about reached its capacity, women started their own gardens on land acquired from the tribal chief. Some women had no feeling for gardening and they decided to start with a small poultry farm where they would raise broilers. Again their endeavour was met with instant success. The result was that a number of women's groups started raising poultry. Within a period of less than a year the market for broilers was totally sated.

>>

In the meantime the original group of women with their garden in the hospital grounds were doing so well with selling the surplus of their produce in the area surrounding the hospital that they could afford to erect a small building in the hospital grounds with a demonstration kitchen and a lecture room. On clinic days they would invite dieticians to come and tell and show them how to prepare food to optimise its nutritional value.

The efforts of the women in food gardening and poultry farming caught the eye of the tribal authority and the service providers in the area. Through the good offices of the authorities and a few NGOs groups were created to develop springs. Because of the mountainous terrain there were many springs in the area. They just had to be developed and the water piped from them to tanks in the various villages. When the first efforts to develop the springs proved to be a fairly easy task, a number of groups sprang up with this in mind and a large number of villages got water in this way. As water became easier to use more food gardens appeared.

At this stage the superintendent realised that he could no longer handle the facilitating of all these projects. Through the good offices of an NGO a project manager was obtained whose salary was paid by the NGO and who got a small flat inside the hospital where she could reside.

The women not involved in food gardens or poultry farming started to talk about doing something for themselves; getting a project going that would improve their income. With the help of the new project manager they identified a possible project, namely the harvesting and selling of the thatch grass that covered a large portion of the area. They began to look for a buyer of the thatch and found one in Johannesburg. They were fortunate to have a siding of the railway line to the north in their area and they arranged with the transport services to park a railway truck at the siding which the women would then fill with thatch grass. They worked out a system whereby the women would receive a token for every bushel of grass they would bring to the truck. Later they could then exchange their tokens for a fixed amount of money. This project was a great success and really brought prosperity to the area.

The tribal authority who had representatives on a steering committee overseeing all of these projects, decided to start a few rehabilitative projects where they invited people to participate with their labour for which they were paid. These projects included rehabilitation of homesteads where huts were fixed and newly thatched and where dilapidated animal kraals were improved. It also included throwing car wrecks lying in the veld into dongas and covering them with diamond mesh wire so that soil and vegetation could take hold.

One of the serious problems at that stage was that there were too few schools and that further schools were only on the waiting list for two or three years hence. Some parents whose children were negatively affected by this came together and decided to build their own school. Through the good offices of the project manager they acquired a deal with an NGO that it would supply and fix the roof of the school if the parents would build the rest. Not one, but three schools were built in this way and every one of them were supplied with water from fountains in the mountains. These schools had so much surplus water that they could make a food garden in every school yard and supply the homes adjacent to the schools with water for their everyday use.

Another educational problem of the area was that many children could not afford school books. The original project of the kwashiorkor mothers was in such a strong position financially at this stage that they decided to start a fund for poor children who could not afford their own books.

After about two years since the first project of the mothers with the kwashiorkor babies, there were about 200 projects in that area and the local people ran these projects with minimal help from the project manager and a few NGOs.

## CASE STUDY 18
### FOOD GARDEN IN MAPAYENI

A new dimension in human development.

Professor H.J. Swanepoel

(Translation of article entitled 'Mapayeni 'n nuwe dimensie in mensontwikkeling', *Lantern*, 34(2) 1985.)

### A general picture of a successful community development project.

Twenty women from the Gazankulu district developed a vegetable garden during one of the driest years of the century, a year when humans and animals were facing starvation. These women produced an enviable harvest, through hard work and perseverance, despite the fact that the once subtropical vegetation in the area was now reduced to red soil and Mopani trees. These women (and it is hoped those who have heard about this project) have learned valuable lessons from this community development project. Mapayeni has shown that poor and isolated people do not necessarily lack potential and energy—these characteristics are just generally hidden. This potential and energy need to be identified and channelled by enthusiastic and passionate people so that these communities are able to achieve more than they ever thought possible.

### The story of Mapayeni

The small group of women who got involved in this project are members of the local Dutch Reformed Church in Africa. They are poor, but they were even more poor until a short time ago. Many of them are their family's breadwinners and some of them are already middle-aged with health problems. Caught as they were in the vicious circle of poverty, the drought and recession were like an insurmountable mountain to these women. This was, however, until something ignited their enthusiasm—something that would change their lives forever.

In 1982, when Gazankulu was reeling from a drought (the residents did not realise that the worst of the drought would hit them in 1983), the local minister from the Dutch Reformed Church in Africa planted cabbages in his garden which he later sold very cheaply to the community. And this got a group of women thinking—they realised that they could develop a garden of their own which would provide for their needs. So they laid their first garden on the premises of an outpost church, but the rains stayed away and the plants shrivelled and died in the extreme heat. Although this attempt was unsuccessful, the women did not become downhearted. They began to look for land on the banks of the Middle Letaba River—a river that runs just a few kilometres past the village—so that there would be sufficient water for the vegetables.

The women chose a piece of land measuring two hectares and obtained the necessary permission from the local tribal chief. A total of 20 women would tackle the project. They elected a committee from this group and were now ready to tackle their project.

Their first task was to clear (deforest) the land. Burning was the easiest option, but that would mean that they would destroy valuable fire wood and that tree stumps under the ground would make the tilling of the land more difficult. The vegetation thus had to be cut down and carted away so that the land was bare; the women did, however, leave a few trees for shade.

The next task was to fence off the area. The women realised that they would need to erect more than a fence made of branches and twigs—the fence needed to prevent hungry goats and other animals from entering the growing area. The women were faced with two problems. Firstly, they did not have sufficient money for a wire fence and, secondly, they did not know how to put up a wire fence. But with the assistance of the local minister, they were able to get an interest-free loan from Church Aid in Need to purchase the necessary wire and poles. They were shown how to put up the fence, but thereafter undertook the work themselves.

>>

The third milestone these women encountered was the ploughing of the land. Thanks to the loan they obtained, the women were able to get someone to do the ploughing for them. This was one of the few tasks they did not undertake themselves.

As soon as the land was cleared, ploughed and fenced off, the women were able to start gardening. The time was ripe. It was already early autumn in 1983–the best time to plant in the Gazankulu district. The women transplanted about 20 000 cabbage, spinach, tomato, onion and pepper plants from the minister's garden which had served as a nursery while they were preparing their garden. It was a team effort. Some measured the distance between the plants, some planted the seedlings, some dug in fertilisers and sprayed for pests where necessary, while others watered the plants.

Watering a garden that is situated on the banks of a river sounds like easy work. The fact is, however, that the river is a good 20 metres lower than the garden–this makes watering an enormous task. The minister, who gave advice whenever necessary, recommended that the women should look at purchasing a pump. He believed that a pump installed on the river bed would eliminate much of the hard work associated with watering the plants. Before the women would consent to this, however, he had to demonstrate the process using a loaned pump. A further loan from Church Aid in Need enabled them to buy the necessary pump, but they had to see to the installation of the pump themselves.

By this time, the drought had become so severe that the river had dried up. The project was facing a huge crisis. The only option was to dig for water in the river bed. At first, all that was needed was a big hole, but with time, the women had to dig a long ditch and additional holes so that each precious drop of water from the supposedly dry river bed could be channelled to the vegetables.

The first vegetables were harvested in August. After months of toil, the women were able to provide their families with fresh vegetables. They were also able to provide the entire community with vegetables at about 60 percent of the market price. So, instead of only feeding 20 women and their families, this group of women were able to assist hundreds in the community. These women also started to make a profit, which enabled them to start paying back their loans and to buy other essential items.

Within a year of the idea being conceived, this group of women who knew very little about gardening and even less about irrigation, water pumps and fencing, had turned their precarious existence around to one of resourcefulness and hope. It is important to note that this group of women did not have exceptional talents; nor were they a unique group of people. What they achieved, therefore, lies within the grasp of each person who lives in similar circumstances.

## The value for the participants

This is not just a good old success story. These women live in poverty, but have turned their lives around. The most important result of this project is the physical improvement of living conditions. A balanced diet for people staring starvation in the face and a little money to buy essential items should not be scorned. These women achieved far more than just the physical improvement of their living conditions.

First, they showed themselves that they can do something about their apparently hopeless situation. They awakened their potential–something they had always underestimated. They now know that a crisis can be overcome by hard work and by working as a team.

Second, these women learned skills which they shall have for the rest of their lives. They have expanded their knowledge of gardening. They now know how to plant seeds and how to keep plants moist. They now have a good understanding of fertilisation and pest control. They have learned something about mechanics by using and maintaining a pump. They can now put up a fence and they know a lot more about marketing and selling.

>>

Third, these women now have increasing respect for human dignity. The knowledge that 'we can' contributes to self-confidence and self-reliance. The fact that they are self-reliant makes them more acceptable to the community. Passers by mocked them when, in excruciating heat, they planted approximately 20 000 cabbage plants in dry ground. But when these selfsame women began selling their produce cheaply to the community, they quickly became 'heroes' and are now seen as pioneers by the community.

Fourth, the women learned to work as a group and they began to understand the value of co-operation. They have proved that people can achieve anything when they stand together–that many hands do, in fact, make light work. No individual would have been able to do what the group has managed to do together. The division of work was an important element of their success. As individuals, they would have been unlikely to have been loaned money, for example.

Lastly, this group has also provided their community with a long-term service. Those who initially mocked and doubted them have since seen the rewards of the project–this has resulted in some of them knuckling down to some hard work themselves. They have realised that the risk factor is not as great as initially anticipated. They have seen what these women have achieved and are attempting to emulate them. The result–a large number of gardens in Mapayeni today. The demonstration effect of this first project was thus overwhelming.

## Lessons for those who wish to help

This project also has a number of lessons for those who would like to help others to help themselves.
In the first place, it is important to limit the number of people involved in a project. The work, organisation and associated costs were also limited in this case. It was thus possible for the minister to keep an eye on the entire project and each participant was able to identify with the total project. Community development projects that get too big can so easily become like a Frankenstein monster–they become unmanageable and make enormous demands on the people involved. The aims of over-large projects gradually become vague and the initial aims are soon replaced by the need to just keep the project going. The problems and work they encountered would have been far more taxing if the project had been bigger. The death-knell of a project sounds as soon as participants feel that they have lost control of the project.

This project was, in the second place, also blessed with good leadership. Leaders often need to be cultivated during a project, but this group already had a clear leader who was accepted by the group. Her strong leadership contributed enormously to the independent nature and behaviour of the group. Weak leadership or a total lack of leadership is often the Achilles heel of a project, because outsiders–such as the minister in this case–must then take on the role of leader. This encroaches on the group's initiative and independence.

In the third place, initiative must be utilised in the right place. People who want to help others often instinctively want to take the initiative. In this case, the minister's actions serve as a good example of how to help others without smothering their initiative. He never told the women what to do. He gave advice when he was asked for it, but he also allowed them to make mistakes. He gradually reduced his visits to the garden so that the women had no choice but to stand on their own two feet. He gave them detailed information about technical matters, but as soon as the women had mastered the technique, he left them to their own devices. One thing he continued to do for the women, however, was to act as their representative. He helped the women to obtain their loans and to acquire an appropriate and well-priced pump–things the women might well have struggled to do on their own. But, it is important to note that he never did anything without first being asked to do so. He never threatened their initiative; neither was he a scapegoat when the women wished to avoid their responsibilities. He was thus very valuable to the project, both as an adviser and as a moral supporter.

>>

Fourth, organisation and self-discipline are key words for the success of any community development project. The women elected a committee right at the beginning and all the obvious leaders were included in this committee. Apart from the project leader, one of the younger women who could read and write was appointed to serve as secretary and treasurer.

Based on this information, it is clear that the committee were thoroughly organised and that they maintained discipline. The women decided early on that each woman was required to attend work each day. Any woman who failed to arrive for work would be fined 30c per day. Those women who already had other work were not excused; they had to make the necessary arrangements to ensure that someone else was available to stand in for them on a temporary basis. Once all the plants had been planted, the committee divided each group of vegetables into equal parts. Each woman was responsible for her section and was entitled to claim her portion of the harvest from her section. It was thus not possible to hide behind the hard work of another woman and then claim an equal portion of the harvest. It was necessary to spend long hours working in the garden to ensure that the plants were properly watered (the women worked long hours for many months). The committee thus divided the women into two shifts, so that there were people on duty from early in the morning until late at night. As soon as the vegetables were selling well, the committee decided that each woman should contribute R5 per month to repay their loans. One of the secrets of any project's success is that each participant is utilised optimally—and the committee was very successful in this regard. One of the older women suffered from asthma and could not keep up with the other women when they were clearing the land. She was thus given the task of collecting and burning thorns. When the pump was installed, she was also given the responsibility of ensuring that the inlet pipe was kept free of branches, leaves and other debris. A younger woman who had attended school for a few years was given the task of maintaining the pump. The minister showed her the ropes and then left her to take full responsibility for the pump.

In the fifth place, it is clear that even the simplest project needs initial capital. It is true that even the poorest communities can generate capital, but then the risk factor becomes so much greater. If they are able to borrow money on reasonable terms (ie that they do not have to pay back the money in the short term), then the risk factor is reduced and the participants can first become entrenched in the project before they are expected to produce physical results.

In the sixth place, this project shows that it is not sufficient to merely convey knowledge to those who need to learn to help themselves. There should be an emotional element to the contact between the outsider and the community. The community must be able to sense a degree of compassion and sincerity on the part of the outsider. They must be able to accept his/her intentions without question.

Once the community realises that the outsider who wishes to help them is just as dependent on them as they are on him/her for the success of the project, then progress can be made.

## Conclusion

The Mapayeni project also has negative elements, because people are, by nature, fallible. This is, however, not of primary importance. What is important, though, is that these women exceeded all expectations in their attempt to do something about their hopeless situations.

The Mapayeni project is not a big and sophisticated attempt to make poor people rich. There was no blueprint that would ensure there was phenomenal growth. It was not necessary to have a group of officials to manage the project or to support the participants. The project did not require any form of advanced technology or large amounts of money. The Mapayeni women are still poor and simple people, but this project has given meaning to their existence. These women have renewed hope, as do their families and those who have followed their example. This project has enabled a group of people to turn away from being victims of their circumstances to being people of self-confidence and independence who wish to improve their lives.

## CASE STUDY 19
### STEALING OR TAKING OWNERSHIP

To illustrate two opposing views of community development workers.

At a trouble shoot session of an NGO conference a middle aged gentleman stood up and said that on the whole he had few problems with running projects. The only problem he had he said was that 'every time that I have a successful project, the people steal it from me'.

A community development worker was responsible for the launching of refuse removal projects in informal settlements in and around the metropolitan area of Johannesburg. These projects did two things. First, it helped clean up the area and second, it created a small income for a group of people who would otherwise be unemployed. She came back one day from one of these areas much earlier than usual. When asked why she was not working that morning in that certain township, she reacted by saying: 'This morning when I arrived at Township X before I could drive into the area I was stopped by a group of people I know well. They are the steering committee of the refuse removal project that we have launched. They stopped me and showed me that they wanted to talk to me. They said to me that they are very thankful for what I have done and for my help to get a project going, but they added that they have decided that they can go it alone now. They don't need me anymore.' The question put to her was: 'Do you feel sad that the people have taken the project?' Her answer: 'No, heavens. This is a fantastic thing! The people have accepted the ownership of a project that was always theirs.'

## CASE STUDY 20
### THE STORY OF KWAMPOFU

To illustrate what usually happens in a rural area.

The rural area of Kwampofu is an extremely poor area with very little opportunity for the population to improve their lives through gainful employment or through small one-person commercial and service enterprises. The area consists of five villages, two under one chieftainship and three under another. Many of the people found some employment in the town about 60 kilometres from the Kwampofu area. Some of them commute daily by way of taxis, but a substantial percentage stay on in town and come home over the weekends. The town is not very big and as a result of brisk influx, it started to fall behind with services. This led directly to a stagnation of commerce and industry so that jobs were not becoming more, but rather fewer.

The provincial government is directly responsible for the wellbeing of this area. It therefore coordinates the various efforts by line departments such as agriculture, health, public works, water, housing and labour, on both provincial government and national government level. Apart from the government there are also a number of NGOs involved in the area. The largest and most sophisticated of these is busy with a project to create day care centres in the three villages falling under the same chieftainship. Unfortunately because of a lack of communication the NGO is frequently at loggerheads with the chief and his council. The chief wants the NGO to discuss its projects with the citizens at public meetings, but the NGO says that will be a political act of which it does not want any part. Nevertheless the NGO is keeping on erecting these day care centres with the blessing of the provincial government and managing them when they become operative. One of the smaller NGOs tried to create small groups of mostly women to start food gardens in the area. They were relatively successful at first until a welfare organisation heard the plight of this area regarding food shortage and decided to approach a large firm to donate fruit and vegetables to the area. The firm saw it as an advertisement for itself and dropped large quantities of fruit and vegetables on the premises of one or other public building where the people could help themselves free of charge.

The government started with the excavation for electricity. It was only when the two tribal councils enquired about the work taking place in their areas, that they were informed of the project. The government then suggested that the tribal councils could draw up lists of those houses that would like to receive electricity. The government representatives pointed out that through the involvement of the tribal councils the project could become really participatory. The reaction from both tribal councils was that all the houses wanted electricity. The government reacted by pointing out the individual costs per house for instalment and deposit. This led to a few angry public meetings and eventually electricity was only provided for street lighting. In the meantime a few of the more affluent members of the community paid their deposit and instalment fees and have electricity in their homes.

Some time ago the government really surprised the people when it started to erect a community centre. The problem was, however, that the centre was built in the most outlying village and that it was therefore difficult for most people to get to the centre. To confound the problem, the government housed a clinic in the centre. This clinic was supposed to serve the five villages of Kwampofu. Most people from the other villages than the one where the clinic is situated, refused to pay for taxis to get to the clinic. They consequently still frequent a private clinic of many years' standing run by the Roman Catholic Church. The community hall which was part of the centre was managed by an NGO situated in the town and quite unknown among the people of the area. No one was ever informed what the function of the hall, and in fact, the whole centre would be. The NGO running the centre tried to organise an expo, but there was very little interest, firstly because the people were ignorant about the format and purpose of such a function and secondly because of the stagnated nature of the local economy. Over a period of time the centre started to fall in disuse and quite a bit of vandalism took place. The government requested the two tribal councils to arrange a public meeting to discuss the community centre. The tribal councils pointed out that each of them should arrange a meeting because that is customary. The officials of the government were however adamant that they could only come to the area on one Sunday.

The result was that members from only the tribe in whose area the meeting took place, attended. The officials tried to explain to those present what functions the centre could play. They stressed that the public should only make use of whatever is arranged by the NGO. Quite a few people, and they received general approval, said that they wanted to participate in the running of the centre. The official reaction was that the NGO was contractually the manager of the centre and that everybody should respect that. The result was that the disuse and the vandalism increased. Eventually the government informed the tribal council in whose area the centre was situated that it was going to put up a fence around the facility. The tribal council requested that local contractors be used for this task, but a firm from the town was appointed. Most of the fence was gone after one week. The NGO in charge of the place withdrew when the car of their employee working as manager of the centre got stolen.

A young youth organiser working in this area drew the attention of the two tribal councils because of the work he was doing. He got a body going calling themselves the youth network for the development of Kwampofu. They operate under the leadership of elected people from their own ranks. They have started to contact other youth groups such as choirs, sports clubs and even the local political party youth league. Their purpose was to launch area wide projects with the active participation of various local youth groups. They have started with a cleanup operation of the whole area. That has led to the training of a number of young people to start their own enterprise of selling bottles and tin cans for a regular income. They have also identified a number of young people to be trained as sports coaches. They made contact with a sports club in town who agreed on a mutual project where the sports club will provide or arrange for the training of people identified by the youth network for the development of Kwampofu.

>>

The government approached this youth group to amalgamate their activities with that of the Department of Education. The youth group welcomed any co-operation, but the government refused to accept their conditions for working together. The government is now considering the creation of an official youth co-ordinating council that could operate from the now dilapidated community centre.

In the area furthest removed from the tarred road going to the town there is quite a bit of agriculture going, mainly because a perennial river runs adjacent to this area. One of the teachers who originally came from this area requested a piece of land as the custom goes. He started to plant maize and vegetables, but he fertilised the soil with the result that his crop looked much better than that of the other farmers. He anticipated correctly that this would lead to suspicion and even animosity. He explained to the farmers what he had done and suggested that they could strengthen one another by forming a co-operative. Some of the farmers liked the idea and started such a co-operative and with the guidance of this teacher they did rather well. Because of this success more and more of the farmers joint with the result that after two years that area is really becoming a prosperous food producing node.

In one of the villages there was a women's chicken raising co-operative. Their big problem was that the feed for broiler chickens was simply too expensive for them. Their enterprises therefore remained small with very little profit for the women. Now, however, they have approached the farmers' co-operative for a deal to buy most of their maize as chicken feed plus some of their vegetables for themselves, but also for the chickens. Now the farmers need not transport their maize to a far off silo at great expense and at the same time the women can get their chicken feed much cheaper than otherwise. Some of the women in this project are so busy that they find it very difficult to look properly after their children. After a lot of soul searching the women have decided to start a day care centre for their children. They were lucky in negotiating a deal with a local church with a church building for the use of it during the week as a day care centre. They started to look for young people who could fulfil the role of child minders. Naturally the youth network for the development of Kwampofu heard about this and they approached the women with an offer to provide the women with two child minders if the women could help to pay for their training. This venture was so successful that the youth body has launched a scheme where young people are trained as child minders and then placed in day care centres in the area.

## CASE STUDY 21
### THE LOVING TEACHER

To illustrate how easily a community development worker can act paternalistically.

We visited the various women's groups created by the community development worker, a twenty three year old unmarried woman. These women's groups were started among the wives of farm labourers on commercial farms with a view to help them gain certain skills and start small development projects. The community worker was totally devoted to her work with a lot of compassion for the women who she tried to organise into groups. We stopped at a farm and under a huge tree about 15 women were waiting for us. The community worker was very glad to see the women and there ensued hearty greetings. What I heard was a condescending overly friendly voice from the community worker: 'Oh Christina, your knitting is wonderful! I never thought you will get it right and now just look at this! And Johanna have you made this beautiful beret? I can't believe it! Oh you are so good!' I wondered where I have heard the same tone of voice and way of speaking before and then remembered it was some time ago when I had visited a day care centre and the very kind teacher communicated with the toddlers in much the way that this community worker did. When I was introduced to the women in this group I found to my amusement (and horror) that all of them were middle aged, any one of them could have been the community worker's mother!

## CASE STUDY 22
### BRUTAL FORCE AMONG THE CABBAGE PLANTS

To illustrate the wrong attitude and action of a community development worker.

I was taken to a large food producing project by the agricultural extension officer who was the community development worker for the project. It was known as a participatory collective garden where the participants were responsible for the garden and had a share of the dividend produced by the garden. The agricultural extension officer had to provide technical advice only.

When we arrived at the garden a large group of people were waiting for us. As we got out of the car the officer, whose door was on the farther side of the waiting group, shouted over the roof of the car and over my head: 'Didn't I tell you to water the cabbage plants? I told you they are going to die, but you don't listen!' As he was moving away from the car towards the garden he was still going at it. The whole group of 'participants' trotted behind him with hanging heads. He was still castigating them as he reached the cabbage plants. He kept on walking and talking while you could see flying cabbage plants in all directions marking his way through them.

## CASE STUDY 23
### THE OLD CHIEF'S STORY

To illustrate how easily someone can be offended by a community development worker.

The other day a smart young man from the government visited me in his smart car. He stopped in front of my homestead. He got out of his car. He didn't greet me properly. He didn't give me the opportunity to greet him properly. His great hurry made him forget all manners of decency. He just came in, sat down and asked me what my weaknesses were.

## CASE STUDY 24
### WATER TO WASTE

To illustrate the necessity for projects to be sustainable.

A certain community living on the slopes of the foothills of a big mountain decided to develop a few of the many springs in the mountain. This was done through a project and the water was then piped from the springs down towards the valley where it was stored in three 5 000 litre tanks. The water stored in these tanks is quite enough for the community of about a thousand people. In fact, when it rains well people need this water solely for household purposes. Added to this is the problem that a number of households lower down in the valley and quite a distance from these tanks make very little use of the water because they need people to walk up the valley and then back down with full holders for their homes. Such labour is not always available with the result that these households go without or obtain their water from dubious sources.

The water from these springs in the mountain is so plentiful that the tanks are overflowing. This causes a serious problem because the waste water is carving out quite a donga that can become deep and dangerous over time. At the moment it is already forming some stagnant pools where mosquitoes are breeding. It is clear that this project has a sustainability problem.

# BIBLIOGRAPHY

About.com.Geography.: http://geography.about.com/od/obtainpopulationdata/a/worldvillage.htm. (Accessed on 8 March 2011)

Abu Samah, A. & Aref, F. 2009. People's participation in community development: a case study in a planned village settlement in Malaysia. *World Rural Observations*, 1(2).

Ackoff, R.L. 1984. On the nature of development and planning. In D.C. Korten & R. Klauss (eds). *People-centred development: Contributions toward theory and planning frameworks*. West Hartford: Kumarian.

Adejunmobi, A. 1990. Self-help community development in selected Nigerian rural communities: Problems and prospects. *Community Development Journal*, 25(3).

Advisory Expert Group. 2006. *Short report of the Fourth Meeting of the Advisory Expert Group on National Accounts*, 30 January—8 February 2006. Frankfurt: European Central Bank.

Altafin, I. 1991. Participatory communication in social development evaluation. *Community Development Journal*, 26(4).

Andersen, P.A., Hecht, M.L., Hoobler, G.D. & Smallwood, M. 2002. Nonverbal communication across cultures. In Gudykunst, W.B. & Mody, B. (Eds). *Handbook of international and intercultural communication*. Second Edition. London: Sage.

Anyanwu, C.N. 1988. The technique of participatory research in community development. *Community Development Journal*, 23(1).

Armor, T., Honadle, G., Olson, C. & Weisel, P. 1979. Organising and supporting integrated rural development projects: A twofold approach to administrative development. *Journal of Administration Overseas*, 18(4).

Arnstein, S.R. 1969. A ladder of citizen participation. *Journal of the American Institute of Planners*, 35(4).

Barker, R. 2001. Communication with communities: A South African experience. *Communicatio*, 27(1).

Beeld. 2005. Meeste informele sake oorleef nèt.

Bhatia, A. 1995. Challenging the new professionals. Moving from Participatory Rural Appraisal to Empowering Rural Appraisal. *Nepal Participatory Action Network Workshop*. Dhulikhel, 20–22 January 1995.

Blanchet, K. 2001. *Participatory development: between hopes and reality.* Unesco Open Forum.

Blunt, P. 1990. Strategies for enhancing organisational effectiveness in the Third World. *Public Administration and Development*, 10(2).

Brokensha, D. & Hodge, P. (1969) *Community development: an interpretation*. San Francisco: Chandler.

Burbidge, J. (ed). 1988. *Approaches that work in rural development: Emerging trends, participatory methods and local initiatives*. München: Saur.

CEFA 2007. *Further education and training certificate in Social Auxiliary Work*. Wellington: CEFA.

Chambers, R. 1978. Project selection for poverty-focused rural development: Simple is optimal. *World Development*, 6(2).

Chambers, R. 1983. *Rural development: Putting the last first*. Essex: Longman.

Chambers, R. 1992. Rapid and participatory rural appraisal. *Africanus*, 22(1&2).

Chambers, R. 1993. *Challenging the professions. Frontiers for rural development*. London: IT Publications.

Chambers, R. 1997. Shortcut and participatory methods for gaining social information for projects. In Sepulveda, S. & Edwards, R. *Sustainable development, social organization, institutional arrangements and rural development*. Selected readings. San Jose: Inter American Institute for Cooperation on Agriculture.

Chambers, R. 2004. Notes for participants in PRA-PLA familiarisation workshops in 2004. Participation group. Brighton: Institute of Development Studies.

Chen, S. and Ravallion, M. 2008. *The developing world is poorer than we thought but no less successful in the fight against poverty*. Policy Research Working Paper No 4703. World Bank: Washington.

Chronic Poverty Research Centre. 2005. *The chronic poverty report 2004-05*. Institute for Development Policy & Management. University of Manchester.

Clark, D.A. 2005. *The Capability Approach: Its Development, Critiques and Recent Advances*. Global Policy Research Group, Institute for Development Policy and Management. Manchester: University of Manchester.

Collyer, S., Warren, C., Hemsley, B. & Stevens, C. 2010. Aim, fire, aim—Project planning styles in dynamic environments. *Project Management Journal*. 41(4).

Cornwell, L. 1986. *Community development: a phoenix too frequent? Working Document in Rural and Community Development*, 2 Dept of Development Administration and Politics.

Cornwell, L. 1996. Using simulation exercises and games in teaching development. *Africanus*, 26(1).

Crovitz, L.G. 2011. Egypt's revolution by social media. *The Wall Street Journal*. 14 February 2011.

Cusworth, J.W. & Franks, T.R. (eds). 1993. *Managing projects in developing countries*. Essex: Longman.

Cuthbert, D. 1995. *Money that matters: An introduction to fundraising in South Africa*. 2nd edn. Pretoria: JP van der Walt.

De Beer, F.C. 1984. *Gemeenskapsontwikkeling, hervestiging en behuising in Steilloopdorp*. Unpublished MA Thesis. Pretoria: University of South Africa.

De Beer, F.C. 1995. Training for community development: Some guidelines for the literature, some lessons from experience. *Social Work/Maatskaplike Werk*, 31(4).

De Beer, F.C. & Swanepoel, H.J. 1994. Energy and the community of the poor: Urban settlements, household needs and participatory development in South Africa. *Energy Policy*, 2(2).

De Beer, F. & Swanepoel, H. 1996. *Training for development. A manual for student trainers*. Halfway House: International Thomson Publishing.

De Beer, F. & Swanepoel, H. 1998. *Community development and beyond. Issues, structures and procedures*. Pretoria: JL Van Schaik.

De Coning, C. & Fick, J. 1995. A development perspective on policy management: From analysis to process facilitation. *Africanus*, 25(2).

De Soto, H. 1998. *The other path. The invisible revolution in the Third World*. New York: Harper & Row.

DFID. 2001. *Poverty: Bridging the Gap—Guidance notes*. DFID Issues paper: Department for International Development, London.

Diale, N.R.2009. *Community group environment for people participation and empowerment*. Doctor of Philosophy Thesis. Pretoria: Unisa.

Doyle, M. & Straus, D. 1976. *How to make meetings work. The new interaction method*. Ridgefield, Connecticut: Wyden Books.

Du Plooy, T. 2000. Ethics in research, in *Research in the Social Sciences: Only Study Guide for RSC201H*. Pretoria: University of South Africa.

Durning, A. 1990. Ending poverty. In Brown, L.R. & Starke, L. (eds). *State of the 990, a Worldwatch Institute report on progress toward a sustainable society*. New York: Norton.

Edwards, A.D. & Jones, D.G. 1976. *Community and community development*. The Hague: Mouton.

Ekins, P. 1992. *A new world order. Grassroots movements for global change* London: Routledge.

Elliott, J.A. 1994. *Introduction to sustainable development: The developing world.* London: Routledge.

El Sherbini, A.A. 1986.Alleviating rural poverty in subSaharan Africa. *Food Policy,* 11(1).

Essama—Nssah, B. 2004. Empowerment and poverty-focused evaluation. *Development Southern Africa.* 21 (3).

Feuerstein, M-T. 1988. Finding the methods to fit the people: Training for participatory evaluation. *Community Development Journal,* 23(1).

Franks, T.R. 1989. Bureaucracy, organisation culture and development. *Public Administration and Development,* 9(4).

Freire, P. 2006. *Pedagogy of the oppressed.* New York: The Continuum International Publishing Group.

Galbraith, J.K. 1979. *The nature of mass poverty.* Cambridge: Harvard University Press.

Gellert, P.K. & Lynch, B.D. 2003. Mega-projects as displacements. *International Social Science Journal.*

Gladding, S.T. 1995. *Group work: A counselling specialty.* Second Edition. Englewood Cliffs: Prentice Hall.

Goulet, D. 1974. Development administration and structures of vulnerability. In Morgan, E.P. (Ed). *The administration of change in Africa.* New York: Dunellen.

Goutier, H. 1994. Health in the developing world—progress despite everything. The Courier-Africa-Carribean-Pacific-European Union, No 143.

Gow, D.D. & Vansant, J. 1983. Beyond the rhetoric of rural development participation: How can it be done? *World Development,* 11(5).

Gran, G. 1983. *Development by people: Citizen construction of a just world.* New York: Praeger.

Guaraldo Choguill, M.B. 1996. A ladder of community participation for underdeveloped countries. *Habitat International,* 20(3).

Gunton, T. 2003. Megaprojects and regional development: Pathologies in project planning. *Regional Studies.* 37(5).

Harrison, P. 1984. *Inside the Third World. The anatomy of poverty.* 2nd edn. Harmondsworth: Penguin.

Holdcroft, L.E. 1982. The rise and fall of community development in developing countries, 1950—1965: A critical analysis and implications. In Jones, G.E. & Rolls, M.J. (Eds). *Progress in rural extension and community development,* Vol 1. Chichester: John Wiley.

Honadle, G. & Cooper, L. 1989. Beyond coordination and control: An interorganizational approach to structural adjustment, service delivery and natural resource management. *World Development,* 17.

IDS. 1997. http://www.ids.ac.uk/pra/intro/whatis.html. [Accessed on 3 April 2011]

International Accounting Standards Board. 2006. *Conceptual Framework. Asset Definition.* Agenda Paper 1A. London: *World Standard Setters Meeting, September 2006.*

James, S. Hosler, S.J. & Allmarsh, T. 1983. Evaluating a community action scheme. *Community Development Journal*, 18(1).

Jeppe, W.J.O. 1985. *Community development: An African rural approach.* Pretoria: Africa Institute.

Jütting, J. 2003. *Institutions and development: a critical review.* Working paper 210. OECD.

Kadushin, A. 1979. *The social work interview.* New York: Columbia University Press.

Khosa, J.H.M. 1991. Coordination in social development in order to combat poverty for the reconstructed society—a rural perspective. *Maatskaplike Werk/Social Work*, 27(3/4).

Kilongi, M. 2011. Chama the best choice for tjommies. *Mail and Guardian.* 18-24 March 2011.

King, C. 1965. *Working with people in community action: An international casebook for trained community workers and volunteer community leaders.* New York: Association Press.

Kingma, S. 1994. Coordination: What does it take? *Contact*, 137.

Korten, D.C. 1980. Community organization and rural development: a learning process approach. *Public Administration Review*, 40(5).

Korten, D.C. 1984. People-centred development: Toward a framework. In Korten, D.C. & Klauss, R. (Eds). *People-centred development: Contributions toward theory and planning frameworks.* West Hartford: Kumarian.

Korten, D.C. 1990. *Getting to the 21ˢᵗ century: voluntary action and the global agenda.* West Hartford: Kumarian.

Korten, D.C. 1991. *Participation and development projects: Fundamental dilemmas.* Unpublished Paper.

Kotze, D.A. 1987. Field administration. In Kotzè, D.A., De Beer, F.C., Swanepoel, H.J. & Bembridge, T.J. *Rural development administration in Southern Africa.* Pretoria: Africa Institute of South Africa.

Kretzmann, J. & McKnight, J. 1993. *Building communities from the inside out.* Chicago, IL: ACTA Publications.

La Fond, A.K. 1992. *Qualitative methods for assessing the acceptability of immunization in Somalia.* RRA Notes. No 16.

Lightfoot, C., Prein, M., & Lopez, T. 1994. *Bioresource flow modelling with farmers.* ILEIA Newsletter.

Lippitt, R. & Van Til, J. 1981. Can we achieve a collaborative community? *Journal of Voluntary Action Research*, 10(3/4).

Majone, G. & Wildavsky, A. 1978. Implementation as evolution. In H. Freeman (ed). *Policy studies review annual.* Beverly Hills: Sage.

Marsden, D. & Oakley, P. 1991. Future issues and perspectives in the evaluation of social development. *Community Development Journal*, 26(4).

Martin, R.L. & Osberg, S. 2007. Social Entrepreneurship: The Case for Definition. *Stanford Social Innovation Review* 37. Stanford: Stanford Graduate School of Business.

Massie, J.L. & Douglas, J. 1981. *Managing. A contemporary introduction.* Englewood Cliffs: Prentice-Hall.

Mathie, A. & Cunningham, G. 2002. From clients to citizens: asset-based community development as a strategy for community-driven development. *Occasional Paper Series*, No. 4.

Max-Neef, M. 1991. *Human scale development: conception, application and further reflections.* New York: Apex.

Mcauley, C. 2003. Ethics. In RL. Miller and JD. Brewer (Eds) *The A-Z of social Research.* London. Sage.

Mersham, J.M., Rensburg, R.S. & Skinner J.C. 1995. *Public relations, development and social investment: A southern African perspective.* Pretoria: JL van Schaik.

Mmakola, D. 1996. The place of policy analysis in South Africa. *Africanus*, 26(2).

Monaheng, T. 2000. Community development and empowerment. In De Beer, F.C. & Swanepoel, H.J. (Eds) *Introduction to development studies.* Cape Town: Oxford University Press.

Morgan, E.P. 1983. The project orthodoxy in development: Reevaluating the cutting edge. *Public Administration and Development*, 3(4).

Morris, R. 1970. The role of the agent in the community development process. In L.J. Carey (ed). *Community development as a process.* Columbia: University of Missouri Press.

Moser, C.O.N. 1983. The problem of evaluating community participation in urban development projects. In Moser, C.O.N. (Ed) *Evaluating community participation in urban development projects.* Unpublished Working Paper no 14. London: Development Planning Unit.

Mutezo, A.T. 2005. *Obstacles in the access to SMME finance: an empirical perspective on Tshwane.* Unpublished MA dissertation. Pretoria: Unisa.

Narayan, D., Chambers, R., Shah, M.K. & Petesch, P. 2000. *Voices of the poor: Crying out for change.* Oxford: Oxford University Press.

Nerfin, M. (Ed) 1977. *Another development: approaches and strategies.* Uppsala: Dag Hammarskjold Foundation.

Nussbaum, M.C. 2000. *Women and human development: The capabilities approach.* Cambridge: Cambridge University Press.

Oakley, P. 1988. Conceptual problems of the monitoring and evaluation of qualitative objectives of rural development. *Community Development Journal*, 23 (1).

Oakley, P. & Marsden, D. 1984. *Approaches to participation in rural development.* Geneva: ILO.

Obaidullah Khan, A.Z.M. 1980. Participatory development: The need for structural reform and people's organisation. In UNAPDI (Ed). *Local level planning and rural development: Alternative strategies*. New Delhi: Concept.

Olivier, B. 2004. Postmodern culture, globalisation, and the lure of 'development'. *Africanus*, 34(1).

Osuga, B. & Mutayisa, D. 1995. *Use of PRA in programme reviews and evaluations: Key strengths, weaknesses and lessons*. Unpublished paper.

Phifer, B.M., List, E.F. & Faulkner, B. 1980. History of community development in America. In Christenson, J.A. & Robinson, J.W. (Eds) *Community development in America*. Armes: Iowa State University Press

Pretty, J.N., Guijt, I., Thompson, J. & Scoones, I. 1995. *A trainer's guide for participatory learning and action*. London: IIED.

Roberts, H. 1979. *Community development: Learning and action*. Toronto: University of Toronto Press.

Robeyns, I. 2005. The Capability Approach: a theoretical survey, *Journal of Human Development*, 6 (1).

Rondinelli, D.A. 1983. Projects as instruments of development administration: A qualified defence and suggestions for improvements. *Public Administration and Development*, 3(4).

Rondinelli, D.A. 1993. *Development projects as policy experiments. An adaptive approach to development administration*. Second Edition. London: Routledge.

Salem, G.W. 1978. Maintaining participation in community organizations. *Journal of Voluntary Action Research*, 7(3/4).

Selener, D. 1997. *Participatory action research and social change*. New York: Cornell University Press.

Selener, D., Endara, N. & Carvajal, J. 1999. *Participatory rural appraisal and planning workbook*. Quito: International Institute of Rural Reconstruction.

Selsky, J.W. 1991. Lessons in community development: An activist approach to stimulating interorganizational collaboration. *Journal of Applied Behavioral Science*, 27(1).

Sen, A. 1981. *Poverty and famines: An essay on entitlement and deprivation*. Oxford: Clarendon.

Servaes, J. & Lie, R. 2003. Media globalisation and culture: Issues and trends. *Communicatio*, 29(1&2).

Sihlongonyane, M.F. 2001. The rhetoric of the community in project management: the case of Mohlakeng township. *Development in Practice*. 11 (1).

Sowman, M. & Gawith, M. 1994. Participation of disadvantaged communities in project planning and decision making: A case study of Hout Bay. *Development Southern Africa*, 11(4).

Spalding, N.L. 1990. The relevance of basic needs for political and economic development. *Studies in Comparative International Development*, 25(3).

Staudt, K. 1985. A planning-centred approach to project evaluation: Women in mainstream development projects. *Public Administration and Development*, 5(1).

Steyn, B. & Nunes, M. 2001. Communication strategy for community development: A case study of the Heifer project—South Africa. *Communicatio*, 27(2).

Swanepoel, H.J. 1985(a). Some guidelines for rural development in Southern Africa. *Africa Insight*, 15(2).

Swanepoel, H.J. 1985(b). Mapayeni. 'n Nuwe dimensie in mensontwikkeling. *Lantern*, 34(2).

Swanepoel, H.J. 1986. *Deelname as beginsel in landelike ontwikkeling. Inaugural lecture.* Pretoria: University of South Africa.

Swanepoel, H.J. 1993. *Population and development.* Paper delivered at a National Conference on Population. Kempton Park.

Swanepoel, H. 1996. Evaluation of community development projects: A human development approach. *Africanus*, 26(1).

Swanepoel, H. 2000. The dynamics of development. In De Beer, F.C. & Swanepoel, H.J. (Eds) *Introduction to development studies.* Cape Town: Oxford University Press.

Swanepoel, H. 2000. The state and development. In De Beer, F.C. & Swanepoel, H.J. (Eds). *Introduction to development studies.* Cape Town: Oxford University Press.

Swanepoel, H.J. & De Beer, F.C. 1994. *Guide for trainee community development workers.* Halfway House: Southern Book Publishers.

Swanepoel, H. & De Beer, F. 1996. *Communication for development. A guide for fieldworkers.* Halfway House: International Thomson Publishing.

Swanepoel, H. & De Beer, F. 1996. *Community capacity building. A guide for fieldworkers and community leaders.* Cape Town: Oxford University Press.

Taconni, L. & Tisdell, C. 1993. Holistic sustainable development. Implications for planning processes, foreign aid and support for research. *Third World Planning Review*, 15(4).

Taylor, L. 1991. Participatory evaluation with non-government organisations (NGOs). Some experiences of informal and exploratory methodologies. *Community Development Journal*, 26(1).

Treurnicht, S. 2000. Sustainable development. In De Beer, F.C. & Swanepoel, H.J. (Eds) *Introduction to development studies.* Cape Town: Oxford University Press.

UNDP. 2001. *Human development report 2001. Making new technologies work for human development.* New York: Oxford University Press.

UNDP. 2011. What are the Millennium Development Goals? http://www.undp.org/mdg/basics.shtml (Accessed on 11 March 2011)

United Nations. 1984. *A systematic and comprehensive approach to training for human settlements.* Nairobi: United Nations Centre for Human Settlements (Habitat).

Uphoff, N. 1989. *A field methodology for participatory self-evaluation of PPPgroup and intergroup association performance.* Rome: FAO.

Uphoff, N. 1991. A field methodology for participatory self-evaluation. *Community Development Journal,* 26(4).

Van Diessen, A. 1998. Keeping hold of the stick and handing over the carrot: Dilemmas arising when agencies use PRA. In Boog, B., Coenen, H., Keune, L.& Lammerts, R. (Eds). *The complexity of relationships in action research.* The Netherlands: Tilburg University Press.

Vargas, L.V. 1991. Reflections on methodology of evaluation. *Community Development Journal,* 26(4).

White, A.T. 1982. Why community participation? *Assignment Children,* 59/60.

White, L.G. 1986. Urban community organizations and local government: Exploring relationships and roles. *Public Administration and Development,* 6(3).

White, S. & Pettit, J. 2004. *Participatory approaches and the measurement of human well-being.* WeD Working Paper 08. Wellbeing in Developing Countries ESRC Research Group (WeD). Bath: University of Bath.

Whitehead, K.A. , Kriel, A.J. & Richter, L.M. 2005. Barriers to conducting a community mobilization intervention among youth in a rural South African community. *Journal of Community Psychology.* 33 (3).

Wiggins, S & Shields, D. 1995. Clarifying the 'logical framework' as a tool for planning and management development projects. *Project Appraisal.* 10(1).

Wileden, A.F. 1970. *Community development: the dynamics of planned change.* Totowa: Bedminster Press.

Wilson, F. & Ramphele, M. 1989. *Uprooting poverty. The South African challenge.* Cape Town: David Philip.

Windell, C. 1988. *The ABC of fund raising.* Pretoria: Serva Publishers.

Wisner, B. 1988. *Power and need in Africa: Basic human needs and development policies.* London: Earthscan.

World Bank. 2003. World Bank Report 2003. *Sustainable Development in a dynamic world. Transforming institutions, growth and quality of life.* New York: Oxford University Press.

Zentner, H. 1964. The state and the community. *Sociology and Social Research,* 48.

# QUESTIONS AND ANSWERS FOR PARTICIPATORY SELF-EVALUATION

Based on the original model of N. Uphoff, but extensively revised by the author. Questions and answers were changed; a number of questions were scrapped; a number were added; process and product questions were separated; and a completely new set of questions to evaluate the work of the community worker has been added.

## Process questions

1. How are group decisions made?
    4 = Decisions are always made with all members' knowledge and participation.
    3 = Decisions are usually made with all members' knowledge and participation.
    2 = Decisions are sometimes made with all members' knowledge and participation.
    1 = Decisions are seldom made with all members' knowledge and participation.

2. How widely are responsibilities for group activities shared?
    4 = Most or all members share responsibility for group activities.
    3 = Many members share responsibility for group activities.
    2 = Some members share responsibility for group activities.
    1 = Only a few members share responsibility for group activities.

3. How much do members scrutinise the activities of their office bearers?
    4 = Members are very active in scrutinising the activities of their office bearers.
    3 = Members are sometimes active in scrutinising the activities of their office bearers.
    2 = Members are seldom active in scrutinising the activities of their office bearers.
    1 = Members are not active in scrutinising the activities of their office bearers.

4. How much sharing of leadership responsibilities is there?
    4 = There is great sharing of leadership responsibilities.
    3 = There is much sharing of leadership responsibilities.
    2 = There is some sharing of leadership responsibilities.
    1 = There is no sharing of leadership responsibilities.

5. How many members are ready, willing and able to assume leadership positions?
    4 = Most to all members are ready, willing and able to assume leadership positions.
    3 = About half of the members are ready, willing and able to assume leadership positions.

2 = Less that a quarter of the members are ready, willing and able to assume leadership positions.

1 = Only very few members are ready, willing and able to assume leadership positions.

6. How good are the chances that decisions made will be implemented?
    4 = The chances that decisions made will be implemented are extremely good.
    3 = The chances that decisions made will be implemented are good.
    2 = The chances that decisions made will be implemented are fairly good.
    1 = The chances that decisions made will be implemented are small.

7. How many members participate in the meetings?
    4 = All members participate in the meetings.
    3 = Most members participate in the meetings.
    2 = Some members participate in the meetings.
    1 = Few members participate in the meetings.

8. How many members participate in other group activities?
    4 = All members participate in other group activities.
    3 = Most members participate in other group activities.
    2 = Some members participate in other group activities.
    1 = Few members participate in other group activities.

9. How productive are group meetings?
    4 = Group meetings are very productive.
    3 = Group meetings are productive.
    2 = Group meetings are fairly productive.
    1 = Group meetings are not very productive.

10. How many members usually come to group meetings?
    4 = Almost all (75%+) members usually come to group meetings.
    3 = Most (50–75%) members usually come to group meetings.
    2 = Less than most (25–50%) members usually come to group meetings.
    1 = A few (25%) members usually come to group meetings.

11. How good is communication within the group?
    4 = Communication within the group is extremely good.
    3 = Communication within the group is good.
    2 = Communication within the group is fairly good.
    1 = Communication within the group is poor.

12. How much information on group activities is communicated within the group?
    4 = A lot of information on group activities is communicated within the group.
    3 = Some information on group activities is communicated within the group.
    2 = Little information on group activities is communicated within the group.
    1 = No information on group activities is communicated within the group.

13. What is the quality of discussion during group meetings?
    4 = The quality of discussion during group meetings is extremely good.
    3 = The quality of discussion during group meetings is good.
    2 = The quality of discussion during group meetings is fair.
    1 = The quality of discussion during group meetings is poor.

14. How able is the group at maintaining discipline in its ranks?
    4 = The group is very able at maintaining discipline in its ranks.
    3 = The group is able at maintaining discipline in its ranks.
    2 = The group ranks.
    1 = The group is not very able at maintaining discipline in its ranks.

15. How able is the group at resolving internal conflict?
    4 = The group is very able at resolving internal conflict.
    3 = The group is able at resolving internal conflict.
    2 = The group is fairly able at resolving internal conflict.
    1 = The group is not very able at resolving internal conflict.

16. How clear are members about their tasks?
    4 = Members are very clear about their tasks.
    3 = Members are clear about their tasks.
    2 = Members are fairly clear about their tasks.
    1 = Members are not very clear about their tasks.

17. How satisfied are members about the fairness with which tasks are assigned?
    4 = Members are very satisfied about the fairness with which tasks are assigned.
    3 = Members are satisfied about the fairness with which tasks are assigned.
    2 = Members are fairly satisfied about the fairness with which tasks are assigned.
    1 = Members are not very satisfied about the fairness with which tasks are assigned.

18. How well are group objectives understood by the members?
    4 = Group objectives are very well understood by the members.
    3 = Group objectives are well understood by the members.
    2 = Group objectives are fairly well understood by the members.
    1 = Group objectives are not very well understood by the members.

19. How clearly is work shared among members?
    4 = Work is very clearly shared among members.
    3 = Work is fairly clearly shared among members.
    2 = Work is not very clearly shared among members.
    1 = Work is not clearly shared among members.

20. How many members contribute nonfinancial resources to the group?
    4 =  All members contribute nonfinancial resources to the group.
    3 = Most members contribute nonfinancial resources to the group.
    2 = Some members contribute nonfinancial resources to the group.
    1 = Few members contribute nonfinancial resources to the group.

21. To what extent are members acquiring knowledge of better technology?
    4 = Members are acquiring knowledge of better technology to a great extent.
    3 = Members are acquiring knowledge of better technology to a large extent.
    2 = Members are acquiring knowledge of better technology to some extent.
    1 = Members are not acquiring knowledge of better technology.

22. To what extent does the group utilise local, indigenous technology?
    4 = The group fully utilises local, indigenous technology.
    3 = The group generally utilises local, indigenous technology.
    2 = The group utilises some local, indigenous technology.
    1 = The group does not utilise local, indigenous technology.

23. To what extent is the group aware of the need to maintain facilities and equipment?
    4 = The group is well aware of the need to maintain facilities and equipment.
    3 = The group is aware of the need to maintain facilities and equipment.
    2 = The group is slightly aware of the need to maintain facilities and equipment.
    1 = The group is unaware of the need to maintain facilities and equipment.

24. How well does the group carry out maintenance on facilities and equipment?
    4 = The group carries out maintenance on facilities and equipment excellently.
    3 = The group carries out maintenance on facilities and equipment well.
    2 = The group carries out maintenance on facilities and equipment fairly well.
    1 = The group does not carry out maintenance on facilities and equipment.

25. How well does the group carry out quality control of production outputs?
    4 = The group carries out quality control of production outputs excellently.
    3 = The group carries out quality control of production outputs well.
    2 = The group carries out quality control of production outputs fairly well.
    1 = The group does not carry out quality control of production outputs.

26. How many members are involved in financial decision making?
    4 = All members are involved in financial decision making.
    3 = Most members are involved in financial decision making.
    2 = Some members are involved in financial decision making.
    1 = Only some office bearers are involved in financial decision making.

27. How well are the financial affairs of the group run?
    4 = The financial affairs of the group are run very well.
    3 = The financial affairs of the group are run well.
    2 = The financial affairs of the group are run fairly well.
    1 = The financial affairs of the group are not very well run.

28. How well does the group progress towards self-reliance?
    4 = The group progresses towards self-reliance very well.
    3 = The group progresses towards self-reliance well.
    2 = The group progresses towards self-reliance fairly well.
    1 = The group is not progressing towards self-reliance.

29. How able is the group to operate without direction from the community worker?
    4 = The group is very able at operating without direction from the community worker.
    3 = The group is fairly able at operating without direction from the community worker.
    2 = The group is not very able at operating without direction from the community worker.
    1 = The group cannot operate without direction from the community worker.

30. To what extent is the group able to mobilise resources from within?
    4 = The group is very able at mobilising resources from within.
    3 = The group is able at mobilising resources from within.
    2 = The group is fairly able at mobilising resources from within.
    1 = The group unable to mobilise resources from within.

31. To what extent do members show increased confidence?
    4 = Members show increased confidence to a great extent.
    3 = Members show increased confidence to a large extent.
    2 = Members show increased confidence to some extent.
    1 = Members show increased confidence to a small extent.

32. To what extent does the group monitor and evaluate its performance?
    4 = The group monitors and evaluates its performance to a great extent.
    3 = The group monitors and evaluates its performance to a large extent.
    2 = The group monitors and evaluates its performance to some extent.
    1 = The group monitors and evaluates its performance to a small extent.

33. To what extent is the group prepared to try something new?
    4 = The group is well prepared to try something new.
    3 = The group is fairly well prepared to try something new.
    2 = The group is not well prepared to try something new.
    1 = The group is not prepared to try something new.

34. To what extent is the group helpful in getting similar projects among other groups off the ground?
    4 = The group is very helpful in getting similar projects among other groups off the ground.
    3 = The group is fairly helpful in getting similar projects among other groups off the ground.
    2 = The group is not really helpful in getting similar projects among other groups off the ground.
    1 = The group is not helpful in getting similar projects among other groups off the ground.

35. How does the group relate to government agencies?
    4 = The group relates excellently to government agencies.
    3 = The group relates well to government agencies.
    2 = The group relates fairly well to government agencies.
    1 = The group relates poorly to government agencies.

36. How does the group relate to NGOs?
    4 = The group relates excellently to NGOs.
    3 = The group relates well to NGOs.
    2 = The group relates fairly well to NGOs.
    1 = The group relates poorly to NGOs.

37. How does the group relate to CBOs?
    4 = The group relates excellently to CBOs.
    3 = The group relates well to CBOs.
    2 = The group relates fairly well to CBOs.
    1 = The group relates poorly to CBOs.

38. How well does the group coordinate with other roleplayers?
    4 = The group coordinates very well with other roleplayers.
    3 = The group coordinates well with other roleplayers.
    2 = The group coordinates fairly well with other roleplayers.
    1 = The group coordinates poorly with other roleplayers.

39. How widely does the group coordinate with other roleplayers?
    4 = The group coordinates very widely with other roleplayers.
    3 = The group coordinates widely with other roleplayers.
    2 = The group coordinates fairly widely with other roleplayers.
    1 = The group does not coordinates with other roleplayers.

40. How regularly does cooperation between the group and other roleplayers take place?
    4 = Cooperation between the group and other roleplayers take place very regularly.
    3 = Cooperation between the group and other roleplayers take place regularly.
    2 = Cooperation between the group and other roleplayers take place fairly regularly.
    1 = Cooperation between the group and other roleplayers does not take place.

41. How much community support does the group enjoy?
    4 = The group enjoys excellent community support.
    3 = The group enjoys good community support.
    2 = The group enjoys fairly good community support.
    1 = The group enjoys little community support.

42. How able is the group at resisting pressure from outside?
    4 = The group is very able at resisting pressure from outside.
    3 = The group is able at resisting pressure from outside.
    2 = The group is fairly able at resisting pressure from outside.
    1 = The group is not very able at resisting pressure from outside.

## Product questions

1.  How well are group objectives achieved?
    4 = Group objectives are fully achieved.
    3 = Group objectives are mostly achieved.

2 = Group objectives are partly achieved.

1 = Group objectives are not achieved.

2. To what extent has the group been successful in generating income for its members?

    4 = The group has been very successful at generating income for its members.

    3 = The group has been successful at generating income for its members.

    2 = The group has been fairly successful at generating income for its members.

    1 = The group has not been very successful at generating income for its members.

3. How successful is the group in expanding its activities?

    4 = The group is very successful in expanding its activities.

    3 = The group is successful in expanding its activities.

    2 = The group is fairly successful in expanding its activities.

    1 = The group is not very successful in expanding its activities.

4. To what extent has production output increased?

    4 = Production output has increased dramatically.

    3 = Production output has increased substantially.

    2 = Production output has increased somewhat.

    1 = Production output has increased very little.

5. How much has the group increased its assets?

    4 = The group has increased its assets very much.

    3 = The group has increased its assets much.

    2 = The group has increased its assets somewhat.

    1 = The group has not increased its assets.

6. How effectively in terms of time was the objective obtained?

    4 = In terms of time was the objective obtained in a very effective way.

    3 = In terms of time was the objective obtained in an effective way.

    2 = In terms of time was the objective obtained in a fairly effective way.

    1 = In terms of time was the objective obtained in an ineffective way.

7. How effectively in terms of economy was the objective obtained?

    4 = In terms of economy the objective was obtained in a very effective way.

    3 = In terms of economy the objective was obtained in an effective way.

    2 = In terms of economy the objective was obtained in a fairly effective way.

    1 = In terms of economy the objective was obtained in an ineffective way.

8. How effectively in terms of effort was the objective obtained?

    4 = In terms of effort the objective was obtained in a very effective way.

    3 = In terms of effort the objective was obtained in an effective way.

    2 = In terms of effort the objective was obtained in a fairly effective way.

    1 = In terms of effort the objective was obtained in an ineffective way.

9. To what extent does the obtained objective serve its planned purpose?

    4 = The obtained objective serves its planned purpose perfectly.

    3 = The obtained objective serves its planned purpose to a large extent.

2 = The obtained objective serves its planned purpose to a lesser extent.

1 = The obtained objective does not serves its planned purpose.

10. To what extent does the obtained objective serve the interests of the larger society?

4 = The obtained objective serve the interests of the larger society very much.

3 = The obtained objective serve the interests of the larger society to a large extent.

2 = The obtained objective serve the interests of the larger society to a limited extent.

1 = The obtained objective does notserve the interests of the larger society.

11. To what extent does the group have the ability to maintain the obtained objective?

4 = The group has great ability to maintain the obtained objective.

3 = The group has some ability to maintain the obtained objective.

2 = The group has little ability to maintain the obtained objective.

1 = The group has no ability to maintain the obtained objective.

12. To what extent does the group have the ability to improve the obtained objective?

4 = The group has great ability to improve the obtained objective.

3 = The group has some ability to improve the obtained objective.

2 = The group has little ability to improve the obtained objective.

1 = The group has no ability to improve the obtained objective.

13. How satisfied is the group with the obtained objective?

4 = The group is extremely satisfied with the obtained objective.

3 = The group is well satisfied with the obtained objective.

2 = The group is fairly satisfied with the obtained objective.

1 = The group is not satisfied with the obtained objective.

14. To what extent has the obtained objective strengthened the group?

4 = The obtained objective has strengthened the group very much.

3 = The obtained objective has strengthened the group somewhat.

2 = The obtained objective has strengthened the group a little.

1 = The obtained objective has not strengthened the group.

## Questions evaluating the community development worker

1.  What is the community development worker's reaction if something is not done on time?

4 = The community development worker establishes with the group the reason for the delay.

3 = The community development worker urges the group to establishes the reason for the delay.

2 = The community development worker urges the group to stamp out delays.

1 = The community development worker castigates the group or the person responsible for the delay.

2.  What is the community worker's reaction if a mistake is made?

4 = The community development worker helps the group to see what they can learn from the mistake.

3 = The community development worker tells the group that they must find the reason for the mistake so that it will not be repeated.

2 = The community development worker urges the group to stamp out mistakes.

1 = The community development worker castigates the group or the person responsible for the mistake.

3. What is the community development worker's attitude during meetings?

4 = The community development worker is part of the group and is learning just as the group is.

3 = The community development worker is sympathetic and tells the group where they go wrong or right.

2 = The community development worker is bored and cannot understand why the group meetings progress so slowly.

1 = The community development worker runs the meetings with strict discipline.

4. What is the community development worker's role in the meetings?

4 = The community development worker participates just like any other member of the group.

3 = The community development worker acts as advisor and guide in the meeting.

2 = The community development worker is the clearing house for all decisions.

1 = The community development worker is the chairperson of the meeting.

5. What role does the community development worker play?

4 = The community development worker only helps the group so that they can make decisions.

3 = The community development worker and the group make decisions together.

2 = The community development worker usually suggests to the group what decisions to make.

1 = The community development worker usually makes the decisions.

6. With whom does the community development worker associate?

4 = The community development worker associates with all members of the group.

3 = The community development worker associates with members who are active.

2 = The community development worker associates with the executive committee members.

1 = The community development worker associates with the chairperson only.

7. What is the community development worker's role in implementing decisions?

4 = The community development worker does his/her bit just as the other members of the group do.

3 = The community development worker does the more complicated tasks with an understudy to learn form him/her.

2 = The community development worker does the more complicated tasks.

1 = The community development worker does not involve him/herself in implementing decisions.

OR

1 = The community development worker does most of the implementation him/herself.

8. How does the community development worker facilitate the learning process?
   4 = The community development worker helps the group to identify items of learning as they come along.
   3 = The community development worker identifies items of learning and indicates them to the group.
   2 = The community development worker identifies items of learning and lectures on them to the group.
   1 = The community development worker does not facilitate the learning process.

9. What is the community development worker's role in evaluation?
   4 = The community development worker helps the group to do proper evaluation.
   3 = The community development worker helps the executive committee to do proper evaluation.
   2 = The community development worker and one or two of the office bearers do the evaluation.
   1 = The community development worker does the evaluation alone.

10. How much does the community development worker know about community development?
   4 = The community development worker knows everything about community development.
   3 = The community development worker knows a lot about community development.
   2 = The community development worker knows a fair amount about community development.
   1 = The community development worker does not know much about community development.

11. To what extent does the community development worker understand the community's situation?
   4 = The community development worker understands the community's situation perfectly.
   3 = The community development worker has a fair understanding of the community's situation.
   2 = The community development worker does not understand the community's situation very well.
   1 = The community development worker does not understand the community's situation.

12. To what extent has the community development worker respect for the people's norms, traditions and wishes?
   4 = The community development worker has great respect.
   3 = The community development worker has respect.
   2 = The community development worker has some respect.
   1 = The community development worker has little respect.

13. How much does the group appreciate the community development worker?
    4 = The group appreciates the community development worker very much.
    3 = The group appreciates the community development worker.
    2 = The group has some appreciation for the community development worker.
    1 = The group does not appreciate the community development worker very much.

# INDEX